RENAISSANCE
SELF-FASHIONING

Holbein, "The Ambassadors" (National Gallery, London).

RENAISSANCE SELF-FASHIONING

From More to Shakespeare

STEPHEN GREENBLATT

THE UNIVERSITY OF CHICAGO PRESS

Chicago & London

PR
429
.S45
G7
1980

THE UNIVERSITY OF CHICAGO PRESS, CHICAGO 60637
THE UNIVERSITY OF CHICAGO PRESS, LTD., LONDON
© 1980 by The University of Chicago
All rights reserved. Published 1980
Paperback edition 1984
Printed in the United States of America
93 92 91   8 7 6

Library of Congress Cataloging in Publication Data

Greenblatt, Stephen Jay.
  Renaissance self-fashioning.

  Includes bibliographical references and index.
  1. English Literature—Early modern, 1500-1700—
History and criticism.   2. Self in literature.
3. Renaissance.   I. Title.
PR429.S45G7   1980   840'.9'353   80-13837
ISBN 0-226-30653-4
ISBN 0-226-30654-2 (pbk.)

To Joshua and Aaron

Contents

Acknowledgments

Versions of several portions of this book have appeared in print: "More, Role-Playing, and *Utopia*," *Yale Review* 67 (©1978 by Yale University); "Marlowe and Renaissance Self-Fashioning," in *Two Renaissance Mythmakers: Christopher Marlowe and Ben Jonson*, edited by Alvin B. Kernan, Selected Papers from the English Institute 1975–76 (Baltimore: Johns Hopkins University Press (©1977 by The English Institute); "Marlowe, Marx, and Anti-Semitism," *Critical Inquiry* 5 (©1978 by The University of Chicago); "The Improvisation of Power," in *Literature and Society*, edited by Edward Said, Selected Papers from the English Institute 1977–78 (Baltimore: Johns Hopkins University Press (©1980 by The English Institute).

I am grateful to the National Endowment for the Humanities, the Guggenheim Foundation, the Howard Foundation, and the University of California for grants that greatly facilitated the research and writing of this book. It is a pleasure to acknowledge as well my many debts to friends, colleagues, and students. I began to list them all and was startled by the sheer numbers, so I will retreat to the expression of special thanks to Paul Alpers, Svetlana Alpers, C. L. Barber, Richard Bridgman, Natalie Zemon Davis, Steven Knapp, Thomas Laqueur, Walter Michaels, Norman Rabkin, Ralph Rader, Michael Rogin, Thomas Rosenmeyer, Richard Strier, and Alex Zwerdling.

As always, my wife, Ellen, had a generous and sustaining influence upon me.

A Note on Texts

I have, in the interest of readability, modernized the spelling and punctuation of all the texts with the exception of those places where the sense or meter is directly affected and the further exception of Spenser's poetry. Given Spenser's attempt to cast the glow of antiquity upon his work, it seemed perverse to rob it of that genuine antiquity that time has conferred upon it.

Introduction

My subject is *self-fashioning* from More to Shakespeare; my starting point is quite simply that in sixteenth-century England there were both selves and a sense that they could be fashioned. Of course, there is some absurdity in so bald a pronouncement of the obvious: after all, there are always selves—a sense of personal order, a characteristic mode of address to the world, a structure of bounded desires—and always some elements of deliberate shaping in the formation and expression of identity. One need only think of Chaucer's extraordinarily subtle and wry manipulations of *persona* to grasp that what I propose to examine does not suddenly spring up from nowhere when 1499 becomes 1500. Moreover, there is considerable empirical evidence that there may well have been less *autonomy* in self-fashioning in the sixteenth century than before, that family, state, and religious institutions impose a more rigid and far-reaching discipline upon their middle-class and aristocratic subjects. Autonomy is an issue but not the sole or even the central issue: the power to impose a shape upon oneself is an aspect of the more general power to control identity—that of others at least as often as one's own.

What *is* central is the perception—as old in academic writing as Burckhardt and Michelet—that there is in the early modern period a change in the intellectual, social, psychological, and aesthetic structures that govern the generation of identities. This change is difficult to characterize in our usual ways because it is not only complex but resolutely dialectical. If we say that there is a new stress on the executive power of the will, we must say that there is the most sustained and relentless assault upon the will; if we say

1

that there is a new social mobility, we must say that there is a new assertion of power by both family and state to determine all movement within the society; if we say that there is a heightened awareness of the existence of alternative modes of social, theological, and psychological organization, we must say that there is a new dedication to the imposition of control upon those modes and ultimately to the destruction of alternatives.

Perhaps the simplest observation we can make is that in the sixteenth century there appears to be an increased self-consciousness about the fashioning of human identity as a manipulable, artful process. Such self-consciousness had been widespread among the elite in the classical world, but Christianity brought a growing suspicion of man's power to shape identity: "Hands off yourself," Augustine declared. "Try to build up yourself, and you build a ruin."[1] This view was not the only one available in succeeding centuries, but it was influential, and a powerful alternative began to be fully articulated only in the early modern period. When in 1589 Spenser writes that the general intention and meaning that he has "fashioned" in *The Faerie Queene* is "to fashion a gentleman," or when he has his knight Calidore declare that "in each mans self . . . / It is, to fashion his owne lyfes estate," or when he tells his beloved in one of the *Amoretti*, "You frame my thoughts, and fashion me within,"[2] he is drawing upon the special connotations for his period of the verb *fashion*, a word that does not occur at all in Chaucer's poetry. As a term for the action or process of making, for particular features or appearance, for a distinct style or pattern, the word had been long in use, but it is in the sixteenth century that *fashion* seems to come into wide currency as a way of designating the forming of a self. This forming may be understood quite literally as the imposition upon a person of physical form—"Did not one fashion us in the womb?" Job asks in the King James Bible,[3] while, following the frequent injunctions to "fashion" children, midwives in the period attempted to mold the skulls of the newborn into the proper shape.[4] But, more significantly for our purposes, fashioning may suggest the achievement of a less tangible shape: a distinctive personality, a characteristic address to the world, a consistent mode of perceiving and behaving. As we might expect, the recurrent model for this latter fashioning is Christ. Those whom God in his foreknowledge has called, Tyndale translates the epistle to the Romans, he "fashioned unto the shape of his son" (8:29), and thus the true Christian, Tyndale writes in the *Obedience*, "feeleth . . . him self . . . altered and fashioned like unto Christ." "We are exhorted,"

Archbishop Sandys remarks in a sermon, "to fashion ourselves according to that similitude and likeness which is in him," while in the 1557 Geneva translation of the New Testament we read that Christ "was disfigured to fashion us, he died for our life." If Christ is the ultimate model, he is not even in the New Testament the only one: "In all things," Paul tells the Corinthians, in Tyndale's translation, "I fashioned my self to all men to save at the least way some" (1 Cor. 9:22). This principle of adaptation is obviously not limited to the propagation of the Gospel: in Richard Taverner's *Garden of Wisdom* (1539), for example, we are told that whoever desires to be conversant with public affairs, "must... fashion himself to the manners of men,"[5] and this counsel is tirelessly reiterated.

Thus separated from the imitation of Christ—a separation that can, as we shall see, give rise to considerable anxiety—self-fashioning acquires a new range of meanings: it describes the practice of parents and teachers; it is linked to manners or demeanor, particularly that of the elite; it may suggest hypocrisy or deception, an adherence to mere outward ceremony; it suggests representation of one's nature or intention in speech or actions. And with representation we return to literature, or rather we may grasp that self-fashioning derives its interest precisely from the fact that it functions without regard for a sharp distinction between literature and social life. It invariably crosses the boundaries between the creation of literary characters, the shaping of one's own identity, the experience of being molded by forces outside one's control, the attempt to fashion other selves. Such boundaries may, to be sure, be strictly observed in criticism, just as we may distinguish between literary and behavioral styles, but in doing so we pay a high price, for we begin to lose a sense of the complex interactions of meaning in a given culture. We wall off literary symbolism from the symbolic structures operative elsewhere, as if art alone were a human creation, as if humans themselves were not, in Clifford Geertz's phrase, cultural artifacts.[6]

"There is no such thing as a human nature independent of culture," Geertz writes, meaning by culture not primarily "complexes of concrete behavior patterns—customs, usages, traditions, habit clusters"—but rather "a set of control mechanisms—plans, recipes, rules, instructions...—for the governing of behavior."[7] Self-fashioning is in effect the Renaissance version of these control mechanisms, the cultural system of meanings that creates specific individuals by governing the passage from abstract potential to concrete historical embodiment. Literature functions within this system in three interlocking ways: as a manifestation of the concrete behavior of its particular author, as itself the expression of the codes by which behavior is shaped, and as a reflection upon those codes. The interpretive practice that I have attempted to exemplify in the essays that follow must concern itself with all three of these functions. If interpretation limits itself to the behavior of the author, it becomes literary biography (in either a conventionally historical or psychoanalytic mode) and risks losing a sense of the larger networks of meaning in which both the author and his works participate. If, alternatively, literature is viewed exclusively as the expression of social rules and instructions, it risks being absorbed entirely into an ideological superstructure. Marx himself vigorously resisted this functional absorption of art, and subsequent Marxist aesthetics, for all its power and sophistication, has never satisfactorily resolved the theoretical problems raised in the *Grundrisse* and elsewhere.[8] Finally, if literature is seen only as a detached reflection upon the prevailing behavioral codes, a view from a safe distance, we drastically diminish our grasp of art's concrete functions in relation to individuals and to institutions, both of which shrink into an obligatory "historical background" that adds little to our understanding. We drift back toward a conception of art as addressed to a timeless, cultureless, universal human essence or, alternatively as a self-regarding, autonomous, closed system—in either case, art as opposed to social life. Self-fashioning then becomes a subject only for sociology, literature for literary criticism.

   I have attempted instead to practice a more cultural or anthropological criticism—if by "anthropological" here we think of interpretive studies of culture by Geertz, James Boon, Mary Douglas, Jean Duvignaud, Paul Rabinow, Victor Turner, and others.[9] These figures do not enlist themselves under a single banner, still less do they share a single scientific method, but they have in common the conviction that men are born "unfinished animals," that the facts of life are less artless than they look, that both particular cultures and the observers of these cultures are inevitably drawn to a metaphorical grasp of reality, that anthropological interpretation must address itself less to the mechanics of customs and institutions than to the interpretive constructions the members of a society apply to their experiences. A literary criticism that has affinities to this practice must be conscious of its own status as interpretation and intent upon understanding literature as a part of the system of signs that constitutes a given culture; its proper goal, however difficult to realize, is a *poetics of culture.* Such an approach is necessarily a balancing act—correcting each of the functional perspectives I sketched in the preceding paragraph against the others—and necessarily impure: its central concerns prevent it from permanently sealing off one type of discourse from another or decisively separating works of art from the minds and lives of their creators and their audiences. I remain concerned, to be sure, with the implications of artistic representation as a distinct human activity—Shakespeare's depiction in *Othello* of his hero's self-construction and destruction is not simply identical to those patterns of self-fashioning and self-cancellation that I explore in the careers of several of my authors—but the way to explore these implications lies neither in denying any relation between the play and social life nor in affirming that the latter is the "thing itself," free from interpretation. Social actions are themselves always embedded in systems of public signification, always grasped, even by their makers, in acts of interpretation, while the words that constitute the works of literature that we discuss here are by their very nature the manifest assurance of a similar embeddedness. Language, like other sign systems, is a collective construction; our interpretive task must be to grasp more sensitively the consequences of this fact by investigating both the social presence to the world of the literary text and the social presence of the world in the literary text. The literary text remains the central object of my attention in this study of self-fashioning in part because, as I hope these chapters will demonstrate, great art is an extraordinarily sensitive register of the complex struggles and harmonies of culture and in part because, by inclination and training, whatever interpretive powers I possess are released by the resonances of literature. I should add that if cultural poetics is conscious of its status as interpretation, this consciousness must extend to an acceptance of the impossibility of fully reconstructing and reentering the culture of the sixteenth century, of leaving behind one's own situation: it is everywhere evident in this book that the questions I ask of my material and indeed the very nature of this material are shaped by the questions I ask of myself.

I do not shrink from these impurities—they are the price and perhaps among the virtues of this approach—but I have tried to compensate for the indeterminacy and incompleteness they generate by constantly returning to particular lives and particular situations, to the material necessities and social pressures that men and women daily confronted, and to a small number of resonant texts. Each of these texts is viewed as the focal point for converging lines of force in sixteenth-century culture; their

significance for us is not that we may see *through* them to underlying and prior historical principles but rather that we may interpret the interplay of their symbolic structures with those perceiv-
able in the careers of their authors and in the larger social world as
constituting a single, complex process of self-fashioning and,
through this interpretation, come closer to understanding how
literary and social identities were formed in this culture. That is,
we are able to achieve a concrete apprehension of the consequences for human expression—for the "I"—of a specific form of
power, power at once localized in particular institutions—the
court, the church, the colonial administration, the patriarchal
family—and diffused in ideological structures of meaning,
characteristic modes of expression, recurrent narrative patterns.

Inevitably, the resonance and centrality we find in our small
group of texts and their authors is our invention and the similar,
cumulative inventions of others. It is we who enlist them in a kind
of historical drama, and we need such a drama in part because
compulsive readers of literature tend to see the world through
literary models and in part because our own lives—quite apart
from professional deformation—are saturated with experience
artfully shaped. If we constantly use devices of selection and
shaping in accounting for our lives, if we insist upon the importance of certain "turning points" and "crises" or, in Freud's
famous modern instance, seize upon the plot of a Sophoclean
tragedy to characterize our shared "family romance," then it is not
surprising that we engage in a similar narrative selection when we
reflect upon our shared historical origins. In attempting to glimpse
the formation of identity in the English Renaissance, we cannot
rest content with statistical tables, nor are we patient enough to
tell over a thousand stories, each with its slight variants. The
problem is not only lack of patience but a sense of hopelessness:
after a thousand, there would be another thousand, then another,
and it is not at all clear that we would be closer to the understanding we seek. So from the thousands, we seize upon a handful of
arresting figures who seem to contain within themselves much of
what we need, who both reward intense, individual attention and
promise access to larger cultural patterns.

That they do so is not, I think, entirely our own critical invention: such at least is one of the enabling presumptions of this
book. We respond to a quality, even a willed or partially willed
quality, in the figures themselves, who are, we assume by analogy
to ourselves, engaged in their own acts of selection and shaping
and who seem to drive themselves toward the most sensitive re-
gions of their culture, to express and even, by design, to embody

its dominant satisfactions and anxieties. Among artists the will to be the culture's voice—to create the abstract and brief chronicles of the time—is a commonplace, but the same will may extend beyond art. Or rather, for the early sixteenth century, art does not pretend to autonomy; the written word is self-consciously embedded in specific communities, life situations, structures of power. We do not have direct access to these figures or their shared culture, but the operative condition of all human understanding—of the speech of our contemporaries as well as of the writings of the dead—is that we have indirect access or at least that we experience our constructions as the lived equivalent of such access.

We should note in the circumstances of the sixteenth-century figures on whom this study focuses a common factor that may help to explain their sensitivity as writers to the construction of identity: they all embody, in one form or another, a profound mobility. In most of the cases, this mobility is social and economic: More, the son of a reasonably successful London lawyer, becomes a knight, Speaker of the House of Commons, Chancellor of the Duchy of Lancaster, Steward of Cambridge University, and finally Lord Chancellor of England, the confidant of Henry VIII; Spenser, the son of a modest free journeyman of the Merchant Taylors Company, becomes a substantial colonial landowner described in royal documents as "a gentleman dwelling in the county of Cork";[10] Marlowe, the son of a shoemaker and parish clerk of Saint Mary's, Canterbury, receives degrees from Cambridge University—a more modest ascent, to be sure, but an ascent nevertheless; Shakespeare, the son of a prosperous glover, is able by the close of his career to acquire, on his father's behalf, a coat of arms and to buy the second largest house in Stratford. All of these talented middle-class men moved out of a narrowly circumscribed social sphere and into a realm that brought them in close contact with the powerful and the great. All were in a position as well, we should add, to know with some intimacy those with no power, status, or education at all. With Tyndale, we have to do not with upward mobility, in the conventional sociological sense, but rather with a highly charged geographical and ideological mobility, a passage from Catholic priest to Protestant, from the Gloucestershire of his successful yeoman farmer family to London and then to Continental exile, from obscurity to the dangerous fame of a leading heretic. Finally, with Wyatt, whose family had risen in status and wealth only in the preceding generation, we have the restless mobility—France, Italy, Spain, Flanders—of the diplomat.

The six writers I consider here then are all displaced in

significant ways from a stable, inherited social world, and they all manifest in powerful and influential form aspects of Renaissance self-fashioning. But the aspects are by no means the same. Indeed my organization in this book depends upon the perception of two radical antitheses, each of which gives way to a complex third term in which the opposition is reiterated and transformed: the conflict between More and Tyndale is reconceived in the figure of Wyatt, that between Spenser and Marlowe in the figure of Shakespeare. Wyatt does not raise the opposition of More and Tyndale to a higher level, though his self-fashioning is profoundly affected by the consequences of that opposition; Shakespeare does not resolve the aesthetic and moral conflict inherent in the works of Spenser and Marlowe, though his theater is enigmatically engaged in both positions. Rather Wyatt and Shakespeare express in literary works more powerful than any produced by their contemporaries the historical pressure of an unresolved and continuing conflict. Moreover, the issues raised at the theological level in the works of More and Tyndale are recapitulated at the secular level in the works of Spenser and Marlowe, while Shakespeare explores in *Othello* and elsewhere the male sexual anxieties—the fear of betrayal, the suspension and release of aggression, the intimations of complicity in one's own torment—voiced in Wyatt's lyrics.

We may posit a direction enacted by these figures in relation to power: for the first triad, a shift from the Church to the Book to the absolutist state; for the second triad, a shift from celebration to rebellion to subversive submission. Similarly, we may posit a direction enacted by the works of literature in relation to society: a shift from absorption by community, religious faith, or diplomacy toward the establishment of literary creation as a profession in its own right. But we must recognize that such approximate and schematic chartings are of limited value. The closer we approach the figures and their works, the less they appear as convenient counters in a grand historical scheme. A series of shifting, unstable pressures is met with a wide range of discursive and behavioral responses, inventions, and counterpressures.

There is no such thing as a single "history of the self" in the sixteenth century, except as the product of our need to reduce the intricacies of complex and creative beings to safe and controllable order. This book will not advance any comprehensive "explanation" of English Renaissance self-fashioning; each of the chapters is intended to stand alone as an exploration whose contours are shaped by our grasp of the specific situation of the author or text. We may, however, conclude by noting a set of governing conditions common to most instances of self-fashioning—whether of the authors themselves or of their characters—examined here:

1. None of the figures inherits a title, an ancient family tradition or hierarchical status that might have rooted personal identity in the identity of a clan or caste. With the partial exception of Wyatt, all of these writers are middle-class.

2. Self-fashioning for such figures involves submission to an absolute power or authority situated at least partially outside the self—God, a sacred book, an institution such as church, court, colonial or military administration. Marlowe is an exception, but his consuming hostility to hierarchical authority has, as we shall see, some of the force of submission.

3. Self-fashioning is achieved in relation to something perceived as alien, strange, or hostile. This threatening Other—heretic, savage, witch, adulteress, traitor, Antichrist—must be discovered or invented in order to be attacked and destroyed.

4. The alien is perceived by the authority either as that which is unformed or chaotic (the absence of order) or that which is false or negative (the demonic parody of order). Since accounts of the former tend inevitably to organize and thematize it, the chaotic constantly slides into the demonic, and consequently the alien is always constructed as a distorted image of the authority.

5. One man's authority is another man's alien.

6. When one authority or alien is destroyed, another takes its place.

7. There is always more than one authority and more than one alien in existence at a given time.

8. If both the authority and the alien are located outside the self, they are at the same time experienced as inward necessities, so that both submission and destruction are always already internalized.

9. Self-fashioning is always, though not exclusively, in language.

10. The power generated to attack the alien in the name of the authority is produced in excess and threatens the authority it sets out to defend. Hence self-fashioning always involves some experience of threat, some effacement or undermining, some loss of self.

To sum up these observations, before we turn to the rich lives and texts that exemplify and complicate them, we may say that self-fashioning occurs at the point of encounter between an authority and an alien, that what is produced in this encounter partakes of both the authority and the alien that is marked for attack, and hence that any achieved identity always contains within itself the signs of its own subversion or loss.

At the Table of the Great: More's Self-Fashioning and Self-Cancellation

"A Part of His Own"

A dinner party at Cardinal Wolsey's. Years later, in the Tower, More recalled the occasion and refashioned it in *A Dialogue of Comfort Against Tribulation* as a "merry tale," one of those sly jokes that interlace his most serious work. The story reaches back to a past that, in the gathering darkness of 1534, might well have seemed to More almost mythical, back before the collapse of his career, the collapse of his whole world. Perhaps as important, it reaches back to a time before More had decided to embark upon his career. He pictures himself as an ambitious, clever young man, eager to make a good impression, but at the same time an outsider: in his fictionalized version, he is a Hungarian visitor to Germany. The vainglorious prelate—transparently Wolsey—had that day made an oration so splendid in his own estimation that he sat as if on thorns until he could hear it commended by his guests. After casting about in vain for a discreet way of introducing the subject, the cardinal finally asked bluntly what the company thought of his oration. Eating and conversation came to an abrupt halt: "Every man was fallen in so deep a study for the finding of some exquisite praise."[1] Then one by one in order, each guest brought forth his flattering speech. When the young More had played his part, he felt confident that he had acquitted himself well, the more so in that he was to be followed by an ignorant priest. But the priest—a "wily fox"—far surpassed him in the craft of flattery, and both in turn were bested by the last to speak, a "good ancient honorable flatterer" who, when he saw that he could not exceed the elaborate compliments already produced, spoke not a word, "but as he that were ravished unto heavenward with the wonder of the wisdom and eloquence that my Lord's grace had uttered in that oration, he fet [i.e., fetched] a long sigh with an "oh" from the bottom of his breast, and held up both hands, and lifted up his head, and cast up his eyes into the welkin, and wept" (215–16).

How much of More is in this little story! The jibes at the ignorant priest who "could speak no Latin at all" and at the rich, worldly cardinal are the last sparks of that humanist indignation at clerical abuses that he once shared with Erasmus and that had somehow survived fifteen years of bitter anti-Protestant polemics. The setting recalls the rich significance for More of the dinner party, emblem of human society both in its foolish vanity and in its precious moments of communion. Above all, the acute observation of social comedy links the story to More's lifelong fascination with the games people play. The particular game in this case is the satisfaction of self-love, played by fools who rejoice to think "how they be continually praised all about as though all the world did nothing else day nor night, but ever sit and sing *sanctus sanctus sanctus* upon them" (212). The rich and powerful have the means to realize this fantasy: in their "pleasant frenzy" they hire flatterers who do nothing but sing their praises.

This is the distillation of More's long career in the dangerous, glittering world of Renaissance politics, the essence of his observation of king and cardinal: bloated vanity, ravenous appetite, folly. The spectacle at once repelled and fascinated him; he could never bring himself simply to renounce the world in holy indignation. On the contrary, he made himself into a consummately successful performer: from modest beginnings in the early 1490s as a young page in the household of Lord Chancellor Morton, four decades of law, diplomacy, parliamentary politics, and courtship brought More in 1529, as Wolsey's successor, to the Lord Chancellorship, the highest office in the realm. Then, as if to confirm all of his darkest reflections on power and privilege, his own position quickly deteriorated beneath the pressure of the king's divorce. In May 1532, attempting to save himself, More resigned the chancellorship on the pretext of ill health, but he was too important and too visible to be granted a silent, unmolested retirement. Refusal to subscribe to the Oath of Supremacy—that is, to acknowledge that the king was Supreme Head of the Church in England—brought him in 1534 to the Tower and, on 6 July 1535, to the scaffold.

This chapter will describe the complex interplay in More's life and writings of self-fashioning and self-cancellation, the crafting of a public role and the profound desire to escape from the identity so crafted, and I propose that we keep in our minds the image of More sitting at the table of the great in a peculiar mood of ambition, ironic amusement, curiosity, and revulsion. It is as if he were watching the enactment of a fiction, and he is equally struck by the unreality of the whole performance and by its immense power to impose itself upon the world. This is, in fact, one of the central perceptions of the *Dialogue of Comfort,* repeated again and again in an endless variety of guises. No sooner is one fantasy laid to rest than another pops up to be grappled with in turn and defeated, until the whole world, the great body of man's longings, anxieties, and goals, shimmers like a mirage, compelling, tenacious, and utterly unreal.

But why should men submit to fantasies that will not nourish or sustain them? In part, More's answer is *power,* whose quintessential sign is the ability to impose one's fictions upon the world: the more outrageous the fiction, the more impressive the manifestation of power. The vain cardinal may be in the grip of madness, but he can compel others to enter the madness and reinforce it. So too, a generation earlier, Richard III cast his ruthless seizure of the throne in the guise of an elaborate process of offer, refusal, renewed offer, and reluctant acceptance. The point is not that anyone is deceived by the charade, but that everyone is forced either to participate in it or to watch it silently. In a brilliant passage of his *History of Richard III,* More imagines the talk among the common people who have just witnessed the sinister farce. They marvel at the whole performance, since no one could be expected to be taken in by it, but then, as one of them observes, "men must sometime for the manner sake not be aknowen what they know."[2] After all, a bishop goes through a similar charade at his consecration, though everyone knows he has paid for his office. And likewise, at a play, everyone may know that the man playing sultan is, in fact, a cobbler, but if anyone is foolish enough to "call him by his own name while he standeth in his majesty, one of his tormentors might hap to break his head."

> And so they said that these matters be king's games, as it were stage plays, and for the more part played upon scaffolds. In which poor men be but the lookers-on. And they that wise be will meddle no farther. For they that sometime step up and play with them, when they cannot play their parts, they disorder the play and do themselves no good. (81)

To try to break through the fiction is dangerous—one can have one's head broken. To try to take a part of one's own, "to step up and play with them," is equally dangerous. On the one hand, the great have the means to enforce their elaborate, theatrical ceremonies of pride; on the other, those ceremonies are usually performed, ominously, on scaffolds.

But if wealth and force are the props on which such ceremonies are based, why should the great bother with the masquerade at all? More's observation that few, if any, among the performers or the audience are taken in by the elaborate pretense obviates a purely political explanation such as Machiavelli, describing similar rituals, provides. For Machiavelli, the prince engages in deceptions for one very clear reason: to survive. The successful prince must be "a great feigner and dissembler; and men are so simple and so ready to obey present necessities, that one who deceives will always find those who allow themselves to be deceived."[3] The observation hovers characteristically between cynicism and revolt, cold counsel and satire, but at least there is only one layer of deception: strip off that layer and you reach the naked realities of appetite and fear. The initiated observer can always see beneath the surface and understand how appearances are manipulated by the cunning prince.

In More, appearances have a more problematical relationship to reality. His is a world in which everyone is profoundly committed to upholding conventions in which no one believes; somehow belief has ceased to be necessary. The conventions serve no evident human purpose, not even deceit, yet king and bishop cannot live without them. Strip off the layer of theatrical delusion and you reach nothing at all. That is why Machiavelli's world seems so much more accessible than More's to the inquiring intellect: "My intention being to write something of use to those who understand, it appears to me more proper to go to the real truth of the matter than to its imagination; and many have imagined republics and principalities which have never been seen or known to exist in reality; for how we live is so far removed from how we ought to live, that he who abandons what is done for what ought to be done, will rather learn to bring about his own ruin than his preservation" (56). There are spiraling ironies in this famous passage from *The Prince*, but the vertigo is arrested by a passionate commitment to life in this world and by a hard, steady confidence that it is possible to penetrate "to the real truth of the matter."

More, of course, could claim with even greater confidence to know the "real truth," but his was a truth of an entirely different order, capable of *canceling*, but not *clarifying*, human politics. In neither of his great political works, the *History of Richard III* and *Utopia*, does he invoke this ultimate religious truth as a decisive explanation: in the former, he writes a historical narrative in imitation of classical models; in the latter, he illuminates contemporary politics with the light not of his faith but of his imagination, inventing one of those republics "which have never been seen or known to exist in reality." His work then has neither the cold clarity of cynicism nor the confident purposefulness of providential history showing God unfold his great plan through the agency of second causes. For Machiavelli and the providential historian alike, the political world is transparent; for More, it is opaque. And his great faith, his sense of the absolute truth, seems only to have increased that opacity, by rendering political life essentially *absurd*.

More did, to be sure, spend much of his career acting as if Parliament, the Privy Council, the law courts, and the royal court were anything but absurd, as if his own considerable gift for compromise, subtle maneuver, and partial reform might well contribute to a rational amelioration of social life and a comfortable position for himself and his family. The tragic drama of his end may obscure for us his remarkable ability to survive and flourish for decades in perilous political waters. After all, the survival rate for those closest to Henry VIII roughly resembles the actuarial record of the First Politburo. More could scarcely have succeeded for as long as he did had his response to power consisted merely of remarking its absurdity. He was evidently a canny judge of human motives, possessed a firm grasp of the complex network of material interests that underlay the intricate formalities of Tudor government, and knew well how to make his own place within these formalities. The actual texture of his long public life is thick with the ceremonies of power. And yet when he tries to explain why the great bother with these ceremonies, why they stage elaborate theatrical rituals, he concludes ultimately not in a sense of rational calculation but in a sense of the absurd: because they are mad, possessed by "fond fantasies," incapable of distinguishing between truth and fiction. It is not only Machiavellian calculation but humanist reform that finds its limits in this madness: political life cannot be resolved into underlying forces, cannot be treated as a code that the initiated understand and manipulate, because it is fundamentally insane, its practitioners in the grip of "frenzies." And it is not only political life, in the narrow sense, that is so judged, but the great body of man's social relations.

To understand More, we must take this haunting perception of universal madness very seriously, not, in other words, simply as a rhetorical device or conventional turn of phrase, but as a central and enduring response to existence. It is a response he shared, like so much else, with Erasmus, whose *Praise of Folly* is its supreme and definitive expression. But *The Praise of Folly* is a dangerous tool for exploiting More's response to life, in part because of the fundamental differences between Erasmus and More (the former a dissatisfied monk, impatient with confinement; the latter a dissatisfied layman, impatient with liberty), in part because of the success and familiarity of Erasmus's great work. Only when we pass from the confidence, flexibility, and charm of the literary masterpiece to the nervous instability over which it triumphed can we feel how disturbing as a lived experience is the sense of the absurd, how it marked for More a profound alienation from his society, from the greater part of his acquaintance, from himself. It is as if, in the midst of intensely valued attachments to family and friends, he carried within himself the perspective of the London Charterhouse in which he had lived, without vow, for four years, a perspective from which not only the ceremonies of the great but most of his own involvements seemed to him manifestations of limitless folly. "I assure thee, on my faith," he told his daughter in his cell in the Tower, "if it had not been for my wife and you that be my children, whom I accompt the chief part of my charge, I would not have failed long ere this to have closed myself in as strait a room—and straiter too."[4]

Admiration for More should not be permitted to efface the disturbing estrangement of this summary utterance at the end of his life. To be sure, More is responding in a characteristically brilliant and one might say witty way to the horrible conditions in which he found himself: he consoles his grieving daughter by transforming the suffering inflicted upon him into a gift, in effect making his destiny his choice. (And indeed that destiny was in a very real sense his choice, though not a choice he actively sought to make.) But there is more than comfort against tribulation here; in his words to Margaret, More gives voice to a lifelong current of contempt for a world reduced in his mind to madness, a rejection not only of all the pride, cruelty, and ambition of men, but of much that he himself seemed to cherish, a desire to escape into the fastness of a cell. In part, this attitude should no doubt be traced less to qualities peculiar to More than to the style of late medieval culture with its intense shiver of revulsion against the world it nonetheless embraced.[5] But our knowledge of More's participation in a larger cultural mood should not diminish our sensitivity to its actual effect in his life and writings.

To grasp the precise character of what I have called More's estrangement, we might compare it with the mood evoked by Holbein's famous work "The Ambassadors" (see frontispiece), painted in London two years before More's execution. Jean de Dinteville, seigneur de Polisy and Francis I's ambassador to the English court, and his friend Georges de Selve, shortly to be bishop of Lavaur, stand at either side of a two-shelved table. They are young, successful men, whose impressively wide-ranging interests and accomplishments are elegantly recorded by the objects scattered with careful casualness on the table: celestial and terrestrial globes, sundials, quadrants and other instruments of astronomy and geometry, a lute, a case of flutes, a German book of arithmetic, kept open by a square, and an open German hymn book, on whose pages may be seen part of Luther's translation of the "Veni Creator Spiritus" and his "Shortened Version of the Ten Commandments." The hymn book suggests more, of course, than the interest in music that is elsewhere indicated; its presence in the portrait of two important Catholic statesmen may signal the French king's attempt, by cynically advancing the Lutheran cause in England, to further tension between Henry VIII and the emperor Charles V, or, alternatively, it may mark that moment in European history in which it still seemed possible to cultivated men of good will that the Catholic Church and the Reformers could meet on common ground and resolve their differences. If More had once harbored such a hope, the moment for him was long past.[6]

Dinteville and Selve are depicted in the context of the highest hopes and achievements of their age. The objects on the table between them, set off splendidly by the rich Turkish cloth and the exquisite mosaic pavement, represent a mastery of the Quadrivium, that portion of the Seven Liberal Arts comprising Music, Arithmetic, Geometry, and Astronomy, while a mastery of the Trivium—Grammar, Logic, and Rhetoric—is implied by the very profession of the two figures.[7] They are thus in possession of the instruments—both literal and symbolic—by which men bring the world into focus, represent it in proper perspective. Indeed, in addition to their significance as emblems of the Liberal Arts, the objects on the table virtually constitute a series of textbook illustrations for a manual on the art of perspective.[8] The Renaissance invested this art with far more than technical significance; for Neoplatonism in particular, the power to map, mirror, or represent the world bore witness to the spark of the divine in man. As Ficino writes, "Since man has observed the order of the heavens, when they move, whither they proceed and with what measures, and what they produce, who could deny that man possesses as it were almost the same genius as the Author of the heavens? And who could deny that man could somehow also make the heavens, could he only obtain the instruments and the heavenly material, since even now he makes them, though of a different material, but still with a very similar order."[9]

The terrestrial and celestial spheres, the sword and the book, the state and the church, Protestantism and Catholicism, the mind as measurer of all things and the mind as unifying force, the arts and the sciences, the power of images and the power of words—all are conjoined then in Holbein's painting and integrated in a design as intricate as the pavement. And yet slashing across the pavement, intruding upon these complex harmonies and disrupting them, is the extraordinary anamorphic representation of the death's-head. Viewed frontally, the skull is an unreadable blur in the center foreground of the painting; only from the proper position at the side of the painting is it suddenly revealed.[10]

The death's-head is most obviously a bravura display of Holbein's virtuosity, elsewhere manifested in his rendering of the complex network of surfaces on the geometrical instruments,[11] but it also bears a more integral relation to the composition as a whole. In a major study of the painting and its subjects, Mary F. S. Hervey observed that Dinteville's cap is adorned by a small brooch on which is engraved a silver skull, and concluded that the ambassador must have adopted the death's-head as his personal badge or *devise*.[12] This theory is plausible, but it should not be made to suggest too ornamental a function for elements that, in one's experience of the painting, are far more disquieting. The skull as *devise* is at once a gesture of self-adornment and a gesture of self-cancellation. Death may be reduced on Dinteville's cap to a fashionable piece of jewelry, an enhancement of the self, but this reduction seems as much mocked as confirmed by the large alien presence that has intruded into this supremely civilized world of human achievement.[13] The anamorphic death's-head draws to itself another discordant element in the painting: the broken string of the lute, an emblematic play upon the very idea of discord.[14] Together these suggest a subtle but powerful countercurrent to the forces of harmony, reconciliation, and confident intellectual

achievement embodied elsewhere in the picture's objects and figures. None of these antitypes is immediately visible—the ornamental skull and broken string reveal themselves only to the
closest scrutiny, only, that is, if one abandons the large, encom-
passing view of the painting and approaches the canvas with such
myopic closeness that the whole gives way to a mass of individual
details. To see the large death's-head requires a still more radical
abandonment of what we take to be "normal" vision; we must
throw the entire painting out of perspective in order to bring into
perspective what our usual mode of perception cannot com-
prehend.

Death's presence in Holbein's painting is at once more elusive
and more disturbing than the conventional representations of
death in late medieval art. In the familiar *transi* tombs, for example, the putrescent, worm-eaten corpse on the bottom level may be
said to mock the figure above, dressed in robes of high office.[15]
But the mockery affirms the viewer's understanding of the relation
between life and death, indeed simplifies that understanding. In
this sense, the *transi* tombs, for all their horrible imagery, are
expressions of a certain kind of confidence: the confidence of a
clear perception of things, a willingness to contemplate the inevitable future of the flesh without mystification or concealment. We
can see the body both in its dignity and in its disgrace. In "The
Ambassadors," such clear, steady sight is impossible; death is
affirmed not in its power to destroy the flesh, or as is familiar from
late medieval literature, in its power to horrify and cause unbearable pain, but in its uncanny inaccessibility and absence. What is
unseen or perceived as only a blur is far more disquieting than
what may be faced boldly and directly, particularly when the limitations of vision are grasped as *structural*, the consequence more
of the nature of perception than of the timidity of the perceiver.

The anamorphic skull casts a shadow on the elegant floor—the
shadow of the shadow of death, Hervey neatly calls it—and thus
demonstrates its substantiality, but the shadow falls in a different
direction from those cast by the ambassadors or the objects on the
table.[16] Its presence is thus at once affirmed and denied; if it can
become visible to us, when we take up the appropriate position at
the angle of the painting, it is manifestly not accessible to the
figures in the painting (in the sense that the books and instruments *are* assumed to be accessible). To be sure, Dinteville has
his silver death's-head brooch, but we feel far more the incommensurability between this ornament and the skull on the
floor than their accord. And this incommensurability is confirmed

by the fact that we must distort and, in essence, efface the figures
in order to see the skull. That this effacement is moving—that it is
felt as a kind of death—is a function of Holbein's mastery of those
representational techniques that pay tribute to the world, that
glorify the surfaces and textures of things, that celebrate man's
relatedness to the objects of his making. For there is nothing in the
painting that is not the product of human fashioning—no flower,
no lapdog, no distant landscape glimpsed through an open window. The heavens and the earth are present only as the objects of
measurement and representation, the objects of the globemaker's
art. It is only when one takes leave of this world—quite literally
takes leave by walking away from the front of the canvas—that one
can see the single alien object, the skull. The skull expresses the
death that the viewer has, in effect, himself brought about by
changing his perspective, by withdrawing his gaze from the figures of the painting. For that gaze is, the skull implies, reality-
conferring; without it, the objects so lovingly represented in their
seeming substantiality vanish. To move a few feet away from the
frontal contemplation of the painting is to efface everything within
it, to bring death into the world.

I have spoken of the skull as alien and inhuman, but to do so is
itself an ironic distortion, for it is the one object in the painting
that is at once human and completely *natural* in the sense of being
untouched by artifice. There are, to be sure, the faces and hands of
Dinteville and Selve, and yet so strong is the sense of *pose* as
Holbein depicts them that they seem, of all the objects in the
painting, the most artificially crafted. They possess a calculated
impenetrability that suggests, in the hands, the carefully
fashioned casualness counseled by Castiglione and, in the faces,
the masking counseled by Machiavelli.[17] The skull then is virtually
unique in its inaccessibility to the power of human shaping affirmed everywhere else in the painting; it is the sole occupant of a
category that nonetheless counterpoises all of the other objects.

Yet paradoxically this skull, emblem of that which resists and
outlasts artifice, is treated aesthetically with the most spectacular
display of the painter's ingenuity and skill, just as paradoxically
the death's-head, emblem of the negation of human achievement,
is worn by Dinteville as a fashionable ornament, a badge of status
akin to the Order of Saint Michael he wears around his neck. The
effect of these paradoxes is to resist any clear location of reality in
the painting, to question the very concept of locatable reality upon
which we conventionally rely in our mappings of the world, to
subordinate the sign systems we so confidently use to a larger

doubt. Holbein fuses a radical questioning of the status of the world with a radical questioning of the status of art. For the painting insists, passionately and profoundly, on the representational power of art, its central role in man's apprehension and control of reality, even as it insists, with uncanny persuasiveness, on the fictional character of that entire so-called reality and the art that pretends to represent it. In the context of our normal relationship to a painting—indeed in the context of the physical stance we conventionally assume before any object we have chosen to perceive—the marginal position is an eccentric flight of fancy, virtually a non-place, just as the skull exists in a non-place in relation to all the other objects Holbein depicts. But to enter this non-place is to alter everything in the painting and to render impossible a simple return to normal vision. Of course, we do return and reassume that perspective that seems to "give" us the world, but we do so in a state of estrangement. In the same artistic moment, the moment of passage from the center of the painting to the periphery, life is effaced by death, representation by artifice. The non-place that is the place of the skull has reached out and touched phenomenal reality, infecting it with its own alienation. Jean de Dinteville and Georges de Selve, so present to us in their almost hallucinatory substantiality, are revealed to be pigments on stretched canvas, an illusionist's trick. They who seem to be present before us exist nowhere, exist then in utopia.

For I justify this long discussion of "The Ambassadors" on the ground that it plunges us, with the sensuous immediacy and simultaneity that only a painting can achieve, into the full complexity of More's estrangement and the richness of his art. The world of Dinteville and Selve was More's world; with the image before us of the table laden with books and instruments, we may recall Roper's account of the period during which More was, in Elton's phrase, Henry VIII's "pet humanist." "When he had done his own devotions," Roper writes, the king would send for More "into his traverse, and there sometime in matters of astronomy, geometry, divinity, and such other faculties, and sometimes of his worldly affairs, to sit and confer with him. And other while would he in the night have him up into his leads, there for to consider with him the diversities, courses, motions, and operations of the stars and planets." [18] The conclusion of the anecdote in Roper is wonderfully revealing: finding himself increasingly trapped by these flattering royal attentions, More "began thereupon somewhat to dissemble his nature," in other words, to become a bore, until his company was no longer so much in demand. If this seems to lead us away from Holbein's ambassadors, presumably vying for the king's attention, it is only because More had in supreme measure those skills of rhetoric and learning that a Dinteville would have assiduously cultivated.

It is not, however, the French humanists whom More most resembles but the genius who painted them (and indeed we may speculate that the magnificent achievement of Holbein's portraits of More and his family owes something to the special bond of understanding that we are trying to sketch here). If More's interests embraced astronomy, music, rhetoric, geometry, geography, and arithmetic, he was also profoundly capable of withdrawing from these interests, altering his perspective in such a way as to unsettle any underlying assumptions upon which all these methods of ordering and measuring the world were based. More important still, this engagement and detachment do not occupy two separate, successive moments in More's career—an early involvement in the world, followed by disillusionment and withdrawal, for example, or even a more complex round of alternating states—but rather are closely bound up with each other throughout his life, while in his greatest works, they are fused with the intensity and power we have encountered in the Holbein painting. This is above all true, of course, of *Utopia*, whose subtle displacements, distortions, and shifts of perspective are the closest equivalent in Renaissance prose to the anamorphic virtuosity of Holbein's art. Like "The Ambassadors," *Utopia* presents two distinct worlds that occupy the same textual space while insisting upon the impossibility of their doing so. We can neither separate them entirely nor bring them into accord, so that the intellectual gratification of radical discontinuity is as impossible to achieve as the pleasure of wholly integrated form. We are constantly tantalized by the resemblances between England and Utopia—analogous to Dinteville's death's-head brooch in relation to the skull—and as constantly frustrated by the abyss that divides them; and no sooner do we confidently take the measure of the abyss than we perceive a new element that seems to establish the unmistakable link between them. This is more than a case of "like in some ways, unlike in others," as if we had two distinct objects that we could hold up to each other and compare, for the two worlds in *Utopia* occupy the same space and are in an essentially unstable relationship to each other. The division of the work into two books is, in this regard, like one of More's straight-faced jokes, for it invites us to establish a simple order of contrast that the work frustrates: Utopia and its analogues inhabit the world of book I just as England inhabits the world of book II. Similarly, the personae More and Hythlodaeus sit in the same garden and converse with each other, but as in Holbein's painting, they cast shadows in different directions and are, in crucial respects, necessarily blind to each other.

This disquieting internal rupture—this sense within the general frame of the work of incompatible perspectives between which the reader restlessly moves—is mirrored at virtually every level of the text, from its largest units of design to its smallest verbal details. Elizabeth McCutcheon has recently called attention to the significance of the latter in a fine discussion of More's extraordinarily frequent use of litotes, a rhetorical figure "in which a thing is affirmed by stating the negative of its opposite."[19] More's use of the figure, she writes, bespeaks "a tendency to see more than one side to a question"; more important, for our purposes, it compels a mental movement, a psychological passage from one point to another and back again.[20] This restless shifting of perspective is, I would suggest, the close equivalent at the verbal level to the visual technique of anamorphosis, whose etymology itself suggests a back-and-forth movement, a constant forming and re-forming.

It would obviously take us too long, even were it in our power, to explicate in detail all of *Utopia*'s anamorphic techniques, but, beyond litotes, we may point to the network of linkages and contradictions worked out with mandarin complexity by Louis Marin in his recent *Utopiques*. Marin demonstrates, with at least partial success, that there are in the smooth surface of Utopian life a series of half-hidden ruptures, ruptures betrayed by subtle inconsistencies and contradictions in topography, economic exchange, the exercise of power, concepts of criminality, and the uses of violence. These ruptures, according to Marin, reveal the presence in the work of the half-effaced signs of its own production, the presence of those sociohistorical forces to which Utopia owes its existence and which it is designed to render invisible. In the midst of Utopian description—timeless, immobile, synchronic, maplike—there survive *traces* of narrative that mark in the finished product the hidden processes by which it was produced. These brief, fragmentary narrative enclaves destroy the structural integrity of the description, tear the canvas, writes Marin, on which the best government is depicted.[21] But where Marin would speak of a canvas torn, I would speak, at least in most of the instances he analyzes, of a subtle anamorphic art that constantly questions its own status and the status of the world it pretends to represent. That is, Marin seems to underestimate

More's self-consciousness, a self-consciousness for once the match of its Gallic counterparts. If there exist highly significant "blind spots" in *Utopia*—for example, an urban design that does not seem to allow for the centralized exercise of power that the system nevertheless calls for—they exist like the great, central blind spot in Holbein's "Ambassadors": as the object of the artist's profound, playful attention.

This playfulness—so easily acknowledged and ignored—deserves special emphasis, for it occupies a central role in both the painting and the book. The arts of mapmaking, calculation, and measurement that figure so prominently in "The Ambassadors" and *Utopia* have important practical functions in everyday life, but they are present here as recreation, the elegant play of distinguished and serious men. This play is not conceived by humanists as an escape from the serious, but as a mode of civility, an enhancement of specifically human powers. As such, the globes and compasses, along with the lute and flutes, sit without contradiction next to the book of merchant's arithmetic, on the one hand, and the book of divine worship, on the other, just as the mock alphabet and maps of *Utopia* are bound up—literally and figuratively—with a searching inquiry into the sources of human misery and the possibilities of human government. The distorted skull in Holbein's painting, for all the grimness of its imagery, is itself an invitation to the viewer to play, while the reader of *Utopia* is invited to enter a carefully demarcated playground that possesses nonetheless a riddling relation to the world outside.[22] That the playfulness in "The Ambassadors" focuses on a skull suggests that the anamorphic technique may derive in part at least from medieval methods of meditation, particularly the concentration upon an object—frequently the death's-head—that enables one to lose the world, to perceive the vanity of human life and the illusory quality of reality.[23] One might argue that Holbein's painting signals the *decay* of such methods, a loss of intensity that can only be partially recuperated through illusionist tricks, but if so, one must conclude that this decay released a magnificent aesthetic byproduct. And while *Utopia* too may owe something to meditative technique, detached from its original purpose, one would be hard pressed from More's works to conclude that the technique was in decay.

In almost all his writings, More returns again and again to the unsettling of man's sense of reality, the questioning of his instruments of measurement and representation, the demonstration of blind spots in his field of vision. In the *Dialogue of Comfort,* Antony challenges Vincent to prove that he is awake and not merely dreaming that he is awake, or dreaming that he has been challenged to prove his wakefulness, or dreaming that he has responded to this challenge by moving his limbs or talking rationally, or dreaming that he is merrily describing such a dream to his friends, or dreaming that he has finally appealed beyond body and words to the unshakable conviction in his soul that he is awake. None of Vincent's responses does anything to arrest the vertiginous fall into an infinite regress of self-mirroring dreams; as with similar games played by Nicholas of Cusa, the mind is driven at once to an acknowledgment of the conjectural status of all its operations and to a profession of faith.[24] In these arguments, Antony says, we must appeal finally to "the Scripture of God" and "the common faith of Christ's Catholic Church."[25] This faith is not, it should be noted, an *answer* to the speculations about sleep and waking; rather it may more fairly be said to license those speculations, to transform into play thoughts that might otherwise lead, as More implies, to suicide or heresy.

We may recall at this point an object in Holbein's painting that until now we barely noted: the crucifix only half visible at the extreme edge of the curtain. This sign is not impervious to effacement—after all, it is turned into a blur, along with everything else, when the skull is brought into focus—yet it may be said to possess a certain cultic imperviousness to the corrosive effects of anamorphosis. In this sense, the marginal presence of the crucifix—symbol of life redeemed from death—sanctions the marginal presence of the skull—emblem of death lurking beneath life. Similarly, Antony's faith is theoretically susceptible to the charge of being a dream, but More refuses to carry the argument that far, for it is precisely faith that invites the speculation even as it closes off the infinite regress. But is there any guarantee of this imperviousness to anamorphic subversion? Not, I think, within the painting or the text themselves: any assurance must be imposed from without, by an individual or by an interpretive community with an interest in establishing a fixed point beyond the ceaseless oscillation of irreconcilable perspectives. Holbein's painting seems deliberately ambiguous about the ultimate origin of this assurance: both the Catholic Church and Lutheran faith are invoked, and we might note that his earlier woodcut series on the Dance of Death was printed, within the space of a few years, by both Catholic and Protestant printers in Lyons.[26] More's *Dialogue of Comfort,* by contrast, is not at all ambiguous: Antony's assurance rests not upon the feeling faith of the individual, but upon the power exercised jointly by the sacred text and by the institution that controls interpretation of that text. The daring of *Utopia* is to be gauged by the extreme marginality of the Scripture of God and the common faith of Christ's Catholic Church: in defense of Utopian principles, Hythlodaeus several times invokes the "doctrine" and "authority" of Christ, but the institutional implications of this authority are unspoken. Like Holbein, More had partially pulled the curtain in front of the crucifix.[27]

What unites *Utopia*—enigmatic in its relation to the ultimate authority of the Church—and the *Dialogue of Comfort*—unambiguously committed to that authority—is More's lifelong interest in the ironies that arise from man's confident belief in illusions. The dreamer who insists that he is awake is only one of a network of such ironies that we may trace all the way back to the pageant verses More composed in his youth. "Old and young, man and woman, rich and poor, prince and page," he writes characteristically in the unfinished *Four Last Things* (1522), "all the while we live in this world, we be but prisoners, and within a sure prison, out of which there can no man escape," but few of us have ever glimpsed the walls, and we strut about as though we were free. Or again, "all our whole life is but a sickness never curable, but as one uncurable canker, with continual swaddling and plastering, botched up to live as long as we may, and in conclusion undoubtedly to die of the same sickness, and though there never came other"[28]—but few of us understand our condition, and we strut about as though we were in health.

We find the same vision expressed in almost the same words in More's early epigrams and again, near the end of his life, in the *Dialogue of Comfort:* they clearly represent a sustained and repeated impulse toward the unsettling of reality. And in their deep disillusionment, they are the foundation of his famous humor whose most characteristic mode is the portrayal of men entangled in their own fantasies:

> If ye shouldest perceive that one were earnestly proud of the wearing of a gay golden gown, while the losel playeth the lord in a stage play, wouldest ye not laugh at his folly, considering that ye are very sure, that when the play is done, he shall go walk a knave in his old coat? Now ye thinkest thy self wise enough while ye art proud in thy players garment, and forgettest that when thy play is done, ye shalt go forth as poor as he. Nor ye

rememberest not that thy pageant may happen to be done as soon as his.[29]

The theatrical metaphor was More's favorite, and for good reason: it is the point in which the disparate and seemingly discontinuous aspects of his existence come together, touch, and resonate. For the stage as emblem of human existence combines, as it were, the competing perspectives of Holbein's painting: the theater pays tribute to a world that it loves—or at the least that it cannot live without—even as it exposes that world as a fiction. More uses theatrical imagery to depict a world living out rituals in which it has ceased fully to believe, to display the folly of human pretensions, to evoke the great leveling power of Death, who strips the king of his rich robes and reduces him at last to the same state as the poorest beggar. The metaphor has a leveling effect even without the invocation of death, for to conceive of kingship as a dramatic part, an expensive costume and some well-rehearsed lines, is potentially at least to demystify it, to reduce its sacral symbolism to tinsel. The dangerous implications of this demystification can be seen quite clearly in More's epigram "On the King and the Peasant." A forest-bred peasant comes to town and sees a royal procession. When the crowd roars out "Long live the king!" and with rapt expressions gazes up at the ruler, the peasant calls out, "Where is the king? Where is the king?"

And one of the bystanders replied, "There he is, the one mounted high on that horse over there." The peasant said, "Is that the king? I think you are fooling me. He seems to me to be a man in an embroidered garment."[30]

From here it is only one step to the revolutionary outrage of John Ball or at the least to the bitter anger of More's own fictional character, Raphael Hythlodaeus, inveighing against the conspiracy of the rich. But far more often in More's works the theatrical metaphor turns inward, expressing his tragicomic perception of life lived at a perpetual remove from reality. All men are caught up in receding layers of fantasy: the spectator laughs or is angry to see another pride himself on a mere fiction, while he himself is no less a player, no less entrameled in fantasy. More's sense of human absurdity then at once leads him to social criticism and undermines that criticism, enabling him to ridicule the ideology of the powerful but severely limiting the practical consequences of that ridicule. Revolution, as Marx understood, can have no traffic with inner intimations of unreality.

It would be a mistake, however, to leave the discussion of the theatrical metaphor in More at the level of his inner life, for the metaphor corresponds quite closely to the actual theatricalization of public life in the society dominated by Henry VIII and Cardinal Wolsey. Henry's taste for lavish dress, ceremonial banquets, pageantry, masque, and festivity astonished his contemporaries and profoundly affected their conception of power. More's humorous sketch of the pompous royal procession is far surpassed in extraordinary elaboration by contemporary accounts of the king, accounts that almost always sound like broad parody and almost never are. Even Henry's vigorous and imposing bulk is fairly lost beneath the sheer mass of stuff—jewels, feathers, yards of rich cloths—with which he bedecked himself; there is nothing in our culture outside the most opulent operatic productions or atavisms like Siena's Palio to suggest even faintly this frantic passion for dressing up:

> The second night were diverse strangers of Maximilian the Emperor's court and ambassadors of Spain with the king at supper; when they had supped, the king willed them to go into the queen's chamber, who so did. And in the mean season, the king with 15 others appareled in Almain [German] jackets of crimson and purple satin, with long quartered sleeves, with hose of the same suit, their bonnets of white velvet, wrapped in flat gold of damask, with visors and white plumes, came in with a mummery, and after a certain time that they had played with the queen and the strangers, they departed. Then suddenly entered 6 minstrels, richly appareled, playing on their instruments, and then followed 14 persons gentlemen, all appareled in yellow satin, cut like Almains, bearing torches. After them came 6 disguised in white satin and green, embroidered and set with letters and castles of fine gold in bullion; the garments were of strange fashion, with also strange cuts, every cut knit with points of fine gold and tassels of the same, their hose cut and tied in likewise, their bonnets of cloth of silver, wound with gold. First of these 6 was the king. . . . Then part of the gentlemen bearing torches departed and shortly returned, after whom came in 6 ladies appareled in garments of crimson satin embroidered and traversed with cloth of gold, cut in pomegranates and yokes, stringed after the fashion of Spain. Then the said 6 men danced with these 6 ladies; and after that they had danced a season, the ladies took off the men's visors, whereby they were

known: Whereof the queen and the strangers much praised the king, and ended the pastime.[31]

It is important to quote such accounts at length (and this is only a small fragment) in order to convey the amazing elaborateness of this "mummery," the staggering opulence, the attention to detail, the sheer energy invested by participants and observers alike. We have come to expect impressionism in accounts of grand pageants; on the contrary, the chronicler and his audience revel in detail, in knowing precisely what kinds of cloth were used, what color, what cut. We think of elegance as allied to simplicity, a minimizing of means; on the contrary, Henry and his court valued superabundance, variety, intricacy, and overpowering insistence on cost. The more conspicuous the consumption the better: the king's fingers "were one mass of jewelled rings," wrote the Venetian ambassador, "and around his neck he wore a gold collar from which hung a diamond as big as a walnut."[32] This is not, of course, simply self-indulgence, though it is certainly that; display shades into diplomacy, amorous dalliance into high politics. But it would be a mistake to pass too quickly to the social, political, or diplomatic uses we may discover in this behavior; to do so is to lose the sense of colossal waste, of inexhaustible appetite, of power utterly materialized in clothes and jewels. If we attend patiently to the multihued silks, damasks, and sarcenets, to the masques, tourneys, and banquets, to the velvet forest created within the palace and the golden palace created within the velvet forest, we find ourselves observing a realm of matter so rich, detailed, and intense that it becomes unreal before our eyes, like a seascape beneath a brilliant sun. We achieve then for a moment an intimation of the world that More observed in the early sixteenth century and found theatrically mad.

More did not simply judge this world; he participated in it as an actor among the rest—if the theatrical metaphor expresses his inner sense of alienation and his observation of the behavior of the great, it also expresses his own mode of engagement in society. That mode began early; in a well-known passage of his *Life of More,* William Roper recalls that as a boy in Cardinal Morton's household More distinguished himself by his extemporaneous performances: "Though he was young of years, yet would he at Christmas-tide suddenly sometimes step in among the players, and never studying for the matter, make a part of his own there presently among them, which made the lookers-on more sport than all the players beside."[33] This youthful talent is, as Roper

understood, brilliantly evocative in its manifestation of dazzling
rhetorical facility and its striking anticipation of the later career, a
career in which More was at once enmeshed in a larger drama and
yet never the mere reciter of lines anyone else had written. Yet
somewhere behind Roper's words, in our mind if not in his, lies
More's own comment on the danger of such playing in the king's
games: "For they that sometime step up and play with them, when
they cannot play their parts, they disorder the play and do themself no good." More was always aware of the tension that underlay
the seemingly effortless performance, and the mingling of this
tension with his evident delight makes his self-consciousness as a
player both compelling and elusive.

Certainly some of More's most fervent admirers were mystified
and even embarrassed by his participation in what he calls the
"stage plays" of the great, embarrassed particularly by his own
professed theatricality. Thus when Nicholas Harpsfield in his Marian biography—hagiography rather—of More retells the anecdote
of the dinner party at Cardinal Wolsey's, he is clearly uncomfortable at the part More cast for himself in his own version, the part
of a willing but somewhat second-rate flatterer. After quoting
More's account, Harpsfield hastens to repair what he evidently
perceives as cracks in the saint's image:

> In this vainglorious pageant of my Lord Cardinal,
> though, as it appeareth, Sir Thomas More was in a
> manner forced, contrary to his sober and well-known
> modest nature, to play a part to accommodate himself
> somewhat to the players in this foolish, fond stage play,
> yet I doubt nothing, if his answer were certainly
> known, he played no other part than might beseem his
> grave, modest person, and kept himself within reason-
> able bounds, and yielded none other than competent
> praise. For in very deed the oration was not to be dis-
> praised or disliked. But, as we began to say, whether it
> were for that, as it is not unlikely, that Sir Thomas More
> would not magnify all the Cardinal's doings and say-
> ings above the stars . . . or for some other causes, he
> never entirely and from the heart loved him.[34]

In three sentences, More's complex irony, his self-conscious
playing in the cardinal's pageant, vanishes: first he is forced,
against his modest nature, to play a part, then the part is none
other than that same modest nature, then the part entirely vanishes in the simple expression of just and reasonable praise, finally

even this praise dissolves, and More emerges as a resolute plain-speaker who incurs the cardinal's secret dislike by refusing to flatter him.

Harpsfield's embarrassment is comical, but it is not merely squeamish: it reflects, in its own way, the peculiar ambivalence that we have already encountered in More's response to the world, ambivalence signaled by the variety of meanings that attach to his use of the theatrical metaphor. More's mode of being is, after all, genuinely perplexing and uncomfortable, the more so in the context of early sixteenth-century England, where it represents something quite exceptional. For his life seems nothing less than this: the invention of a disturbingly unfamiliar form of consciousness, tense, ironic, witty, poised between engagement and detachment, and above all, fully aware of its own status as an invention. These elements may be perceived in the lives of others who preceded him, but scattered, isolated; in More, they are self-consciously integrated and set in motion both in literary discourse and in the actual social world. Indeed, a distinction between text and lived reality such as may be implied by the close of the preceding sentence is precisely abrogated by More's mode of existence. For one consequence of life lived as histrionic improvisation is that the category of the real merges with that of the fictive; the historical More is a narrative fiction. To make a part of one's own, to live one's life as a character thrust into a play, constantly renewing oneself extemporaneously and forever aware of one's own unreality—such was More's condition, such, one might say, his project. Small wonder that Harpsfield felt uncomfortable!

What is haunting about such a project is the perpetual self-reflexiveness it demands, and, with this self-reflexiveness, perpetual self-estrangement. More is committed to asking himself at all times "What would 'More' say about this?" and to ask such a question implies the possibility of other identities unfulfilled by the particular role that he is in the act of projecting. From this, the peculiar shadows that hover about him throughout his career, not only the shadow of the designing consciousness manipulating the mask but the shadow of other selves, crouched in the darkness. Occasionally a shaft of light catches one of these for an instant, as when More tells Margaret that, had it not been for his family, he would long ago have shut himself in a narrow cell, or when he writes about his distracting engagements in the letter to Peter Giles that prefaces *Utopia:*

> I am constantly engaged in legal business, either pleading or hearing, either giving an award as arbiter

or deciding a case as judge. I pay a visit of courtesy to one man and go on business to another. I devote almost the whole day in public to other men's affairs and the remainder to my own. I leave to myself, that is to learning, nothing at all.

When I have returned home, I must talk with my wife, chat with my children, and confer with my servants. All this activity I count as business when it must be done—and it must be unless you want to be a stranger in your own home.[35]

There is always, it seems, a "real" self—humanistic scholar or monk—buried or neglected, and More's nature is such that one suspects that, had he pursued wholeheartedly one of these other identities, he would have continued to feel the same way. For there is behind these shadowy selves still another, darker shadow: the dream of a cancellation of identity itself, an end to all improvisation, an escape from narrative. The dream, as I shall argue, is played out in *Utopia*, and its consequence is that More's life, and not simply his public life in the law court or the royal administration but his private life in his household or among his friends, seems *composed, made up*. If we may believe Roper, this quality extended even to his choice of a wife: More, the story goes, loved the second daughter of Master Colt, but when he considered that the elder daughter would be shamed by being passed over, he "of a certain pity framed his fancy towards her, and soon after married her" (199). A family myth perhaps, but there is ample evidence elsewhere, including More's own eloquent testimony in his letter to Giles, for his willingness to "frame his fancy." "Although . . . because of a certain unique perspicacity in your make-up you are accustomed to dissent sharply from the crowd," Erasmus writes to More in the preface to *Praise of Folly*, "at the same time because of your incredibly affable and easy ways you can play the man of all hours with all men, and enjoy doing so." More "is not offended even by professed clowns," Erasmus tells Ulrich von Hutten some years later, "as he adapts himself with marvelous dexterity to the tastes of all; while with ladies generally and even with his wife, his conversation is made up of humour and playfulness."[36]

This protean adaptability is closely linked to More's constant recourse in his writing to the hypothetical situation. This is, to be sure, one of the characteristic devices of the lawyer and rhetorician, but in its pervasiveness and intensity it seems much more than a device for More. "Suppose that," "what if," "put the case that," "picture," "imagine"—his mind works brilliantly and, it seems, inevitably in this mode.[37] Certainly More's enemies were highly aware of his penchant for fictions: "Mr. More hath so long used his figures of poetry," writes Tyndale, "that (I suppose) when he erreth most, he now by the reason of long custom believeth himself that he saith most true."[38] For Tyndale, poetry is synonymous with lying; it is a term of abuse: "O poet, without shame!" His one concession to a richer meaning is to allow that More may have been taken in by his own falsehoods. But for More, as we have seen, fictions have a far more complex and elusive function. He does not, it should be stressed, simply exclude Tyndale's meaning; he has a powerful sense both of the way men use the "figures of poetry" to lie and of the way men get entangled in their own fabrications. But then he makes up a part of his own and plays it alongside the other actors. And if this self-fashioning is the mark of an alienation that extends to his own life, private as well as public, it is also, as Erasmus's tribute makes clear, the source of much that is delightful, inventive, and energetic in More. The hypothetical situations and histrionic improvisations are, after all, manifestations of that brilliant playfulness that issued in *Utopia*.

Utopia

Utopia offers the profoundest commentary on those aspects of More's life that we have been discussing; it is at once the perfect expression of his self-conscious role-playing and an intense meditation upon its limitations. At the heart of this meditation is the character of Raphael Hythlodaeus and his relation to the "More" who appears in the work as both presenter (or recorder) and character. Hythlodaeus, in effect, represents all that More deliberately excluded from the personality he created and played; he is the sign of More's awareness of his own self-creation, hence his own incompleteness.

The poignancy of this sense of incompleteness is heightened by the fact that More presents himself in *Utopia* in all of his circumstantial reality. The "I" of the work is a man tied in a hundred ways to his particular time and place, to his offices, responsibilities, family and friends. Rarely before had a work created so successful an illusion of reality; with a few deft strokes More evokes a whole world of busy men immersed in their careers: Cuthbert Tunstal, whom the king "has just created Master of the Rolls to everyone's immense satisfaction"; the burgomaster of Bruges, "a figure of magnificence"; Georges de Themsecke, provost of Cassel, "a man not only trained in eloquence but a natural orator"; Peter Giles, "a native of Antwerp, an honorable man of high position in his home town." And at the center of this group is Thomas More, "citizen and sheriff of the famous city of Great Britain, London," the king's "orator" in certain complex negotiations in the Netherlands. This is a man linked to other men, a man with a well-defined, widely acknowledged public identity, and that identity is further substantiated in the flurry of letters and commendations that preface the work. Erasmus to John Froben, William Budé to Thomas Lupset, Peter Giles to Jerome Busleyden, John Desmarais of Cassel to Peter Giles, Busleyden to More, More to Giles—the letters establish More in the midst of a distinguished community of Northern European humanists, men who know More personally or by reputation and who discuss his work among themselves in that special personal spirit one reserves for the books of friends.[39]

One notable effect of this circumstantiality is to heighten the realism that attaches to Hythlodaeus and his account of his travels, a realism that More and his friends have fun with in their maps, vocabulary, and solemn pedantry. But there are other effects as well. Into this mutual admiration society of successful men erupts a figure who does not fit, who steadfastly refuses to fit. If Hythlodaeus seems real to us, rubbing elbows as he does with well-known historical personages, he seems, by the same token, the very embodiment of the stranger, "a man of advanced years, with sunburnt countenance and long beard and cloak hanging carelessly from his shoulder" (49). And More deliberately renders this strangeness more striking, even in the midst of his careful realism, by immediately identifying Hythlodaeus with the fabulous and imaginary. As Hythlodaeus establishes himself with ever greater power in the conversation with More and Giles, a process takes place that is the very opposite of heightened realism. Thomas More, the solid, middle-aged, smiling public man, is, as it were, fictionalized by his relationship to the stranger. More's acute sense in his life of being "More," a made-up figure played as on a stage, is manifested directly in his becoming just that: *Morus*, a character in an imaginary dialogue. And in a moment of quite extraordinary self-consciousness and irony, Morus and Hythlodaeus discuss precisely this process of fictionalization.

The context of this discussion is the debate on the question of state service. Hythlodaeus flatly rejects Peter Giles's suggestion that, as an enlightened and eloquent man, he "attach himself to some king." Nothing, he objects, could be more frustrating or futile, and to prove his case, he imagines himself in the council of the French king, arguing for peace where everyone else is war-mongering, advising the king to amend his own indolence and arrogance where everyone else is busy puffing them up, warning the king to adjust his expenses to his revenues where everyone else is counseling him to pillage his people. "To sum it all up, if I tried to obtrude these and like ideas on men inclined to the oppo-site way of thinking, to what deaf ears should I tell the tale!" (97). Morus is forced to grant Hythlodaeus's point, but he counters by arguing that it is mere foolishness to thrust radical ideas upon individuals who cannot possibly be expected to accept them or even consider them seriously. There is no room for academic phi-losophy with rulers,

> but there is another philosophy, more practical for statesmen, which knows its stage, adapts itself to the play in hand, and performs its role neatly and appropri-ately. This is the philosophy which you must employ. Otherwise we have the situation in which a comedy of Plautus is being performed and the household slaves are making trivial jokes at one another and then you come on the stage in a philosopher's attire and recite the passage from the *Octavia* where Seneca is disputing with Nero. Would it not have been preferable to take a part without words than by reciting something in-appropriate to make a hodgepodge of comedy and tragedy? You would have spoiled and upset the actual play by bringing in irrelevant matter—even if your contribution would have been superior in itself. What-ever play is being performed, perform it as best you can, and do not upset it all simply because you think of another which has more interest. (99)

Hythlodaeus, the fictional character, speaks for directness, for what we would now call authenticity; Morus, the "real" man, speaks for submission to fiction, for accommodation to the play at hand. Indeed, Morus tries to reduce Hythlodaeus's authenticity itself to a part, in this context a particularly ridiculous and in-appropriate part. To insist upon reciting one's stiff-necked and solemn lines regardless of the other characters is to make oneself both absurd and ineffectual; the man who wishes to contribute to the betterment of society learns how to adapt himself. Hythlodaeus, in reply, rejects the implication that he too is merely playing a part and argues that the accommodation to fictions *(fabulae)* Morus counsels is tantamount to the telling of lies *(falsa)*, corruption all the more dangerous for being cloaked as public service. Not only will nothing good be accomplished in the public realm, but the would-be virtuous councillor will lose his liberty and become, in effect, an actor in the prince's play, a play that is both sinister and insane.

This debate, with its self-conscious recollections of Plato and Seneca, is a literary set-piece, as *Utopia*'s early readers would have recognized, but it also represents a real and pressing problem, both in More's personal life and in his culture. There are periods in which the relation between intellectuals and power is redefined, in which the old forms have decayed and new forms have yet to be developed. The Renaissance was such a period: as intellectuals emerged from the Church into an independent lay status, they had to reconceive their relation to power and particularly to the increasing power of the royal courts. For most, not surprisingly, this simply meant an eager, blind rush into the service of the prince; as Hamlet says of Rosencranz and Guildenstern, they did make love to this employment. But there was also a substantial and serious exploration of the implications of such employment, its responsibilities and dangers, and a few men like Pico della Mirandola and Erasmus hesitated, resisted, and cautioned. More, at once ambitious and deeply influenced by both Pico and Erasmus, was, as it were, poised at the center of these issues. As he wrote book I of *Utopia,* he was trying to decide the extent of his commitment to the service of Henry VIII, a decision which he well knew would shape the course of his life.[40] And at stake, as I have suggested, was not simply his career but his whole sense of himself, the dialectic between his engagement in the world as a character he had fashioned for himself and his perception of such role-playing as unreal and insane.

In the debate that opens *Utopia* then, More isolates, on the one hand, his public self and, on the other, all within him that is excluded from this carefully crafted identity, calls the former *Morus* and the latter *Hythlodaeus* and permits them to fight it out. Gradually, the positions become clearer, until, in the exchange we have just discussed, the fundamental, irreconcilable opposition is expressed and the debate nears its climax. And it is at this point that we hear once again, after a long hiatus, of Utopia and learn, for the first time, its central innovation: the abolition of private property. What is the relation between this new theme—Utopian communism—and the extended argument that has preceded it? J. H. Hexter, the most astute student of the structure of More's work, has argued precisely that there is no relation, that this is one of the points at which we may perceive More stitching together pieces that he wrote quite independently and that represent "two different and separate sets of intention."[41] For Hexter, Hythlodaeus's praise of Utopian communism at the close of book I is simply a convenient structural device, a formal bridge to book II. The eulogy of the Utopian community of all things does function in this way, but I would suggest that it serves a deeper purpose: it is, exactly as it appears to be, the climax of book I, a debate not simply over public service but over one's whole mode of being.

Communism is Hythlodaeus's radical response to the role-playing which More both argued for and embodied. Against the "philosophy...which knows its stage," he offers an uncompromising vision of root-and-branch changes in the structure of society and hence in the structure of the individual. Like Marx's early *Economic and Philosophical Manuscripts,* More's work propounds communism less as a coherent economic program than as a weapon against certain tendencies in human nature: selfishness and pride, to be sure, but also that complex, self-conscious, theatrical accommodation to the world which we recognize as a characteristic mode of modern individuality. *Utopia* then is not only a brilliant attack on the social and economic injustices of early sixteenth-century England but a work of profound self-criticism, directed at the identity More had fashioned for himself and that he would play for increasing amounts of his time, should he accept the proffered royal appointment. It is not that More turns against himself in self-disgust; rather he sees his mode of being as a deliberate stratagem against the evils of his time. And through Hythlodaeus, he permits himself both to question the effectiveness of the stratagem and to imagine a radical alternative.

The heart of this alternative is an uncompromising rejection of private property: "It appears to me," Hythlodaeus states flatly, "that wherever you have private property and all men measure all things by cash values, there it is scarcely possible for a commonwealth to have justice or prosperity—unless you think justice exists where all the best things flow into the hands of the worst citizens or prosperity prevails where all is divided among very few" (103). At a stroke, Hythlodaeus dismisses the elaborate ideology of status and custom that provided a time-honored justification for the unequal distributions of wealth in society. Indeed he scarcely has to attack this ideology because no one in the work rises to defend it. When Morus objects to communism, he does so on the grounds that it impoverishes the commonwealth and ignores human psychology—"Life cannot be satisfactory where all things are common" (107)—not that it violates the privileges of the feudal nobility.[42] If the middle-class More cannot rest easy with his own carefully fashioned social identity, he will not, at the same time, allow an identity to be given fully formed by an exalted name and title. The pretensions of the social hierarchy to embody a "natural" moral order are ridiculed in *Utopia*. There is no rebuttal even when, at the work's end, Hythlodaeus carries his version of contemporary society to its extreme conclusion: "When I consider and turn over in my mind the state of all commonwealths flourishing anywhere today, so help me God, I can see nothing else than a kind of conspiracy of the rich, who are aiming at their own interests under the name and title of the commonwealth" (241).

All measures that aim at reform and stop short of a complete abolition of private property are inadequate: "There is no hope . . . of a cure and a return to a healthy condition as long as each individual is master of his own property. Nay, while you are intent upon the cure of one part, you make worse the malady of the other parts. Thus, the healing of the one member reciprocally breeds the disease of the other as long as nothing can so be added to one as not to be taken away from another" (105–7). Without the communal ownership of property, every man is set against every other man, for it is impossible to possess anything without wresting it somehow from the possession of another.[43] The resulting competitiveness is reflected in the rancorous debates Hythlodaeus describes; it is as if even ideas were possessed as private property, each man fiercely defending his own. In such a society, individuals are isolated, unattached save where their material interests chance to coincide, while at the same time there is no true independence: all value depends upon the admiration or envy excited by what is displayed and consumed. Men become acutely sensitive to all they are permitting others to see and all that they are concealing within themselves. Even the few virtuous men who wish to have no part in the competition must develop the same sensitivity; after all, this is just what Morus counsels Hythlodaeus to do. By implication then, private ownership of property is causally linked in *Utopia* to private ownership of self, what C. B. Macpherson calls "possessive individualism";[44] to abolish private property is to render such self-conscious individuality obsolete.

Utopian institutions are cunningly designed to reduce the scope of the ego: avenues of self-aggrandizement are blocked, individuation is sharply limited. In a society based on private property, all things are acquired *at the expense of* someone else; the pleasure of possession is, at least in part, the knowledge that someone else desires and does *not* possess what you do. In Utopia, pride of possession and pride of place are obliterated. Clothes "are of one and the same pattern throughout the island and down the centuries" (127); the capes worn over these clothes are "of one color throughout the island and that the natural color" (133). Food is divided equally, and meals are taken in common. The houses, all three stories high, "are set together in a long row, continuous through the block and faced by a corresponding one" (121); lest anyone become personally attached to one of these identical buildings, "every ten years they actually exchange their very homes by lot" (121). Presumably, few Utopians notice the change.

There is no place in Utopia then for the dazzling extravagance, the sumptuous waste that fascinated and repelled More; no Wolsey or Henry VIII could indulge his inexhaustible appetite and swell with the immense accumulation of possessions. If the king and cardinal seemed larger than life, it was because they were just that, unnaturally bloated with the labors, the very lives, of others. In Utopia, occupations that cater to luxury or licentiousness are eliminated, so that not only is there an abundance of necessary goods but no man may be said either to labor in the service of another's will or merely to consume the labor of another. Virtually all men work; every thirty families annually choose an official called a syphogrant, whose "chief and almost . . . only function . . . is to manage and provide that no one sit idle, but that each apply himself industriously to his trade" (127). The syphogrants themselves, though legally exempted from work, take no advantage of this privilege. Occupations are distributed equitably, and the worst tasks—those that degrade or deaden a person—are performed by slaves. This latter feature is chilling, but then More has asked himself questions that the writers of such fantasies almost never ask: who slaughters the meat? who disposes of the filth? If Utopia is designed to reduce the size of the ego, to eliminate the possibility of a Henry VIII and to obviate the necessity of a More, it is equally designed to prevent the existence of a class of laborers reduced to the condition of animals. The syphogrants provide that no one sit idle, but they also provide that no citizen be "wearied like a beast of burden with constant toil from early morning till late at night." Such wretchedness, observes Hythlodaeus, "is worse than the lot of slaves, and yet it is almost everywhere the life of workingmen—except for the Utopians" (127).

The Utopian workday of six hours is astonishingly short by the standards set in Tudor statutes;[45] we could argue then that, far from discouraging individuation, Utopian institutions are designed to permit its greatest possible flourishing. After all, "the constitution of their commonwealth looks in the first place to this sole object: that for all the citizens, as far as the public needs permit, as much time as possible should be withdrawn from the service of the body and devoted to the freedom and culture of the mind" (135). Such a goal, unbounded by distinctions of class, caste, or sex, is genuinely radical. But here we encounter a crucial characteristic of Utopia: the steady constriction of an initially limitless freedom. The English translation accurately renders the syntactic movement of the original: "The intervals between the hours of work, sleep, and food are left to every man's discretion, not to waste in revelry or idleness, but to devote the time free from work to some other occupation according to taste" (127–29). These occupations turn out to be two in number: attendance at pre-dawn public lectures or, "as is the case with many minds which do not reach the level for any of the higher intellectual disciplines," voluntary continuation of the regular labor. The endless day prescribed by the Statute of Artificers[46] is scarcely longer than that envisaged here, though one should add that there is, after supper, an hour's recreation, in the summer in the gardens, in the winter in the dining halls.

Similarly, the account of Utopian travel begins with almost unlimited license and ends with almost total restriction. A citizen can go where he chooses . . . provided he has a letter from the governor granting him leave to travel and fixing the date of his return. (For travel within the territory belonging to his own city, he needs only the consent of his wife and father.) Wherever he goes, he must continue to practice his trade. These regulations are not to be taken lightly: "If any person gives himself leave to stray out of his territorial limits and is caught without the governor's certificate, he is treated with contempt, brought back as a runaway, and severely punished. A rash repetition of the offense entails the sentence of slavery" (147).[47]

The pattern is repeated again and again in Hythlodaeus's account: freedoms are heralded, only to shrink in the course of the description. The cause is not cynicism; rather prohibitions are placed solely on what the Utopians take to be unnatural behavior. Presumably, it is only from a corrupt point of view—one tainted by individuality, a thirst for variety and novelty, a conviction that each person possesses his existence as a piece of private property—that what remains after the unnatural has been weeded out seems hopelessly thin and limited. The Utopians believe quite otherwise, and they take pains to reduce sharply the number of points of reference by which men mark themselves off from each other. Indeed, even the larger units of differentiation within society are obliterated. The uniformity of dress strikes out not only against vanity but against the elaborate distinctions of rank and occupation that were reflected (and legally regulated) in Tudor dress. Even so basic a distinction as city versus country is eliminated; all men and women are trained in agriculture and spend at least some years farming. A reader of a work like Fernand Braudel's *The Mediterranean and the Mediterranean World in the Age of Philip the Second* will appreciate how deep and fundamental are the network of distinctions that the Utopians thus overturn; he will appreciate too how radical is More's vision of national uniformity: "The island contains fifty-four city-states, all spacious and magnificent, identical in language, traditions, customs, and laws. They are similar also in layout and everywhere, as far as the nature of the group permits, similar even in appearance.... The person who knows one of their cities will know them all" (113–17). More dreams here of sweeping away the centuries-old accumulation of local and particular culture, marked seemingly indelibly in all the varieties of dress, speech, architecture, behavior. And we may perceive this dream—as men have always perceived it in its recurrent forms through the centuries—in two quite different ways: on the one hand, as the sweeping away of the clutter of generations, all that resists improvement and justice, all the stubborn insularity, selfishness, and invidious distinctions that make life unbearable for the great mass of mankind; on the other hand, as a failure to appreciate the opacity of social existence, to grasp that men thrive on particularity and variety, to understand that endless sameness destroys the individual.

But then the destruction of the individual as a private and self-regarding entity is a positive goal in Utopia; at the least, the ways in which a person could constitute himself as a being distinct from those around him are radically reduced. As we have seen, More's sense of his own distinct identity is compounded of a highly social role, fashioned from his participation in a complex set of interlocking corporate bodies—law, parliament, court, city, church, family—and a secret reserve, a sense of a life elsewhere, unrealized in public performance. Utopia cancels such an identity by eliminating, among other things, most of the highly particularized corporate categories in which a man could locate himself and by means of which he could say,"I am *this* and not *that*." There remain, to be sure, hierarchical distinctions between the sexes and between the generations—"Wives wait on their husbands, children on their parents, and generally the younger on their elders" (137)—but even these are carefully designed to prevent a high degree of particularization.

If, as Hexter has persuasively argued, Utopia is founded on patriarchal familism,[48] it is important to grasp what elements of the early modern family the Utopians reflect and what elements are noticeably missing. In Utopia, marriage is the rule, even for priests (thereby eliminating concubinage as a widespread, if somewhat disreputable, alternative); adultery is punished "by the strictest form of slavery" and, in the case of a second offense, by death (191); mothers nurse their own offspring (a practice that even the urgent counsel of Renaissance physicians could not bring about for the middle and upper classes);[49] families lodge together; husbands discipline their wives, parents their children. Sectarian religious rites, as distinct from the common worship of Mithras, take place in the home, and even confession is a family affair: "Wives fall down at the feet of their husbands, children at the feet of their parents" (233). For Lawrence Stone, Utopia gives ideal expression to the "rise of the nuclear family in early modern England" and the decline of other, competing affective bonds: "Where Plato's ideal had involved the destruction of the family, that of More involved the destruction of all other social units."[50]

At the same time, we must remember that the sick are cared for not in the home but in hospitals; that houses do not reflect the individual identity of the families that inhabit them; that "though nobody is forbidden to dine at home, yet no one does it willingly since the practice is considered not decent [*honestum*] and since it is foolish to take the trouble of preparing an inferior dinner when an excellent and sumptuous one is ready at hand in the hall nearby" (141). The strictly enforced monogamy and sexual exclusiveness are not necessarily signs of the emotional intensity of the marriage bond; the reason that Utopians punish extramarital intercourse so severely, Hythlodaeus reports, "is their foreknowledge that, unless persons are carefully restrained from promiscuous intercourse, few will unite in married love, in which state a whole life must be spent with one companion and all the troubles incidental to it must be patiently borne" (187). And lest such an explanation seem to place a high value on sexual pleasure, we are told that the Utopians classify intercourse, along with defecation and scratching, as an agreeable but decidedly low form of pleasure:[51] "If a person thinks that his felicity consists in this kind of pleasure, he must admit that he will be in the greatest happiness if his lot happens to be a life which is spent in perpetual hunger, thirst, itching, eating, drinking, scratching, and rubbing. Who does not see that such a life is not only disgusting but wretched?" (177). Utopian marriage then does not strive for a deep affective union between husband and wife based upon their sexual intimacy; the latter serves the interest of generation, which in turn serves the general interest of the community rather than the particular interest of the family. A belief in inherited family characteristics, such as was widespread in the Renaissance and survives to our own time, would be counter to the Utopian commitment to human malleability and interchangeability, and hence there is no concern for a family "line" or for the purity of the "blood." No household may have fewer than ten or more than sixteen adults: "This limit is easily observed by transferring those who exceed the number in larger families into those that are under the prescribed number" (137).

Above all, there is no family inheritance, no transfer of property in marriage, no sense of the family fortune. For the most part, each child is brought up "in his father's craft, for which most have a natural inclination" (127), but this is merely a practical convenience: "If anyone is attracted to another occupation, he is transferred by adoption to a family pursuing that craft for which he has a liking" (127). Without patrimony, there is no need for planning, no sense of the family's future across the generations. Such planning is not an incidental feature of family life in More's age but, according to Natalie Davis, one of its central and defining concerns:

> Some want merely to pass on the family's patrimony as intact as possible to those of the next generation who will stand for the house or its name in the father's line. Others want to enhance that patrimony; still others want to create a patrimony if it does not already exist.

And what is being planned for here is not merely lands, cattle, houses, barns, pensions, rents, offices, workshops, looms, masterships, partnerships, and shares, but also occupations or careers and the marriages of children. These, too, must be designed so as to maintain, and perhaps increase, the family's store and reputation.[52]

Not one of these characteristic features survives in Utopia, where family strategies are entirely subsumed under state strategies. If Utopia is founded on the institution of the family, that institution bears only partial resemblance to the actual families of early modern Europe.

More has, in effect, imagined a split in the family as he would have known it, so as to preserve its disciplinary power while discarding its exclusiveness and particularity. Children kneel at the feet of their parents, as the adult More, Chancellor of England, still knelt publicly to receive his father's blessing, but the family is not permitted to develop a grasp of its own identity and property in itself, a sense of the "arrow" of its fortunes in historical time.[53]

It is no accident that Hythlodaeus does not give us the name of a single Utopian except, of course, Utopus himself; it is difficult to think, even in this most patriarchal of societies, of the father's name being passed on as the property of his heirs, just as it is difficult to think of individual Utopians. The problem with envisaging such distinct, named individuals is not simply that More has used the family to eliminate the dense network of corporate bodies that once differentiated man and then used communism to eliminate the individuating power of the family, but that he has greatly restricted any sense of *personal* inwardness that might have compensated for the effacement of differences in the social world. Even pleasure, which would seem irreducibly personal and subjective, is understood by the Utopians to be an entirely objective phenomenon. To be sure, they profess to value pleasure very highly: "They seem to lean more than they should," Hythlodaeus says gravely, "to the school that espouses pleasure as the object by which to define either the whole or the chief part of human happiness" (161). But here again, what at first seems to be a limitless vista turns out to be something less. The Utopians do not embrace every kind of pleasure, but only "good and decent" pleasure. Indeed, as in Plato, such virtuous pleasure is all that is held to exist; other sensations may be perceived as pleasurable, but such perceptions are illusory. What then of the enjoyment that a person may feel in the course of unacceptable pursuits? The Utopians are unimpressed by the testimony of the senses: "The enjoyment does not arise from the nature of the thing itself but from their own perverse habit. The latter failing makes them take what is bitter for sweet, just as pregnant women by their vitiated taste suppose pitch and tallow sweeter than honey. Yet it is impossible for any man's judgment, depraved either by disease or by habit, to change the nature of pleasure any more than that of anything else" (173). There are a limited number of pleasures then, and these may be ranked hierarchically. Pleasure is something located *outside* men; indeed there is scarcely any inside.

With this drastic diminution of self-differentiation and private inwardness, we approach the heart of More's strategy of imagined self-cancellation in *Utopia,* for his engagement in the world involved precisely the maintaining of a calculated distance between his public persona and his inner self. How else could he have sat at Wolsey's table? How could he make his way in a world he perceived as insane and riddled with vicious injustice? Even in his own family he kept back a part of himself from all except, perhaps, his daughter Margaret. His whole identity depended upon the existence of a private retreat; his silences were filled with unexpressed judgments, inner thoughts. It is not surprising to find that in the 1520s More quite literally constructed such a retreat for himself. Not only was his house in Chelsea a place set apart from the scenes of More's public life, but, as Roper tells us, "because he was desirous for godly purpose sometime to be solitary, and sequester himself from worldly company, a good distance from his mansion house builded he a place called the New Building, wherein there was a chapel, a library, and a gallery" (221). Here, alone from morning to evening, More spent his Fridays "in devout prayers and spiritual exercises." In *A Dialogue of Comfort,* Anthony, More's spokesman, counsels such a retreat as a weapon against pride:

> Let him also choose himself some secret solitary place in
> his own house, as far from noise and company as he
> conveniently can, and thither let him some time secretly
> resort alone, imagining himself as one going out of the
> world even straight unto the giving up his reckoning
> unto God of his sinful living. Then let him there before
> an altar or some pitiful image of Christ's bitter pas-
> sion . . . kneel down or fall prostrate as at the feet of
> almighty God, verily believing him to be there invisibly

> present as without any doubt he is. There let him open
> his heart to God, and confess his faults such as he can call
> to mind, and pray God forgiveness. (242–43)

There can be little doubt that this is an account of More's own
practice.

Meditative withdrawal or informal confession was not, of
course, unique to More; in the early fifteenth century, we find
Saint Bernardino of Siena exhorting his hearers to retire to some
closet and look unto themselves, and this counsel is frequently
repeated.[54] As the public, civic world made increasing claims on
men's lives, so, correspondingly, men turned in upon themselves,
sought privacy, withdrew for privileged moments from urban pressures.[55] This dialectic of engagement and detachment is among
those forces that generated the intense individuality that, since
Burckhardt, has been recognized as one of the legacies of the Renaissance. Burckhardt, to be sure, viewed such individuality as a
largely secular phenomenon, but it now seems clear that both
secular and religious impulses contributed to the same psychic
structure. Thus if More piously urges a frequent retreat to "some
secret solitary place," so does Montaigne, though his retreat is
detached from explicitly religious content and infused with the
spirit of ethical stoicism:

> A man that is able may have wives, children, goods,
> and chiefly health, but not so tie himself unto them that
> his felicity depend on them. We should reserve a
> storehouse for ourselves, what need soever chance;
> altogether ours, and wholly free, wherein we may
> hoard up and establish our true liberty and principal
> retreat and solitariness, wherein we must go alone to
> ourselves, take our ordinary entertainment, and so pri-
> vately that no acquaintance or communication of any
> strange thing may therein find place: there to discourse,
> to meditate and laugh, as, without wife, without chil-
> dren and goods, without train or servants, that if by any
> occasion they be lost, it seem not strange to us to pass it
> over; we have a mind moving and turning in itself; it
> may keep itself company.[56]

The word Florio translates as "storehouse" is *arrière-boutique*,
literally a room behind the shop; the word conjures up a world of
negotium, in effect a world of private property. If Montaigne counsels a retreat from this world, he is, at the same time, assuming its
existence; that is, his sense of self is inseparable from his sense of
the *boutique* and all it represents. We are returned forcefully to

More's insight in *Utopia* that there is an essential relationship between private property and private selves. Significantly, in Utopia, there are no *arrière-boutiques* because there are no *boutiques* to begin with.[57] The public realm stretches out into all spaces, physical and psychic. Withdrawal into a "secret solitary place" within one's home is rendered quite literally impossible by the design of the houses: "Every home has not only a door into the street but a back door into the garden. What is more, folding doors, easily opened by hand and then closing of themselves, give admission to anyone. As a result, nothing is private property anywhere" (121). The original is even more to the point: *ita nihil usquam priuati est,* "thus nothing is private anywhere."

This psychological remodeling provides at least a partial answer to the charges that Morus had leveled against communism: that men would not work if they could not keep the products of their labor for themselves or if they could rely on the labor of others; that, in times of want, there would be continual bloodshed and riot, exacerbated by the inevitable breakdown of the authority of magistrates or respect for their office—"for how there can be any place for these among men who are all on the same level I cannot even conceive" (107). Such arguments assume a selfishness that is canceled by the Utopian reduction of the self. In place of the anxious striving of the individual, the Utopians share a powerful sense of relatedness: "The whole island is like a single family" (140). The close attention to occupations, resources, defense, and planning for the future that More excludes from the individual Utopian family is reinstated at the level of the entire community. Respect for magistrates (who are called "fathers" [195]) is sustained not by the unequal distribution of wealth but by each man's absorption into the community and indoctrination in its patriarchal values; disorder is checked not by fines or seizure of property but chiefly by *shaming.*

In the vast literature on *Utopia,* the extremely important role of shame seems to have been neglected, perhaps because readers are struck so powerfully by the penal institution of slavery. A citizen of Utopia can be enslaved for committing "heinous crimes," traveling without leave (second offense), tempting another to an impure act, insisting too vehemently upon religious views, and committing adultery. (One may also choose to accompany into slavery a spouse found guilty of adultery.) Certainly by sixteenth-century standards—and by our own—this is a remarkably short list of punishable offenses, and the absence of the death penalty would have seemed then, as it does to millions now, a dangerous sign of weakness. Granted that there can be no crimes against property, there remain the innumerable minor offenses that, outside Utopia, are adjudicated in court. But in Utopia the whole judicial system is radically simplified: the legal profession, in which More founded his public identity, is nonexistent, and there are very few laws. Social control is maintained in large part by the intense communal pressure of honor and blame:

> If anyone should prefer to devote this [free] time to his trade . . . he is not hindered; in fact, he is even praised as useful to the commonwealth. (129)

> Though nobody is forbidden to dine at home, yet no one does it willingly since the practice is considered not decent. (141)

> [If illness or death prevent a mother from nursing her child, there are many volunteer wet-nurses,] since everybody praises this kind of pity. (143)

> If any person gives himself leave to stray out of his territorial limits and is caught without the governor's certificate, he is treated with contempt. (147)

> [In the case of premarital intercourse, not only is the couple severely punished, but] both father and mother of the family in whose house the offense was committed incur great disgrace as having been neglectful in doing their duties. (187)

> To great men who have done conspicuous service to their country they set up in the market place statues to stand as a record of noble exploits and, at the same time, to have the glory of forefathers serve their descendents as a spur and stimulus to virtue. (193)

> If the women are anxious to accompany their husbands on military service, not only do they not forbid them but actually encourage them and incite them by expressions of praise. . . . It is the greatest reproach for a husband to return without his wife or for a son to come back having lost his father. (209–11)

> [A person who believes that the soul perishes with the body or that the world is a mere sport of chance] is tendered no honor, is entrusted with no office, and is put in charge of no function. He is universally regarded as of a sluggish and low disposition. (223)

It is above all in their famous use of precious metals and gems that the Utopians manifest their full reliance on shame as a method of social control. Out of gold and silver they make chamber pots and other "humble vessels," as well as the chains and solid fetters they put on their slaves. Those who bear "the stigma of disgrace" for some crime have "gold ornaments hanging around their necks, and, as a last touch, a gold crown binding their temples" (153). As a result, of course, gold and silver become "a mark of ill fame." Similarly, pearls, diamonds, and rubies are used to adorn little children; "when they have grown somewhat older and perceive that only children use such toys, they lay them aside, not by any order of their parents, but through their own feeling of shame, just as our own children, when they grow up, throw away their marbles, rattles, and dolls" (153). This Utopian practice is the occasion for the memorable story of the Anemolian ambassadors who arrive in Utopia decked out in their costly garments and are assumed by the common people to be slaves or clowns. After seeing the contempt in which Utopians hold gold and jewels, the ambassadors are "crestfallen and for shame put away all the finery with which they had made themselves haughtily conspicuous" (157). The fantasy must have had a particular piquancy for More, who was serving at the time as royal ambassador: he manages, at a stroke, to metamorphose the king into a despised slave and to devalue the role that he himself had taken in the king's service.

As the experience of the Anemolian ambassadors suggests, slavery functions not only as a penal and economic institution but as an extreme form of shaming.[58] The slave's shame is a significant part of his punishment and serves as well as a deterrent to others. Malefactors are not executed or shut away from public view but forced to do nasty or demeaning work under the gaze of all. The public quality of Utopian space renders this gaze inescapable, for ordinary citizens as well as slaves. Being seen is central to the experience of shame (and, for that matter, of praise), and thus Utopia is constructed so that one is always under observation. In the dining halls, the syphogrants and priests sit in the middle of the first table, "which is the highest place and which allows them to have the whole company in view" (143). Old and young are seated together, so that "the grave and reverent behavior of the old may restrain the younger people from mischievous freedom in word and gesture, since nothing can be done or said at table which escapes the notice of the old present on every side" (143). Similarly, at the religious observances, the heads of the households are seated where they may overlook their families; "every gesture of everyone abroad is observed by those whose authority and discipline govern them at home" (235). Those homes, as we have seen, have no locks on any of the doors, and there are, in addition, no hiding places in the community at large: "Nowhere is there any license to waste time, nowhere any pretext to evade work—no wine shop, no alehouse, no brothel anywhere, no opportunity for corruption, no lurking hole, no secret meeting place. On the contrary, being under the eyes of all, people are bound either to be performing the usual labor or to be enjoying their leisure in a fashion not without decency" (147).

The danger of a social system that depends so heavily upon the constant surveillance of its members is that there are inevitably moments in which physical observation simply fails. Since honor is only lost in the disapproving gaze of others, the absence of the threat of shame would seem to license acts of robbery and violence.[59] The Utopians correct for this problem by inculcating a belief in a constant, invisible surveillance. Even if a man should find a rare moment of privacy in this society where there is nothing but public space, he would be pursued by the sense of being observed and hence by the threat of shame. For the Utopians believe that the dead "move about among the living and are witnesses of their words and actions," and this belief keeps men "from any secret dishonorable deed" (225). Honor and shame being social evaluations, they participate, as J. G. Peristiany observes, in "the nature of social sanctions: the more monolithic the jury, the more trenchant the judgment."[60] The extension of surveillance to the dead in effect renders the jury supremely monolithic and always in session.

There is a further problem in an ethos of honor and shame that should be noted: the inequality of rules. In societies organized around a code of honor, the code normally applies only to those who are worthy of it. "A single system of values of honour," writes Pierre Bourdieu, "establishes two opposing sets of rules of conduct—on the one hand that which governs relationships between kinsmen and in general all personal relationships that conform to the same pattern as those between kinsmen; and on the other hand, that which is valid in one's relationships with strangers."[61] We may see this double standard at work in Utopian foreign relations, where behavior is sanctioned that would be severely punished at home, but within Utopian society the opposition is collapsed by extending the family to the entire island: all

Utopians (with the exception of slaves) are considered kinsmen and hence share the same interest in the preservation of honor.

In Utopia then the greatest moral force in men's lives is respect for public opinion. Citizens are drawn toward virtue by the prospect of honor, the highest honor being rewarded to "the very best among the good," the priests (229). Conversely, to be exposed to ridicule or disgrace—to be laden with gold ornaments or to be regarded "as of a sluggish and low disposition"—is felt to be unbearable; the pressure is enough to ensure a high level of social conformity.

In keeping with our general conception of his character and situation, we may ask ourselves what a culture shaped by the force of shame and honor might have canceled or effaced in More's existence. The answer, I think, is *guilt*, by which I mean pangs of conscience, the inner conviction of sinfulness, the anxious awareness of having violated a law or distanced oneself from God.[62] As we shall see, such feelings are by no means entirely eliminated in Utopia, but the coercive power of public opinion—the collective judgment of the community, perceived as an objective, external fact—diminishes the logical necessity for a mechanism of social control operating within the inner recesses of an individual consciousness such as More's own. There are many signs in More's life of a powerful sense of guilt and sinfulness, whose most striking outward manifestations are the hair shirt he secretly wore and the flagellation he secretly practiced to mortify his flesh. Both of these penitential practices reflect the structure we have come to expect: a public equability, good humor, and self-possession concealing private suffering and judgment.

It would be misleading, I think, to interpret this self-punishment as a consequence of personal pathology or even exclusively as the attempted expiation of an insupportable guilt. The practices were widespread in the period—even Wolsey owned no fewer than three hair shirts, though there is no evidence that he actually wore any of them[63]—and they were conceived as acts of remembrance and almsgiving as well as expiation. But there can be little question that More did experience intense and sustained guilt feelings: quite apart from any deeper psychological roots, his whole mode of life, with its mingled accommodation and resistance to the world, would have called such feelings into being, and they would have been confirmed by the religious ideal of purity that he never eschewed. We may recall that the young More had translated a letter in which Pico della Mirandola writes that "a perfect man should abstain, not only from unlawful pleasure, but also from lawful, to the end that he may altogether wholly have his mind into heavenward and the more purely intend unto the contemplation of heavenly things." And in the *Life* of Pico that More translated, it is reported that "he many days (and namely those days which represent unto us the passion and death that Christ suffered for our sake) beat and scourged his own flesh in the remembrance of that great benefit and for cleansing of his old offenses."[64]

When, at the end of his life, More prays "To know mine own vility and wretchedness," he expresses a lifelong perception of his condition, ritualized in such practices as self-scourging and the daily recitation of the Seven Penitential Psalms.[65] To these symbolic acknowledgments of guilt, we may add the longing for confinement that More voiced at the end of his life, and we may speculate that in 1516, at the turning point in his career, he may have felt with particular intensity the distance that separated him from the monastic life he had rejected. With its theoretical celebration of pleasure and its partial displacement of guilt by shame, Utopia was at least in part a response to this deep current in his life, a dream of relief.

The strong emphasis in Utopia on shame and communal solidarity may have represented as well More's response to certain elements he perceived as dangerous in the religious climate of his time. Protestantism obviously did not spring up from nowhere in 1517; Luther's crisis of guilt was symptomatic of a far broader cultural crisis, as the events of the 1520s and '30s make abundantly clear. Again and again we encounter the same pattern: grave spiritual anxiety, an intense feeling of being in a false or sinful relationship to God, a despairing sense of the impossibility of redemption despite scrupulous ritual observance, suddenly transformed into inner conviction of salvation through faith in God's love. Luther's brilliant exposition of this pattern became, of course, a model, but only because it spoke so powerfully to the psychological and spiritual state already in existence.

More's own spiritual anxieties were contained and consoled by the tenets and practices of the Catholic Church, but by 1516 he may have already seen ample evidence of the condition that would be literally brought home to him several years later in the figure of his son-in-law, William Roper. According to Harpsfield, Roper was a Lutheran when he married Margaret More in 1521. The "fall into heresy" began when a "scruple" of Roper's conscience was not assuaged by the outward observances of the faith; his anxiety grew and was finally laid to rest by the conviction that "faith only did justify," that "only belief should be sufficient."[66] Of course, this experience took place some years after More wrote *Utopia;* in 1516 More had almost certainly never heard of Luther. But it would not have taken a miraculous prescience on More's part to be sensitive to those elements that emerged shortly thereafter at the center of the psychological experience of those who were drawn to Protestantism. And if we may credit More with such sensitivity, we may observe that in emphasizing shame rather than guilt as a social force, Utopia would diminish the possibility of that psychological experience by reducing the inner life and strengthening communal consciousness.

Such reflections may help us to understand how More, who was to become a staunch persecutor of heresy and an undeviating apologist for Catholic orthodoxy, could have conceived for Utopia what was, in the early sixteenth century, a radical policy of religious toleration. The Utopians believe that no one should suffer for his religion, that everyone should be free to follow the doctrine of his choice and to attempt to persuade others of the truth of this doctrine, provided that such attempts remain modest and nonviolent. If this allows a lassitude of belief beyond that permitted in any Renaissance European state and far beyond More's own subsequent policy, it is the logical consequence of a society designed to reduce the scope of the inner life: the Utopians concern themselves far more with what men do than with what they believe. In Utopia that which is not manifested in public behavior has little claim to existence and hence is not the serious concern of the community.

There are, to be sure, restrictions placed on the policy of toleration—here too the broad vista turns out to have its bounds—but these restrictions are attributed to moral rather than dogmatic considerations: the Utopians believe that he who denies the existence of divine providence and the immortality of the soul will inevitably seek to evade the public laws "or to break them by violence in order to serve his own private desires" (223). Dogmatism inevitably enters into this conviction, for there can be no empirical basis for such certainty about the consequences of unbelief, but significantly the dogmatism is virtually hidden from the Utopians themselves: they see themselves not as imposing the tenets of a particular religious faith but rather as defending the public interest against private desires. Characteristically, they defend this interest not by threats and torture—the standard European treatment—but by the withdrawal of honor, public office, and the right to argue in the presence of the common people. In short, the nonbeliever is shamed.

We may add that *Utopia* as a whole acts upon its readers precisely through the ethos of shame; in R. W. Chambers's well-known formulation, "The underlying thought of *Utopia* always is, *With nothing save Reason to guide them, the Utopians do this; and yet we Christian Englishmen, we Christian Europeans . . .!*"[67] Each particular feature of Utopian life holds up to scorn a complementary negative feature in the ordinary world and demonstrates how the abuse of corruption or distortion could be blocked. Utopian shame opposes the undesirable development of inwardness through guilt, as its communism opposes the development of a sense of self-ownership; both are viewed as traps or nightmares. Marx too, it might be observed, saw guilt and private ownership as forces imprisoning men, but not before they had liberated men from other, prior forces; they in turn would have to be destroyed, but they were necessary, indeed inevitable elements in the process of human emancipation. More does not see history in this way; he wishes, as it were, to stop modern history before it starts, even as he wishes to cancel his own identity.

Having come this far, we must quickly qualify our last statement, as we must qualify almost everything we say about More. We must remind ourselves that "Hythlodaeus" means "Well-learned in nonsense," that More deliberately introduces comic and ironic elements that distance his fantasy from himself and his readers, and that More remains ambivalent about many of his most intensely felt perceptions. If *Utopia* is, as I have argued, a work of profound self-criticism, the expression of a longing for self-cancellation, that self has remarkable sustaining power. The imagined existence of Utopia may function as a reproach to a corrupt social order, it may signal the limitations of the usual accommodation to power and property, it may expose the process whereby the established order of things lays claim to reality itself and denies the possibility of alternatives, but *Utopia* is always an imagined existence and vulnerable to the doubts and ironies and civilized demurrals of its creator. The work is, after all, an expression of More's inner life, the life that it dreams of engineering out of existence. The more intense and plausible the dream, the more profound its confirmation of precisely the inner life that engendered it. And if this confirmation is a maddening tribute to the power of that vicious existence that Utopia would obliterate if it could, it is at the same time a pleasing reassurance that the fantasy of self-annihilation may be indulged in playfully without real loss.

We may recall that More finally decided to accept the royal appointment, that he had a strong streak of personal ambition and a complex involvement in the world of competitive enterprise and politic compromise. Significantly, when in 1516, in a letter to Erasmus, he records a playful daydream about Utopia, he imagines himself not as a nameless citizen, attending early morning lectures and plying his useful trade, but as a great prince: "You have no idea how thrilled I am; I feel so expanded, and I hold my head high. For in my daydreams I have been marked out by my Utopians to be their king forever; I can see myself now marching along, crowned with a diadem of wheat, very striking in my Franciscan frock, carrying a handful of wheat as my sacred scepter, thronged by a distinguished retinue of Amautotians, and, with this huge entourage, giving audience to foreign ambassadors and sovereigns."[68] The ego that was to have shrunk to nothing has instead swollen, if only in jest, to heroic size, and we are reminded that far from being effaced by his creation, More was made famous by it. The fame is no accident, thrust upon him, as Roper wishes us to believe was the case with all his worldly successes; More himself conceived the flattering tributes to his genius that accompanied the text, and he asked Erasmus, to whom he had entrusted his work for publication, to supply recommendations not only by scholars but especially by statesmen.[69]

Moreover, within Utopia itself, and particularly in Utopian religion, there are important elements that seem to cut across the communal ethos of shame and honor. Thus we would expect the Utopians, with their prizing of health and comfort, to treat asceticism with derision, but their spirit of ridicule pulls up short before the sect called the Buthrescae, who undertake the most miserable tasks, eschew all sexual activity, abstain from meat, and entirely reject the pleasures of this life. "The more that these men put themselves in the position of slaves"—that is, the more they assume the stigmata of shame—"the more are they honored by all" (227). Hythlodaeus is quite conscious of the anomaly: "If the [Buthrescae] based upon arguments from reason their preference of celibacy to matrimony and of a hard life to a comfortable one, they would laugh them to scorn. Now, however, since they say they are prompted by religion, they look up to and reverence them" (227).

Shame and honor are not, of course, abrogated here but rather are reversed. Elsewhere, however, there are signs that a quite different ethos operates in Utopia alongside the dominant one. Criminals, for example, have their sentences lightened or remitted only "if they show such repentance as testifies that they are more sorry for their sin [*peccatum*] than for their punishment" (191). The distinction shows a surprising concern for an inner state, a concern evidently based on a theological and intentional, rather than purely behavioral, conception of crime. Indeed, despite their mastery of techniques to regulate behavior, the Utopians have little faith in the social basis of morality; they see to it, Hythlodaeus reports, that their children pay attention at religious services, lest they "spend in childish foolery the time in which they ought to be conceiving a religious fear towards the gods, the greatest and almost the only stimulus to the practice of virtues" (235).

One would have thought that there were stimuli enough—massive, constant, relentless inducements to virtue—without the addition of "religious fear," but the Utopians believe otherwise. Shame is a very important part of the enforcement of conformity, but it is not trusted to work alone. The full complement of disciplinary forces may be seen quite clearly in the account of priestly admonition: "It is counted a great disgrace for a man to be summoned or rebuked by them as not being of upright life. It is their function to give advice or admonition, but to check and punish offenders belongs to the governor and the other civil officials. The priests, however, do exclude from divine services persons whom they find to be unusually bad. There is almost no punishment which is more dreaded: they incur very great disgrace and are tortured by a secret fear of religion" (227–29). The public disgrace of excommunication is reinforced by a secret fear which is, in turn, reinforced by the threat of physical punishment: "Even their bodies will not long go scot-free. If they do not demonstrate to the priests their speedy repentance, they are seized and punished by the senate for their impiety" (229). It is here, in this crushing of impiety, that all the coercive powers of Utopian society—shame, guilt, and bodily harm—come together. And the form of their union, in this commonwealth celebrated for its tolerance, is the precise form of the operation of the Holy Inquisition: excommunication, public shaming, the attempt to awaken guilt, the grim transfer of the unrepentant sinner from the religious to the secular arm.[70]

At a moment like this, we realize how tenuous is the balance of forces in *Utopia*—intellectual ambition and self-effacement, Christian humanism and realpolitik, radicalism and the craving for order, reforming zeal and detached irony, confidence in human power and misanthropy, expansiveness and the longing for strict confinement. *Utopia* does not reconcile these forces, nor does it organize them into a coherent, overarching opposition, a clear choice. Rather, it functions as a playground in which a shifting series of apparently incompatible impulses can find intense expression without flying apart or turning violently on each other. Of course, within the work there is a powerful sense of opposing positions—all discussions of *Utopia*, including the present one, invariably acknowledge this feature—but the formal design and the known details of composition have tended to obscure the fact that the work's most vital antinomies are expressed in the same artistic moments. More's act of self-fashioning is precisely an act of self-cancellation, just as his most daringly iconoclastic fantasy expresses his most insistent desire for absolute order.

More brings together then a near-chaos of conflicting psychological, social, and religious pressures and fashions them into a vision that seems at once utterly clear and utterly elusive. I have spoken of the place where this vision occurs as a playground: More's term for it is a *libellus*, a handbook. For the paradoxical unity of *Utopia* depends in large part upon the physical existence of the book, upon the reduction in its printed pages of the conflicting moments of composition to the timeless uniformity of mechanical reproduction, upon its effacement of the hand of the author so as to permit his reintroduction as a fictional character, upon its collapse of the fabulous and the mimetic into the poker-faced neutrality of movable type. And beyond the physical existence of the book, *Utopia* depends upon the simple circumstance— so obvious as to be virtually invisible—that there are not two forms of language, one referential and the other nonreferential, one for truth and the other for fiction. Morus and Hythlodaeus speak the same language; England and Utopia are present by virtue of a single methodology of representation. If this circumstance licenses the realistic description of "no-place," it licenses at the same time the perception that we encountered with "The Ambassadors," namely that the reality we assume in our daily existence is also a construction, as is the identity we deploy in our relations with power.

More felt himself, as I have argued, to be a supremely *constructed* self, and he devised his *libellus* as an exploration of the conditions of this construction, and the possibility of its undoing. But if he imagines the dismantling of the structure of his identity—the transformation of the family, the abolition of private property and private space, the displacement of guilt by shame— he will not, and indeed cannot, finally cancel that identity. For all its anamorphic strangeness, Utopia is not, as we have just seen, absolutely other, and More's undoing of himself is not

represented as a chaotic dissemination of the energies so rigidly
structured in his life but rather as a more intense and monolithic
structuring. If Thomas More is not present in this new order, his
very absence is paradoxically a deep expression of his sense of
himself, for, as we have seen, his self-fashioning rests upon his
perception of all that it excludes, all that lies in perpetual darkness,
all that is known only as absence.

Our reading of *Utopia* has shuttled back and forth between the
postulate of More's self-fashioning and the postulate of his self-
cancellation; both are simultaneously present, but as with Holbein's painting, interpretation depends upon one's position at a
given moment in relation to the work. If, for over four hundred
years, criticism has, more often than not, consisted of attempted
seizures of the *libellus*—for the Church, the British Empire, the
Revolution, or even Liberal Democracy—it is both because *Utopia*
insists that any interpretation depends upon the reader's position
and because the stakes seem surprisingly high. The struggle is not
merely over an isolated work of genius but over a whole culture.

"The Whole Corps of Christendom"

Utopia appears almost timeless, reaching effortlessly back to Plato
and forward to our own age, but its existence is nonetheless the
result of a daring grasp of a single propitious moment: five years
earlier or later More could not have written it. Of course, all great
works of art strike us in just this way, but with *Utopia* the subsequent events were so epochal that we may look back on 1516 as
an almost magical year, equivalent, in its way, to 1788 in France or
1913 in the whole of Europe. Certainly, if we chart in More's life
and writings the subsequent course of the elements fused in
Utopia, we discover a virtual disintegration.

Thus we may recognize essential aspects of Hythlodaeus in the
vicious protraits More draws of Luther and Tyndale. The reformers, for More, are desperate and isolated fanatics, wildly flailing
out at the familiar, time-honored institutions and beliefs. Failing
to find everything perfect and all men good, they flatly condemn
the whole existing order of things. And in the name of what do
they do so? In the name of a completely imaginary church that they
alone have seen, that they alone insist is real. This church has no
place for the familiar, ineradicable vices of mankind; it is, of
course, without blemish, without so much as the possibility of
blemish. Hythlodaeus's steadfast confidence, his dismissal of all
objections, his scathing, prophetic voice become by 1523 Luther's

hysterical and intolerant certainty. Hythlodaeus's argument from his experience of Utopia—"You should have been with me in Utopia and personally seen their manners and customs as I did" (107)—becomes in More's parody Luther's comical and demonic insistence on the truth of his calling:

> "By what reason, father, do you prove that you alone must be believed?"
> To this he returns this cause: "Because I am certain," he says, "that I have my teachings from heaven."
> Again we ask: "By what reason are you certain that you have your teachings from heaven?"
> "Because God has seized me unawares," he says, "and carried me into the midst of these turmoils."
> Again therefore we demand: "How do you know that God has seized you?"
> "Because I am certain," he says, "that my teaching is from God."
> "How do you know that?"
> "Because God has seized me."
> "How do you know this?"
> "Because I am certain."
> "How are you certain?"
> "Because I know."
> "But how do you know?"
> "Because I am certain."[71]

Certainty about that which does not exist becomes for More the very emblem of what is maddening and satanic about the heretics. Luther's power over the unsuspecting, who long for a release from an uncertain, imperfect, and guilt-ridden existence, derives from his unscrupulous understanding that, in the absence of reality, the mere forms of reality will suffice. He has grasped that the conventional techniques of representation may be employed in the service of that which cannot *truly* be represented because it does not and cannot exist. He has then mastered not only the dogmatic confidence of Hythlodaeus but the aesthetic cunning of Hythlodaeus's creator.

At a point in the *Responsio ad Lutherum* in which More is reiterating his endless challenge to Luther to bring forward his invisible church, the marginal gloss, by More or by his publisher, Richard Pynson, mocks, *Eam fortasse uidit in Vtopia*—"Perhaps he has seen it in Utopia."[72] How revealing and melancholy this sarcasm is: by 1523, Utopia could be invoked not as an image of the ideal commonwealth but as an image of a madman's fantasy. It could be invoked with precisely the ridicule and contempt that Protestant polemicists would use against More. Thus the Protestant martyrologist John Foxe, rebutting More's assertion that the heretic Bilney abjured before his death, indignantly asks, "And how is this proved? By three or four mighty arguments—as big as mill-posts, fetched out of Utopia, from whence thou must know, reader, can come no fictions, but all fine poetry."[73]

In all of his controversial literature, More responds to the Protestant charge that the Catholics worship idols of their own making with the countercharge, tirelessly repeated, that the heretics have constructed an imaginary world and have come to believe in it, or at least to claim that they believe in it. It is impossible, More writes in the *Dialogue Concerning Heresies,* to dispute with the heretics: "When their hearts are once fired upon their blind affections, a man may with as much fruit preach to a post, as reason with them to the contrary. For they nothing ponder what is reasonably spoken to them, but whereto their fond affection inclineth, that thing they lean to, and that they believe, or at the least wise that way they walk and say they believe it. For in good faith, that they do believe in deed, their matters be so mad that I believe it not."[74] Protestant belief, for More, is constantly revealed to be something else: madness, effrontery, blindness, hypocrisy, demonic possession, buffoonery, lying.

More's wavering on the status of heretical "belief" may look incidental—the effect of haste or rhetorical striving for effect—but it is in fact central to an understanding of his bitter turn against the Utopian mode. For belief—not so much the precise doctrines held but the experience of holding them—is, with the assistance of the Holy Ghost, constitutive of religious truth itself. That is, for More, conviction does not follow upon an objective assessment of the facts but is the prior condition for establishing those facts. Thus far, More may sound surprisingly like Luther, for whom faith alone is the path to redemption. But for Luther, faith is an illumination received by the individual in direct communion with God; for More, belief is a *social* phenomenon, the shared conviction of the community, the *consensus fidelium.* Individual conviction, no matter how intensely held, no matter how carefully buttressed by apparently irrefutable "evidence," is, if it conflicts with the common consensus, at best irrelevant, at worst criminal or mad. Thus in conducting his argument with Tyndale, More does not hesitate to ignore Erasmus's text of the Bible, despite its evident scholarly authority, when its readings threaten to conflict with the consensus. And Erasmus himself would be hardpressed to object to More's procedure, since he shared the same funda-mental conception of belief.[75]

Now it should be stressed that for More consensual belief is constitutive only of religious truth; its force over men's minds is no less powerful elsewhere, but in realms apart from what is essential to man's salvation, consensual belief can constitute *meaning*, that is, it can determine what men consider *real*, but it cannot constitute truth. Thus in such realms, reality, however powerfully felt, can always be shown to exclude other meanings; one can always construct, at least in imagination, a counterreality. All configurations are not thereby collapsed into a single, undif-ferentiated mass: judgments are possible, even necessary, but ab-solute certainty—the certainty one may possess concerning those doctrines essential to salvation—is not. Of course, some rash indi-viduals within any given reality-construction will always be per-suaded that theirs is the only conceivable reality; the wise man, however, will understand that, in matters apart from the truth of the faith, he must always live with doubt, with the nagging con-sciousness of distortion and indeterminacy, with the silent sub-versiveness of anamorphosis.

Only the timeless, universal truth of religious belief will admit to no subversion, no countertruths, for it is guaranteed by what More takes as the irrefutable fact that the Holy Spirit would not have allowed his flock to be in mortal error for over fifteen hundred years.[76] The essence of God's promise then lies in the continuity of the solid, public consensus of Christian men and women through the centuries; the sign of the covenant is precisely that the church is known and visible. Christian faith dwells in the light of public knowledge, not in the dark, hidden recesses of the individual soul or in the "no place" of an invisible church: "The church is as Saint Paul saith, the pillar and the foot or ground, that is to say the sure strength or fastening of the truth. And this church must be that known Catholic Church of which from age to age the scripture hath been received, and the people taught and not a church unknown of only good men or elects only, in which is neither preacher nor people assembled to preach unto, nor sacra-ments ministered by any man as a minister of that unknown church, nor people of an unknown church to minister them unto among whom can be no such assembly for no man can know where to call another, nor how to know another if they came to gather by hap."[77]

In the "unknown" church of the heretics, men are isolated and adrift, cut off from the past, from the ceremonies and preaching that confirm the faith, from fellow believers. Indeed, More asks Luther, should a Turk wish to become a Christian, where would he go to learn the faith? and who would distinguish for him the orthodox teacher from the heretic? Without the prop of the known, acknowledged church, everything is radically uncertain, not merely for the hypothetical Turk but for the ordinary Christian: "From this church you must learn about the mass, if you wish to speak correctly about the mass. Otherwise you will be borne about in doubt and uncertainty by every wind of doctrine, and you will reduce everything to doubt."[78] Luther was, of course, hardly the apostle of radical doubt, and it is difficult to locate in this period instances of the gnawing uncertainty More claims that the Reformers spawned. Even those who passed back and forth several times between Catholicism and Protestantism seem to have experienced not corrosive skepticism but successive and incompatible states of certainty. But More does not need actual instances of uncertainty; the specter of interpretive anarchy needs to be invoked as much to stabilize his own position as to attack another's. Not only order and security, but truth itself for More is to be found only in the visible community of believers; truth apart from community, truth that resides solely in the secret conviction of the heart, is a dangerous illusion that must be destroyed.

If in the 1520s Hythlodaeus is transformed into a dangerous heresiarch, Utopia itself is not entirely reconceived as the invisible church about which he raves. Rather it is split: its nonexistence is bequeathed to Luther and company, while its massive communal solidarity becomes the consensus of the Catholic Church. As Utopian society is designed to efface the individual, swelling with self-importance or nursing a private reserve of judgment, so the Church as More represents it vehemently opposes those who dare to set themselves off from the community and to lay claim to a private truth. Luther, More charges, "persuades everyone that nothing is anywhere certain but that each one believes at his own risk," and the consequence is interpretative anarchy: "Despising the authority of the whole church, despising the holy fathers and the doctors and all the ancient interpreters, each one will interpret sacred scripture according to his own understanding and form for himself whatever faith he chooses. For since Luther has made each person the judge of Peter and also of Paul, each person may mount the tribunal in his own heart and judge both men: here Paul speaks well, here badly. Here Peter teaches rightly, here he teaches wrongly."[79] This situation seems to More self-evidently monstrous, and he repeatedly provides his readers with models of the correct response to authority and tradition: "The whole church of Christ for more than a thousand years past tells you this [that water should be poured into the wine]. Whatever her spouse has inspired in her for so long a time surely must be so, however much a new heretic may now deny and contemn it."[80]

The bedrock conviction of Christ's sustaining presence in his visible church saves More from the drastic implications of his conception of belief, or rather it allows him to play intensely and ironically with those implications without, however, sliding toward a final, vertiginous centerlessness. In all of the works of religious controversy, any intimation that reality is not given but rather constructed by the shared convictions and institutions of men depends upon the certain existence of a sole, ultimate community, the Catholic Church. When the *consensus fidelium* is threatened, the possibility of playful, subversive fantasy—what we have called the playground—is virtually destroyed. There are, to be sure, tattered remnants in the merry tales and in the masks to which More remains attached, but, as More himself seems to acknowledge, the essential spirit is gone.[81] It was once possible for Erasmus, in *The Praise of Folly*, to "jest upon the abuses" of saints' images, holy relics, and the like, "after the manner of the dysours [i.e., jester's] part in a play, ... yet hath Tyndale by erroneous books in setting forth Luther's pestilent heresies, so envenomed the hearts of lewdly disposed persons that men can not almost now speak of such things in so much as a play, but that such evil hearers wax a great deal the worse."[82] If *The Praise of Folly* or certain of his own works were translated into English, More writes, he would help to burn them with his own hands.[83]

We may be virtually certain that *Utopia* would have been consigned to the holocaust, for its jests upon abuses, its playful exploration of alternative structures, its daring mobility are precisely the qualities More now finds dangerous. If we wish to understand the fate of *Utopia* in More's own thought after 1516, we must continually remind ourselves that for More, as for Erasmus, the consensus of the faithful, embodied in the visible church, is "the principle of intelligibility itself."[84] By undermining that consensus, by fostering discord, doubt, and individual judgment, the Reformers threaten for More the very possibility of a final haven of meaning and hence deprive him of that license for subversive play on which he once relied. Utopia has not vanished; rather, the estrangement embedded in More's work, the perception that reality is a construction and identity, a mask, suddenly bids fair to engulf everything. And this engulfment heralds not a higher,

more rational order but the collapse of society itself: "The people
would neither be ruled by laws nor obey rulers, nor listen to doctors, but would be so free and unbridled, . . . that no one would be
forced, nor commanded, nor counselled, nor taught anything, nor
would anyone venerate the saints." The specter of anarchy—"not
only will the papacy not endure but also royal power, and supreme
magistracy, and the consulate and every administrative office
whatever will fall into ruin and the people will be without a ruler,
without law and order."[85]—must be checked by the secular
authorities who should, in their interest, repress the heretics with
"grievous punishment." The passion for social justice, the conviction that pride and private property are causally linked, the daring
attack on "the conspiracy of the rich" give way to the demand for
discipline and the extirpation of dissent.

If this shift marks the immense, melancholy distance that sepa-
rates *Utopia* from the works of religious controversy, we must recognize that More's faith in a single, unchallengeable religious
consensus remains a constant, largely invisible in the earlier work,
massively visible in the later. There is no moment in More's work
in which he grants that there could be a counterconsensus in religion, for were he to do so, he would in effect abandon his faith.
The Utopians, to be sure, cheerfully declare that they are prepared
to accept a superior faith, should they ever encounter one, but this
flexibility does not signal More's acceptance of the principle that
the religious consensus—and hence, religious truth—could
change, still less that there should be a kind of competitive
marketplace of doctrines. The Utopian attitude is More's
Cockayne-like fantasy of a people for whom conversion to the
truth faith would be no trauma, a fantasy akin to that indulged in
by Christopher Columbus on 12 October 1492.[86] No wonder that
we are told of a prelate who burned with the desire to be named
apostle to the Utopians: they would be a blissfully easy assign-
ment. "After they had heard from us," reports Hythlodaeus, "the
name of Christ, His teaching, His character, His miracles, and the
no less wonderful constancy of the many martyrs whose blood
freely shed had drawn so many nations far and wide into their
fellowship, you would not believe how readily disposed they, too,
were to join it, whether through the rather mysterious inspiration
of God or because they thought it nearest to that belief which has
the widest prevalence among them" (219). There is no question of
Christianity being absorbed by the Utopian cult of Mithras; rather
the Utopians will in time join the fellowship of the Catholic faithful.
When Luther challenges the consensus, when he charges that

the pope is the Antichrist and that the doctrinal unity of the Church is maintained by persecuting the authentic faithful, More responds, as he must, with horror. He resists even the notion that the Protestants actually believe their false doctrines, since belief constitutes truth and the consensus must be immune from rift; instead, as we have seen, he argues that the heretics are either mad or diabolically willful. As a whole class, the controversial writings of the Catholics and Protestants alike are, as E. M. Cioran says of early Christian apologetics, "a series of libels camouflaged as treatises,"[87] but we should not for this reason discount the personal intensity of More's rhetorical violence: "For as long as your reverend paternity will be determined to tell these shameless lies, others will be permitted, on behalf of his English majesty, to throw back into your paternity's shitty mouth, truly the shit-pool of all shit, all the muck and shit which your damnable rottenness has vomited up, and to empty out all the sewers and privies onto your crown."[88] This is the raw voice of hatred, hatred that would gladly kill what it perceives as demonic. We may sense the hatred even in passages that display more of More's characteristic irony and control:

> If our father Tyndale had been in paradise in the stead of our father Adam, he should never have needed any serpent or woman either to tempt him to eat the apple of the tree of knowledge. For when God had forbade him the eating thereof upon pain of death, as he for-biddeth us lechery upon pain of damnation: then would he have searched for the cause of the command-ment. And when his wit would have founden none because the flesh had there no need of taming: then would he have eaten on a good pace, and have thought that God almighty had but played the wanton with him, and would not be angry with him for an apple and so would he by his own rule of searching have found out as much mischief as the woman and the serpent and the devil and all.[89]

The woman, the serpent, and the devil—an ascending triad of wickedness—are all collapsed into Tyndale who is cast, in a mini-ature satirical drama, as father Adam. But the identification of the heretic with all that is most alien—the feminine, the bestial, and the demonic—is not perhaps the deepest source of More's vio-lence. More has recast as hateful, as deserving extermination, some of the qualities of mind we most associate with the author of *Utopia*. To search for causes, to question the given, to rely on one's

own probing "wit" are now manifest signs of evil, evil that must
be ridiculed in print and persecuted remorselessly by both church
and state. Of course, neither in *Utopia* nor in *Richard III* nor in the
letters to Martin Dorp, Edward Lee, and the Monk, John Batman-
son, did More ever intend to use his intelligence to question God's
authority, but as Hythlodaeus's story of the ignorant, zealous friar
in Cardinal Morton's entourage suggests, More well understood in
1516 that his wit and independence might strike some careless or
bigoted observers as heterodox and that the blanket appeal to
religious authority could be used to stifle all challenging thought:
"We have a papal bull," the enraged friar shouts, "by which all
who scoff at us are excommunicated!" (85). Now in his attacks on
the Reformers it is More, voicing the rage of threatened orthodoxy,
who invokes excommunication, and he strikes out at a demonic
version of himself.

Just as Utopia is split between the heretics' "unknown church"
and the *consensus fidelium,* so More is split: the garden in which
Morus and Hythlodaeus once talked together has been destroyed.
The part of More's identity that refused to be swept up in the
opinions of the multitude, that cultivated a stubbornly independent and ironic judgment of human affairs, that regarded
the stage plays of the great as madness or evil—the part given
expression in Hythlodaeus—is transformed into the heretic's isolation, stubbornness, and galling insistence upon his right to judge.
And what of Morus? what of the More who accommodated himself
to those stage plays and attempted to influence state policy from
within the circle of power? He may be glimpsed, in part, in the
theatrical flexibility manifested by the writer of those hundreds
upon hundreds of pages of polemics, in the ability to shift voices
to suit the particular scene: patient with the perplexed, violent
with the violent, solemnly intellectual, savagely mocking, coarsely
popular, or gently funny. He may be seen still more clearly in the
king's good servant, heightening as Lord Chancellor the persecution of heretics, keeping discretely silent in the face of abuses he
could not prevent, participating tactfully, if G. R. Elton is correct,
in a circumspect but perilous internal opposition to royal policies
that threatened the liberties of the Church.[90]

As More knew from the beginning, there were dangerous potential conflicts inherent in such a part, for the flexible, realistic
adviser to the national monarch was also the man who believed
that all coherence ultimately derived from the universal Catholic
Church. As long as the national and international authorities were
linked in uneasy union, or at least not working in opposition, he

could function, but when they drifted toward increasingly bitter conflict over the issue of the king's divorce and royal supremacy, More was put into an impossible position. Hall's *Chronicle* gives us a glimpse of Morus in extremity, straining almost to the breaking point that "philosophy, more practical for statesmen, which knows its stage, adapts itself to the play in hand, and performs its role neatly and appropriately." The stage in question was parliament, the role presenter of the opinions in favor of Henry's divorce that had been obtained from continental universities. This was a command performance, and More neatly and appropriately complied, "not showing," Roper writes, "of what mind himself was therein."[91] More's closing words to the Commons, after the reading of the learned opinions, suggest both his extraordinary skill at fashioning his part and the difficulty of his moral and political situation: "Now you of this Common House may report in your countries what you have seen and heard and then all men shall openly perceive that the King hath not attempted this matter of will or pleasure, as some strangers report, but only for the discharge of his conscience and surety of the succession of his realm: This is the cause of our repair hither to you, and now we will depart."[92] The general impression is that the Lord Chancellor supports his master's position, but, considered closely, the words say far less: not only does More refrain from personally affirming the justice of the king's position, he does not even quite endorse the king's claim to be acting on the basis of religious scruple and national policy. The little speech is a minor masterpiece of evasion, but it leads one to recall Hythlodaeus's skeptical response to the *obliquus ductus,* the "indirect approach," that Morus had counseled: to the extent that one praises evil policies, one furthers them; to the extent that one praises them faintly, one risks being "counted a spy and almost a traitor" (103).

Such is the fate of Morus, such the extent to which accommodation has been stretched. This extreme theatrical improvisation at the very center of power, this tense, cunning suppression of his true beliefs could not be long sustained, either at the level of politics or at the level of More's own soul. On 16 May 1532 More resigned his office and attempted to withdraw into the fastness of a quiet, private life, but the public identity with its national and international stature could not be so easily shed. In the letters he wrote during the months preceding his arrest and imprisonment, we may watch More desperately trying to sustain that blend of compliance and inner counsel that he had fashioned throughout his career. Thus in an extraordinary letter to Cromwell on 5 March

1534 More disclaims any competence to pass judgment or even to comment on the issues involved in the marriage to Anne Boleyn: "So am I he that among other his Grace's faithful subjects, his Highness being in possession of his marriage and this noble woman really anointed Queen, neither murmur at it nor dispute upon it, nor never did nor will, but without any other manner meddling of the matter among his other faithful subjects faithfully pray to God for his Grace and hers both, long to live and well and their noble issue too, in such wise as may be to the pleasure of God, honor and surety to themself, rest, peace, wealth, and profit unto this noble realm."[93]

Obviously, More was willing to go very far indeed to accommodate himself to the play at hand; in his great Marian edition of More's *Collected Works*, his nephew William Rastell quietly omitted this passage from the letter. But this and similar concessions are not an aberrant and desperate response to intolerable pressure; they are the climax of a life-strategy, the maintenance, as we have put it, of a calculated distance between the public *persona* and the inner self.

It is supremely appropriate that the heart of More's legal position in his last months was the right to remain silent. On 13 April 1534 he was summoned to Lambeth and shown the Act of Succession and the conjoined Oath of Supremacy. The former renounced Henry's marriage with Catherine, declared that the king's marriage with Anne Boleyn was "consonant to the laws of Almighty God," and established that Henry's heirs of that marriage alone were to be successors to the crown; the latter in effect affirmed that the king was the Supreme Head on earth of the Church in England. More declared himself prepared to swear to the succession, but he refused the Oath of Supremacy and also refused to give a reason for his refusal. For refusing the oath he was imprisoned and, on 1 July 1535, brought to trail on charges of treason. In his defense, he declared that "for this my silence neither your law nor any law in the world is able justly and rightly to punish me."[94] The prosecution did not concede this argument, but they did indirectly acknowledge its force by producing, in the form of Richard Rich's testimony, evidence—almost certainly perjured—that More had in fact broken his silence and spoken treasonous words against the king's supremacy.

When in *Utopia* More imagines the effacement of what I have called his life strategy, he imagines a state that would reduce the inner life to a cipher and hence would have no interest in oaths;

the modern state, by contrast, accepts the inner life of each individual but demands that it be rendered discursive. From the viewpoint of the prosecution, More was hiding essential testimony (as to his affirmation or denial of the oath) within himself; his silence then "is a sure token and demonstration of a nature maligning against the statute." More responds with what Chambers calls "his great plea for the liberty of silence": "I assure you," he declares, "that I have not hitherto to this hour disclosed and opened my conscience and mind to any person living in all the world."[95] More appeals, in effect, to his profound isolation and estrangement, to the concealment of his innermost thoughts; he promises to maintain that estrangement until death.

But from this extreme position of outward compliance and inward silence, this sense of conscience as something walled up within the individual, More proceeds, even before he decisively breaks his silence in the wake of the verdict against him, to work his way toward the opposite stance. On the subject of the primacy of the pope, the same letter to Cromwell continues, "I nothing meddle in the matter." But he recalls that his initial reservations about papal supremacy were overcome by the king's own arguments and those of others, and from here he passes to the heart of the consensual position: "And therefore sith all Christendom is one corps, I cannot perceive how any member thereof may without the common assent of the body depart from the common head."[96] With this "one corps," with this single Christian world and its "common head," goes a supreme, universal authority to declare those truths that must be believed and obeyed, an authority that "ought to be taken for undoubtable, or else were there in nothing no certainty, but through Christendom upon every man's affectionate reason, all things might be brought from day to day to continual ruffle and confusion."

"Or else were there in nothing no certainty"—here after the accommodation to practical realities and the clever rhetorical arguments and the politic silence, we reach the belief that More will not under any circumstances alter or suspend. To do so would be to render his whole world meaningless, to plunge into a chaos of uncertainty. "I am not then bounden," he writes several weeks later from his cell in the Tower, "to change my conscience and confirm it to the council of one realm, against the general council of Christendom."[97] Indeed, in the last letters, More's conscience comes to be identified more and more powerfully and directly with this communal solidarity, as if the final weeks had burned away all that stood between his intimate sense of himself and the great consensus of Christendom with which he longed to merge. At the end when he speaks of his *conscience,* he speaks at once of his innermost being and his participation in the community, the communion, of all true Christians, past, present, and future, in the visible body of the Catholic Church.

But, of course, that visibility was increasingly a matter of doubt in England in the 1530s. At least as early as 1531, with the submission of the clergy at the Convocation of Canterbury to Henry's claim to supremacy "as far as the law of God permits," the "one corps" of Christendom began to recede from view. By the time of More's imprisonment in the Tower, on 17 April 1534, its existence was far more an affirmation of religious belief than a recognized, tangible, institutional presence. More's appeals to the consensus do not express doubt—if anything, they are more serene and confident in the late writings than in the strident works of controversy—but they are appeals to something seen with the eyes of faith.

In June 1535, Thomas Cromwell asked More how he distinguished between the Church's right to demand a precise answer to the question of papal supremacy and the king's right to demand a precise answer to the question of royal supremacy—"they were as well burned for the denying of that as they be beheaded for the denying of this." More replied by differentiating between a local law and "the whole corps of Christendom."[98] But in the mid-1530s, England was scarcely an isolated, local problem, and consensus is proclaimed in the face of a drastic and manifest disintegration of consensus. Where, the skeptic may ask, is the single, universal body of all Christian believers to be seen?

Precisely at this point we may recall Hythlodaeus's reply to the skeptical Morus: "You should have been with me in Utopia and personally seen their manners and customs as I did" (107). For in his growing isolation—even among the religious orders very few refused their assent—More in effect recovers that part of himself that he had consigned to the heretics. True, he had never wavered from his adherence to the consensus, but when he held power and seemed, as he put it to Roper, "to sit upon the mountains treading heretics under our feet like ants,"[99] this adherence scarcely had a visionary character. Now he spoke, at the peril of his life, for a community no more visible in England than the "unknown church" he had mocked. The Catholic Church, to be sure, was highly visible elsewhere—Rome was not, after all, the mythical Amaurotum—but More's sense of the Church had never rested exclusively on Rome. He could appeal, of course, to the unity of the "holy saints in heaven," but this appeal only heightens the sense that to affirm in 1535 the essential singleness of the "whole corps of Christendom" was to affirm that which ordinary, earthly vision could not see.

It is tempting to argue that at the end Hythlodaeus, metamorphosed for long, bitter years into the hateful parodies of Luther and Tyndale, returns to his original form and displaces Morus: just as Hythlodaeus had predicted, the adaptable, well-meaning servant of the prince has been ruined, his strategy of tactful performance exposed as hopelessly inadequate. But has Morus been so utterly routed? More's writing and behavior in his final months suggests that here too he is adapting himself to the play in hand, though the play is a more solemn and fearful one than any in which he had ever performed. If one remembers More for his upholding unto death of the Catholic Church as the sole principle of intelligibility and certainty, one also remembers him for his remarkable ironic humor in the face of horror, for the insistent infusion of his distinctive personality into apparently impersonal procedures of state, for the innumerable ways he contrived to signal the ongoing process of his adaptation to the role thrust upon him.

More had long conditioned himself, I have argued, to ask himself on all public occasions, "What would 'More' say about this?" and he relies deeply upon this conditioning throughout the final months. His humor is, no doubt, a spontaneous expression of his personality, but it is also something more deliberately fashioned, as we can perhaps most clearly perceive at those moments in which the jests seem forced.[100] As a strategy, humor could hardly save More's life, but it could fulfill an overlapping series of important functions. It was the expression of an oblique resistance to authority. The unsympathetic Hall speaks of More's ceaseless "taunting and mocking,"[101] and while this seems too negative a response, it is true to the authentic element of aggression in the jesting. It is, moreover, a sign of More's embodiment of a cultural ideal: a posture of nonchalance, *disinvoltura*, at the imminent prospect of death. This attitude may reflect in part the influence of stoicism on Renaissance humanism, in part the bourgeois adoption of an aristocratic ethos, but its deepest roots lie in religious faith: merriment was the manifest sign of that certainty More's beliefs conferred upon him.[102] Finally, More's humor is a way of mastering the terror of his situation, a terror that can be gauged by enduring a detailed account of the execution of the Carthusian monks. And he had to face not only the physical horror but, in the weeks preceding his trial, the ease with which he could obtain his release. Thus when his daughter Margaret wrote to urge him to take the oath, More first responded with an anguished expression of "deadly grief," then in the subsequent weeks contrived to deal with such exchanges with characteristic irony: he dubs Margaret "Mistress Eve" and likens her to an actress in a play.[103]

Humor was not More's only response to fear, nor his only way of marking the complex distance that separated him from the martyr's role he simultaneously resisted and embraced. The most moving and personal moments of the Tower Works are those in which More reflects not upon the heroic martyr who "rushes forth eagerly to his death," but upon the martyr who "creeps out hesitantly and fearfully."[104] Whoever is "utterly crushed by feelings of anxiety and . . . tortured by the fear that he may yield to despair," More writes in the *De tristitia*, must meditate upon Christ's sufferings in the Garden; we may recall that at the end of his grief-stricken letter to Margaret, before the irony masked over the naked anguish, More prayed for the grace "devoutly to resort prostrate unto the remembrance of that bitter agony, which our Savior suffered before his passion at the Mount."[105] In the timorous martyr then, the martyr who must struggle to accommodate himself to his part, More depicts himself. The merriment performed for the world is on the other side of an intense anxiety that is also performed. As the merriment is a sign of certainty, so paradoxically is the fear, for it signalled his humble resistance to a martyrdom that could only then be thrust upon him by God. In a moving reversal of expectations, More imagines not that he is reenacting Jesus's part, imitating Christ, but rather that with supreme generosity Christ has rehearsed the part that More must now play: "For here he will see the loving shepherd lifting the weak lamb on his shoulders, playing the same role as he himself does, expressing his very own feelings, and for this reason: so that anyone who later feels himself disturbed by similar feelings might take courage and not think that he must despair."[106]

At such a moment as this, More's role-playing, that highly complex consciousness of fashioning himself that marked his intense individuality, is absorbed into a larger totality, into the total life of Christ, into the total institution that claims to be the guardian of that life's meaning. This merger explains, I think, a very odd quality of the Tower Works, namely, their mysterious passage from intensely personal meditation to what appears to be dry, tedious elaborations of scholastic theology.[107] These elaborations of the words of Aquinas or Gerson are the voice of the total institution in which More longed all his life to be absorbed, just as the fearful meditations and the humor are the voice of his ironic, complex sense of self; though we may still mark the differences between them, the two voices are no longer opposed. In the Tower Works, in his cell, and at last in his death, More once again brought together in dialogue Morus and Hythlodaeus, aspects of his identity and his culture that had for so long been violently sundered. But now it is not in a garden that they converse; they triumph and are destroyed together on a scaffold.

The Word of God in the Age of Mechanical Reproduction

In 1531 a lawyer named James Bainham, son of a Gloucestershire knight, was accused of heresy, arrested, and taken from the Middle Temple to Lord Chancellor More's house in Chelsea, where he was detained while More tried to persuade him to abjure his Protestant beliefs. The failure of this attempt called forth sterner measures until, after torture and the threat of execution, Bainham finally did abjure, paying a £20 fine to the king and standing as a penitent before the priest during the Sunday sermon at Paul's Cross. But scarcely a month after his release, according to John Foxe, Bainham regretted his abjuration "and was never quiet in mind and conscience until the time he had uttered his fall to all his acquaintance, and asked God and all the world forgiveness, before the congregation in those days, in a warehouse in Bow lane."[1] On the following Sunday, Bainham came openly to Saint Austin's church, stood up "with the New Testament in his hand in English and the Obedience of a Christian Man in his bosom," and, weeping, declared to the congregants that he had denied God. He prayed the people to forgive him, exhorted them to beware his own weakness to die rather than to do as he had done, "for he would not feel such a hell again as he did feel, for all the world's good." He was, of course, signing his own death warrant, which he sealed with letters to the bishop of London and others. He was promptly arrested and, after reexamination, burned at the stake as a relapsed heretic.

More's role in this grim story reflects his hatred of heresy and his direct engagement in a campaign to eradicate it. He was surely not the sadistic inquisitor of "The Book of Martyrs"—Foxe has him whipping Bainham at a tree in his garden—but he was just as surely not the sweet soul conjured up by those who speak admiringly of More's "hearty, loving labor for the man's amendment."[2] Behind this labor lay a threat the Lord Chancellor fully endorsed: "to thieves, murderers and heretics grievous," he wrote in his own epitaph.[3] "Now the spirit of error and lying," More concludes venemously of one Protestant martyr, "hath taken his wretched soul with him straight from the shore fire to the fire everlasting."[4] The spiritual violence here enables us to understand how More's Chelsea—for Erasmus, "Plato's Academy on a Christian footing"; for R. W. Chambers, "this small patriarchal, monastic Utopia"—could function, for brief periods, as a prison house.[5] This disturbing fact shatters that careful separation of public and private to which More himself, as we have seen, clung as long as he could.

The immediate occasion for this shattering was More's high office—the judicial functions of the chancellorship and More's determination to use his position to war against heresy. But the public and private spheres were always interlocked, even when More himself most struggled to keep them apart: the private life made possible the public by making it morally bearable; the public life defined the private by giving it a reason to exist. From William Roper's early biography to Robert Bolt's *Man for All Seasons,* we have been led to picture Chelsea as a kind of ideal suburb—a magical haven of wit, humanism, and familial tenderness. When, in Roper's superb account, More, under arrest, bids farewell to his family, he "pulled the wicket after him and shut them all from him":[6] we have passed poignantly from the enclosed, loving, domestic retreat to the murderous world of Tudor power. This sense of Chelsea is by no means a mere myth: More had, I have argued, a stake in building a high wall between his public engagements and his private existence. But the intense pressure of the 1520s and '30s rendered that separation increasingly tenuous: after all, it was in effect what transpired in the chapel of New Building—that retreat within a retreat, that place of conscience and solitude—that led to More's arrest, trial, and execution. At the end, as we have seen, More's innermost private conscience had become precisely his public adherence to the known, visible consensus of the Catholic Church.

The wicket that allowed More to pass between carefully demarcated worlds allowed others to pass as well; if Chelsea was a suburban retreat, it was one to which the Lord Chancellor brought home pressing business in the person of the occasional heretical prisoner. To James Bainham, More's house must have seemed anything but a haven from the world. As we have tried to grasp the principles governing More's self-fashioning, so we must turn now to the shaping of the identities of those he so much loathed. Here again, as we shall see, identity is achieved at the intersection of an absolute authority and a demonic Other, but the authority has shifted from the visible church to the book. This investment of power in the book has, I hope to demonstrate, important consequences both for self-fashioning and for the way we read.

Neither Bainham's beliefs nor his ultimate fate are particularly unusual. He had read works by the English Lutherans, Tyndale, Frith, and Joye and "never saw any error" in them; he affirmed that "Christ's body is not chewed with teeth, but received by faith"; he did not believe in praying to departed saints, thought that Saint Paul would have condemned the doctrine of purgatory as heretical, doubted the necessity of confession to a priest, and believed that repentance alone was sufficient for God's forgiveness. Though More found him a chatterer—"Bainham the jangler," he calls him[7]—the record of his interrogations shows him rather circumspect: he denied, for example, having said that "he had as lief to pray to Joan his wife, as to our lady," pleaded ignorance on such issues as psychopannychism, and was careful to frame most of his answers in the words of Scripture. What rivets our interest in the case, almost lost in the great mass of Foxe's famous work, is the critical role taken, at the height of the drama of abjuration and relapse, by the printed book.

To understand the role of the book we must understand the drama itself, and the key to such understanding is a recognition of its dialectical structure: Bainham's actions after his release were generated directly and systematically by the constituent elements of the process that led to his abjuration. That process consisted of a progressive revelation of power, a movement from the private to the public, from rational discourse to intolerable pressure, from civil conversation to humiliation and violence. It is as if we were watching the stripping away of masks from the face of power: a conversation with Thomas More at Chelsea gave way to imprisonment within his house, then transfer to the Tower, then interrogations, the rack and the threat of burning, then the signing of the bill of abjuration and final public disgrace.

This disclosure of the force that always underlies even the most apparently calm and benign discourse of the authorities is one of the recurrent motifs in early Protestant accounts of persecution. Subtle arguments over finely drawn theological points are taken with the utmost seriousness by both heretic and inquisitor, as if they were engaged in an academic disputation, but these are in fact shadow arguments, as in a ritual or a play, for actual persuasion is out of the question: the heretic will either abjure for fear of punishment or stand firm and be punished. Protestant historiography insists that recourse to violence did not always characterize the Church's relation to dissent; Augustine and Jerome, Foxe declares, relied only on the strength of intellect to contend with heresy, and such was their learning and eloquence that they easily prevailed; "but in their place, there is such posterity crept in, as which, with mere power and violence, do for the most part defend that which they cannot judge or discern, when they are not able to accomplish the matter by learning."[8]

Protestants described and seem to have experienced the inquisitorial process as a kind of demonic theater; the long scenes of doctrinal debate have to be played out, with each of the actors performing his preordained part, until the inevitable epiphany of "mere power and violence." Thus in the Lollard William Thorpe's account of his examination in 1407, the authorities, interrogating him in detail on each of his heretical positions, become increasingly enraged by his refusal to submit, until the archbishop of Canterbury—"striking with his hand fiercely upon a cupboard"—threatens to have him imprisoned like a thief. When this histrionic outburst fails to break Thorpe's will, the show of violence increases until the heretic takes refuge in silence: "And then, I was rebuked, scorned, and menaced on every side; and yet, after this, divers persons cried upon me to kneel down and submit me: but I stood still, and spake no word. And then there was spoken of me and to me many great words; and I stood, and heard them menace, curse, and scorn me: but I said nothing."[9] A long tradition of suffering for the faith lies behind this eloquent silence, a tradition reaching back to Christ's own initial silence before Caiaphas: "And the chief priest arose and said to him: answerest thou nothing? how is it that these bear witness against thee? but Jesus held his peace" (Matt. 26:29–31).[10] Caught in a terrifying situation and facing the rage of the great and powerful, the heretic William Thorpe, like the imprisoned Thomas More, found refuge in an identification with Christ: "And the men that stood about Jesus mocked him and smote him and blindfolded him and smote his face" (Luke 22:37–39). This identification lies deeper than literary artifice, pastoral consolation, or religious doctrine, though it partakes of all three; it marks, as we have seen with More, a simultaneous affirmation and effacement of personal identity.

The sense of the inquisitorial process as theater culminates in a revelation of the ultimate roles, the truth in which all partial representations find their meaning and ground. Christ's suffering constitutes more than a powerful similitude to the suffering of the heretic; it is the latter's underlying reality, and hence identification is as much somatic as metaphoric. The point is worth stressing, since the Protestant emphasis on *inward* grace tends to obscure the implication of the body and hence to render public behavior incomprehensible or irrelevant. Christ is present not only in the mind of William Thorpe but in his situation; to put the matter somewhat differently, the outward physical compulsion of the authorities is overmastered by an inward compulsion that is no less physical. We may see this countercompulsion, this somatic imitation of Christ, most clearly in another account of a heresy investigation, that of Sir John Oldcastle, Lord Cobham, who led an abortive Lollard rebellion in 1414. Near the close of the interrogation, one of the inquisitors asked Oldcastle if he would worship images and, more particularly, the Cross of Christ:

> "Where is it?" said the lord Cobham.
> The friar said: "I put you the case, Sir, that it were here, even now before you."—The lord Cobham answered; "This is a great wise man, to put me an earnest question of a thing, and yet he himself knoweth not where the thing itself is. Yet once again I ask you, What worship I should do unto it?"
> A clerk said unto him: "Such worship as Paul speaketh of, and that is this; God forbid that I should joy, but only in the cross of Jesus Christ."—Then said the lord Cobham, and spread his arms abroad: 'This is the very cross, yea, and so much better than your cross of wood, in that it was created of God, yet will not I seek to have it worshipped."[11]

In his Goya-like gesture, Oldcastle at once identifies himself with Christ on the cross and carefully avoids either a blasphemous self-exaltation or a celebration of images. The physical gesture is both an expression of his faith and a condemnation of the inquisitorial procedure. It is a brilliant piece of histrionic improvisation, identifying his tormentors with the tormentors of Christ and transforming his situation into a symbolic reenactment of the crucifixion.

Oldcastle, like William Thorpe or, indeed, like any individual or group confronting a hostile institution that possesses vastly superior force, has recourse to the weapon of the powerless: the seizure of *symbolic* initiative. He may be crushed, but his martyrdom will only confirm his construction of reality, for the very success of the dominant institution is exposed as a sign not of its rightness but of the power of the Antichrist. We may argue, of course, that such a symbolic victory is trivial—in 1419, after eluding the authorities for several years, Oldcastle was "hanged up there by the middle, in chains of iron, and so consumed alive in the fire"[12]—but though large numbers of individuals may be dealt with in this fashion, it is only in a concentration camp that a monopoly of violence alone is sufficient to control a whole society. The Catholic Church had neither the will nor the technical means to create such a world; like all significant and durable human institutions, it relied for its preservation and reproduction upon a thick network of symbolic bonds as well as an apparatus of repression. Against the symbolic initiatives of the heretics, the Church opposed not only violence but its own powerful symbolism, and yet the final recourse to force undermined this symbolism even as it seemed to confirm its power. For each public exercise of violence, each torture and burning, could suggest to onlookers that the Church ultimately depended not upon its truth but upon its power.[13]

If Foxe's immensely influential "Book of Martyrs"—more properly, *Acts and Monuments* (1563)—dwelt lovingly upon scenes of horror, if it insisted again and again that beneath the institutions and symbolic language of the Catholic Church lay "mere power and violence," it was not because of a private fixation nor even primarily because of the rhetorical capital in unmerited suffering, but because the revelation of such violence attacked that consensual unity for which More went to the scaffold. A consensus held together by threats of torture and the stake is no consensus at all. Catholic authorities for their own part denied that they were trying to compel belief and insisted that the heretic could only return to the Holy Mother Church "purely and unfeignedly." When a heretic like James Bainham agreed to submit—and it was to obtain such submission that the Church directed all its efforts—he had to declare in the bill of abjuration that he "voluntarily, as a true penitent person" abjured his heresies. The prosecution of heresy then—as is inevitable in the prosecution of thought-crime—combined extreme duress with the insistence on the purely voluntary character of the penitent's act.[14] And, to be sure, the prisoner did have a certain grim freedom: he could choose to return to the "truth" or to embrace the stake.

It is the authorities themselves, both secular and religious, who adamantly insist that they have no power over the heretic's soul; as Augustine had argued, *credere non potest homo nisi volens*, "Man cannot believe against his will." But Augustine had also written, *Quae peior mors animae quam libertas erroris?* "What death is worse for the soul than the liberty to err?" and this conviction was strengthened by the urgent determination to prevent the infection of others.[15] If power does not extend to the soul, it may be exercised upon the body; indeed secular power *is* essentially the ability to perform certain operations upon the body: to remove it from one place to another, to confine it, to cause it extreme pain, to reduce it to ashes. The conviction that the soul is entirely separate from the body licenses the exercise of such power, while the exercise of such power helps to produce the conviction that the soul is entirely separate from the body. For it is preeminently when the Church is involved in the corporal discipline of an unwilling subject (as opposed, that is, to a willing penitent) that it invokes the aid of the secular arm and hence reserves to itself the cure of the soul, while consigning to the state the punishment of the body. And it is preeminently when his body is subjected to torment that the obstinate heretic is most suffused with the conviction that his soul is inviolable. To this extent the exercise of power—of violence or the threat of violence, in this world or the next—confirms for both inquisitor and heretic the separateness and incorporeality of the soul.

Michel Foucault has carried this argument to its extreme, claiming that the soul is not, as Christian theology holds, born guilty and punishable, but rather is engendered by the very process of punishment, surveillance, discipline, and constraint.[16] If this is too radical a reduction, it is nonetheless clear in a case like James Bainham's that the object of the authorities' inquiry—the state of the heretic's soul—is itself significantly shaped by such inquiries, performed throughout the course of his life from earliest childhood. The individual conscience as a fertile field of knowledge is at least in part the product of a complex operation of power—of watching, training, correcting, questioning, confessing. And in the case of a heretic, the threat of punishment that underlies this operation, always present if only in a veiled, symbolic, or allegorized form, is at last completely realized, for the edification not only of the victim but of the entire community. Hence the publicity of a punishment that in a later age would take place, if at all, in a dank cellar or behind barbed wire: in the Church's symbolic system, as opposed to the heretic's, the rack and the fire are at once foretaste and confirmation of those other-worldly tortures that were sculpted in stone, painted in vivid colors, described in rich rhetorical detail. "From the short fire to the fire everlasting." The heretic is enrolled in a virtual *theater* of torments; early editions of Foxe's work include a woodcut of Bainham standing on a stage before the congregation at Paul's Cross and holding a faggot of wood and a candle, symbols of the fate he has averted by means of his penitence.[17]

This public ceremony is the climax of a procedure designed to assure that the external performance of abjuration before the community reflects a sincere inner repentance; the authorities are by no means only interested in a public show undertaken to save one's skin. Their object is knowledge of the genuineness of the heretic's return to the truth, in token whereof Bainham had to swear an oath to the articles of abjuration and to sign and kiss the book in which these articles were recorded. It is the cross of power that it can only know the inner state it has brought into being through outer gestures; even as it asserts the incorporeality of the soul, it must accept a physical sign. The act of kissing the book is a sign devised to assure that the physical has indeed given way to the spiritual, for the book's physical existence is only the carrier of its incorporeal meaning, while in the kiss, whose erotic quality seems to contradict any charge of compulsion, the soul itself is conceived to be present.[18]

In the month following his release, Bainham reenacted the elements of the process of abjuration, only turning them inside out. Where before he had been free in mind while under extreme physical duress, now he was free in body while under extreme mental or spiritual duress. Indeed, Bainham seems to have experienced this condition not as an inner conflict but as an external pressure, weighing upon his conscience: "If I should not return again unto the truth," he said, holding the New Testament in his hand, "this word of God would damn me both body and soul at the day of judgment" (4:702). Instead of the Catholic Church and the state then, God himself and his revealed word threaten Bainham with torments. The close parallel is not accidental, for Bainham conceives of the Catholic Church as a demonic parody of the true church: "there were two churches," he told his inquisitors at the first interrogation, "the church of Christ militant, and the church of Antichrist; and ... this church of Antichrist may and doth err; but the church of Christ doth not" (4:699). We have already encountered this conception of a demonic church in More:

neither side could resist invoking it, for it had both powerful doctrinal precedent and psychic force, but it was dangerously reversible.[19] And there was a danger beyond reversibility: its effect here was to force Bainham to repeat the actions of his oppressor on himself in order to translate them from the realm of Antichrist to the realm of Christ militant, to restore their true significance.

Thus he could not achieve quiet in mind and conscience simply by dismissing the actions of the Catholic Church as a horrible injustice or even by repenting inwardly. Since his abjuration had had a public as well as an inner aspect, so too his return to God would have to be *performed* publicly. Had not Christ said, "whosoever shall deny me before men, him will I also deny before my Father which is in heaven" (Matt. 10:33)? Bainham had to affirm Christ before men as he had denied him before men. At first, he "uttered his fall to all his acquaintance," but apparently he felt this informal confession—the equivalent of the early informal interrogation—to be incomplete. He then appeared before the Protestant congregation, the Brethren, and asked their forgiveness and God's.[20] In the symmetry of Bainham's symbolic acts, this confession to the group of fellow believers, meeting secretly in the warehouse, was the equivalent to the formal interrogation in the Tower.

As the Tower interrogation was situated between the relative privacy of More's Chelsea and the full publicity of Paul's Cross, Bainham's discourse with the heretical congregation linked his private anguish and his decisive public appearance at Saint Austin's Church. Indeed the meeting at Bow Lane seems to have given Bainham the strength to pass from one to the other. Hunted, contacting each other with code words and covert signs, meeting secretly in warehouses and private rooms, reading together from prohibited books, the Brethren seem to have been profoundly energized by their sense of community. Individually, they could be treated as the madmen and fools that More, in the optimism of his hatred, called them; together they possessed the strength to unsettle the immense weight, the vast equilibrium, of the Catholic establishment. The pages of Foxe and Tyndale are full of this energy, just as the voluminous controversial writings of More are haunted by a terrible weariness, by a sense of grinding labor through sleepless nights.

As the name Brethren suggests, members of the early Protestant groups were charged with intense familial emotion toward one another: "For so did we not only call one another," writes Antony Dalaber, "but were in deed one to the other."[21] Dalaber, who as a student at Oxford in 1528 fell afoul of the clerical authorities, has left a particularly vivid account of this emotion in an unfinished memoir printed by Foxe. His natural brother, a "rank Papist" and "the most mortal enemy that ever I had for the Gospel's sake," is supplanted by his adopted brothers in Christ whose perils he shares: "Then kneeled we both down together on our knees, lifting up our hearts and hands to God, our heavenly Father, . . . and then we embraced, and kissed the one the other, the tears so abundantly flowing out from both our eyes, that we all bewet both our faces, and scarcely for sorrow could we speak one to the other; and so he departed from me" (5:423). Dalaber finds in the movement not only new brothers but a new father, his teacher John Clark: "He came to me, and took me up in his arms, kissed me, the tears trickling down from his eyes, and said unto me: . . . from henceforth forever take me for your father, and I will take you for my son in Christ" (5:427). The fellow believers were thus bound to each other in passionate rituals of kinship, and the new family was a bridge between individual experience and the alien, largely Catholic, public world.

It was as a member of such a group then that Bainham made his confession before the conventicle in the warehouse in Bow Lane. If this confession, like his earlier informal expressions of remorse, left him unsatisfied, if the act of repentance was still incomplete, the support of the group apparently gave him the immense, reckless courage needed to take the next and decisive step: the public confession at Saint Austin's, where he testified not to his brothers and sisters in Christ but to an indifferent and possibly hostile community. Only in standing before such an audience and "declaring openly, with weeping tears, that he had denied God" could Bainham annul the denial at Paul's Cross and find the release, the "quiet," that had eluded him. His model perhaps was Saint Peter, who thrice denied Christ, wept bitterly at his weakness, and went on to fulfill his calling. That calling, according to legend, included martyrdom, and it certainly appears that Bainham sought such a fate. At the least, he must have known what was likely to happen, but he was compelled to act as he did.[22] It is as if only by embracing the stake—as Foxe reports he did at the end—could he annul the kiss that had confirmed his abjuration.

This sense of compulsion in Bainham's behavior may lead one plausibly to Freud's concept of *undoing what has been done*—"ungeschehenmachen" or, literally, "making unhappened." Undoing, writes Freud, "is, as it were, negative magic, and endeavours, by means of motor symbolism, to 'blow away' not merely the *consequences* of some event (or experience or impression) but the event itself."[23] Such a notion can help us understand the elements of ritual expiation, annulment, and above all symmetry at work in the heretic's relapse: each separate phase of the polluting process of abjuration must be blown away by a corresponding symbolic act of undoing. But Freud's "negative magic" is unconscious, a neurotic defense against impulses that threaten the structures of the conscious mind and hence must be repressed; to invoke *undoing* as an explanation rather than an analog seems to me misleading.[24] The dangers of such a reduction are exemplified by a recent psychohistorical study that, while it does not discuss undoing, does characterize the Tudor martyrs as "compulsive neurotics" taking "the self-willed, self-inflicted path of suicide" rather than the self-preserving path of "cooperation with the magistrates."[25] The Reformers' bitter denials that they were seeking death by refusing to embrace orthodoxy are dismissed as defensive reductions of guilt. But are there then ever moments in which a man may legitimately determine, in order to save his soul, not to cooperate with the magistrates, even if execution is the certain consequence? Is to be chained to a stake and burned to death so unmistakably "suicide"? The actions of a man like Bainham were not neurotic symptoms in the midst of a presumptively sane society, but symbolic actions fully understood by both friends and enemies and explicable in terms of a complex theological and political system. This does not, of course, obviate the possible functioning of "unconscious" forces, but it does suggest that these forces were organized and given expression by a fully conscious, public discourse. And this discourse is manifested most concretely in the case of Bainham and dozens like him in the crucial significance of the printed book.

At Saint Austin's, it will be recalled, Bainham stood up "with the New Testament in his hand in English and the Obedience of a Christian Man in his bosom." It is hard to tell if there is one book here or two, for "the Obedience of a Christian Man" may refer to Bainham's inner state or to Tyndale's book of the same name, which Bainham owned and may have carried next to his heart. The ambiguity here is felicitous, for Tyndale's manual, which he wrote in exile, probably in Worms, in 1527, is precisely designed to be absorbed: one should not, in principle, be able to say where the book stops and identity begins. This absorption of the book at once provides a way of being in the world and shapes the reader's inner life; Christian obedience is simultaneously a form of action and an internal state. Such fashioning of action and identity is essential because in breaking images, radical Protestants have rejected a central Catholic mode of generating inward reflection—recall More's advice to meditate in private "before an altar or some pitiful image of Christ's bitter passion"—while in abandoning formal auricular confession, they have rejected the primary Catholic mode of maintaining the obedience of the Christian man by ordering this inward reflection. Since the momentous decree of the Fourth Lateran Council of 1215, *Omnis utriusque sexus,* which commanded yearly confession, there had arisen a vast literature for confessors and penitents detailing a complex methodology for the examination and formal cleansing of conscience.[26] It is this systematic, institutionalized form of self-scrutiny in the service of discipline and consolation that caused the young Augustinian monk Martin Luther such anguish and is violently rejected by virtually every reformer. "Shrift in the ear," writes Tyndale in the *Obedience,* "is verily a work of Satan."[27]

Because of subsequent developments, we associate Protestantism with a still more intense self-scrutiny, the alternately anguished and joyful self-reflection of Bunyan's *Grace Abounding* or Fox's *Journal.* But significantly, among the early Protestants we find almost no formal autobiography and remarkably little private, personal testimony.[28] The kind of self-consciousness voiced in these forms, the sense of being set apart from the world and of taking a stance toward it, the endless, daily discursiveness of later generations, is only in the process of being shaped, while the traditional methodology for the examination of conscience and the ritual forgiveness of sin by virtue of the Church's power of the keys have been bitterly renounced. There is a powerful ideology of inwardness but few sustained expressions of inwardness that may stand apart from the hated institutional structure. What we find then in the early sixteenth century is a crucial moment of passage from one mode of interiority to another. Tyndale's *Obedience of a Christian Man* is located at this liminal moment; in his book and the others of its type, we may watch the fashioning of the Protestant discourse of self out of conflicting impulses: rage against authority and identification with authority, hatred of the father and ardent longing for union with the father, confidence in oneself and an anxious sense of weakness and sinfulness, justification and guilt.

A spiritual guide, written by hand for a family or circle of friends, a manuscript patiently copied for a monastic library, a saint's life lovingly recorded in a private collection—all of these have a certain innate intimacy and presence: they possess, in

Walter Benjamin's term, an *aura* linking them to a ritual function or, at the least, to a particular, specific human community.[29] We are accustomed to believe that print culture moved away from that presence, lost that aura: after all, there is no longer the visible sign of the recording hand, the sense of unique production. Print is, in these terms, a form of depersonalization. But we must balance this perspective with that afforded by Tyndale's work: that in the early period of print culture the book could have a special kind of presence that perhaps no manuscript ever had. For with the rejection of formal auricular confession and the power of the keys, works like Tyndale's are, in effect, among the primary sources of self-fashioning. In the symmetry of unmaking and displacement, they occupy the structural position of the confessional manual, but they refuse the institutional framework that seems to have controlled the experience or at least the representation of interiority in the Middle Ages. That framework insisted that interiority be subordinated to an intimate verbal transaction, that it be embedded in a ritual of confession and absolution within the visible fabric of the Church. Tyndale's *Obedience* and similar Protestant guides to the inner life have no such end in view; the printed word does not serve the spoken, but has a kind of absoluteness, integrity, and finality. Distance from the scribal hand, production in relatively large quantities, mechanisms of distribution far distant from the author and printer, refusal of subordination to a ritualized verbal transaction, the very lack of aura—all that we may call the *abstractness* of the early Protestant printed book—give it an intensity, a shaping power, an element of compulsion that the late medieval manuals of confession never had.[30]

Works like the *Obedience* differ as well from the printed or, for that matter, manuscript accounts of the inner life in the next century. In seventeenth-century spiritual autobiography, the inner life is *represented* in outward discourse; that is, the reader encounters the record of events that have already transpired, that have been registered and brought from the darkness within to the clear light of the page. In the early sixteenth century there is not yet so clearly a fluid, continuous inner voice—a dramatic monologue—to be recorded. The words on the page in *The Obedience of a Christian Man* are aspects of the inner life, awkward and eloquent, half-formed, coming into existence. These words are not carried out into the light but are destined for the opposite process: they will be studied, absorbed, internalized, colored by a thousand personal histories. It is as if for a brief moment we see the thing itself, not represented but *presented* in its original and originating form. The phenomenon I describe—this *presence* in the written word of identity—has its last brilliant flowering in the essays of Montaigne and, by transference from script back to voice, in the soliloquies of *Hamlet,* words that claim not access to the inner life but existence as the inner life. And the characteristic of these words—as opposed to modern attempts to record the discourse of interiority—is their public character, the apparent impersonality of their rhetorical structure, their performative mode. If the revelation of Hamlet's innermost thoughts is a highly formal *quaestio* on the problem of being and nonbeing, delivered in direct address to an enormous, outdoor, public assembly, we may understand some of the force of this peculiar convention by recalling works like the *Obedience* whose apparently impersonal rhetoric fashioned their readers' most intimate sense of themselves.

James Bainham had every reason to clutch the *Obedience* to his bosom as he stood up at Saint Austin's. He had abjured, but the book spoke directly to the humiliation, the "fall" as he called it, that he had undergone: "If any man clean against his heart (but overcome with the weakness of the flesh), for fear of persecution, have denied, as Peter did, or have delivered his book, or put it away secretly; let him (if he repent) come again, and take better hold, and not despair" (143–44). He was casting himself into the hands of his enemies, but the book told him that tribulation for righteousness was a blessing, a gift that God who "worketh backward" only gives to his elect: "If God promise riches, the way thereto is poverty. Whom he loveth, him he chasteneth: whom he exalteth, he casteth down: whom he saveth, he damneth first. He bringeth no man to heaven, except he send him to hell first. If he promise life, he slayeth first: when he buildeth, he casteth all down first. He is no patcher; he cannot build on another man's foundation" (135).[31] More's attack seems at its most odious when he charges that Tyndale's books killed men; the killing was done by the state More served and in defense of the church More loved.[32] But there is truth in the charge that the *Obedience* virtually produced a heretic like Bainham. He was a creature of the book.

The shaping power of the *Obedience* may be seen as an extreme version of the less drastic but widespread influence exerted in the period by conduct manuals of which the most famous are Machiavelli's *Prince* (1513) and Castiglione's *Courtier* (1528). Tyndale himself may have translated Erasmus's important contribution to the genre, the *Enchiridion militis Christiani* (1501).[33] That the most significant and enduring works of this kind appeared

during the first decades of the sixteenth century suggests the great
"unmooring" that men were experiencing, their sense that fixed
positions had somehow become unstuck, their anxious awareness
that the moral landscape was shifting. "Men live among themselves in such a manner," writes Luther, "that no consideration is
given to the state or household . . . . who does not see that God is
compelled, as it were, to punish, yes, even to destroy Germany?"[34]

The complex sources of this anxiety may be rooted in momentous changes in the material world: a sharp population increase,
the growth of cities, the first stages of an "agrarian revolution,"
the rapid expansion of certain key industries, the realignment of
European-wide economic forces.[35] These changes were present in
varying degrees to the consciousness of the men of the early sixteenth century; still more present, however, were shifts in societal
definitions of institutions and of the alien, and it is at the intersection of these two, we have argued, that identity is fashioned. The
Obedience, like virtually all major guides to conduct in the period,
grasps that the shaping of the individual, even at the most intimate level, depends both on the' institutional mode of secular
power and religious doctrine and on the communal perception of
the alien and the devilish. Where in his later career More exalts the
existing institution of the Catholic Church and identifies heresy as
the alien force that must be destroyed, Tyndale, for his part, exalts
the monarchy as the essential, saving secular institution and
defines the Catholic Church as the demonic other.

The immediate occasion of the *Obedience* was the charge that the
Protestants fomented rebellion, a charge fueled by the German
Peasants' Revolt of 1525. Tyndale's reply takes the form of that
strategy of reversal we have already seen several times and that
derives, like so much else, directly from Luther: "it is the bloody
doctrine of the pope which causeth disobedience, rebellion, and
insurrection" (166). The Catholic Church teaches us from earliest
childhood "to kill a Turk, to slay a Jew, to burn an heretic, to fight
for the liberties and right of the church, as they call it"; when "we
have sucked in such bloody imaginations into the bottom of our
hearts, even with our mother's milk" (166), what wonder that we
mistakenly think it lawful to fight for the true word of God and
hence are lured into disobedience? It is the goal of the *Obedience*
then to free men from their own corrupted imaginations, to restore
them to that obedience that Christ himself taught.

From the passage I have just quoted, one might imagine that
Tyndale goes on to preach toleration and mildness. He does

nothing of the kind. He preaches, rather, what one might call a violent obedience. His work is addressed to a soul conceived as the domain of power, the point at which all the lines of force in the universe converge. He exhorts the child to remember that he is the "good and possession" of his parents; such is the will of God who has "cast thee under the power and authority of them, to obey and serve them in his stead." Likewise, the husband's commandments are, to the wife, as God's commandments. "Sara," Tyndale writes, "before she was married, was Abraham's sister, and equal with him; but, as soon as she was married, was in subjection, and became without comparison inferior; for so is the nature of wedlock, by the ordinance of God" (171). Servants too must understand that they are the property of their masters, "as his ox or his horse" (172). And all men must understand that "God hath made the king in every realm judge over all, and over him is there no judge." He who judges the king judges God; he who lays hands on the king lays hands on God; he who resists the king resists God. If a subject sins, he must be brought to the king's judgment; "if the king sins, he must be reserved unto the judgment, wrath, and vengeance of God. And as it is to resist the king, so is it to resist his officer, which is set, or sent, to execute the king's commandment" (177).

Tyndale obliterates here more than the competing rights of the Church. As *Utopia* had envisaged the reduction of all men to citizens with the identical language, traditions, customs, and laws, the *Obedience* reduces all men to the common condition of subjects: this includes dukes and earls, as well as cardinals and bishops. Tyndale's silence in this regard is eloquent in its dismissal of the vast and intricate feudal network of rights and obligations. By contrast, even the Elizabethan *Homily on Obedience* (1559) is careful to speak of the "high powers, which be set in authority by God" as "God's lieutenants, God's presidents, God's officers, God's commissioners, God's judges."[36] Tyndale simply jumps from the power of masters over servants, which he conceives as the ownership of property, to the power of the king over subjects: there is room for the king's officers but not for individuals with independent, divinely or humanly sanctioned claims to power. And he does not shrink before the full implications of his argument: "the king is, in this world, without law; and may at his lust do right or wrong, and shall give accounts but to God only" (178). At Anne Boleyn's urging, Henry VIII read the *Obedience* and is reported to have said when he had finished it, "This is a book for me and for all kings to read."[37]

But it would be a mistake to imagine that Tyndale wrote the *Obedience* to please or reassure Henry VIII; two years later the reformer did not hesitate to write and publish *The Practice of Prelates,* a work that opposed the royal divorce and won the king's lasting enmity.[38] The extremity, the violence, of his vision of obedience reflects other motives. As a rebel against the Catholic Church, Tyndale, like virtually all the early reformers, needs to see that Church as profoundly disobedient; he constructs a universe in which all men are locked into a rigid code of obedience, a code utterly beyond their control or volition, fixed by God himself, and then observes, angrily and triumphantly, that there is no place in this universe for the Catholic Church. Any claim the Church might make for men's obedience is a competitive claim, an attempt to divert obedience due elsewhere; and the Church compounds this crime by failing itself to obey its rulers, the temporal princes.

Tyndale juxtaposes then a call for violent disobedience to the Church and a call for absolute submission to the king. Such is the individual's relation to the great, patriarchal institutions of the world: one father must be destroyed; the other exalted to supreme temporal authority. In the individual's relation to God, the split is resolved by the transformation of rebellion into proper boldness and of submission into proper observance: "Let a child have never so merciful a father," Tyndale writes in the *Exposition of I John* (1513), "yet if he break his father's commandments, though he be not under damnation, yet he is ever chid and rebuked and now and then lashed with the rod: by the reason whereof he is never bold in his father's presence. But the child that keepeth his father's commandments is sure of him self and bold in his father's presence to speak and ask what he will."[39] It is precisely in strict obedience to God that men become "sure of themselves," and this assurance contrasts with the groveling idolatry Tyndale claims that the Catholic Church desires from its members.

The *Obedience* sets out to expose and dismantle those false practices—superstitious ceremonies, factitious sacraments, confession, the worship of saints, monasticism, typology, clerical celibacy, purgatory, indulgences, excommunication—that constitute the means by which the Church transforms good Christians into abject idolaters. If some Catholic practices bear a curious resemblance to true doctrine and observance, it is because they have been cunningly designed to do so. The preaching of God's word inevitably involves an attack on the Church's perversion of that word: "It is impossible to preach Christ, except thou preach against Antichrist" (185). For though both Christ's teachings and the Catholic Church's abuses are easy, according to Tyndale, for all to grasp, nevertheless, as the contemporary embodiment of Antichrist, the Church has the uncanny power to simulate certain aspects of authentic Christian faith, to construct a holy mask sufficiently convincing to deceive the unenlightened, to *perform* as in a theater the truth that it should actually embody. This histrionic power is one of the marks of Antichrist and a source of his enduring power: "his nature is (when he is uttered and overcome with the word of God) to go out of the play for a season and to disguise himself, and then to come in again with a new name and a new raiment."[40] Such masquerading is, of course, antithetical to the true nature of God, for "Christ is not hypocrite" who "playeth a part in a play and representeth a person of state which he is not." He "is always that his name signifieth: he is ever a saver."[41]

The *Obedience* must strip away the Antichrist's mask, but the task is difficult, for the Church is a vast, devious, international conspiracy, with tentacles reaching everywhere from the poorest hamlets to the council chambers of the great: "In every parish have they spies, and in every great man's house, and in every tavern and alehouse. And through confession know they all secrets, so that no man may open his mouth to rebuke whatsoever they do, but that he shall be shortly made a heretic. In all councils is one of them; yea, the most part and chief rulers of the councils are of them: but of their council is no man" (191). All classes have been dupes and victims of the Church, from the peasant who believes that a few mumbled Latin verses will make his corn grow better to the gentleman who must support an army of clerical drones. The false shepherds do not overlook a shred of the fleece: "The parson sheareth, the vicar shaveth, the parish priest polleth, the friar scrapeth, and the pardoner pareth; we lack but a butcher to pull off the skin" (238). And the greatest dupes are the kings, "nothing now-a-days, but even hangmen unto the pope and bishops, to kill whomsoever they condemn without any more ado" (242).

What begins as a doctrine of obedience ends as ruthless criticism: it is as if the former makes the latter possible, by assuring a firm ground on which to stand, boundaries within which to contain violent anger. The more rigid, harsh, and absolute the law of obedience, the more far-reaching and daring the attack on the corruptions of authority. Having exalted fathers to the status of domestic gods, Tyndale can turn around and write, of the churchmen: "And when they cry, 'Fathers, fathers,' remember that it were the fathers that blinded and robbed the whole world, and brought us into this captivity, wherein these enforce to keep us still. Furthermore, as they of the old time are fathers to us, so shall these foul monsters be fathers to them that come after us; and the hypocrites that follow us will cry of these and of their doings, "Fathers, fathers," as these cry "Fathers, fathers," of them that are past" (324). Having similarly exalted kings, Tyndale can attack them as either tyrants or mere shadows; combining both charges, and with a sly glance at Henry's title "Defender of the Faith" he can urge them not to let the pope any longer make them so drunk with vain names and other baubles, "as it were puppetry for children," that they will bankrupt their realms and murder their people "for defending of our holy father's tyranny" (204–5). For all his vehemence, however, Tyndale's attack is bounded by the order that enables it to exist: he will denounce the Church and expose kings and emperors as corrupt tools, he will long for God to come like a thief in the night and destroy the great ones of the earth, but he will not exhort the people to act for themselves. He is no Thomas Müntzer at the head of a revolutionary party; the commons are urged to take patience and suffer the abuses under which they groan. Violent anger has been released only, it seems, to be swallowed up again. But not completely.

Historians frequently divide early Protestants into conservatives and radicals, with Tyndale placed squarely among the former, as a preacher of passive obedience.[42] But such a distinction, though virtually inevitable, may be misleading, for even in the *Obedience*'s opening catalogue of ineluctable authorities, there is a subtle yet highly significant shift when we reach "The Obedience of Subjects unto Kings, Princes, and Rulers." We expect a further discourse on obedience; we hear instead of the necessity of *submission*. And there is a great difference, as James Bainham could testify. For there are certain extreme situations in which a man *must* disobey the king, even as the king is exhorted to disobey the pope and to break those vows which were unlawful to begin with. These are situations in which a man has been commanded to perform an action or express a belief directly contrary to the law of God and the faith of Christ. Such cases compel dissent, though the individual so compelled must at the same time bear patiently and without resistance the full punishment meted out by the authority he has disobeyed. He must, that is, act as James Bainham acted. The *Obedience*, as More quickly pointed out, is in fact a guide to *disobedience* of church and state.[43]

Such disobedience is not, of course, a rejection of the principle of authority but is obedience to a higher authority at whose command all lesser restraints fall away: "Jacob robbed Laban his uncle; Moses robbed the Egyptians; and Abraham is about to slay and burn his own son; and all are holy works, because they are wrought in faith at God's commandments. To steal, rob, and murder are no holy works before worldly people, but unto them that have their trust in God: they are holy when God commandeth them."[44] Thomas More was not alone in expressing horror at the queasy possibilities opened by this view. In the absence of a visible church, how is a man to be sure of his position—sure enough, that is, to take the far less spectacular but still drastic steps that led a man like Bainham to the stake? There did not exist in the early sixteenth century, after all, a coherent ideology of dissent: the medieval past bore witness to innumerable conspiracies, rebellions, jacqueries, heresies, millennial outbursts, but provided no principle of negation. If the movements led by Wycliffe and Hus offered the glimmerings of such an ideology, these movements were certainly not sufficient by themselves to sustain disobedience; the *Obedience* scarcely alludes to the Lollards, and it would take Foxe's massive rewriting of history in the middle decades of the sixteenth century to establish a "tradition" of resistance to illegitimate spiritual authority. Tyndale does not seek to set up a vanguard party that will make the necessary decisions nor to ally himself with a discontented social class or status group; such developments, insofar as they happen at all, begin considerably later in the century and do not assume clear form until the following century.[45] What Tyndale seeks is rather a principle powerful enough to uphold individuals in daring acts of dissent against overwhelming spiritual and political authority and to sustain these individuals during the sufferings that would follow such acts.

For Tyndale, this principle is found in the other book James Bainham held in his hand at Saint Austin's Church: the Bible, freed of the Church's false hermeneutics, translated into the vernacular, printed in quantities large enough for all men to possess or at least have access to a copy. The vernacular Bible, to which Tyndale devoted his life, was one of the principles of the earlier heretical movements, but neither technology nor the individual conscience had been fully prepared; now it was possible to put into the hands of literate and at least make accessible to illiterate believers an infallible rule by which to judge the words and deeds of those who set themselves up as absolute authorities: "Forasmuch now as thou partly seest the falsehood of our prelates, how all their study is to deceive us and to keep us in darkness, to sit as gods in our consciences, and handle us at their pleasure, and to lead us whither they lust; therefore I read thee, get thee to God's word, and thereby try all doctrine, and against that receive nothing" (324). "Get thee to God's word": so Tyndale voices that fetishism of Scripture preached by all of the early Protestants. More, defending the position of the Catholic Church, argued that we are bound "not only to believe against our own reason the points that God shewed us in Scripture; but also that God teacheth his church without Scripture against our own mind also."[46] We are bound, Tyndale countered, "to look in the Scripture, whether our fathers have done right or wrong, and ought to believe nothing without a reason of the Scripture and authority of God's word" (330).

A reader who took this counsel to heart and looked into the English New Testament of 1525 could learn almost the whole of the heretical creed from the prologue and glosses. Following Luther, Tyndale dwells on man's utter worthlessness, the bondage of his will: "The devil is our lord, and our ruler, our head, governor, our prince, yea, and our god. And our will is locked and knit faster unto the will of the devil, than could an hundred thousand chains bind a man unto a post. . . . Whatsoever we do, think, or imagine, is abominable in the sight of God."[47] This depravity is not the consequence of the observable behavior of particular individuals but rather the condition of existence; a human fetus is equally abominable: "By nature, through the fall of Adam, are we the children of wrath, heirs of the vengeance of God by birth, yea, and from our conception. And we have our fellowship with the damned devils, under the power of darkness and rule of Satan, while we are yet in our mother's wombs. . . . And as an adder, a toad, or a snake, is hated of man, not for the evil that it hath done, but for the poison that is in it, and hurt which it cannot but do: so are we hated of God, for that natural poison, which is conceived and born with us, before we do any outward evil" (14).

This vision of human loathsomeness is proclaimed, of course, only to be redeemed by the glad tidings: Christ "hath fought with sin, with death, and the devil, and overcome them; whereby all men that were in bondage to sin, wounded with death, overcome of the devil, are, without their own merits or deservings, loosed, justified, restored to life and saved, brought to liberty and reconciled unto the favour of God, and set at one with him again" (9). Man has been driven to desperation by the law in order to be saved by the gospel; hearing and believing this news, a Christian "cannot but be glad, and laugh from the low bottom of his heart" (9). This joyful redemption comes only through man's faith in

Christ's sacrifice and not through good works: "By faith are we saved only" (15) declares Tyndale's prologue, echoing Luther's famous *sola fide*.

When he turned from this prologue to the text itself, the reader found ample confirmation of the Reformer's doctrines. More likened Tyndale's translation to "poisoned bread" and counted over a thousand "faults" in it; he was surely correct in pointing out the Lutheran intent behind the use of "congregation" instead of "church," "love" instead of "charity," "senior" instead of "priest," "knowledge" instead of "confession," and so on.[48] And the subversiveness of the translation was heightened by the simple fact that charges like More's could be so plausibly reversed and the Vulgate exposed as a partisan, partial translation, slanted to favor the interests of the Catholic Church. The success of this reversal may be gauged by the decree of the Council of Trent, dated 8 April 1546, which ordains that "the Vulgate approved through long usage during so many centuries be held authentic in public lectures, disputations, preachings and exposition, and that nobody dare or presume to reject it under any pretext."[49] An unspoken assumption over centuries that the Vulgate was the authentic version is one thing; a decree to that effect is quite another. The Protestant translators had forced the Church into the declaration that the "authentic" version was to be preferred in all instances to the original. By contrast, Tyndale could, in the prologue to the 1525 New Testament, exhort "those that are better seen in the tongues than I, and that have better gifts of grace, to interpret the sense of the Scripture" to mend the translation wherever necessary.[50]

The printing of the English New Testament in 1525 marked for men like Bainham a turning point in human history: God once more spoke directly to men. "The truth of holy Scripture," Bainham declared at his first interrogation, "was never, these eight hundred years past, so plainly and expressly declared unto the people, as it hath been within these six years" (698). Bainham himself had no need of a vernacular translation to understand Scripture; according to Foxe, he was learned in both Latin and Greek. The issue then is not his own personal access to the Bible; a text in English and in print rather than script are for the Reformers keys to the *repossession* of God's word by the Christian people. The vernacular wrests the Bible from the hands of the priests, and the printing press assures that this liberation of the word is irreversible. For manuscript copies of the New Testament alone, even copies prepared by a competent scriptorium, were necessarily time-consuming to make and hence both costly and scarce. By seizing and destroying such manuscripts, the authorities could seriously impede the dissemination of God's word. But printed books were quite another matter. When in 1529 More went to Antwerp with his friend Cuthbert Tunstall, the bishop of London, the latter bought up and burned as many copies of Tyndale's New Testament and other heretical works as he could find, but this was a pre-Gutenberg strategy. The money Tunstall spent for the books only helped Tyndale to hasten the production of the second edition of his translation, which appeared in 1534.[51]

The word of God in the age of mechanical reproduction—fifty thousand copies by the time of Tyndale's death—has a new, direct force: "All mercy that is shewed there is a promise unto thee, if thou turn to God. And all vengeance and wrath shewed there is threatened to thee, if thou be stubborn and resist. And this learning and comfort shalt thou evermore find in the plain text and literal sense."[52] "The plain text and literal sense": translation is not the imposition of an intermediary between God's word and man but just the opposite—the tearing aside of a veil of deceit in order to present the text in full immediacy. If God's word was to be experienced by more than a handful of clerks as an unmediated address to the soul, then the language of the Bible could only be the vernacular. Even for a man well trained in Latin, the English Scriptures spoke to the heart in a way the Vulgate never could; the vernacular was the unself-conscious language of the inner man.[53] Bainham's interrogators offered him the embrace of the Holy Mother Church—"the bosom of his mother was open for him" (700), they told him. The Reformers offered a different intimacy, the intimacy not of the institution, imaged as the nurturing female body, but of the book, imaged, in terms displaced from that body, as self, food, and protection: "As thou readest," Tyndale writes in the *Prologue to Genesis*, "think that every syllable pertaineth to thine own self, and suck out the pith of the Scripture, and arm thyself against all assaults."[54]

The power of the English Bible was at its height precisely in the years when copies were publicly burned by the authorities, when readers put their lives in danger to read it.[55] By their opposition to vernacular translation, by seeing to it that not a single English Bible had been produced since the invention of printing, the Catholic authorities in England vastly heightened the impact of Tyndale's work. Only those who had been brought up to think of the Bible as a Latin work could experience the full shock of the voice of God speaking to them in English from its pages. Add to this the threat of persecution, and the effect must have seemed overpowering, almost irresistible. This is surely one of the reasons why, during a brief period, Protestantism in England could survive and spread without any significant institutional framework, on the force of the word. When Tyndale writes of arming oneself with the syllables of Scripture or Bainham speaks of his fear that this word of God—pointing to the book in his hand—would damn him, we must take them at very close to the literal meaning: the printed English New Testament is, above all, *a form of power*. It is invested with the ability to control, guide, discipline, console, exalt, and punish that the Church had arrogated to itself for centuries. And lest this be thought inflated rhetoric, let us recall that James Bainham simply could not live with the pain of what he took to be his betrayal of the book; he preferred death.

Bainham is by no means unique. Of the numerous comparable instances, we may recall Latimer's moving account of Thomas Bilney, who had abjured in 1527 and done public penance—"borne his faggot"—at Paul's Cross. Upon his return to Cambridge, Bilney "had such conflict within himself" that his friends were afraid to leave him by himself; day and night they attempted to comfort him, but no comfort would serve. "As for the comfortable places in Scripture, to bring them unto him it was as though a man would run him through the heart with a sword."[56] After two years of such pain, he went to Norfolk, began again to preach Lutheran teachings, and was arrested as a relapsed heretic. According to Foxe, while awaiting execution Bilney thrust his hand into the flame of a candle, recalling as he did so a passage from Isaiah: "When thou walkest in the fire, it shall not burn thee, and the flame shall not kindle upon thee, for I am the Lord thy God, the holy One of Israel."[57] Where the Scripture had literally tormented Bilney after abjuration, it now shields him from agony. At the end, as More relates, Bilney was taken "and Tyndale's books with him too, and both two burned together," with "more profit unto his soul," More adds, than had he "lived longer and after died in his bed."[58]

These and other testimonials to the magical power of the Word are the extreme expressions of a far more pervasive influence that would make the English Bible, when its dissemination became a matter of national policy, by far the single most significant book in the language. Access to the Bible was a decisive force behind the extraordinary spread of literacy to the masses, so that by the middle of the seventeenth century perhaps as many as 60 percent of men in the larger towns of the South and at least 30 percent in the country as a whole could read.[59] By royal command, reiterated in a proclamation in 1541, "Bibles containing the Old and New Testament in the English tongue" were "to be fixed and set up openly in every of the said parish churches" so that "every of the King's majesty's loving subjects" might read in the Scriptures.[60] Immediately after the proclamation, William Malden tells us, "divers poor men in the town of Chelmsford in the county of Essex ...brought the New Testament of Jesus Christ, and on Sundays did sit reading in [the] lower end of the Church, and many would flock about them to hear the reading."[61] Indeed, interest was sufficiently popular and intense for a 1538 Declaration to warn the unlearned against engaging in biblical exegesis "in your open Taverns or Alehouses," an admonition, as one scholar notes, no doubt honored more in the breach.[62] Over two hundred editions of the Holy Scriptures were produced between 1521 and 1600, 480 between 1601 and 1700; by the early eighteenth century, well over 500,000 copies of the Bible, by conservative estimate, had been printed. Tyndale had unleashed an immense force.

This force receives its supreme literary tribute more than a century after Tyndale's death in the works of Bunyan. According to *Grace Abounding*, particular biblical passages had an obsessional force in Bunyan's life, hammering at his mind, striking him across the face, pursuing him relentlessly: "Now about a week or fortnight after this, I was much followed by this scripture, *Simon, Simon, behold, Satan hath desired to have you*, Luk. 22, 31. And sometimes it would sound so loud within me, yea, and as it were call so strongly after me, that once above all the rest, I turned my head over my shoulder, thinking verily that some man had behind me called to me...."[63] Texts "tear and rend" his soul, "touch" him, "seize" him, "fall like a hot thunder-bolt" upon his conscience; and even the consoling visitations have something violent about them: "And as I was thus before the Lord, that Scripture fastned on my heart, *O man, great is thy Faith*, Matt. 15.28, even as if one had clapt me on the back" (65). A massive cultural investment of power in the book culminates in this uncanny, uncontrollable presence.

That it is Bunyan, imprisoned for preaching without the permission of the authorities, who testifies to this presence reminds us that once they had displaced Catholicism, the Protestants had to reinforce and control the power of God's word with more obviously physical punishments and with the whole apparatus of patriarchal family, church, school, and state. But in the first years the power was almost uniquely present in the book itself. "The Lord began to work for his Church," writes Foxe, "not with sword and target to subdue His exalted adversary, but with printing, writing and reading.... How many printing presses there be in the world, so many blockhouses there be against the high castle of St Angelo, so that either the pope must abolish knowledge and printing or printing at length will root him out."[64]

The Bible has displaced the *consensus fidelium* as the principle of intelligibility and the justification of all action: "Without God's word do nothing" (330).[65] The authority of God's word is assured by the *inner experience* of God's word; the true interpretation of Scripture is made possible by the feeling faith of the believer.[66] More, like all Catholic apologists, argued that we are bound "to give diligent hearing, firm credence, and faithful obedience to the Church of Christ concerning the sense and understanding of holy Scripture, not doubting but since he hath commanded his sheep to be fed, he hath provided for them wholesome meat and true doctrine."[67] If we waver in this acceptance of the Church's hermeneutic authority, we will be plunged into uncertainty and doubt, for how else can we know that the Scripture comes from God? Tyndale's most eloquent and radical reply to this question came three years after the *Obedience*, in his *Answer to Sir Thomas More's Dialogue:* "Who taught the eagles to spy out their prey? Even so the children of God spy out their Father; and Christ's elect spy out their Lord, and trace out the paths of his feet, and follow; yea, though he go upon the plain and liquid water, which will receive no step, and yet there they find out his foot."[68] In response, More tried, with several jokes, to dissipate the force of this vision and, more seriously, to expose its violence; the Scripture is the heretics' prey, "to spoil and kill and devour it as they list, even by the special inspiration of God."[69] But Tyndale fully intended the violence of his metaphors; a Christian does not need elaborate training to understand God's word; he seizes upon it, by instinct, for his very survival.

Tyndale thus is able to reject the mediation of the Church and its tradition; the individual has sufficient means within his own conscience to grasp the truth of God's word as revealed in Scripture. In response to this challenge, Catholic apologists tend to affirm an increasingly external authority, but it is important to note that the sharp opposition which thus emerged is historically misleading. For, as we have seen, it is precisely the Church that had, over several centuries, slowly developed and enriched the inner life of the individual, as a locus of its power, a means of discipline and consolation. Reformers like Tyndale are attempting, in effect, a seizure of power.

With the 1525 translation of the New Testament and the 1530 translation of the Pentateuch—the first five books of the Old Testament—Tyndale took what he felt were the essential steps toward this seizure that he, of course, conceived as the triumph of God's word. But even in 1525 he recognized that a reading alone, without any instruction as to *how* to read the Bible, might not be sufficient. Most of his subsequent writings may be understood as attempts to provide such instruction and to clear away impediments; for Tyndale all human enterprises rest ultimately on the fate of reading. Thus, in its long concluding sections, the *Obedience* turns from an analysis of the responsibilities of rulers and subjects to an attack on the four-fold method of scriptural interpretation, an attack mounted in the name of what Tyndale calls "the literal sense." Tyndale's notion of the literal sense by no means amounts to a coherent theory of interpretation; more often than not it is merely a stick to beat a reading he dislikes. But it reflected and no doubt strengthened certain tendencies that proved immensely influential not only in the reading of Scripture but in the reading and writing of imaginative literature in this period and beyond. In the first place, and perhaps most important, Tyndale's "literal sense" is the expression of a powerful *confidence:* it is easy to understand Scripture, its meaning lies directly in front of us, competing interpretations are perverse mystifications. There is no need of advanced degrees, the mastery of difficult languages, the juggling of arcane symbolisms, prodigious memory, an expensive library; the truth is as accessible to a shoemaker as to a theologian, perhaps more accessible, for the latter has been poisoned by popish sophistry.

Secondly, the stress on the literal sense means that one should avoid, wherever possible, looking behind the words of the Scripture for some hidden, mystical meaning. Paul's words in 2 Corinthians 3, "The letter killeth, but the spirit giveth life," do not refer to the literal and spiritual sense of Scripture, but to the contrast of the law and the gospel. There is no division between the literal and spiritual sense, for "God is a Spirit"; "His literal sense is spiritual, and all his words are spiritual" (309). To understand the significance of Tyndale's position here, we can compare it to Erasmus's discussion of Scripture in the *Enchiridion*. The whole Bible, he writes, including the Gospel, has both a flesh and a spirit, and it is our task to despise the former and search out the latter. The "plain sense" is worthless; only the "mystery" deserves our reverent attention. Indeed if you take at face value the stories of Adam formed of moist clay or Eve plucked out of the rib, or the talking serpent, you might just as well "sing of the image of clay made by Prometheus, or of fire stolen from heaven by subtlety and put into the image to give life to the clay."[70] And if Erasmus thus struggles rather poignantly with the palpably fictional appearance of certain books of the Bible, with the disturbing resemblance to pagan myths of origin, he struggles equally with the purely historical appearance of other books: "What difference is there whether thou read the book of Kings or of the Judges in the Old Testament, or else the history of Titus Livyus, so thou have respect to the allegory nere nother [i.e., if you look at the veiled meaning in neither]? For in the one, that is to say Titus Livyus, be many things which would amend the common manners; in the other be some things, yea, ungodly as they seem at the first looking on, which also if they be understood superficially should hurt good manners" (147). The solution to the problem is to discard "the rind or outer part" of Scripture and nourish oneself on the allegory. One cannot uncover these mysteries by means of one's own mind, but only by a "known and certain craft" which is taught in works like the Pseudo-Dionysius's *De divinus nominibus.* Erasmus may have preached a simple "philosophy of Christ," available to fools and wise men alike, but the place to acquire this philosophy was clearly not the literal sense of the Bible.

By contrast, Tyndale insists, as we have seen, that the most readily accessible sense of Scripture is always the heart of the meaning: "There is no story nor gest, seem it never so simple or so vile unto the world, but that thou shalt find therein spirit and life and edifying in the literal sense" (319). Even he is forced to acknowledge that the Scripture uses "proverbs, similitudes, riddles, or allegories, as all other speeches do," but the meaning of these devices "is ever the literal sense" (304). From the examples he proceeds to give, it appears that by the "literal sense" here Tyndale means a clear, moral lesson or principle of faith that is openly stated elsewhere in the Bible. Allegorical interpretation is permissible if it is a self-conscious and provisional process, with no inherent claim to truth: "allegories are no sense of the Scripture, but free things besides the Scripture, and altogether in the liberty of the Spirit" (305). By themselves, "allegories prove nothing" and can make no more claim upon our faith than any fiction: "if I could not prove with an open text that which the allegory doth express, then were the allegory a thing to be jested at, and of no greater value than a tale of Robin Hood" (306). Allegory, along with the related forms of similitude, example, and figure, are not used to express a dark mystery but rather to heighten the effect upon the reader, for such indirect or metaphorical speech "doth print a thing much deeper in the wits of a man than doth a plain speaking, and leaveth behind him as it were a sting to prick him forward, and to awake him withal" (306).

The third major effect of Tyndale's insistence on the "literal sense" follows directly from this view: an emphasis on the *rhetorical* nature of Scripture. Nowhere is the influence of humanism on the early Protestants clearer. The Bible is not a vast network of occult signs but a divine work of persuasion, designed to strengthen the reader's faith and to deter him from evil. Thus, for example, the reader should concern himself less with the ultimate, abstract significance of a word than with its function in a particular, highly specific context: " A serpent figureth Christ in one place, and the devil in another; and a lion doth likewise" (208). The meaning of key words is established not by institutional definition but by the reader's grasp of context: "if this word *congregation* were a more general term than this word *church*, it hurteth not, for the circumstance doth ever declare what thing is meant thereby." More replies that if this is so, Tyndale may translate any word as he wishes: "For so he may translate the world into a football if he join therewith certain circumstances, and say this round rolling football that men walk upon and ships sail upon, in the people whereof there is no rest nor stability, and so forth a great long tale; with such circumstances he might as I say make any word understanden as it like himself, whatsoever the word before signified of itself."[71]

In the controversial works this argument leads only to a reaffirmation of familiar positions: for Tyndale, a willingness to have his translation improved upon by others, provided they submit themselves to God's word; for More, a conviction that "good Christian men," perceiving the heretical intent of the translation, should "abhor and burn up his books and likers of them with them."[72] But the effect on the translation itself of Tyndale's interest in "circumstance" and in rhetorical power is more significant; it is reflected in the clarity of the narrative, its impressive coherence, its commitment to the constant engaging of the reader's ready understanding:

> The elder brother was in the field, and when he came and drew nigh to the house, he heard minstrelsy and dancing and called one of his servants and asked what those things meant. And he said unto him: thy brother is come, and thy father had killed the fatted calf, because he hath received him safe and sound. And he was

angry, and would not go in. Then came his father out
and entreated him. He answered and said to his father:
Lo these many years have I done thee service, neither
break at any time thy commandment, and yet gavest
thou me never so much as a kid to make merry with my
lovers: but as soon as this thy son was come, which
hath devoured thy goods with harlots, thou hast for his
pleasure killed the fatted calf. And he said unto him:
Son, thou was ever with me, and all that I have is thine:
it was meet that we should make merry and be glad: for
this thy brother was dead and is alive again: and was
lost, and is found. (Luke 15:25–32)[73]

Our familiarity with the Authorized Version, which, as always,
follows Tyndale quite closely, may inhibit our grasp of Tyndale's remarkable advance in simple, loving eloquence—in "open-
ness"—over the Wycliffite translations. The second Wycliffite
version, for example, renders the close of verse 29, "and thou
never gave to me a kid: that I with my friends should have
eat." The Authorized Version loses in intensity what it gains in
accuracy: "and yet thou never gavest me a kid, that I might make
merry with my friends."

Tyndale's interest in "circumstance" is reflected still more
closely in his conviction that the reader must be sensitive to the
natural order of a text, even one that does not tell a story, and must
not jumble the beginning and the end. God's word cannot be cut
and spliced; to do so, indeed, can be dangerous, as Tyndale, following Luther, explains in the Prologue to Romans. The "unquiet,
busy, and high-climbing" spirit that rushes to chapters 9–11 of
Paul's epistle in the hope of understanding predestination runs
the risk of falling into despair. Only when the reader has fully
experienced the meaning of the first seven chapters is he ready for
the eighth, which, in turn, is the necessary introduction to those
that follow: "After that, when thou art come to the eighth chapter,
and art under the cross and suffering of tribulation, the necessity of
predestination will wax sweet, and thou shalt well feel how precious a thing it is. For except thou have born the cross of adversity
and temptation, and hast felt thyself brought unto the very brim of
desperation, yea, and unto hell-gates, thou canst never meddle
with the sentence of predestination without thine own harm, and
without secret wrath and grudging inwardly against God; for
otherwise it shall not be possible for thee to think that God is
righteous and just."[74] The *order* of the reading experience is all-
important; the chapters have been arranged rhetorically to produce essential psychological effects which are at the same time

doctrinal truths. There is a kind of historicity and narrativity built into the experience of faith through the act of reading: by following the text in its proper sequence, the reader reenacts in his own spirit the passage from the Old Testament to the New, from the law that kills to God's free gift of grace.

This sense of necessary sequence marks much of Tyndale's prose and distinguishes it sharply from More's. The *Confutation of Tyndale's Answer,* as More acknowledges in responding to his enemies, is almost unreadable; the brethren, he writes in the *Apology,* complain that his work is too long "and therefore tedious to read." More justifies this elaphantine text on the paradoxical ground that many of his readers would grow weary in the attempt to read a long book, "and therefore have I taken the more pain upon every chapter, to the intent that they shall not need to read over any chapter but one, and that it shall not force greatly which one throughout all the book." There is no need to read the book through or to read its chapters in sequence; More's goal rather is to compile an encyclopedia of antiheretical arguments, but a strange kind of encyclopedia, since its ultimate aim is to be unnecessary, unread: "Now he that will therefore read any one chapter, either at adventure, or else some chosen piece in which himself had weened [i.e., thought] that his evangelical father Tyndale had said wonderful well, . . . when he shall in that chapter as I am sure he shall, find his holy prophet plainly proved a fool, he may be soon eased of any further labor. For then hath he good cause to cast him quite off, and never meddle more with him, and then shall he never need to read more of my book neither, and so shall he make it short enough."[75]

It is crucially important for More to demolish the texts of the Reformers, while not crucially important to put his own text in their place. Hence the odd sense of the disposability of More's discourse; his work longs to disappear, to cede place to multiple voices, to tradition and ultimately to the institution as the living expression of the Christian consensus. More's commitment to the disappearance of his text paradoxically commits him to an endless text. He cannot allow his controversial works to possess form, because form would grant to the heretics a narrative coherence, a "free-standing" perspective that More denies.

If More's controversial writings want to be absorbed back into the community, Tyndale's can perhaps be thought to cede place too, but only to another, superior, and finally irreducible text. Where in More the text must always give way to the institution that lies behind it and controls interpretation, in Tyndale the text strives to establish itself beyond interpretation as the personal history of the individual reader: "Then go to and read the stories of the Bible for thy learning and comfort, and see every thing practised before thine eyes; for according to those ensamples shall it go with thee and all men until the world's end."[76] The rhetorical force of the Bible depends upon the reader's grasp of the *stories* in their full narrative power and upon the *presentness* of the language. Where the first Wycliffite translation had striven for the literal sense in an almost totemic way—that is, preserving the Latin word order at the expense of English syntax—Tyndale follows Wycliffe's disciple, John Purvey, in the attempt to render Scripture in what the latter called "open" English.[77] The more "open" the text, the less dependent upon an institutional interpretation.

More himself, we should add, did not object to the rhetorical force of Tyndale's translation, nor did he or the clerical authorities oppose on principle an English Bible. But approval of such a project, they argued, would have to wait until the heresy was crushed and the authority of the Church reaffirmed. Tyndale's Bible was hateful to More not because it was in English but because its "false" translations and its glosses lured men to their destruction, while Tyndale himself watched from the safety of the Continent. After all, unlike many of those who were shaped by *The Obedience of a Christian Man,* Tyndale did not passively suffer the consequences of disobedience; at every point in his career when his views threatened to bring down upon him the rage of authority, he chose to move in search of less constraining, less menacing circumstances where he could pursue his work. In 1523, running afoul of his clerical superiors in Little Sodbury where, on leaving the university, he had gone to teach, Tyndale did not simply submit. "When I came before the chancellor [of the Gloucestershire diocese]," he bitterly recalls, "he threatened me grievously, and reviled me, and rated me as though I had been a dog." In the midst of this humiliation, Tyndale remembered that the bishop of London had been praised for his learning: "Then thought I, if I might come to this man's service, I were happy. And so I gat me to London."[78] And when the bishop of London, More's friend Tunstall, refused to help, Tyndale betook himself into exile, from whence he flooded England with his words and the words of Scripture. How did he reconcile his social ethic and his actions?

The answer seems to lie in his reply to Cromwell's agent, Stephen Vaughan, who tried to persuade him to return to England, submit himself "to the obedience and good order of the world," and trust in the king's mercy. "I assure you," Vaughan reports Tyndale as saying, "if it would stand with the King's most gracious pleasure to grant only a bare text of the Scripture to be put forth among his people, like as is put forth among the subjects of the Emperor in these parts, and of other Christian princes, be it of the translation of what person soever shall please his Majesty, I shall immediately make faithful promise never to write more, nor abide two days in these parts after the same; but immediately to repair into his realm, and there most humbly submit myself at the feet of his Royal Majesty, offering my body to suffer what pain or torture, yea, what death his Grace will, so that this be obtained."[79] The mission of putting forth the Scripture in the vernacular has priority over everything else in his life including his social ethic; let such a translation freely circulate and he will, in effect, cease to exist. He will fall silent, he will die. And in a sense his own life, as something autonomous, something he possessed, had already ceased to exist. It had been fully absorbed in his great project.

According to a plausible if suspiciously prophetic account in Foxe, Tyndale first expressed that project at the height of an argument with a learned divine who had declared, "We were better to be without God's laws than the Pope's." Tyndale replied, "I defy the Pope and all his laws. If God spare my life, ere many years I will cause a boy that driveth the plough shall know more of the Scripture than thou doest."[80] The words are strikingly reminiscent of the hope Erasmus expressed in 1516 in the *Paraclesis,* the preface to his Greek and Latin edition of the New Testament: "I disagree very much with those who are unwilling that Holy Scripture, translated into the vulgar tongue be read by the uneducated .... I would that even the lowliest women read the Gospels and the Pauline Epistles. And I would that they were translated into all languages so that they could be read and understood not only by Scots and Irish but also by Turks and Saracens .... Would that, as a result, the farmer sing some portion of them at the plow, the weaver hum some parts of them to the movement of his shuttle, the traveller lighten the weariness of the journey with stories of this kind!"[81] Tyndale may indeed have conceived his project from this vision of Erasmus; have we not just witnessed the way a man's whole sense of himself may be shaped by another's words? But we must also note the vast difference between Erasmus's "Would that" and Tyndale's "I will cause," a difference compounded of the intertwining conflicts between generations, temperaments, and cultures. What Erasmus is willing to express as a wish, Tyndale puts as his personal mission.

The mission is conceived in anger and rebellion and expressed with a considerable sense of self-importance. "I defy the Pope, and all his laws," the obscure, powerless country priest grandly declares, and the inflated sense of personal significance carries over to the vaunt that follows. We may glimpse this egotism throughout his subsequent career, in his stinging attacks on the character and competence of his fellow workers William Roy and George Joye, in his increasing defensiveness about the validity of his own translation; but, significantly, all of its manifestations are closely related to his mission as translator. Though he insists on the interiority of faith, we have at the end of his work very little sense of his presence, of *personal* suffering and redemption. The most intimate anecdote in his writings is the account of his unsuccessful attempt to acquire Tunstall's patronage for the long labor of translation. Tyndale published the 1525 New Testament anonymously and claims that he would have continued this practice—for Christ "exhorteth men (Matt. 6) to do their good deeds secretly"—had he not been compelled to distinguish his own work from the scurrilous work of his former associate Roye.[82] Unlike Luther, Tyndale never gives us a sense of inner depth, of the powerful imprint of his own experience, of the effect of others upon his consciousness; what he gives us is a *voice,* the voice of the English Bible. Our sense of supreme eloquence in English is still largely derived from Tyndale—attempts at sublimity in our language tend to be imitations, most often unconscious and frequently inept, of the style of the English Bible—and he seems to have accomplished this remarkable achievement by transforming his whole self into that voice.

Tyndale's is a life lived as a *project.* When, in a letter of advice and comfort to John Frith, he reflects on his own career, he thinks exclusively of his relationship to God's Word: "I call God to record against the day we shall appear before our Lord Jesus, to give a reckoning of our doings, that I never altered one syllable of God's Word against my conscience, nor would this day, if all that is in the earth, whether it be pleasure, honour, or riches, might be given me."[83] Having made this assertion and disturbed perhaps by its element of pride, he follows, a few sentences later, with an unconvincing expression of humility: "God hath made me evil-favoured in this world, and without grace in the sight of men, speechless and rude, dull and slow-witted." This little exercise in self-denigration does not matter; his ego is fully realized in the work as translator. It is of this work that he still thinks at the close of his life.

In 1535 Tyndale, who was living with an English merchant in
Antwerp, was lured from the safety of his house by one Henry
Phillips, a treacherous Englishman who claimed to be a fellow
Protestant, and betrayed into the hands of the Catholic authorities.[84] Accused of heresy, Tyndale was imprisoned for over a
year, awaiting his trial, at Vilvorde Castle, near Brussels. From
this period of imprisonment, there survives a Latin letter he wrote
to the governor of the castle; the prisoner requests warmer clothes,
but, above all, he continues, "I beg and beseech your clemency to
be urgent with the commissary, that he will kindly permit me to
have my Hebrew Bible, Hebrew Grammar, and Hebrew Dictionary, that I may pass my time in that study."[85] As Bainham seems
to have thought of himself as Saint Peter, Tyndale quite possibly is
thinking here of Saint Paul, who asked, in his second epistle to
Timothy, for his "cloak . . . and the books, but specially the parch-
ment" (2 Tim. 4:13).

It is not known if Tyndale's request for books was granted. In
August, 1536, he was convicted of heresy and degraded from the
priesthood. The ceremony of degradation recalls those theatrical
rites of undoing with which this chapter began: the bishops sat on
a high platform either in church or in the town square, and the
priest condemned to be unhallowed was led, dressed in clerical
vestments, before them. He was made to kneel. "His hands were
scraped with a knife or a piece of glass, as a symbol of the loss of
the anointing oil; the bread and the wine were placed in his hands
and then taken away; and lastly his vestments were stripped from
him one by one, and he was clothed in the garments of a
layman."[86] Tyndale was then turned over to the secular authorities, who condemned him to be strangled and burned. The
sentence was carried out in October 1536. It must, I think, have
been to the need for a vernacular Bible, for which he labored all his
adult life, that Tyndale was referring when at the stake he cried
with a fervent zeal and a loud voice, "Lord, open the King of England's eyes!"[87]

More and Tyndale were profoundly divided. More's literary
interests were despised by Tyndale; the Catholic Church loved by
the one was regarded by the other as the very Antichrist; the cultic
observances More prized as an integral part of his communion
with the body of Christendom seemed to Tyndale a vicious fraud.
Tyndale's English Bible appeared to More a cunning piece of
heretical propaganda, the attack on purgatory a satanic device to
torment poor souls, the doctrine of justification by faith alone a
mere cloak for worldly transgressions. Tyndale thought More a

cruel and venal politician who had sold his services to the highest bidder; More thought Tyndale an immoral madman. There can scarcely be any doubt that More would have worked actively to bring about the execution of Tyndale as he had worked actively to bring about his capture; there is little question that Tyndale would have celebrated More's execution as a blow struck against an agent of the Antichrist. With his famous genius for friendships, and brilliant wit, his complex balance between council chamber and cloister, law court and scholar's study, Parliament and family, More's life seems richer and fuller than Tyndale's, wholly given over to the single-minded pursuit of the English Scripture. But eleven months after Tyndale's death, the English Bible—essentially Tyndale's Bible—was legally authorized in an England whose king had been declared Supreme Head of the national church.

For all the violent division, however, there are certain significant similarities between More and Tyndale. Though he was comfortable with ceremony and defended it in print, the heart of More's faith was not ritual practice but a spirit of communion that manifested itself at once in inner assurance and a virtuous life. For his part, Tyndale, though deeply influenced by Luther, was never completely at home in Lutheran theology and, it has been argued, in the course of his career moved steadily away from it. He did not, to be sure, soften his hatred of the Catholic Church, but his increasing commitment to the law, to morality as the fulfillment of the contract between God and man, led him surprisingly close to the position of Catholics like More or Colet.[88] The movement may be illustrated by a characteristic example of the changes Tyndale made between the Prologue to the 1525 New Testament and 1530 revision of that prologue printed separately as *The Pathway to the Scripture*. Men of right faith, he writes, "have delectation in the law (notwithstanding that they cannot fulfill it [as they would] for their weakness); and they abhor whatsoever the law forbiddeth, though they cannot [always] avoid it."[89] The words in brackets were added in 1531 and radically change the meaning: the first version More would have abhorred as heretical, the second he might almost himself have written.

The link here between the two enemies, Catholic and Reformer, is humanism. More, to be sure, came to feel very uneasy about his own and Erasmus's early works, while Tyndale harshly condemns "all the moral virtue of Aristotle, Plato, and Socrates" as pride abominable to God. All the same, both men continue throughout their careers to be deeply influenced by the Christian humanists' preoccupation with *right living.* "It is better to will the good than to know the truth," Petrarch had written,[90] and this conviction makes itself felt even in the midst of intense *theological* controversies.

At the same time, More and Tyndale share certain ambiguous feelings about even virtuous and moral living in the world. This is easier to see in More, with his sense of the way good men may be manipulated and his still deeper sense—Augustinian in character—of a fundamental chasm between the city of man and the city of God. This chasm makes even the most virtuous man fulfilling his duties to the best of his ability seem like an actor on a stage, lifelike but nevertheless at a fundamental distance from reality. Tyndale seems far removed from this sensibility; but, in fact, no sooner has he woven his hierarchy of authorities, each ordained by God and standing in the place of God, than he begins to unravel it again, until it vanishes altogether: "In Christ there is neither father nor son, neither master nor servant, neither husband nor wife, neither king nor subject: but the father is the son's self, and the son the father's own self; and the king is the subject's own self, and the subject is the king's own self; and so forth. I am thou thyself, and thou are I myself, and can be no nearer of kin" (*Obedience,* 296). Of course, such a total collapse of identity is only "in Christ"; in the temporal world, the distinctions still hold. But this neat resolution is more apparent than real, because, after all, Christ and the temporal world are not simple opposites. Christ had a historical reality, on which Tyndale insists; we pray to him, and try to fulfill his commands in this world; the man who thinks that his order and the world's order are entirely separate and distinct is foolish or evil or both. What then is the relationship between the utterly sanctified roles—father, master, king—and the obliteration of these roles? Precisely none. At times, social identities seem as fixed and inflexible as granite; at times, they shimmer like a mirage.

This ambiguity deepens when we consider the complex dialectic of external manifestation and inner conviction in Tyndale, a dialectic already glimpsed in the story of Bainham. On the one hand, all that matters is the justifying faith; on the other, that faith inevitably and irresistibly blossoms in works in the world. The absence of such works is a clear sign that the faith is merely feigned or imagined, but by themselves works are worthless, no matter how virtuous they may appear in the world's eyes. To be sure, most often in Protestant writings, these "works" divide themselves into two quite different categories: the works of the hypocrites tend to be cultic observances—prodigious numbers of *Ave*

Marias recited or candles burned or fasts undertaken—while the works of the elect tend to be acts of kindness or generosity or compassion. But the distinction is by no means absolute or reliable; Tyndale goes out of his way to condemn the classical moral virtues when pursued for their own sake and to assert that actions which seem worthless or evil in the world's eyes—even robbery and murder—may in fact be the fulfillment of God's commandments and the manifestation of true faith.

This position, which horrified More, paradoxically provides the setting for the deepest link between himself and Tyndale, for it drives Tyndale to an intense need for something external to himself in which he could totally merge his identity. We have already seen how More was drawn to such a merger, which he characteristically conceived as an identification with an institution or consensus. Tyndale, of course, defied the existing church, reviled monasticism, and ridiculed Utopia, but he committed himself with passionate totalism to God's Word as manifested in the Bible. Human actions by themselves are always problematical; they must constantly be referred to an inner state that must, nonetheless, be experienced as the irresistible operation of a force outside the self, indeed alien to the self. The man of faith is seized, destroyed, and made new by God's Word. He gives up his resistance, his irony, his sense of his own shaping powers, and experiences instead the absolute certainty of a total commitment, a binding, irrevocable covenant.

For Tyndale, the Mosaic law, with the exception of certain cultic practices, formed the very core of this covenant which the New Testament enabled man to fulfill. And this contract was equally binding on God and man: all scriptural promises, Tyndale writes in the prologue to the 1534 Pentateuch, "include a convenant: that is, God bindeth himself to fulfill that mercy unto thee only if thou wilt endeavour thyself to keep his laws."[91] The Bible then is the point of absolute, unwavering contact between God and man, the written assurance that God will not be arbitrary, the guarantee that human destiny is not ruled merely by chance, cunning, or force. It provides for Tyndale what the Church provides for More: not simply a point of vantage but a means to absorb the ambiguities of identity, the individual's mingled egotism and self-loathing, into a larger, redeeming certainty. For More, to be sure, the assurance rests in an institution, while for Tyndale it rests in a sacred text illuminated by faith, but both achieve guaranteed access to a truth that lies beyond individual or social construction, beyond doubt or rebellion.

The spiritual violence that marks this achievement in both More and Tyndale no doubt reflects the harsh temper of the age and the conviction that the immortal souls of thousands of fellow Christians hung in the balance, but it may also be viewed in the context of the urgent need to discipline certain impulses highly characteristic of each of them. The appeal of the total institution to More is in direct proportion to all the elements in his personality and career that pull against such an institution: his complex subversive irony, his sense of role-playing, his playful imagination. These elements are not crushed in More's later career, but they are split and reorganized, transformed and absorbed so that it takes a scholarly effort to recognize the author of *Utopia* in the author of the *Confutation*. There is no comparable shift in Tyndale, and C. S. Lewis can even speak of "the beautiful, cheerful integration" of his world.[92] But though it is quite true that Tyndale utterly denies the medieval distinction between religion and secular life that continued to haunt More, Tyndale's rebelliousness, rejection of institutions, and fierce independence exist more in nervous alliance than cheerful integration with his affirmation of the absolute authority of the Bible. If he seems at moments to set himself against the whole established order of things, if he exalts "sure feeling" over "historical faith," if he asserts that "the kingdom of heaven is within us,"[93] he is saved from the most disturbing and radical implications of such positions by his sense of the inflexible and external compulsion of the law, the absolute *otherness* of God's word.

He is saved too from the imagination. For just as More charged that the Protestants had fashioned an unreal church out of their own fevered imagination, Tyndale characteristically reverses the charge and asserts that at the heart of the Catholic Church—which at first seems too alien and external to man—there is nothing else than man's own imagination idolatrously worshiped. The same Church that forbids laymen to read Scripture in their own language permits them to read "Robin Hood, and Bevis of Hampton, Hercules, Hector, and Troilus, with a thousand histories and fables of love and wantonness, and of ribaldry, as filthy as heart can think."[94] The same Church that conspires against the saving faith of Christ enjoins its members "to build an abbey of thine own imagination, trusting to be saved by the feigned works of hypocrites."[95] The Church is comfortable with such corruptions, since its own essence is *fiction*. As soon as they acquired worldly power, the spirituality "gave themselves only unto poetry, and shut up the Scripture."[96] The mass, penance, confession to a priest, purgatory, indulgences, all are works of the human imagination tricked out to appear divine. Thus in choosing More, the pope and his agents "did well to choose a poet to be their defender."[97] But ultimately, all the mummery and poetry will be brought low, for nothing, Tyndale writes in the *Obedience*, "bringeth the wrath of God so soon and so sore on a man, as the idolatry of his own imagination" (292).

To a reader who believes, as I do, that all religious practices and beliefs are the product of the human imagination, these charges have a melancholy and desperate sound. It is as if the great crisis in the Church had forced into the consciousness of Catholics and Protestants alike the wrenching possibility that their theological system was a fictional construction; that the whole, vast edifice of church and state rested on certain imaginary postulates; that social hierarchy, the distribution of property, sexual and political order bore no guaranteed corresondence to the actual structure of the cosmos. "God is not man's imagination," Tyndale declared, but there was a time when such a declaration would have seemed unnecessary and absurd. To be sure, this is spoken against the Catholics; it is their faith that is damnable idolatry, just as More charged that it was the Protestant church that was to be found only in the realm of man's imagination. But the extreme violence on both sides exists precisely so as to deny the contaminating presence of the imagination—of human making—in one's own beliefs. Only by destroying the other will one assure the absolute reality and necessity of the order to which one has submitted oneself and hence fully justify this submission.

Tyndale in the *Obedience* and elsewhere saw the existing church as a conspiracy of the rich against the poor, the educated against the ignorant, the priestly caste against the laymen. More in *Utopia* saw the existing state as organized, respectable robbery, "a kind of conspiracy of the rich, who are aiming at their own interests under the name and title of the commonwealth." Between them, they undermined the two great pillars of the European social order from feudal times, exposing their pretensions to divine sanction as mere ideology, ridiculing their attempts at mystification, insisting on their human origin and their material interests. If we stand back for a moment from the fierce quarrel between More and Tyndale and view them together, they suggest a radical and momentous social crisis: the disintegration of the stable world order, the desacramentalization of church and state, the subversive perception of the role of the mind, and specifically the imagination, in the creation of oppressive institutions. Sharing these perceptions, a God-haunted revolutionary like Thomas Müntzer will respond by attempting to destroy both church and state, to liberate men from their oppressors and usher in the millennium; More and Tyndale, on the contrary, both search ever more insistently for a new basis of control, more powerful and total than the one they have helped to undermine. They seek to order their own lives and with them the physical and spiritual lives of all men. They struggle, in the words of Saint Paul, to cast down "imaginations, and every high thing that exalteth itself against the knowledge of God" and to bring "into captivity every thought to the obedience of Christ" (2 Cor. 10:3–5). Both More and Tyndale die in the attempt.

Power, Sexuality, and Inwardness in Wyatt's Poetry

There is no translation that is not at the same time an interpretation. This conviction, stamped indelibly in the mind by the fact that men went to the stake in the early sixteenth century over the rendering of certain Greek and Latin words into English, lies at the heart of virtually all of Wyatt's translations, never more so than in his version of the penitential psalms—the traditional grouping of psalms 6, 32, 38, 51, 102, 130, and 143—that were, in the climate of the 1530s and '40s, essentially and unavoidably controversial.[1] Rejecting the relatively mild formulations of his major contemporary sources, Wyatt captures the authentic voice of early English Protestantism, its mingled humility and militancy, its desire to submit without intermediary directly to God's will, and above all its inwardness.[2] Where the Vulgate still clearly speaks at the close of the 51st psalm of a historical Zion and Jerusalem, where John Fisher, the martyred Catholic bishop of Rochester whose devotional work Wyatt had before him, speaks of the "heavenly city of the Church Triumphant," Wyatt speaks, in words of his own invention, of "Inward Sion, the Sion of the ghost" and of the "heart's Jerusalem."[3] He thus heightens the significance of the psalmist's refusal to offer outward sacrifices, a refusal grounded on the conviction that God "delightest not in no such gloze / Of outward deed as men dream and devise" (498–99). The last clause is also Wyatt's addition and serves to distinguish, in the manner of Tyndale and Luther, between the idolatrous worship of the products of the human imagination and the true inwardness of faith.[4]

My initial purpose in this chapter will be to examine the extent to which the intense inwardness Wyatt voices in the penitential psalms is brought into being by the forces sketched in the preceding chapter. Unlike More, Wyatt has no supreme consensus, set apart from royal power and made visible in an enduring institution, that absorbs into itself all individual voices and confers ultimate meaning on human lives. But unlike Tyndale, Wyatt does not give himself over entirely to the Word: theological self-fashioning—the power of the book over identity—cannot be long separated from secular self-fashioning—the power of sexual and political struggles at court. The church in England has become an adjunct of the state, and a discussion of Wyatt's psalms will be drawn irresistibly from the presentation of the self in the court of God to the presentation of the self in the court of Henry VIII, that is, to the court lyrics. With these and the satires, we move decisively away from the religious context that governed inwardness in More and Tyndale. Indeed it is likely that even in the presence of God, Wyatt casts a nervous glance at the king; the two irascible autocrats seem, in any case, to bear a striking resemblance to each other.

We must not, however, pass too quickly to a sense of the immediate occasion, biographical or more broadly historical, of Wyatt's poetry, even in its most intimate moments. Though Wyatt gives it both a personal and markedly Protestant cast, the inwardness of the penitential psalms is by no means either his own innovation or the invention of the early sixteenth-century Reformers. It is embedded in the poems themselves, which are among the most influential expressions of soul-sickness in the Judeo-Christian tradition. They speak of stain and cleansing, guilt and redemption; they address a God who "desirest truth in the inward parts" (51:6); they cry out from isolation and persecution and express an intimate longing, fear, and trust. Inwardness, to be sure, is not their only dimension: they express an intense fear of physical assault, unmerited when it comes from malicious enemies, all too justified when it comes from God. But the body's pain is inseparable from the pain of the "heart": an insupportable dread, a sense of worthlessness and insignificance, a tormenting awareness of having ruptured a personal bond essential to life itself. Likewise, there are expressions of a communal, indeed specifically national character, particularly at the close of psalm 130, but the concerns of the whole society are reached only by way of the individual; the primordial penitential experience takes place at the level of the isolated, suffering soul. This soul may be said, of course, to embody humanity as a whole, but such representative status only heightens the importance of the individual.[5] The psalms enact not a communal confession of sin, a guilt born by the entire community and purged by a shared ritual of absolution, but an unmistakably *personal* crisis of consciousness. It is the individual, cut off from his kinsmen and followers, who acknowledges his fault and suffers divine chastisement. And if this chastisement bears eloquent witness to the otherness of God *before* whom and *against* whom one has sinned, it is felt at the same time as the lash of conscience, the secret sense of guilt in the innermost reaches of one's being.[6]

Taken together, as they appear to have been for centuries, the penitential psalms seem to express not only powerful states of defilement, sin, and guilt and the complementary longing for cleansing, forgiveness, and redemption but a movement, a psychological and moral pattern, which other men can experience—reenact—in their own lives. The movement may be likened to the course of an illness in which the initial onslaught is followed by a brief remission, then succeeded by progressively graver assaults and remissions until an intense crisis is experienced and passed, whereupon the disease slowly wanes. Each of the psalms thus expresses a version of the whole, but in graded degrees of intensity and elaboration; the movement is at once repetitive and linear. Such considerations have far more than formal, aesthetic importance, for these poems bear a powerful functional significance from a very early date; they constitute, in effect, a dynamic mold, one of the models by which men organize their experience. As the Church's penitential system develops, this pattern becomes institutionalized, prescriptive. Thus in a canon from the monk Regino's *Ecclesiastical Discipline* (ca. 906), the bishop is instructed to lead the penitents into the church, where "prostrate upon the floor, he shall chant with tears, together with all the clergy, the seven penitential psalms, for their absolution."[7] At this point, penance still reflects the wholly public character of the system of forgiveness and reconciliation that characterizes the early Middle Ages; the inwardness of the psalms is not thereby canceled, but it is absorbed into a ritual that marks the entry of the penitent, once and for all, into a formal social category, with rigid obligations and severe disabilities that continue until death. By the twelfth and thirteenth centuries, however, this system had been largely replaced by the momentously different penitential practice that we glimpsed in the previous chapter: a system that called for regular, individualized, and "private" confession to a priest. The privacy should not be overemphasized: the confessional box was a mid-sixteenth-century innovation, and, until its widespread use, confession was relatively open and would have been audible (and no doubt interesting) to those waiting their turn to confess. But at least in comparison with the earlier period, the confession of the High Middle Ages is profoundly private in the sense of its intense interest in the inward state of the individual penitent, a state that must be repeatedly and convincingly rendered in discourse, narrated to the priest. The Church's concern for the penitent's willingness to perform overwhelming disciplinary exercises gives way to a concern for the sincerity of the penitent's *contrition*, which now becomes the central part of the sacrament of penance.[8]

The seven psalms take their place in this new system not only as a ritual practice—part of the penitent's public "satisfaction"—but, more significantly, as a guide to a desired spiritual condition. Accordingly, the psalms' traditional attribution to King David is insisted upon with increasing elaboration of details; David comes to function as a kind of model penitent whom the worshiper can imitate.

The poems' formal characteristics as a group—their fusion of the cyclical and the linear, their passage through anguish and dread to consolation and security—are now seen clearly as a depiction of the penitent's spiritual progress, one that must be repeated on a regular basis. The recitation that in the tenth century marked a decisive, unrepeatable act becomes by the early sixteenth century the daily practice of a pious layman like Thomas More. This is not to say that the psalms have now become a strictly psychological expression, the representation of a particular cast of mind at a moment of crisis. Such a perception of psychological processes is indeed possible, almost inevitable by the late Middle Ages, but even when there is a lengthy discussion of the character of David, as in Fisher's commentary, the psychological is carefully subordinated to the doctrinal. Everywhere in the seven psalms, Fisher sees injunctions of the proper threefold method of doing penance: contrition, confession, and satisfaction. The three stages, he comments, may be likened to the erasure of writing: with each step the marks are further effaced until the paper is once again perfectly clear. And the "paper" in question is not simply the mind of the penitent: he may "feel" cleansed after contrition and confession, but there remains in the soul "a certain taxation or duty" that must be satisfied with pain in this life or in purgatory.[9]

Luther, Calvin, and Zwingli all attacked this threefold penance, though they disagreed about the extent to which any confession to a minister of God's word was to be allowed. Tyndale, as we have seen, carried this attack to England, asserting that confession was the key to the Church's spy network and hence a mainstay of its corrupt power. But the Protestant assault did not extend to the inwardness fostered by the penitential system or to psychological models like the penitential psalms. On the contrary, contrition becomes for Luther still more the essence of repentance, precisely because the insitutional role in absolution—the power of the keys—has been cast away. The presence of Protestant ideology in Wyatt's version of the penitential psalms, in the lines we have quoted and elsewhere, may be likened (as I have already suggested in another context) to a seizure of power, a coup carried out in the very heart of the individual. At stake, as Luther suggested in his commentary on the 51st psalm, was virtually the whole doctrine of the Reformed faith: the nature of sin, repentance, grace, justification, and worship.[10]

Thus the inwardness of these poems can in no way be conceived as Wyatt's private affair, any more than can the controversial writings of More and Tyndale. The intensely personal moment—the withdrawal into the darkness of the self, the anguished acknowledgment of festering guilt, the solitary straining for reconciliation with God—is intertwined with the great public crisis of the period, with religious doctrine and the nature of power.[11] The consequence for the penitential psalms as poetry is that now more than ever the text does not respect aesthetic limits, indeed is scarcely even "poetry" in the sense in which we usually use the term: that is, rhythmical language formally marked off from the ordinary, practical functions of discourse. To be sure, the penitential psalms are decisively marked off from the everyday; they are, after all, sacred, but their sacredness only intensifies the insistence upon the interpenetration of text and reader, and by "reader" we must include as the first and most important instance Wyatt himself in his psychological and spiritual particularity. This particularity had always been implicit in the psalms, we have argued, even in the Church's institutional framework: a man "shall not confess another man's trespass," Fisher comments, "but only his own."[12] Still, the sacrament of penance directed attention toward the consoling and disciplining power of the Church. With the rejection of the penitential system, as we have already seen in the case of Bainham, the book assumes a still greater compulsion and intimacy. The penitential psalms must be experienced as expressions of the reader's own consciousness: the distance between reader and text is effaced and the poems absorbed into the reader's inner life, which is in turn the legitimate object of both secular and religious power. And if this conception seems to exalt the reader (or the translator), such exaltation is sharply tempered by the fact that here, as with Tyndale's *Obedience,* the reader is virtually created by the text he absorbs. In Wyatt, as in Tyndale, translation is the supreme expression of this paradoxical relationship, for the translator at once pays homage to the original text and transforms it into the representation of his own voice and culture.[13]

Discussions not only of the penitential psalms but of virtually all of Wyatt's poetry have generally reflected either the belief that Wyatt inherited an inert mass of clichés and, by virtue of his intense individuality, managed at his best to infuse this frozen material with warmth and life, or the belief that his poetry exemplified "the clash between a desperate personal need and the impersonal and ceremonial forms which such needs assumed in the court of Henry VIII."[14] Such views posit an opposition between the constraining, repressive force of literary and social convention and the vivifying force of personality, emotional need, honesty—an opposition that seems to me a romantic misreading of the early sixteenth century. I would suggest that there is no privileged sphere of individuality in Wyatt, set off from linguistic convention, from social pressure, from the shaping force of religious and political power. Wyatt may complain about the abuses of the court, he may declare his independence from a corrupting sexual or political entanglement, but he always does so from within a context governed by the essential values of domination and submission, the values of a system of power that has an absolute monarch as head of both church and state. For all his impulse to negate, Wyatt cannot fashion himself in opposition to power and the conventions power deploys; on the contrary, those conventions are precisely what constitute Wyatt's self-fashioning. If as a poet Wyatt seems to be set off from his contemporaries, it is not because he managed to burst through imprisoning clichés, but because in this aspect of a cultural competition he proved himself a superior performer. Far from struggling against the supposed anonymity of received forms, Wyatt seems to me to have been almost incapable of both genuine anonymity and detachment from received forms. He could, of course, play with masks—the translations are all a kind of elaborate masking—but the masks are part of the social game in which he is fully implicated as a competing player. They do not permit an authentic detachment.

It is in the light of such a general conception of Wyatt's self-fashioning, I suggest, that we must understand his attempt to "dramatize" the penitential psalms by borrowing from Aretino the "historical" prologues that set the poems in the context of a notorious abuse of power, King David's adultery with Bathsheba and his responsibility for the death of her husband Uriah. The psalms are conceived as dramatic soliloquies, David's anguished response to the prophet Nathan's denunciations, and it would first appear that such a setting would have the opposite effect from the one I have described: that is, the historical framework would seem to *distance* the poems from both poet and reader by insisting upon the local and particular circumstances of their original composition. But the dramatic setting—which is handled awkwardly and, for the modern reader, lends little but histrionic vulgarity to the entire sequence—seems to have appealed to Wyatt precisely because it embeds the poems firmly in a world of royal power he inhabited. That is, we must conceive the drama not as a performance that takes place behind a proscenium arch that frames and isolates the represented action but as an interlude that is thrust in among the ordinary lives of the beholders.

If, as H. A. Mason suggests, Wyatt wrote the work in 1536, when he was imprisoned and nearly executed in the aftermath of the fall of Anne Boleyn, the invocation of David may glance, slyly and indirectly, at Henry VIII himself. Instead of behaving with self-righteous and murderous indignation, the king should emulate David—the implication would run—and repent his own scandalous abuse of power in the service of his lust. In Wyatt's psalms, wrote Surrey, "Rulers may see in a mirror clear / The bitter fruit of false concupiscence."[15] The setting, if this reading is accurate, provided Wyatt not only with a mirror to hold up to the king—something akin to the parable Nathan first uses to awaken David's conscience—but with a mask to protect himself against the king's wrath, for the Tudor monarch bore scant resemblance to the king of Israel, and it would have been fatal for a subject to point his finger directly at him and say, "Thou art the man." As Morus and Hythlodaeus both grasped, anything short of abject flattery had to be put to the autocratic ruler with tactful indirection; the principle was stated memorably by Sir Walter Ralegh when asked why he chose to write about the ancient past rather than his own times: "whosoever in writing a modern History, shall follow truth too near the heels, it may haply strike out his teeth."[16] As if to protect his teeth, Wyatt's mask in the psalms is of double thickness: not only is the moral drawn from the life of the biblical ruler, but the setting is a translation from the Italian. The implied reflection upon Henry VIII has what government spokesmen now call "deniability."

Quite apart from these considerations of self-preservation, the allusion to the king, if present at all (and the dating of Wyatt's poetry remains uncertain), seems to me subordinated to interests at once more personal and more general. Wyatt's poetic individuality is not something uncovered, disclosed as by the lifting of a veil, but something put on, created by the brilliant assimilation of literary materials. In the case of the psalms, those materials focus particular attention on the interplay of power and desire: by using the Bathsheba story as the context for the entire sequence, the Renaissance in effect sexualizes what in the original is a broader expression of sinfulness and anxiety. The speaker of the psalms—the voice seems unmistakably Wyatt's, the condition his own—is surrounded by enemies who conspire against him, but his worst enemies are the "mermaids" within himself, his senses, who have contrived to "usurp a power in all excess" and who must be forced "by constraint" to "Obey the rule that reason shall express" (175). Under the "tyranny of sin," the poet has been entrained into "filthiness," his "entrails infect with fervent sore" (353).[17] Where the Vulgate describes the psalmist's nightly grief as an aspect of that misery which he begs the Lord to heal, Wyatt and his contemporary sources describe it as a kind of prophylactic discipline:

> By nightly plaints, instead of pleasures old,
> I wash my bed with tears continual,
> To dull my sight that it be never bold
> To stir my heart again to such a fall.
>
> (148–51)

As a result of this discipline, and with the help of God, the poet can "stop his ears" to the mermaids' songs and block the sensual tempters from reaching his fortified heart. The repentant David, we are told in the prologue to psalm 39, is now "Inflamed with far more hot affect / Of God than he was erst of Bersabe" (317–18).

This transference of "hot affect" from mistress to the Lord is at the center of Wyatt's rendering of the penitential psalms, and the force of the transformation of desire is intensified by the fact that God is present not only as merciful friend but as stern judge:

> O Lord, I dread, and that I did not dread
> I me repent, and evermore desire
> Thee, thee to dread.
>
> (83–85)

To love God is to love the smiter, the punisher whose heavy hand was so "increased" upon him both day and night, in Wyatt's elaboration of psalm 32,

> and held my heart in press
> With pricking thoughts bereaving me my rest,
> That withered is my lustiness away.
>
> (246–48)

The turning of eros from Bathsheba to God, the transformation of desire from "filth" to worship, is effected through submission to domination:

> I, lo, from mine error
> Am plunged up, as horse out of the mire
> With stroke of spur: such is thy hand on me,
> That in my flesh for terror of thy ire
> Is not one point of firm stability,
> Nor in my bones there is no steadfastness:
> Such is my dread of mutability.
>
> (333–39)

It is not until we reach the phrase "with stroke of spur" that we realize that the peculiar expression "Am plunged up" is a full passive; it captures with uncanny accuracy the paradoxical act of rising beneath and because of immense downward pressure. This ascent through the acceptance of domination from on high is for Wyatt the quintessential penitential experience.[18]

Submission to domination is, as we have seen, at the center of Tyndale's Lutheran politics and theology. In Wyatt's psalms we encounter one of the psychological aspects of this ideology: sexuality in its natural, that is sinful, state is aggressive and predatory; in its redeemed state, passive. Sexual aggression—that which motivated David's abuse of power—is transferred entirely to the sphere of transcendent power, where it serves to bring about penitence.

If the penitential experience is marked by a loss of "firm stability," a sense that the body has no "steadfastness," the pain of this uncertainty—as the language implies, this impotence—is welcome insofar as it leads to a higher stability and firmness grounded outside the body. The goal, to reverse one of the tenets of phenomenology, is to *lose* the body as our "point of view on the world, the place where the spirit takes on a certain physical and historical situation."[19] This centrality of the body, a given of modern consciousness, is seen as unbearable, at once vulnerable to mutability and presumptuously independent: the senses must be checked, the body not permitted to be our central human expression in the world.[20] By the time he composed his translations of the psalms, Wyatt had encountered the Inquisition and endured two imprisonments, the latter extremely perilous. In 1536 from his cell in the Tower, he appears to have watched the execution of Anne Boleyn: "The bell-tower showed me such sight / That in my head sticks day and night."[21] In the late 1530s, Wyatt wrote to his son of the "thousand dangers and hazards, enmities, hatreds, prisonments, despites, and indignations" he had faced, and his father had endured the same: if "the grace of God that the fear of God always kept with him, had not been, the changes of this troublesome world that he was in had long ago overwhelmed him. This preserved him in prison from the hands of the tyrant [Richard III] that could find in his heart to see him racked, from two years and more prisonment in Scotland, in Irons and Stocks, from the danger of sudden changes and commotions."[22] The son to whom this brief family chronicle was written was beheaded for treason by Queen Mary.

In such a world, an obsession with "steadfastness" and a mistrust of the body are hardly surprising. The psalms at once reproduce the experience of power, by celebrating a crushing disciplinary force, and transfer this experience to a "higher" level, where the spirit is secured from the vulnerability of the body. The victim of both the homage to secular power and its transcendence is the body as the perceiving center of human existence. Repentence entails an assault upon the primacy of perception, an assault signaled by David's withdrawal from the world of light—the world in which his senses are kindled by the vision of "Barsabe the bright"—to the cave "wherein he might him hide / Fleeing the light, as in prison or grave" (61–62). The first psalms are sung in total darkness, relieved midway through the sequence by a mysterious beam of divine light that pierces the cave striking the harp and, by reflection, David's eyes, "Surprised with joy by penance of the heart" (316). This is the light not of bodily but of spiritual perception, a distinction underscored by the fact that David stares "as in a trance" upon the ground and, still more, by the frequent descriptions of David's prone or kneeling position—his humble abandonment of the upright posture that establishes human beings in perceptual opposition to the world of objects.[23] The body itself must be reduced from the presumptuous independence of the perceiver to the status of an object in the world, gazed upon by the creator as by a jailor. Imprisonment (and we should recall that Wyatt probably translated the psalms just after his re-

lease from the Tower) becomes not an object of fearful contemplation but a metaphor for the state of grace.

The psalmist thus pleads with God, "Do not from me turn thy
merciful face," and Wyatt adds, revealingly, "Unto my self leaving
my government" (543–44). To be left alone, unregarded and self-
governing, is far worse than to be punished, for as in Tyndale or,
more familiarly, in Donne's Holy Sonnets, identity is achieved in
moments of chastisement: "For thou didst lift me up to throw me
down, / To teach me how to know myself again" (575–76).[24] Self-
knowledge—and the second line here is Wyatt's own—is achieved
by submitting the body to discipline, a conception that accorded
well with Renaissance child-rearing and educational practices.
The sequence closes with a clear indication that his prayers have
been answered, that identity has been established outside of himself, beyond his own live bodily being: "For thine am I, thy servant aye most bound" (775). The phrase "aye most bound," the
assurance of eternal domination, is Wyatt's addition and responds
to his intense "dread of mutability," his longing for "steadfastness." At moments the poet conceives of sin as bondage (341–44)
and hence penitence as liberation, but his most persistent wish is
for a state of perpetual bound servitude to God:

> The greatest comfort that I can pretend
> Is that the children of thy servants dear,
> That in thy word are got, shall without end
> Before thy face be stablished all in fere.
>
> (628–31)

The final phrase, again Wyatt's addition, plays on the now archaic
sense of "fere" as "companion" as well as the obvious "fear": a
community is finally fashioned out of dread, a congregation locked
into the desired domination. To be "stablished"—bounded and
unchanging, all avenues of escape blocked off, forever under the
gaze of the Lord—is to be saved from the radical instability that is
the poet's fears and hence to approach the timelessness of God:
"thou thyself the self remainest well / That thou was erst, and shalt
thy years extend" (625–26).

The goal of steadfastness or boundedness was, as we have seen,
central to the careers of both More and Tyndale; it is for both
Catholic and Protestant the response to a crisis in political and
spiritual authority. Wyatt's penitential psalms offer us an almost
formulaic reduction of the historical, psychological, and literary
forces that we have repeatedly encountered: *power over sexuality
produces inwardness.* In other words, the inner life expressed in the

penitential psalms owes its existence to a wrathful God's power over sexuality; before the Lord's anger was stirred up by "filthy life," David was blind to his own inwardness, an inwardness he is now driven to render in speech. Hence divine power over adulterous sexuality produces penitential inwardness. The imposition of secular power has its place in the production of penitential inwardness as well, particularly if the impetus behind Wyatt's translation was the king's violent wrath against his adulterous wife and her alleged lovers.

Each of the terms of the formula we have extracted from the psalms represents a rich interaction of meanings. David's abuse of his political power—the monopoly of legitimate force that enables him to send Uriah to his death—is the result of the sensual usurpation of reason's power within him. This ursurpation in turn is an aspect of the war between sin and faith in which God is invoked as a merciful ally against the feared enemy, but God is at the same time the threatening, wrathful judge whom men must fear and to whom they must submit. The proper mode of relation to this divine power is directly linked to the struggle between Catholicism and Protestantism, and hence to the temporal as well as spiritual power of the Church. As even this brief sketch should make clear, not only is the term *power* itself multivalent but it insistently involves the other multivalent terms *sexuality* and *inwardness*. Sexuality is both the sinful desire that must be resisted and the "hot affect" to God, both the rebellious longing to gratify the senses and the passionate, tearful craving for self-abasement and submission. Inwardness is a psychological state (and hence subjective) and a spiritual condition (and hence objective); it bespeaks withdrawal and yet is insistently public, for we may only encounter a *discursive* inwardness, one dependent not only upon language but upon an audience. Indeed it is precisely this audience, in the figure of God as ultimate reader, who has brought the psalms into being by the pressure of his hand, and so we are returned from inwardness to divine power. The overarching effect of the penitential psalms as poetry (insofar as they succeed at all) is to insist upon the interdependence of categories which, in ordinary discourse, have an illusory distinctness. The poems express a single, unified process which we may describe in religious terms as penitence or in psychological terms as loving submission to domination. And Wyatt attempts to convey this process by fashioning a new poetic technique, introducing *terza rima* into English and, as important, forging a language sufficiently forceful and subtle to represent the fusion of power, sexuality, and inwardness.

This sense of an intimate relationship between Wyatt's poetry and the forces that shape his identity may be confirmed by examining his other *terza rima* poems, the satires. Like the psalms, the satires appear to have been written in the wake of a personal crisis, quite possibly the same crisis: in 1536, following a quarrel with the Duke of Suffolk and coincident with the arrest of Anne Boleyn and her alleged lovers, Wyatt was imprisoned in the Tower, from which, after several anxious weeks, he was released with the command to return home to Allington Castle and learn, under his father's eye, "to address him better."[25] Both sets of poems then may jointly represent his response to this command, a struggle to clear himself of the entanglements that had nearly brought him to the scaffold and to achieve a new mode of "address." Both invoke the pressure of power; both turn in revulsion from the allurements of lust; both depict retreat from the locus of corruption to safer ground, in the psalms a "dark Cave," in the satires "Kent and Christendom." The psalms express, as one critic notes, certain aspects of the secular stoic doctrine of the satires: the longing for steadfastness, "firm stability," wholeness and integrity. The satires, for their part, have at moments a homiletical fervor that links them to the psalms.[26] In both, through the experience of power the poet discovers his true voice.

But if the similarities between the two sets of poems are sufficient to suggest that they both emerged from the same or at least highly similar circumstances, the differences between them are too great to be bridged with a single term, such as "Christian stoicism"; rather, they seem to represent alternative and even competing modes of self-fashioning. We may recall Thomas More in 1516, torn between those versions of himself that he calls Hythlodaeus and Morus; in just such a spirit, Wyatt may have represented to himself in poetry contrasting ways of facing his circumstances and shaping his identity. Thus though both the psalms and the satires self-consciously give voice to a "true" self, stripped of falsification and corruption, we encounter two distinct versions, the former produced by *submission*, the latter by *negation*. Where the psalmist longs to be utterly bound by God's will, to accept eternal domination, the satirist discovers himself in the act of saying no. Where the psalmist prays, "Do me to know what way thou wilt I bend" (760), the satirist lists all that he cannot do—"I cannot frame my tongue to feign," "I cannot crouch nor kneel," "I

cannot with my work complain and moan," "I cannot speak and
look a saint," and so on for dozens of verses—until he bursts forth
in a general cry of negation: "I cannot, I; no, no, it will not be."[27]
Of course, though distinct, submission and negation are not
necessarily incompatible; we have already seen them yoked in a
powerful ideological form in Tyndale's *Obedience*, a work that may
well have influenced Wyatt's inwardness. The attack on the corruptions of the great is carefully qualified by the satirist's denial
that he scorns or mocks "The power of them to whom fortune hath
lent / Charge over us, of Right, to strike the stroke" ("Mine Own
John Poins," 8–9), while the psalmist's turn to God presupposes
something like the satirist's rejection of the court. Yet already in
Tyndale, submission and negation pull tensely against each other;
in Wyatt's psalms and satires they appear to strain toward opposing expressions.[28]

Where David pleads with God not to run away, "Unto my self
leaving my government," the speaker of the second satire, "My
Mother's Maids," counsels self-possession:

> Then seek no more out of thy self to find
> The thing that thou hast sought so long before,
> For thou shalt feel it sitting in thy mind.
>
> (97–99)

Where the psalms are solitary expressions of anguish, sinfulness,
and faith, the satires are confident, moralizing, and self-justifying
conversations with friends. Where the psalms long for an end to
the isolated self by means of submission to God's domination, the
satires call for retrenchment, renunciation of the longing for power
and wealth, acceptance of limitation in the name of freedom and
security. The psalms represent an attempt to break away from
enveloping corruption by means of a radical reformation of the
self, a plunge into the intense emotions of dread, love, and willing
servitude. The satires counsel a retreat from anxiety; the individual does not seek to be driven or possessed or crushed but to be
steadfast and independent. He grants the right of rulers "To strike
the stroke," but then quickly turns to his own integrity, untouched by any outward force, incapable of compromise, hypocrisy and doubleness. This "self-content," a value far from the
spirit of the psalms, is the key to a mastery over the accidents of
existence, the answer to the restlessness, anxiety, and posing of
court society. The goal of the satires is not as in More to find the
institutional guarantee of certainty nor as in Tyndale to reach un-

mediated union with the Word; the goal is to take control of one's life by finding within oneself a sustaining center.

The worst pain that the satirist can ask God to visit upon the fools he attacks in "My Mother's Maids" is that "looking backward" they may see the bright figure of virtue and, "whilst they clasp their lusts in arms across," "fret inward for losing such a loss." That is, illicit desire is dismissed not, as in the psalms, because it is mortally sinful and arouses the wrath of a jealous God, but because sexual pleasure is inevitably disappointing:

> Live in delight even as thy lust would
> And thou shalt find when lust doth most thee please
> It irketh straight and by itself doth fade.
>
> ("My Mother's Maids," 81–83)[29]

This is the closest Wyatt comes in the satires to the Stoic's outright rejection of the body epitomized in Seneca's flat pronouncement: "Refusal to be influenced by one's body assures one's freedom."[30] Accordingly, "My Mother's Maids" comes closest to Seneca's conviction that it is possible to live invulnerable in the midst of viciousness and depravity. Elsewhere Wyatt suggests either that the individual must condemn court corruption and accept the consequences or, alternatively, withdraw to the country simplicity and spareness depicted so delightfully in "Mine Own John Poins":

> This maketh me at home to hunt and hawk
> And in foul weather at my book to sit.
> In frost and snow then with my bow to stalk
> No man doth mark whereso I ride or go;
> In lusty leas at liberty I walk.
>
> (80–84)

This simplicity is both a life style and a literary style, a conjunction captured most perfectly perhaps in the deliberately proverbial flatness of "But here I am in Kent and Christendom." This is spoken in contrast not only to the foreign countries where as diplomat he would have had to practice "Rather than to be, outwardly to seem" (92) but to the London where as courtier he would have had to call the crow a swan and the lion a coward, praise flattery as eloquence and cruelty as justice. "Mine Own John Poins" bitterly assails that divorce between the tongue and the heart which is the constant lament of humanists throughout the sixteenth century. The great enemy is hypocrisy, the ability to feign and play parts:

> My Poins, I cannot frame my tongue to feign,
> To cloak the truth for praise, without desert,
> Of them that list all vice for to retain.
>
> (19–21)

As the long catalog that follows makes clear, most of the vices that the satirist attacks involve what Jürgen Habermas has called "distorted communication"—self-censorship, deceit, false reverence, mystification, inversion—and the strength of the attack lies in its recognition of the essential link between language and power. When speech enters the milieu of the court, it is inevitably perverted; indeed, its perversion is precisely the privilege and the achievement of power which is, as Habermas claims, itself a form of distorted communication.[31] The satires on court abuses written later in the sixteenth century almost always have recourse to an idealized version of court life, a proper use of power usually located in the figure of the queen and a handful of "perfect" courtiers. It is against this visionary model that particular vices are measured, so that the very attack upon deviations bears witness to the triumph of normative court ideology.[32] In Wyatt, by contrast, the essence of power is to prevent a clear grasp of norms of any kind by compelling a systematic perversion of standards:

> And he that dieth for hunger of the gold
> Call him Alexander, and say that Pan
> Passeth Apollo in music manifold,
> Praise Sir Thopas for a noble tale
> And scorn the story that the knight told.
>
> ("Mine Own John Poins," 47–51)

What is lost in this topsy-turvy world is not only a grasp of the nature of virtue and truth but an understanding of the self; these, the satire suggests, can only be achieved elsewhere, at a safe distance from power. Wyatt makes his forced retirement seem a noble attempt to purge himself of that cynical role-playing in which he and his poetry had been involved by virtue of participation in the intrigues of court and diplomacy, an attempt to cleanse his speech of its Machiavellian manipulation of appearances. He will discover himself not through the exercise of protean powers of self-transformation, but through a grasp of all that he cannot do, all that his nature will not permit him to learn. And in its clarity and leanness his poetry will be a model of undistorted communication, exemplified by that intimate exchange with a close friend that must have made the form of the verse epistle particularly appealing to him. Wyatt forges for himself a blend of a conversational directness and moral earnestness that enables him to pass gracefully from the lively retelling of a fable—

> "Peep," quoth the other, "Sister, I am here,"
> "Peace," quoth the towny mouse, "why speakest thou so loud?"—

to exalted reflections on its moral:

> Alas! my Poins, how men do seek the best
> And find the worse, by error as they stray!
> And no marvel, when sight is so oppressed
> And blind the guide.
>> ("My Mother's Maids," 70–73)

The poetic voice here and the values expressed are familiar from the hundreds of similar performances in the centuries that followed; this is the classic voice of what Courthope in 1897 called with perfect precision "an English gentleman conversant with affairs."[33] Like all such successful models, this voice gradually came to seem inevitable, natural, an object in reality; in Wyatt we may witness one of the crucial moments in its invention. And the purpose it serves is to free the speaker from any implication in the world he attacks; unlike the court lyrics, here he stands safely apart, in firm moral rectitude. Having withdrawn from the court to the country, Wyatt achieves a sense of self-confidence and self-content, of integrity and invulnerability.

Until recently the satires were Wyatt's most admired poems: Warton speaks of "these spirited and manly reflections," written "with the honest indignation of an independent philosopher, and the freedom and pleasantly of Horace," Nott of their "force and dignity," Courthope of their "strength of individual feeling," and Tillyard of their "air of unaffected self-expression."[34] In their energetic expression of a confident wholeness and independence, they reflected and helped to shape a powerful, enduring sentiment among the English gentry, a sentiment that found its full poetic flowering in the Horatian imitations of the eighteenth century. But it is important to understand how much of the self is left out of this self-presentation, how tightly the nexus of power, sexuality, and inwardness has been reined in.

What is left to express in this "unaffected self-expression"? Inwardness is eloquently praised—

Then seek no more out of thyself to find
The thing that thou hast sought so long before,
For thou shalt feel it sitting in thy mind—
                        ("My Mother's Maids," 97–99)

but is defined almost entirely negatively. The satirist claims to
have a *center* in his life from which he speaks with secure assurance, but he pays for this claim in the coldness that lurks beneath
the surface energy, the stiffening that seems to preclude the possibility of full emotional life. Sexuality has diminished to nothing:
the satirist defines himself by his attack on sexual viciousness in
the court and his stoic dismissal of the pursuit of pleasure. Power
is denounced as the very essence of corruption: the satirist defines
himself by his distance from the pursuit of power and wealth.
There is, to be sure, both money and social standing associated
with the speaker—hunting and hawking, servants, land on which
to walk and ride "at liberty"—but he is not at all implicated in the
processes by which this wealth is secured. We may remind ourselves that the estate to which the poet retreats from power is the
reward for royal service and that the pleasant acres are swelled
with confiscated monastic lands. We may point out the ironic connection between the comfortable means evoked by the phrase "My
mother's maids" and the grinding rural poverty so eloquently depicted in the fable of the country mouse and the town mouse; we
may observe that the high moral tone of the fable's close counsels
an acceptance of wretchedness that is not, after all, the condition
of the speaker but of those nameless men and women who support
him; we may conclude that the probity and rectitude, the confident individuality, the honest indignation of the speaker feed
upon what Raymond Williams eloquently calls the "brief and ach-
ing lives of the permanently cheated."[35] But we do so only by
standing outside the poems and questioning their fundamental
assumptions about the world. To be sure, in "Mine Own John
Poins" the poet qualifies his delighted celebration of rural liberty
by noting that "a clog doth hang yet at my heel" (86), but the
nature of this clog is left unclear and the acknowledgment of its
existence is immediately followed by a denial that it constitutes a
genuine constraint: "No force for that, for it is ordered so, / That I
may leap both hedge and dike full well" (87–88). For the briefest
moment we glimpse an unpleasant answer to the question with
which the poem has begun—"The cause why that homeward I me
draw": the poet's country freedom is in fact a kind of house arrest.
But the thought is dispelled with the image of the gentleman

leaping across boundaries, though a lingering reservation survives in "it is ordered so."

Only in "A Spending Hand," which may have been written later than the first two satires, is there somewhat more than a perfunctory acknowledgment of the limiting conditions of the rural life and the voice Wyatt has fashioned to praise it. The poem combines the preoccupations of the other satires: it pillories the duplicities of court life—

> In word alone to make thy language sweet,
> And of the deed yet do not as thou says—
>
> (38–39)

while it exposes the self-deception by which Sir Francis Brian thinks he can successfully combine a career as courtier and diplomat with an "honest name" and a "free tongue." Yet the celebration of country rectitude that we might have expected is instead both lightly travestied in the speaker's own encomium—"drink good ale so nappy for the nonce, / Feed thyself fat and heap up pound by pound"—and vigorously attacked in Brian's reply: "For swine so groans / In sty and chaw the turds moulded on the ground." For Wyatt's Brian, the rural retreat is nothing more than bestial sloth, no better than the life of idle monks: "So sacks of dirt be filled up in the cloister." Against this excremental existence, Brian holds up the ideal of service: "Yet will I serve my prince, my lord and thine." This is the ideal Wyatt himself inherited from his father, the self-conception of his profession and indeed of his whole social class. This is the principle they repeatedly invoke to explain to others and above all to themselves their difficult, anxious careers, to make moral sense out of apparent moral chaos, to ward off the claims of competing conceptions of service, such as those embraced by More or Tyndale. This is, in one line of monosyllabic verse, the justification of an entire existence.

At the comparable moment in book 1 of *Utopia,* Hythlodaeus confronts Peter Giles with what service to the prince entails in the real world: the inevitable and progressive corruption of one's own moral position in pandering to the debased will and pleasure of the ruler. Wyatt here mounts a similar attack by pretending to instruct his friend in the duplicitous arts of advancement at court: if you want to succeed, say one thing and do another, pander to the rich, court wealthy old widows, sell your sister or daughter, and so forth.

"We"—the implied intimate audience constituted by the poem,

the audience that assumes Brian's place as recipient of the mock advice—do not take the cynical counsel at face value; we know for a certainty that the pose is a "thrifty jest," a pointed dramatic irony that heightens rather than undermines the speaker's integrity. How we know this is more difficult to say with precision—we assume that Wyatt is not deliberately exposing his own degradation, we assume that such advice, if seriously intended, would not be committed to paper and that the terms of moral capitulation would be softened, we assume from the model of Horace's satire on legacy hunters or from mock encomia that Wyatt is working in a familiar satiric tradition. And the close of the poem supports these assumptions: the corrupt, worldly proverbs are invoked to be rejected. The rejection, however, only leads back to the unsatisfactory state with which the poem began: to trot still up and down and never rest, running day and night from realm to realm, wearing oneself out to no apparent purpose. To be sure, by the poem's end, this choice is given a certain dignity, the dignity of honest poverty and the acceptance of occasional adversity for speaking the truth. Yet this ethos of selfless, loyal service—the ethos of *Lear*'s noble and true-hearted Kent—seems in Wyatt's poem pallid and abstract, an ideal that can be voiced only by guarding it from all contact with lived experience.

To accept the "free tongue" that the poem celebrates in its last lines as anything more than a hopeless fantasy is to forget everything that the preceding lines have implied: that the corruptions listed with such bitter energy are not those of isolated individuals but of a whole system, that they constitute the rules of the game. It is precisely such a forgetting that the poem seems to demand, and this may be only the extremest instance of that ideological obscuring of unpleasant contradictions or qualifications that we have already witnessed in the first two satires. Wyatt and his peers need to view themselves in a favorable light, to fashion their images as independent, courageous, freedom-loving gentlemen who condemn the viciousness of others, the craven "beasts" who cheat and lie and curry favor. Having rejected the praise of rural retreat, "A Spending Hand" has no alternative but to uphold a vague ideal of service to a prince whose court has been vigorously condemned.

But "A Spending Hand" offers at least one indication that Wyatt is quite conscious of the forgetting: the choice of Francis Brian as the contemner of cynical advice and the spokesman for the values of godliness and an honest name. These are the very last things the historical Francis Brian possessed or represented: wit, bravery, and the ability to survive, yes, but not an honest name. Already by 1519 he had earned notoriety by riding, in company that included the king of France himself, "daily disguised through Paris, throwing eggs, stones and other foolish trifles at the people";[36] Brian was evidently the kind of man a king would take along when he felt the urge to amuse himself in this fashion. His was a career of conniving, betrayal, politic marriage, sycophancy, and pandering. Though Wyatt's poem seems quite deliberately to avoid turning its satire against Brian, more than one of the vices it catalogues bear an uncanny resemblance to well-known incidents in Brian's life.[37] There is no explicit internal evidence for an ironic reversal, an exposure of his unscrupulous boon companion as a mock honest man (just as the speaker had pretended to be a mock corrupt man), but some such thought must at least have crossed Wyatt's mind. At a minimum, any contemporary reader of the poem would have had to be dimly conscious of the work of forgetting that he had to undertake to make Brian the spokesman for honesty. The effect of this consciousness is to raise a faint but significant uneasiness about the comfortable stance of gentlemanly rectitude, to signal the potential deviousness of this apparently straightforward discourse. Power, with its distorting influence, was supposed to be "out there," the object of high-minded contempt, but the satirist himself stands on morally uncertain ground—his position may be itself a kind of pose taken in response to the dictates of power. Men like Brian—and possibly Wyatt himself—find it diplomatically useful to assume a rough honesty and incorruptibility, an air of satirical truth-telling. It is as if Wyatt felt compelled to acknowledge the distance between this stance and reality, to deflect this acknowledgment from himself onto a blatant timeserver like Brian, and then to deflect it further by presenting Brian as an honest man. What should be solid and unambiguous—the poetic alternative to the duplicity of the court—threatens to crack apart, and if the reader hastens to repair the cracks, by excluding as "irrelevant" what he knows about Brian, there remains an unsettling awareness of having done so.

But why should Wyatt have risked subverting his own moral authority? The answer seems to lie in the force of his extraordinary intelligence, in the need to give vent in however indirect a form to his perception of his situation. More accurately, the poetry itself constitutes this perception—the penitential psalms and the satires are, by virtue of their poetic mode, *enactments* of Wyatt's condition, functional registers of his relation to the world. The force of Wyatt's poetry consists precisely in its full, painful engagement in the anxieties, bad faith, and betrayals of his career, even as the poetry is written to serve the ends of that career. The point is worth stressing because of the tendency to read back into the Renaissance the modern notion—not wholly adequate even for our own period in which art has far more autonomy—that poetic technique is developed entirely for its own sake out of a disinterested aesthetic concern for form and apart from both personal interests and the general interests of the culture as a whole. No doubt Wyatt *was* fascinated with literary form and may have been, in Patricia Thomson's phrase, a "born experimenter."[38] "The English language was rough and its verses worthless," wrote John Leland in a Latin elegy. "Now, learned Wyatt, it has had the benefit of your file."[39] For Puttenham, in the 1580s, Wyatt and Surrey "were the two chieftains, who having travelled into Italy, and there tasted the sweet and stately measure and style of the Italian Poesy . . ., greatly polished our rude and homely manner of vulgar Poesy, from that it had been before, and for that cause may justly be said the first reformers of our English metre and style."[40] But as Puttenham's whole work makes clear, this manner of "courtly making" is not at all set apart from the dominant social and political concerns of the culture; "while the *Arte of English Poesie* is ostensibly a treatise on poetry," a perceptive critic has recently noted, "it is at the same time one of the most significant arts of conduct of the Elizabethan age."[41] Wyatt's poetry is, in effect, a species of conduct.

To be sure, the court of Henry VIII has been frequently invoked in discussions of Wyatt's poetry, but, more often than not, for the purpose of dismissing any claims the poetry might make to be taken seriously:

> Wyatt, like the other court writers, was merely supplying material for social occasions. Consequently, the study of these poems belongs to sociology rather than to literature. (H. A. Mason)[42]

> The whole scene comes before us . . . . We are having a little music after supper. In that atmosphere all the confessional or autobiographical tone of the songs falls away. (C. S. Lewis)[43]

But is this really what it meant to write from within the court? Entertainments in the court of Henry VIII were perhaps less lighthearted than Lewis's charming account suggests; conversation with the king himself must have been like small talk with Stalin. And Mason's sense of the trivializing force of "social occasion" may likewise be misleading.[44] Certainly when we consider even the relatively slight lyrics in the Devonshire MS, we find very little verse that is merely "occasional" (in the sense of those lines still turned out by the poet laureate on the occasion of the queen's birthday). On the contrary, however much these poems impress us as entertainments, fashioned to be read or sung in a sophisticated group of courtiers and ladies, they convince us at the same time that the poet has a *stake* in them, though the precise nature of that stake may be obscure. Indeed it is precisely their blend of playfulness and danger that marks them as the product of the court; we must imagine a game in which idealism and cynicism, aggression and vulnerability, self-revelation and hypocrisy are tensely conjoined. The game seems often childish, the stakes are enormous and, on occasion, fatal: we would do well to reread *The Charterhouse of Parma* or to recall More's sense that the great and powerful of his time were madmen performing plays on a scaffold.

Wyatt is a master of this game. He rehearses the familiar tropes and stale paradoxes, parades the appropriate proverbs and turns of phrase, assumes the expected poses, and yet convinces us again and again of the reality of his pain and disillusionment. It is as if the daring of the game consisted in freighting fragile artifice with an unexpected weight of passion. And though Wyatt seems to have had this daring in greater measure than his contemporaries, he was by no means alone: the poems only make sense in a society of competing players. The aggression, anxiety, and vulgarity inherent in all such competitions are, on occasion, undisguised, as in the following lyric that cannot be atrributed with certainty to Wyatt but is clearly a product of the world in which his poems were written:

> To wet your eye withouten tear,
> And in good health to feign disease,
> That you thereby mine eye might blear,
> Therewith your friends to please;
> And though ye think ye need not fear,
> Yet so ye cannot me appease;
> But as you list, feign, flatter, or gloze,
> You shall not win if I do lose.
>
> Prate and paint and spare not,
> Ye know I can me wreak;
> And if so be ye care not,

Be sure I do not reck:
And though ye swear it were not,
I can both swear and speak;
By god and by the cross,
If I have the mock, ye shall have the loss.[45]

The poem derives its effect from convincing us that the menace is real, that its moments of roughness and irregularity and obscurity are the result of its embeddedness in a specific, highly charged situation. That situation is a tense sexual struggle, and the lines suggest moves and countermoves that express themselves in a kind of intimate shorthand. Thus the rather obscure exchange, "And if so be ye care not, / Be sure I do not reck," seems to say, "If you are indifferent to my power to wreak revenge on you—because you do not think me capable of it or because you are counting on my restraint and even my own self-interest—you should understand first, that I do not care about your indifference and second, that I am reckless, that is, I do not care, finally, how badly I am hurt in the revelations that will come out so long as you are hurt even more badly."[46] The poet does not shrink in the slightest from the full nastiness of this menace: "You shall not win if I do lose."

C. S. Lewis writes that when he starts to take the voice and implied sexual relationships in such poems seriously, his sympathy deserts his own sex: "I feel how very disagreeable it must be for a woman to have a lover like Wyatt." Still, Lewis continues, "I know this reaction to be unjust; it comes from using the songs as they were not meant to be used."[47] But the notion that these are merely after-dinner entertainments, distanced and generalized to the point of anonymity, does not really lay to rest the perceptions Lewis so acutely voices only to disavow. As with the penitential psalms, personal intensity and inwardness, the felt reality of expressed relationships, is not diminished by literary convention but rather created by it.

The conventions of lyric poetry from the nineteenth century to the present lead us to demand as proof of experiential stringency in art a certain self-conscious opposition to the dominant culture and a high degree of particularity; neither was a requirement of the early sixteenth century. On the contrary, the sense of social compulsion is precisely what gives lyrics like "To Wet Your Eye" their force. The fact that such lyrics are called forth by an entire social ambiance, that they are its most familiar and characteristic expressions, does not mean that the expressions are thereby trivialized. Melancholy was fashionable in the late sixteenth century, as was hysteria in the late nineteenth: neither condition was any the less intense or "real" for being the manifestation of a cultural norm, as much "sociosis" as "neurosis."[48] So too, in the wake of the dismantling of the cult of the Virgin, in the absence of a fully articulated celebration of married love, in a cultural milieu dominated by a ruthless despot and pervaded by intrigue and envy, it may not surprise us that court entertainments habitually express disillusionment, frustration, menace, hostility to the very women who are courted, and craving for a security that erotic love cannot offer. The frequency of such expressions, their conventionality, is here the virtual assurance of their lived reality. It is only if one is convinced that poetry emanates spontaneously from an inviolable core of subjectivity and has no significant relation to power that one could conclude, with Mason, that the conventionality of the court lyrics is proof that there is in them "not the slightest trace of poetic activity."[49] We must grasp instead that in helping to create the subjectivity they express, these poems are the secular equivalent of the penitential psalms. Wyatt and the other court poets are as much written by their conventional lyrics as writers of them.

Wyatt's poetic technique, his fasioning of a powerfully expressive idiom, is inseparably linked to his participation in the court. His language is a tool, a weapon, in a dangerous contest, as the poet of "To Wet Your Eye" is intensely aware:

> And though ye swear it were not,
> I can both swear and speak;
> By god and by the cross,
> If I have the mock, ye shall have the loss.

The poet's ability to swear and speak more forcefully and persuasively than his mistress is the heart of his power, the power to hurt her more terribly than she can hurt him, and the poem not only affirms this power but attempts to embody it. This accounts for the curious fusion of recklessness and calculation in the final lines: "By god and by the cross" is at once an impulsive exclamation of anger, a solemn oath to strengthen the force of the threat that follows, and a measured display of that ability to swear that he has just affirmed. As such, it is true to its status as a line in a poem: recklessness in poetry is always calculated recklessness. And calculated recklessness, as Machiavelli observed, is one of the essential techniques for sexual and political survival.

It is not only the ambiance of the English court that should be invoked here but the methods and ethos of that other world in which Wyatt and many of his fellow poets were engaged, Renaissance diplomacy. "You shall not win if I do lose" is a time-honored diplomatic maneuver, "perfected" in the nuclear diplomacy of our age, and this sense of sexual relations as diplomacy extends throughout the poem: masking and unmasking, alliances and appeasement, the threat of losing face (to "have the mock") and the counterthreat of reprisal. To be sure, there is nothing in this poem that had to come from diplomacy, but the overlapping of themes, here and in many poems by Wyatt and his circle, is striking.[50]

In 1527 Wyatt accompanied Sir John Russell's embassy to the papal court of Clement VII, scheming futilely as the imperial troops, virtually beyond the control of their own officers, advanced toward Rome. The twenty-four-year-old Englishman glimpsed a world that still seems, in Ralegh's phrase, to glow and shine like rotten wood, a world of treachery, sophistication, and boundless corruption. It is above all a world in which *power* seems to be man's supreme product and goal, power directly linked, as always, to wealth, status, and the monopoly of violence, but also thought of as something quite independent, a possession to be wrested from another, an object of intellectual interest, a consummate manifestation of human energy. This energy is conceived in remarkably personal terms; it is the emanation of the emperor, king, prince, or *condottiere* in his concrete individuality. This is perhaps why the physical presence of the European rulers—the actual body of Henry VIII, Wolsey, Francis I, Charles V—impresses us intensely for the first time during this period. The ruler's social identity seems to be absorbed into his personal being; his power, for all its dependance upon loyal troops, merchant fleets, treasuries, natural resources, seems to breathe forth from his body. This too is perhaps why the punishment of rebels and traitors in the period becomes so much more protractedly and agonizingly brutal. The fairly straightforward executions, if we may so term them, of the Middle Ages become virtuoso performances of torture, as if the physical torment of the traitor had to correspond fully to the incorporation of power in the body of the prince. Finally, this is perhaps why power and sexuality seem so closely intertwined, manifestations of the same energy of the body. Rebels were castrated, their sexual organs burned before their eyes, prior to execution. Conversely, the prince's sexual acts were affairs of state.[51]

Power, conceived in these personal and physical terms, is not only the ability to levy taxes or raise an army but the ability to enforce submission, manifested in those signs of secular worship—bowing, kneeling, kissing of rings—that European rulers increasingly insist upon. If these signs always have an air of fiction about them—and indeed in England they become increasingly fantastic until they reach the aesthetic mania of the court of Charles I—so much the better, because, as we have argued, one of the highest achievements of power is to impose fictions upon the world and one of its supreme pleasures is to enforce the acceptance of fictions that are known to be fictions.

As a diplomat for most of his adult life, Wyatt was engaged at once in the assertion of his master's power (and hence the imposition of his fictions) and in the attempt to weaken and resist the competing power of other rulers. The two functions are inseparable, at least in this period, for the Renaissance seems to have conceived of diplomacy as it conceived of trade: it posited a severely limited substance (power or wealth) and hence assumed that the gain of one party is inevitably the loss of the other. "To think of exchange as advantageous to both parties," Louis Dumont has recently observed, "represented a basic change and signalled the advent of economics."[52] The earlier model of exchange, I would argue, permeated the consciousness of Wyatt and the other male poets of his circle, and helped shape not only political but sexual relations, so that a failure in love is like the rupture of a treaty and a consequent loss of power, while even an erotic triumph seems most often to be achieved at the expense of one or the other of the lovers, as well as of a third party. "I love an other," Wyatt writes in a moment of stark simplicity, "and thus I hate myself."[53] Any expression of need or dependence or longing is thus perceived as a significant defeat; the characteristic male as well as national dream is for an unshakable self-sufficiency that would render all relations with others superfluous: "I am as I am and so will I be."[54] But such a hard, indifferent identity—in conflict, after all, with the Protestant conviction of man's utter helplessness—cannot be sustained; even its few expressions are tinged with anxious defiance or calculating regard for those opinions that are supposedly being scorned. The single self, the affirmation of wholeness or stoic apathy or quiet of mind, is a rhetorical construct designed to enhance the speaker's power, allay his fear, disguise his need. The man's singleness is played off against the woman's doubleness—the fear that she embodies a destructive mutability, that she wears a mask, that she must not under any circumstances be trusted, that she inevitably repays love with betrayal. The woman is that which is essentially foreign to the man, yet the man is irresistably drawn into relations with her; hence the need for the diplomat's art.

Diplomacy then, along with courtiership, seems to have influenced Wyatt's conception of the essential function of discourse which he grasped as a shifting, often devious series of strategic maneuvers designed to enhance the power of the speaker, or rather of the party whom the speaker represents, at the expense of the power of some other party. The distinction between the speaker and the power he represents is worth emphasizing, for it is reproduced at the level of court poetry; that is, the poem itself is a kind of agent, sent forth to perform the bidding of its master. The poem is clearly not the *direct* expression of its author's mind—it is shaped by the complex aesthetic and social rules of literary production and possesses a certain leeway that ordinary speech does not normally possess. But it is governed by its overarching purpose which is to enhance its creator's personal position, to manifest and augment his power. We may note, in this regard, that Renaissance diplomacy is distinguished by its abandonment of the customary medieval phrases about an ambassador's office, phrases that defined the position in terms of the "public good," the "general welfare," the "commonwealth of Christendom," and the "pursuit of peace." When, in the late fifteenth century, the Venetian Ermolao Barbaro writes of diplomacy, he states quite simply, "The first duty of an ambassador is exactly the same as that of any other servant of a government, that is, to do, say, advise and think whatever may best serve the preservation and aggrandizement of his own state."[55] Wyatt's poetry serves a comparable function in relation to his position at court; and even at a distance from the court, in the psalms and satires, it is above all power that shapes his poetic discourse.

A court lyric, to be sure, may be considered apart from its creator and its immediate context: it finds its way into commonplace books, is set to music, and circulated outside the court, is included in anthologies and quoted in handbooks on the art of poetry. And, after all, we know little enough about the precise circumstances of these poems, many of which have come to us without clear attribution, since appearance in print was something courtiers actively avoided. But if we grasp the extent to which Wyatt and others like him were defined by their relation to power, the extent to which they were at once attracted and repelled by Henry VIII and the world he represented, we grasp more readily in their poetry the heightened awareness of techniques of self-presentation and concealment. As ambassador, courtier, and poet, Wyatt seems to have self-consciously cultivated a bluff manner and a taste for homely proverbs, cultivated, that is, a manner that denies its own cunning. We may recall More's comparable diplomatic masquerading—"full of craft and subtlety," his foreign rivals reported, concealed "by smooth speech and calm expression in the English way."⁵⁶ As his dispatches to Henry VIII and Cromwell show, Wyatt developed a fine sensitivity to such nuances of feigning, to the deviously indignant denial of deviousness, to plausible lies and passionate insincerity:

> And for the other part that they [the emperor's diplomats] be about the clearing of their purposes with France, I suppose the conclusion of that clearing will be but cloudy. And that they would set out some appearance thereof to win time; for I cannot see that it should be for their purpose if they thought that clearing should come to conclusion to tell it me, unless they would have it hindered rather than furthered, for so they take that we would, or else to see if thereby we would make to them any offer with declaring whereof they might recompense the Frenchmen with the like. But in sum, they of the court that dare a little more liberally speak with their friends make here a mock unto the Frenchmen.⁵⁷

This sensitivity to doubleness, this sense of discourse as a calculated series of deceptive moves, this constant apprehension of betrayal and mockery, is familiar to any reader of Wyatt's lyrical expressions of disillusionment in love: the poet either realizes in the bitter aftermath of betrayal that he has been duped or vows, on the basis of his experience, never to be duped again. The relation between this erotic disillusionment and Wyatt's experience of deception in diplomatic service and the court is clearest in a poem like "What 'vaileth Truth":

> What 'vaileth truth? or, by it, to take pain?
> To strive by steadfastness, for to attain,
> To be just, and true: and flee from doubleness:
> Sithens all alike, where ruleth craftiness,
> Rewarded is both false, and plain.
> Soonest he speedeth, that most can fain;
> True meaning heart is had in disdain.
> Against deceit and doubleness
>   What 'vaileth truth?
> Deceived is he by crafty train
> That meaneth no guile and doth remain

Within the trap, without redress,
But for to love, lo, such a mistress,
Whose cruelty nothing can refrain,
     What 'vaileth truth?

So completely are the realms of love and power interchangeable
that it is not until the last lines that we know that Wyatt is writing
about his mistress at all. Indeed the revelation of this interchangeability is the heart of the reader's experience, for we are induced to
read the poem as a brooding reflection on career, rule, and reward
until the close jars us into connecting the disillusioned perception
of power with the disillusioned perception of love.[58]

Even the formal skill involved in the structuring of such a lyric
may derive in part from diplomacy, for beyond imparting a
sensitivity to doubleness, Wyatt's ambassadorial experience
shaped his consciousness of calculated effect, above all through
the manipulation of language in the game of power. In 1540, for
example, Wyatt was instructed to call the emperor Charles V an
"ingrate" for his refusal to hand over a Welshman in his train,
Robert Brancetour, whom Henry VIII wanted arrested for treason
and brought to England. According to the account Wyatt sent to
the king, Charles was (understandably) incensed at the charge:

> "For I would ye know I am not Ingrate and if the king
> your master hath done me a good turn, I have done him
> as good or better. And I take it so that I can not be
> toward him Ingrate. The inferior may be Ingrate to the
> greater, and the term is scant sufferable between like.
> But peradventure because the language is not your nat-
> ural tongue ye may mistake the term."
> "Sir," quod I, "I do not know that I misdo in using
> the term that I am commanded."
> "Then," quod he, "I tell it you to th'end your master
> know it, and ye how to utter his commandment."
> "Nor I see not," quod I, "sir, under your supporta-
> tion that that term should infer prejudice to your great-
> ness. And though yourself, sir, excuseth me by the
> tongue, yet I can not render that term in my tongue into
> the French tongue by any other term which I know also
> to descend out of the Latin, and in the original it hath
> no such relation to lesserness or greaterness of persons.
> Although I know it be not so meant to charge your
> majesty in so evil part that you should so be moved
> thereby."[59]

Once the word "ingrate" is used, the focus of attention shifts
from Brancetour to what Mattingly calls the "chief burden" of the

Renaissance diplomat, "maintaining the dignity of his master's crown in the eternal wrangle over precedence."[60] And the nuances of language are the heart of this wrangle: Wyatt grasps immediately that the emperor's seemingly gracious allowance of a possible mistake in translation is a slight, a move to regain the initiative. There is, as both emperor and ambassador know, something outlandish about English: "Nobody in the sixteenth century," writes Mattingly, "except an Englishman was expected to speak English, not even the perfect ambassador."[61] Wyatt responds with a clever mixture of firmness, pedantry, and qualification, so that, as he tells it at least, he comes close to "winning" this little encounter. But, we should add, Brancetour was not handed over.[62]

In this anecdote we not only see again the intimate relation in Wyatt's experience between language and power, the subtle engagement of words in the struggle to dominate, but we glimpse too the central place of translation. Once again criticism has treated Wyatt's remarkable translations as a purely literary affair, whereas in fact their very existence almost certainly depends on his ambassadorial experience. I am speaking not simply of Wyatt's intimate acquaintance, through living abroad, with French and Italian culture, but with the context of that acquaintance. His experience, as we have just seen, made Wyatt highly conscious of the potential shifts in meaning as words pass from one language to another, and this sensitivity intersects with an acute awareness of the way conventions of courtesy and friendliness may conceal hostility and aggression, on the one hand, or weakness and anxiety, on the other. The effects of this subtle art of implication are felt most powerfully in Wyatt's brilliant translation of Petrarch's "Una candida cerva":

> Whoso list to hunt, I know where is an hind,
> But as for me, alas, I may no more:
> The vain travail hath wearied me so sore.
> I am of them that farthest cometh behind.
> Yet may I by no means my wearied mind
> Draw from the Deer: but as she fleeth afore,
> Fainting I follow. I leave off therefore,
> Since in a net I seek to hold the wind.
> Who list her hunt I put him out of doubt,
> As well as I may spend his time in vain:
> And, graven with Diamonds, in letters plain
> There is written her fair neck round about:
> *Noli me tangere*, for Caesar's I am,
> And wild for to hold though I seem tame.

Wyatt's debt to Petrarch is clear, but so is his deliberate and careful refashioning of the original poem, his transformation of transcendental idealism into exhaustion and bitterness. Petrarch's pictorialism is discarded, as is his loving attention to time, place, and season; the mystical vision becomes the hunt; the focus shifts from the longed-for object in its exquisite landscape to the mind of the poet. Petrarch depicts an experience of illumination and loss; Wyatt an attempt at renunciation; the former is alone with his unattainable beloved, the latter withdraws from a crowd of hunters. Petrarch's sonnet ends with the poet's fall into the water and the disappearance of the hind; Wyatt's with the inscription on the diamond collar, and this collar, emblematic in Petrarch of the beloved's unattainability, her absolute freedom in and for God, seems in Wyatt a sign of her *possession* by one vastly more powerful than the poet. "Caesar's I am" is the cold assertion that explicates the string of earlier assertions around which the poem is structured: "I know where is an hind," "I may no more," "I leave off therefore," "I put him out of doubt." The intimation of power spreads backward like a stain through the preceding lines, so that the whole poem comes to be colored by it.

So rooted does "Whoso List" seem in the cynical realities of court intrigue that critics have confidently identified the hind as Anne Boleyn, who is rumored to have been Wyatt's mistress before she became the possession of Caesar, Henry VIII. This identification is plausible—it follows, after all, from the embeddedness of Wyatt's verse in the politics of the court—but stated thus baldly it seems to me to diminish the effect of the poem, an effect that depends on the poet's immense power of *implication*, a power heightened, as I have argued, by Wyatt's ambassadorial experience. The poem's brilliance is linked precisely with its restraint and suggestiveness.[63] There is, in fact, nothing in the poem that is unequivocally about worldly power and appropriation; even the words "Caesar's I am" may refer, as they do in Petrarch, to the motto inscribed on the collars of the emperor's hinds so that they would be left alone and thence, by the conventional symbolic exchange, to the hind's dedication to God. They do not suggest this transcendental meaning, but that they do not is purely by implication. The poem seems *suspended* between transcendentalism and cynicism, and the decisive movement in one direction or the other is left to the reader.

This reliance on implication may above all else be simply prudence; it would have been suicidal folly to write directly about the loss of Anne Boleyn to Henry. But it results in a richness of resonance that seems more than a mere side effect. The whole poem is caught up in a series of suspensions, or alternately, in *passages* from one state to another. The poet has not withdrawn from the hunt; rather he is in the act of trying to disengage himself. Thus the poem opens on a note of detachment and superiority belied by the "alas," as if a carefully plotted show of cool indifference were undermined by an involuntary expression of grief. The poet then places himself among those "that farthest cometh behind," only to reveal that this knowledge of his position, this consciousness of his own weariness and the emptiness and vanity of the effort, is to no avail: he cannot detach himself and fully renounce the hunt. No sooner does he acknowledge this inability—"Fainting I follow"—than he affirms, in the same line, his renunciation: "I leave off therefore." There seem to be two separate, indeed opposing intentions held in tense juxtaposition. As if recognizing this impasse, at line 10 the poet writes as if he were beginning the poem over again, this time not to attempt a clear disengagement of himself from the hunt but a clear statement of its hopelessness, its "vanity." The reader is left with the impression that, despite the poet's attempts at decisiveness, he never quite "leaves off," that he is incapable of fully drawing his mind from the "deer": the poem itself bears witness to his continued obsession even as it records the attempt to disengage himself from it.

And it is not only the poet who is suspended or in passage: just at the point that the hind seems most wild, as free and untouchable as the wind, she is revealed by her diamond collar as tame, and just at the point that she seems most tame, she is revealed as most wild. The collar which is the manifest sign of her tameness is at the same time the manifest sign of her wildness. The phrase "wild for to hold" is richly suggestive: at the simplest level, it means "impossible to grasp," as the proverb of trying to hold the wind in a net had earlier suggested. The hind is unconfined and uncontrollable; she moves freely without restraint, subject only to her own will. But here, as in other poems by Wyatt, we find the proverb invoked only to be complicated and qualified. "Wild" suggests not only elusiveness but the uncanny menace associated with the medieval tradition of the wild man or wild woman: a being who has fallen away from a state of tameness or civilization to the savage condition of animal, a creature dissolute, licentious, and potentially violent, living outside the bounds of human convention, living outside human *bonds*. This figure is the focus for some of the deepest fears of medieval and Renaissance culture, for wildness exposes the tenuousness and artificiality of society's elaborate codes and challenges the stable order imposed upon sexuality, sustenance, and government. The wild man or woman represents the radically alien being, unassimilated and unknowable.[64]

"Wild" in this sense signals *danger* and thus crystallizes that transformation of the hunter into the hunted subtly implied in the poet's inability to draw his wearied mind from the deer. The danger lies not only in the hind's own wildness—her irresistible yet unattainable beauty, her otherness—but in the power of "Caesar": it is, paradoxically, within the power of the ruler to confer wildness. And, by a further paradox, this wildness is a form of protection for the hind; the collar stops the hunt, transforms the hind from prey to pet or possession. The deer seems tame, and this seeming tameness protects her wildness.

This subtle play on the sense of "wild" is the climax of Wyatt's powers of implication; while remaining ambiguous and elusive, it compels a profound reevaluation of all the preceding terms, above all rendering it impossible to take *noli me tangere* in its original religious context. That context is evoked only to be violated, so that the reader experiences the wrenching transformation of the sacred to the profane which is the essence of Wyatt's treatment of Petrarch. Petrarch's *nessun mi tocchi* clearly recalls not only Caesar's protected hinds but John 20:15–17, the apparition of Jesus to Mary Magdalene at the sepulcher. "Jesus saith unto her, Woman, why weepest thou? whom seekest thou? She, supposing him to be the gardener, saith unto him, Sir, if thou have borne him hence, tell me where thou hast laid him, and I will take him away. Jesus saith unto her, Mary. She turned herself, and saith unto him, Rabboni; which is to say, Master. Jesus saith unto her, Touch me not; for I am not yet ascended to my Father." This is the quintessential moment of suspension, of poise between states of being, evoked by Petrarch as the key to his own moment of vision, with its wondrous sense of presence and distance, joy and loss.

In Wyatt, the allusion, made even stronger by the direct quotation of the Vulgate, is bitterly ironic, and the spiraling ironies seem to embrace the whole scholastic theory of the nature of Christ's body as he appeared to Mary and the disciples after his death. According to this theory, Christ's Glorified Body, as it was called, has four qualities, qualities which are at least implicitly present in Petrarch's poem and which seem to be parodied in Wyatt's poem: *impassibility*, or freedom from suffering, becomes cold indifference; *clarity*, or glorious beauty, becomes the irresistible lure of the woman; *agility*, or the ability to pass from place to place with great speed, becomes the lady's maddening elusiveness; and *subtlety,* or the complete subjection of the body to the soul, becomes the subtlety of the courtesan.

What we have been calling suspension or passage is here revealed as *translation.* In its subtle restraint and power of implication, "Whoso List" makes part of its meaning the complex process of transformation from one language to another, from one culture to another. The drama of the lyric is the passage from Petrarch's vision of the world to Wyatt's or rather to the vision we ourselves constitute on the basis of the poet's deliberately allusive self-representation. Of course, the effect is diminished if we are unfamiliar with the source, but it is by no means entirely lost, for the reader is in any case implicated in the sonnet's essential activity, the transformation of values. The poet twice addresses the reader as a potential hunter—"Whoso list to hunt," "Who list her hunt"—both inviting and dissuading him, making him reenact the poet's own drama of involvement and disillusionment. We share the passage from fascination to bitterness, longing to weariness, and we do more than share: we are forced to take responsibility as translators in our own right. It is we, after all, who refuse to take *noli me tangere* in a religious sense, we who understand Caesar not as God but as an all too human protector, we who hear—as Wyatt's contemporaries may have done—Anne Boleyn and Henry VIII where there is only talk of a hind and her hunters. It is as if a whole mystical visionary ethos gives way before our eyes and *under our pressure* to a corrupt and dangerous game of power.

This sense of our own implication in the act of translation coincides with the faint but disturbing intimations that the poet himself bears some responsibility for his frustration. The last line, as we have already seen, is a complex reversal of expectations: from the point of view of the hunter it should be the tameness rather than the wildness of the hind that is the disabling surprise. And this reversal subverts the speaker's implied innocence and self-righteousness: the hind was hunted as a wild animal, so it is scarcely surprising that she turns out to be wild. What did the hunter expect? What else could she have been? She is fulfilling not only the laws of kind but the nature of the speaker's own approach, the structure of the relationship. The transformation from idealism to disillusionment was foreordained in the very first line with the mention of the hunt.

But perhaps the transformation has even deeper roots, for if we argue that a radical shift from the sacred to the profane is part of

the experience of Wyatt's poem, we may at the same time observe
that the *connection* between them remains deeply felt, and not
simply as the relatedness of diametrical opposites. I have already
spoken of this connection in regard to the penitential psalms with
their poetic revelation of the linkage between power, sexuality,
and inwardness. This is precisely the nexus of both "Una candida
cerva" and "Whoso List To Hunt," where the poet's inner life in
each case is shaped by the relation of Caesar and the object of
desire. Petrarch's poem, after all, is as much about frustration and
loss as Wyatt's, and if the former does not speak of a hunt, it has
its own disturbing image for the pursuit: the miser's search for
treasure. There is, I suggest, a sense in which this shared emotional state and the structure of relations that brings it about are
more important than the contrasting identifications of Caesar with
God and with the king. From this perspective, Petrarch's idealism
is not *replaced* by Wyatt's sense of weariness and emptiness but
rather *fulfilled* by it.[65]

I am not suggesting that the relation between transcendental
vision and cynical betrayal was present to Wyatt's consciousness
nor that the subtle complicity of the lover in his own failure was
fully intended; rather they are intimations at the edges of his finest
poems, as if the act of representation itself, in its highest achievements, had its own powers of implication. Few of Wyatt's poems
have this resonance, but it seems unmistakably present in moments of the penitential psalms, in "Whoso List," and in his
greatest achievement, "They Flee from Me":

> They flee from me that sometime did me seek
>   With naked foot stalking in my chamber.
>   I have seen them gentle, tame, and meek
>   That now are wild and do not remember
>   That sometime they put themself in danger
>   To take bread at my hand, and now they range
>   Busily seeking with a continual change.
> Thanked be fortune it hath been otherwise
>   Twenty times better, but once in special,
>   In thin array after a pleasant guise
>   When her loose gown from her shoulders did fall
>   And she me caught in her arms long and small,
>   Therewithal sweetly did me kiss
>   And softly said, Dear heart how like you this?
> It was no dream: I lay broad waking.
>   But all is turned thorough my gentleness
>   Into a strange fashion of forsaking,
>   And I have leave to go of her goodness,

And she also to use newfangleness.
But since that I so kindly am served,
I would fain know what she hath deserved.

In one of the best recent discussions of this poem, Donald Friedman suggests that we consider the speaker a "fully imagined *persona*" deliberately distanced from Wyatt himself who subjects his creation to a searching "dramatic analysis." This analysis "reveals a man whose sensibility has been warped by subservience to a code he has just learned is false and impermanent."[66] Such an approach enables us to confront the bad faith in the speaker's self-righteous resentment, the ironies that underlie and subvert the claim that "all is turned thorough my gentleness / Into a strange fashion of forsaking." "Gentleness" has, by this point, been so charged with inner contradiction and aggression that the speaker's simple attempt at irony turns against him: his "gentleness"—the code that governs his sexual betrayal—may indeed have led to what he perceives as betrayal. "I would fain know what she hath deserved." Excluded from the predominantly male rhetorical culture, "she" has no opportunity to respond, but were she to do so, we might imagine her saying, "Dear heart, what did you expect?"

The speaker's relations with women are charged with that will to power, that dialectic of domination and submission, whose presence we have viewed elsewhere in Wyatt's poetry.[67] The creatures who now flee from him once put themselves "in danger / To take bread at my hand," a relationship he remembers with bitter satisfaction. But the image is already more than a simple assertion of successful domination; it conveys a complex interweaving of condescension, menace, and entreaty. The wild creatures are induced to place themselves in submissive postures only if the man suspends all signs of aggression and holds himself perfectly still. The paradox of a power suspended, rendered passive, in order to exist at all is intensified in the second stanza where the bravado of "twenty times better" gives way to the highly particularized recollection of a moment of perfect passivity. Friedman finds this stanza "an anticlimax that reveals the poverty of moral imagination that underlies an elaborate, exalted, and idealizing vision of human conduct"; the scene, he writes, is "a sketch of rapacious appetite, its outlines blurred and made glamorous by ritualized manners and by the compressed meanings of a conventional diction."[68] This response is the outcome of the view that the speaker is a *persona* from whom both poet and audience are wholly detached, but I think it is precisely here that the limitations of this view become evident. For the remembered scene, far from being anticlimactic, seems in the context of both this poem and of early Tudor poetry remarkably intense, almost haunting in its *presence*. The erotic experience is indeed the object of critical reflection, but from *within*, from the midst of a powerful engagement. And the criticism is not of "rapacious appetite," which is little in evidence in either the man or the woman, but of the almost infantile passivity that is the other side of manly domination.

That passivity is tantalizingly ambiguous: in the first stanza, it seems to be disguised aggression; in the second, an ecstatic release from aggression; in the third, a form of victimization. And this progression suggests an emotional pattern that characterizes not only a particular relationship but, as the initial "they" suggests, a whole series of relationships. The pattern is roughly as follows: the man is sexually aggressive; his desire can only be satisfied through the transformation of aggression into passivity; this passivity—at once masked aggression and its negation— invites both embrace and flight; the flight, perceived as a betrayal of his "gentleness," leads the man to turn his passivity back into aggression against the woman for whose embrace he still longs.

The powerful intensity of "They Flee from Me," like that of "Whoso List," derives from the fact that neither audience nor poet is permitted to stand at a comfortable distance from the speaker. It is misleading to conceive of the poem as if it were one of Browning's dramatic monologues, even if such a conception enables us to isolate certain important elements, for this places us at a moral remove where the poem itself insists that we are participants. The experience at the heart of the poem is less a matter of individual character, isolated like a laboratory specimen for our scrutiny, than a matter of shared language, of deep cultural assumptions, of collective mentality. Hence the ambiguity of the speaker's passivity has its roots not in the quirks of a complex personality—there is little individuation of this kind in Wyatt's poetry—but rather in the conflicting cultural codes that fashion male identity in Tudor court lyrics. If, as I have suggested, those lyrics reflect both the religious and secular institutions that dominated their creators' lives, we might note that in the Lutheran context, passivity, understood as submission to nurturing domination, is a transcendent value, while in the context of Henrician diplomacy, passivity, understood as the failure to manifest one's power, is a sign of dangerous vulnerability, recuperable only if the failure is implied to be a mask for a more potent aggression. Now neither the religious nor the diplomatic code directly determines the sexual relations implied by love poetry in the court, but they both affect the way erotic experience will be represented and understood.

The deep disquiet occasioned by "They Flee from Me" emerges then from the contradictions inherent in the code by which the speaker lives and in which we ourselves as readers are implicated (just as Wyatt's first audience would have been implicated); bad faith is not confronted face to face but glimpsed on the periphery, in the hollowness that attaches to words like "gentle, tame, and meek," in the darkness that hovers about the false phrases of politeness—"I have leave to go of her goodness," "since that I so kindely am served"—to which the speaker still ironically clings.

As in "Whoso List," the process portrayed as betrayal turns out to be a fulfillment, but there is no evidence that Wyatt set out to depict the disappointed lover's involvement in his own failure. A subversive awareness intrudes itself into the work of art but is inaccessible to a lover who views himself as a gentleman betrayed by a fickle mistress and asks bitterly what she deserves. From within this dominant perspective, one is aware only of a painful striving toward a perception that remains just beyond the field of vision, an unsettling intimation that the link between male sexuality and power has produced this mingled frustration, anxiety, and contempt. For Wyatt to articulate this perception would be to write a different kind of poem—a psalm or a satire—and in so doing the perception would be utterly changed, for as we have seen, the psalms transfer "hot affect" to an all-powerful God while the satires attempt to withdraw from both power and sexuality.

If Wyatt's best court lyrics make us perceive in a critical form the lived experience of sexual politics at court, they do so in the manner that Balzac's art gives us a critical view of the lived experience of capitalist society: not, that is, because the artist has abandoned his ideology but, paradoxically, because he has clung to it. Balzac and Solzhenitsyn, writes Louis Althusser, "give us a 'view' of the ideology to which their work alludes and with which it is constantly fed, a view which presupposes a *retreat*, an *internal distantiation* from the very ideology from which their novels emerged. They make us 'perceive' . . . in some sense *from the inside*, by an *internal distance*, the very ideology in which they are held."[69] To understand how this internal distance, this gap between discourse and intention, is generated in Wyatt's lyrics, we must return to the conditions of his poetic creation. As courtier and ambassador, Wyatt developed techniques of self-fashioning that he brings to bear on his poetry; these techniques are weapons in a struggle for power and precedence in which sexual relations are fully implicated. The goal, both politically and sexually, is domination and possession (for which Wyatt provides powerful images in the hunt and the diamond collar), but such a goal cannot be openly avowed; instead both diplomats and lovers constantly invoke and half believe in the values of "service," "gentleness," and "truth."

Encountering the same contradictions, Thomas More was drawn to irony and to dreams of self-cancellation or absorption into a transcendent consensus. Wyatt too, under the scourge of royal discipline, expresses the longing for both transcendence and withdrawal, but he lacks More's absolute institution just as he lacks Tyndale's unwavering and consuming adherence to an absolute text. Wyatt is far more purely dependent than either More or Tyndale upon secular power, and it is in relation to this power that his identity is shaped. In the competitive struggle to express himself more powerfully, intensely, and persuasively than anyone else in the court—to win sympathy, command respect, hurt his enemies, in short, to dominate—Wyatt enlists and helps to create the forces of realism, manliness, individuality, and inwardness. These forces are intertwined, and it is in their complex relation that the resonance, the crucial internal distance, of his lyric poetry arises.

Critics have long celebrated Wyatt's "manliness." The modern anthology's observation of his "manly independence in love" is in a line of such comments stretching back to Surrey's praise of Wyatt as "manhood's shape."[70] The qualities that seem to evoke this term are sarcasm, the will to dominate, aggression toward women, concern for liberty and invulnerability and hence resistance to the romantic worship of the lady, a deliberate harshness of accent and phrasing, and—for Surrey at least—a constant and unappeasable restlessness. This last seems to me a particularly fruitful term for the shape of manhood in Wyatt, for it suggests the blend in his works of defiance, assertiveness, energy, inventiveness, dissatisfaction, and passionate incompleteness. These qualities are not, of course, Wyatt's own invention, but it is important to see how little appropriate would "manliness" so understood be as a description of any poet before him or, for that matter, of More or Tyndale. Wyatt appears to have fashioned it as his literary and social identity, in part perhaps as a flattering imitation of Henry VIII. The notion of manliness has, of course, undergone numerous complex transformations since the early sixteenth century, but a certain underlying continuity is suggested by the frequency with which the term continues to be employed in descriptions of Wyatt's poetry. Wyatt's manliness becomes, in its way, as profound and influential a pattern for the future as More's ironic blend of engagement and detachment and Tyndale's passionate identification with the Word.

The principal expressive mode of manliness in Wyatt's discourse is realism, exemplified in the unsentimental weighing of motives in the diplomatic dispatches or the "plain speaking" of such poems as "Madam, Withouten Many Words" and "You Old Mule." Wyatt presents himself as a man suspicious of aureate diction and the subtle indirections of rhetoric, fond of homey tales and proverbial wisdom. That this stance was identified as Wyatt's and perhaps cultivated by him is suggested by his charge that his enemies, in inventing a speech that they then attributed to him, strewed it with oaths and proverbial expressions to make it sound like his own. These enemies nearly had his head by charging that he had said that he wished the king "cast out of a cart's arse," that is, hanged like a thief; Wyatt countered that he had merely said he feared the king has been "left out of the cart's arse," that is, that his interests had been overlooked.[71]

Realism as a discursive technique in Wyatt is closely linked with a heightened sense of individuality, dramatized superbly in his poetry by means of innovative metrical techniques.[72] The verse swells and buckles, the stress suddenly shifts, the translation veers away from its original, to register the pressures of the poet's powerful ego. The natural environment and even the mistress herself play relatively little part; always squarely at the center is the speaker, complaining, threatening, resolving to make an end, recording his doubts and hopes. There is no more insistent expression of the "I" in Tudor literature. This insistence is by no means the equivalent of security; on the contrary, the self manifested so urgently has all of the instability of egotism, at once threatening to swallow up the whole world and terribly vulnerable:

> for suddenly me thought
> My heart was torn out of his place.[73]

But of the *importance* of his identity, Wyatt has no doubt whatever; there is none of the diffidence that colors self-presentation from Chaucer to More.

This faith in the centrality of the self is not simply a sign of egotism but is validated—justified in a quasi-theological sense—by the inwardness that Protestantism held to be one of the signs of truth, the inwardness celebrated in the penitential psalms. By achieving this powerful interiority, the court poetry does not appear to be concerned only with histrionic self-manifestation but with the *revelation* of the self in discourse. The audience is not being manipulated but invited to experience the movement of the poet's mind through assurance, doubt, dread, and longing. This painstaking rendering of the inner life seems to surpass any social game, though the poems remain clearly embedded in such a game.

We are now prepared to grasp how the gap between discourse and intention opens up in Wyatt and hence how it is possible for his greatest poems to engage in complex reflections upon the system of values that has generated them. The skillful merger of manliness, realism, individuality, and inwardness succeeds in making Wyatt's poetry, at its best, distinctly more convincing, more deeply moving, than any written not only in his generation but in the preceding century. But his achievement is dialectical: if, through the logic of its development, courtly self-fashioning seizes upon inwardness to heighten its histrionic power, inwardness turns upon self-fashioning and exposes its underlying motives, its origins in aggression, bad faith, self-interest, and frustrated longing. Wyatt's poetry originates in a kind of diplomacy, but the ambassadorial expression is given greater and greater power until it intimates a perception of its own situation that subverts its official purpose. Wyatt's great lyrics are the expression of this dialectic; they give voice to competing modes of self-presentation, one a manipulation of appearances to achieve a desired end, the other a rendering in language, an exposure, of that which is hidden within. The result is the complex response evoked by a poem like "They Flee from Me": on the one hand, acceptance of the speaker's claim to injured merit, admiration for his mastery of experience, complicity in his "manly" contempt for women's bestial faithlessness; on the other hand, recognition of the speaker's implication in his own betrayal, acknowledgment of the link between the other's imputed bad faith and his own, perception of an interior distance in the ideology so passionately espoused. We sense, in short, a continual conflict between diplomatic self-presentation, struggling to appropriate inwardness, and inwardness struggling to achieve critical independence from self-presentation. Neither triumphs: hence the *suspension* of Wyatt's court lyrics between impositions of the self on the world and critical exploration of inwardness.

To Fashion a Gentleman: Spenser and the Destruction of the Bower of Bliss

More, Tyndale, and Wyatt all make strong, independent claims upon our attention, but they also come to stand for more than their own private visions or personal destinies. They give voice to longings and fears that are deeply embedded in the nation's social and psychological character; taken together, they may be said to enact the momentous ideological shift in early modern England from the *consensus fidelium* embodied in the universal Catholic Church to the absolutist claims of the Book and the King. It may be helpful at this point to review briefly and somewhat schematically the ground that has been covered.

For More the self is poised between an ironic, self-conscious performance, grounded upon hidden reserves of private judgment and silent faith, and an absorption into a corporate unity that has no need for pockets of privacy. In the former state, identity is a mask to be fashioned and manipulated; in the latter, it is a status firmly established by the corporate entity and comprehensible only as a projection of that entity. There are moments in More's career and writings in which he seems to veer sharply in one or the other of these directions, as when he flatters Wolsey or when he lives as a lay member of the Charterhouse. But more often the two states are intertwined: thus he writes *Utopia,* with its vision of the entire absorption of the individual into the larger body of the community, at the moment in which he is most intensely engaged in calculated self-presentation. Or again, in the midst of subtle maneuvers designed to placate the king and hence in the midst of his most demanding improvisational performance, More slides into an increasingly powerful identification with the Church's martyrs, until at the end he has become one of their number. We may, I think, argue that the moments both of the greatest creative force and of the greatest estrangement and violence occur when the self-conscious, self-concealing, theatrical identity touches the corporate identity. These conjunctions did not happen spontaneously; they took place under intense pressure brought to bear upon More because of his relation to power and to the heretics he sought to destroy.

For Tyndale the self is likewise poised, but between poles quite different from those glimpsed in More. There is, to be sure, a highly individuated identity, but it is not at all conceived as a threatrical role, a mask behind which one conceals private judgments. Such theatricality is repugnant to Tyndale; he associates it with what he takes to be the hypocrisy of Catholic prelates and their lay agents, with the refined hostility of Cuthbert Tunstall and the smooth temporizing of More. The righteous individual, for Tyndale, has no scope for feigning, indirection, or hidden judgment; he seizes directly, as it were rapaciously, upon the truth. Any more devious path bears witness to bad faith and backsliding, or, at best, to an unwilling, enforced concession to the overwhelming pressures of a corrupt social world. To take delight in social performance as distinct from inward reality is unthinkable or rather thinkable only as a characteristic mode of the followers of Satan.

Tyndale's own sense of his identity is marked precisely by his refusal to make a part for himself in the midst of the ongoing performance. As a tutor in Gloucestershire he did not keep silent, cloaking his judgments behind a cover of affability, but quarreled openly and violently with those whose views of the Church he could not accept, until he was forced to depart for London. And when it became clear that he could not do as he wished in London, he left there too. These departures signal a pattern of rejections in Tyndale's life that centers on the crucial rejection of the Catholic Church. Man must live outside the institution, must not accept it as mediator between himself and other men or God. There is no longer a dense body of offices, ceremonies, rituals, traditions passed down from generation to generation, in the midst of which a man takes his place.

If there is none of More's calculated role-playing, there is equally none of his absorption into a visible corporate body. Thus Tyndale can speak of man in a kind of isolation that is entirely alien to More, can claim that a single, unaided man's judgment is sufficient unto itself to distinguish the true from the false, to find and understand God. To be sure, there is isolation in More as well, as the vigils in the New Building attest, but this isolation is not complete, for the believer is never entirely detached from the body of all Christians, from the visible, tangible guarantor and preserver of the unity of mankind. In Tyndale those bonds are cut with the rejection of the Church: "Who taught the eagles to spy out their prey?"

The violence, both literal and metaphoric, that accompanies this rejection indicates how threatening it seems; nonetheless, it is the necessary self-constituting act. The self must have at its core a principle of negation powerful enough to tear itself away from the body of the Church, to attack its communal rituals, to refuse even a theatrical accommodation to its sacraments. One cannot preach Christ without preaching Antichrist; one cannot achieve an identity without rejecting an identity.

At the same time, the principle of negation, though necessary, is not sufficient to the fashioning of the self. Alongside rejection of the Church—and hence alongside individuation, isolation, singleness of being—there is a powerful counterforce of obedience. This obedience, it should be noted, is quite different from More's membership in the *corpus Christianorum*. Where the latter implies absorption, oneness, the former implies the separation of individuals, a distance transcended but never entirely effaced. Protestants and Catholics alike use the traditional Pauline concept of the Church as body, but, as a social historian has recently argued, the more authentic biological image of the Protestant community is the network of ligaments and nerves.[1] The network, fittingly, is not tangible or visible, save to the anatomist; it is a concept most men take on faith. Identity then is not defined by participation in a body—hence in visible, communal rituals—but by a place in a schema of communication, legal relationships, obedience. The principle of negation in each man ultimately derives from the divine power that animates the network in which he has a place, and the expression of that power, the master key to the encoded system of relationships, is the Bible. The book—for Tyndale, the printed book in the vernacular—displaces the communal body.

No successful synthesis of these two modes of being was possible: even an irenic genius like Erasmus could not convincingly argue that one might select good qualities from each and combine them into a new, comprehensive totality. What was possible was a complex, unstable yoking of aspects of both in a secular context. Thomas Wyatt's court poetry insists that it has no inner silences, that it obeys its own principle of individuation. The self stands alone, defined by its rejection of the doubleness that in a corrupt world assures sexual and political success. For Wyatt this doubleness is, above all, characteristic of women; hence singleness, fidelity, the identity of inner state and external appearance, are attributes of the virtuous man. Wyatt's verse is a constant affirmation of his manliness, manifested not only in professions of singleness, but in deliberate stylistic roughness, coarse directness, aggression toward women, restlessness. This manliness is, I suggest, the equivalent in court poetry of Tyndale's eagle-self, deliberately cut off from false social rituals, refusing to play a corrupt game, whole. But of course, in the secular context, there is no sacred book by means of which man is reintegrated into a larger social network. There is only secular power, the ground and end not of a just order of things but of a vicious competition. Where Tyndale's singleness then is set in the context of his participation in a vast system of obedience, Wyatt's is caught up in a struggle for secular power. Consequently, Wyatt's declarations of self-absorbed independence and hatred of feigning are counterpoised by intimations of their opposites. The contempt for doubleness is itself a theatrical manipulation of appearances; the bluff honesty is a subtle, diplomatic maneuver in an elaborate and dangerous contest. Wyatt's Tyndale-like singleness then has been made over into a More-like theatricality.

But as Tyndale's isolation was transcended by his religious project, More's role-playing was transcended by his longing for absorption into the Church. Wyatt has neither More's Church nor Tyndale's passionate obedience to the Word of God: he has only secular power, the will to domination that governs both political and sexual relations at court. And in this bleak context, Wyatt's manipulation of his manly honesty affords glimpses of a bad faith that receives its definitive depiction in honest Iago. In his most brilliant court poems, Wyatt hovers on the brink of reflecting directly upon his condition, exploring his complicity in his own failure, his inability to free himself from the dialectic of domination and submission, but he cannot ever succeed in rendering this reflection fully conscious and deliberate. For, in the midst of an ongoing engagement in precisely those competitive conditions that shape his identity and determine the purposes of his speech, how could he establish a position from which to conduct such an exploration? If More was able to do so, it was only by virtue of his ardent adherence to an institution that had for Wyatt been discredited and driven out of England. Wyatt does, to be sure, turn to other poetic forms that signal the unraveling of his uneasy courtly identity, but the psalms succeed only in transferring the nexus of power, sexuality, and inwardness to a higher court, while the satires, for all their attempt to establish a hard, well-defended identity secured by withdrawal from dangerous relations to women and power, are drawn back toward the contradictions and role-playing from which they sought to escape.

For someone in Wyatt's situation, role-playing seems virtually inescapable, for both the concentration of power in the court and Protestant ideology lead to a heightened consciousness of identity, an increased attention to its expression, and an intensified effort to shape and control it. The fashioning of the self is raised to the status of a problem or a program. The pressure brought to bear on identity—the pressure of consciousness and power, in the individual and in the society of which he is a part—has profound literary consequences, some of which we have already glimpsed in the three figures we have examined. In the chapters that follow we will consider a second triad—Spenser, Marlowe, and Shakespeare—focusing now more on the particular texts and less on direct links between the authors and their works. This narrowing of focus is due to the greater illusion of independence in the art, to the fact that we must now consider more complex and seemingly autonomous characters in fully realized fictional worlds. As the pressure toward self-fashioning that we have already viewed in More, Tyndale, and Wyatt reaches over higher levels of conscious artistry, the literature of the later sixteenth century becomes increasingly adept at rendering such characters in highly individuated situations. Moreover, it becomes increasingly possible for at least a small number of men to conceive of literature as their primary activity: as we pass from Spenser to Marlowe to Shakespeare, we move toward a heightened investment of professional identity in artistic creation. Consequently, it becomes easier to discuss the formation and undermining of identity *within* individual works without formally referring beyond them to the lives of the creators, though we must remind ourselves that the very existence of such apparent inwardness depends upon the lived experience of a self-fashioning culture.[2] Before turning to Spenser, we will attempt to sketch very briefly some of the salient characteristics of this culture.

Despite its age and its well-documented limitations, one of the best introductions to Renaissance self-fashioning remains Burckhardt's *Civilization of the Renaissance in Italy*.[3] Burckhardt's crucial perception was that the political upheavals in Italy in the later

Middle Ages, the transition from feudalism to despotism, fostered
a radical change in consciousness: the princes and *condottieri*, and
their secretaries, ministers, poets, and followers, were cut off from
established forms of identity and forced by their relation to power
to fashion a new sense of themselves and their world: the self and
the state as works of art. But his related assertion that, in the
process, these men emerged at last as free individuals must be
sharply qualified. While not only in Italy, but in France and England as well, the old feudal models gradually crumbled and fell
into ruins, men created new models, precisely as a way of containing and channeling the energies which had been released.

The chief intellectual and linguistic tool in this creation was
rhetoric, which held the central place in the humanist education to
which most gentlemen were at least exposed.[4] Rhetoric was the
common ground of poetry, history, and oratory; it could mediate
both between the past and the present and between the imagination and the realm of public affairs. Encouraging men to think of
all forms of human discourse as argument, it conceived of poetry
as a performing art, literature as a storehouse of models. It offered
men the power to shape their worlds, calculate the probabilities,
and master the contingent, and it implied that human character
itself could be similarly fashioned, with an eye to audience and
effect. Rhetoric served to theatricalize culture, or rather it was the
instrument of a society which was already deeply theatrical.[5]

Theatricality, in the sense of both disguise and histrionic self-
presentation, arose from conditions common to almost all Renaissance courts: a group of men and women alienated from the customary roles and revolving uneasily around a center of power, a
constant struggle for recognition and attention, and a virtually
fetishistic emphasis upon manner.[6] The manuals of court behavior
which became popular in the sixteenth century are essentially
handbooks for actors, practical guides for a society whose members were nearly always on stage. These books are closely related
to the rhetorical handbooks that were also in vogue—both
essentially compilations of verbal strategies and both based upon
the principle of imitation. The former simply expand the scope of
the latter, offering an integrated rhetoric of the self, a model for the
formation of an artificial identity.

The greatest and most familiar of these manuals of behavior,
Castiglione's *Book of the Courtier*, portrays a world in which social
frictions, sexual combat, and power are all carefully masked by the
fiction of an elegant *otium*. Because of its mastery of its own precepts, Castiglione's work masks the tedious conning of lines and

secret rehearsals which underlie the successful performance. For a sense of these, we must turn to the cruder manuals, such as *The Court of Civil Courtesy* (1577), a handbook designed to help its reader to thread his way successfully through the labyrinth of social distinctions, to win at the game of rank. For example, if a host of equal or lower social rank seats a gentleman below an inferior, the author suggests that the gentleman casually sit down two or three places *below* even his assigned place; then if his host tries to move him back, he should say nonchalantly, "As long as I find good meat, I never use to study for my place."[7] The point, of course, is that this is spoken by someone who has intensely studied for his place.

Dissimulation and feigning are an important part of the instruction given by almost every court manual, from this comedy of manners, to Guazzo's defense of the pretence necessary to achieve an agreeable social presence, to Castiglione's idea of the sugercoated pill of political virtue.[8] One of the most penetrating Renaissance studies of this feigning and indeed of the whole mentality of the courtier is Philibert de Vienne's brilliant mock encomium, *The Philosopher of the Court* (1547). According to the speaker of this little-known work, translated by George North in 1575, "Our new and moral *Philosophy* may thus be defined: A certain and sound judgment, how to live according to the good grace and fashion of the Court."[9] Where old-fashioned philosophers used to struggle to probe below the appearance of things to their essence, modern moralists need only pay scrupulous attention to surfaces: "the semblances and appearances of all things cunningly couched, are the principal supporters of our Philosophy: for such as we seem, such are we judged here..." (56–57). Acts which have plausible "coverings and pretty pretexts" (50) are to be condoned; acts without them are condemned as crimes. This is not presented as the voice of conscious cynicism; quite the contrary, the speaker considers himself highly moral. He talks of commutative and distributive justice, of prudence, temperance, and magnanimity. Above all, he prizes honor, in defense of which a man may lawfully fight and, if need be, kill. But such extreme measures are rare; as in *The Courtier*, a man wins honor less by the sword than by the possession of grace, a quality which may be acquired through careful study and practice.[10]

Philibert's target is not the craftiness of a confidence man but the idealism, the high moral tone, that serves at once to advance the courtier's career and to conceal his rapacity from himself. The philosopher of the court has no intention of forgoing the pleasures of an unspotted conscience; indeed that conscience is one of the choicest products of the humanistic education that his social world requires of its participants. But the problem is to maintain this conscience in the face of the violations of its tenets in the reality of behavior at court. If those violations are invisible for much of the time, there are nonetheless moments at which a life pervaded by dissimulation must confront a moral tradition that insists, in the teachings of Socrates for example, that dissimulation is immoral. Philibert's interest is the working of the court mind at such moments, the social accommodation of an ethical embarrassment: "*Socrates* forbids such masking and general disguising, because we should not appear to be others than we are: and we also allow the same . . . . But *Socrates* letteth us not, that having no desire to show ourselves contrary to that we would be esteemed, notwithstanding we dissemble, and accommodate ourselves to the imperfections of everyone, when the same doth present us danger, and is prejudicial unto us. . . . Himself doeth serve us for example, for although he was ever like unto himself . . . yet was he the greatest dissembler in the world" (97–98).

By virtue of several convenient distortions and the discreet omission of the circumstances of his death, Socrates is absorbed into the ethos of rhetorical self-fashioning that Plato, in *Theaetetus* and *Gorgias*, has him condemn. For the philosopher of the court, Socrates is no longer opposed to a sophistic view of the world—"the virtue of man consisteth not in that which is only good of itself, following the opinion of Philosophy: but in that which seemeth to them good" (12)—but one of its supreme practitioners. The potentially disillusioning conflict between social ideals and social behavior has been averted, and Philibert's speaker can conclude with a celebration of Protean man: "This facility of the Spirit is not therefore to be blamed which makes men according to the pleasure of others, to change and transform himself. For in so doing he shall be accounted wise, win honor, and be free of reprehension everywhere: which *Proteus* knew very well, to whom his diverse Metamorphosis and oft transfiguration was very commodious" (101).[11]

Philibert has seen deeply into the mind he satirizes and cunningly mimics its forms of thought and expression. Indeed, there is some evidence that *The Philosopher of the Court* may have been taken at face value in England as a manual of court behavior.[12] If so, it is a startling tribute to the accuracy of Philibert's perception of the pressure on the court mind to preserve its idealism by transforming disruptive criticism into histrionic celebration and confirmation. This pressure intensifies as one moves closer to the center of power; at the very center even hostility and frustration wear the face of perfervid worship. Thus Sir Walter Ralegh may have chafed at Elizabeth's Spanish policy, wishing it more militant, but he did so only in the context of the "romance" which he carried on with his royal mistress. She was Cynthia and he was the Ocean, she was Diana and he an adoring follower, she was the heroine of a chivalric romance and he her devoted knight. When he had incurred the disfavor of his sixty-year-old mistress, the middle-aged lover declared himself heartsick with loneliness and grief: "While she was yet near at hand, that I might hear of her once in two or three days, my sorrows were the less: but even now my heart is cast into the depth of all misery. I that am wont to behold her riding like *Alexander*, hunting like *Diana*, walking like *Venus*, the gentle wind blowing her fair hair about her pure cheeks, like a nymph [etc.]."[13]

To accompany such fine sentiments, Ralegh even staged a scene of violent passion, modeled on the twenty-third canto of *Orlando Furioso*. His kinsman, Sir Arthur Gorges—no doubt acting upon instructions—carefully described the "strange Tragedy" in a letter to Cecil, concluding "I fear Sir W. Ralegh will shortly grow to be Orlando Furioso, if the bright Angelica persevere against him a little longer." The key to the performance is provided in a postscript: "I could wish her Majesty knew."[14]

Ralegh was more flamboyant than most, but the phenomenon as a whole is familiar. Sir Robert Carey has left a record of the way he was caught up in Elizabeth's theatricals. In 1597, smarting at not having been paid for his services as Warden of the East Marches, he rode to Theobalds uninvited and requested an audience with the queen. Both Cecil and Carey's brother (who was then Lord Chamberlain) advised him to leave at once without letting the queen know of his rash visit, for they assured him she would be furious. But a courtier friend, William Killigrew, devised a better plan: he told the queen that she was beholden to Carey, "who not having seen her for a twelvemonth and more, could no longer endure to be deprived of so great a happiness; but took post with all speed to come up to see your Majesty, and to kiss your hand, and so to return instantly again."[15] Carey was then granted an audience and was given the money due to him.

How are we to take a story like this? Carey implies in his account that the queen was taken in. Perhaps; and yet without denying her a jot of her enormous vanity, we may be virtually certain that Elizabeth was well aware that he had not ridden from the

Scottish marches in order to kiss her hand. By insisting upon the romantic fiction, she determined the whole tone of their subsequent dealings: Carey was no longer a civil servant demanding his pay, but a lover at the feet of his mistress. He had been absorbed into Petrarchan politics.

Not surprisingly, one of the most acute contemporary observers of these tactics was Sir Francis Bacon. If the courting and professions of love which the queen encouraged are viewed indulgently, "they are much like the accounts we find in romances of the Queen in the blessed islands, and her court and institutions, who allows of amorous admiration but prohibits desire. But if you take them seriously, they challenge admiration of another kind and of a very high order; for certain it is that these dalliances detracted but little from her fame and nothing at all from her majesty, and neither weakened her power nor sensibly hindered her business."[16] Bacon perceives first, that the romantic atmosphere of the court had a distinctly literary cast, and second, that it did not interfere with royal control. The two were in fact intertwined: Elizabeth's exercise of power was closely bound up with her use of fictions.[17] A surviving holograph of one of her speeches, at the close of a difficult session, enables us to glimpse the queen's characteristic strategy: "Let this my discipline stand you in stead of sorer strokes," she writes, "never to tempt too far a Prince's pow . . ." The last letters are crossed out, and in their place she writes "patience."[18]

In an intensification of that political mode described by More, everyone perceives that power has been made to mask as patience or that it has assumed romantic trappings, but the perception that a fiction is being imposed is rarely turned against Elizabeth as it will be turned against James and Charles. The reasons for the queen's relative success are many and complex; they may be summarized by observing that it did not seem in the interest of a substantial segment of the population to attempt to demystify the queen's power, and hence it was enormously difficult to do so.

The queen's power was linked with fictions in a more technical sense as well: her reign, according to Ernst Kantorowicz, witnessed the first major secular elaboration of the mystical legal fiction of "the King's Two Bodies." "I am but one body, naturally considered," Elizabeth declared in her accession speech, "though by [God's] permission a Body Politic to govern." When she ascended the throne, according to the crown lawyers, her very being was profoundly altered; in her mortal "Body natural" was incarnated the immortal and infallible "Body politic." Her body of flesh would age and die, but the Body politic, as Plowden wrote, "is not subject to Passions as the other is, nor to Death, for as to this Body the King never dies." Her visible being was a hieroglyphic of the timeless corporate being with its absolute perfection, just as, in the words of Coke, "a king's crown was a hieroglyphic of the laws."[19] She was a living representation of the immutable within time, a fiction of permanence. Through her, society achieved symbolic immortality and acted out the myth of a perfectly stable world, a world which replaces the flux of history.

Even without this elaborate doctrine, of course, kingship always involves fictions, theatricalism, and the mystification of power. The notion of "the King's Two Bodies" may, however, have heightened Elizabeth's conscious sense of her identity as at least in part a *persona ficta* and her world as a theater. She believed deeply—virtually to the point of religious conviction[20]—in display, ceremony, and decorum, the whole theatrical apparatus of royal power. "We Princes," she told a deputation of Lords and Commons in 1586, "are set on stages, in the sight and view of all the world duly observed."[21]

In the official spectacles and pageants, everything was calculated to enhance her transformation into an almost magical being, a creature of infinite beauty, wisdom, and power. But even her ordinary public appearances were theatrically impressive. A contemporary, Bishop Goodman, recalled in later years having seen the queen emerge from council on a December evening in 1588: "This wrought such an impression upon us, *for shows and pageants are ever best seen by torchlight,* that all the way long we did nothing but talk of what an admirable queen she was, and how we would adventure our lives to do her service."[22] Goodman was anything but a cynic, but, in recollection at least, he could see the royal appearance as a performance calculated to arouse precisely the emotions that he felt. And a performance it was. The queen's words to the crowd on that occasion—"You may well have a greater prince, but you shall never have a more loving prince"— were repeated with variations throughout her reign. They were part of a stock of such phrases upon which she was able to draw when need arose. Her famous "Golden Speech" of 1601 was little more than a particularly felicitous combination of these refrains—there is scarcely a phrase in it which she had not used again and again.

The whole public character was formed very early, then to be played and replayed with few changes for the next forty years. Already in her formal procession through the City on the day before her coronation, the keynotes were sounded. "If a man should say well," wrote one observer, "he could not better term the city of London that time, than a stage wherein was showed the wonderful spectacle, of a noble hearted princess toward her most loving people, and the people's exceeding comfort in beholding so worthy a sovereign." Where her sister Mary had been silent and aloof at her accession, Elizabeth bestowed her gratitude and affection on all. "I will be as good unto you," she assured her well-wishers, "as ever queen was to her people . . . . And persuade yourselves, that for the safety and quietness of you all, I will not spare, if need be, to spend my blood."[23]

Mutual love and royal self-sacrifice—in her first address to Parliament some weeks later, she reiterated these themes and added a third, perhaps the most important of all: "And in the end, this shall be for me sufficient, that a marble stone shall declare that a Queen, having reigned such a time, lived and died a virgin" (Neale, 1:49). The secular cult of the virgin was born, and it was not long before the young Elizabeth was portraying herself as a Virgin Mother: "And so I assure you all," she told Commons in 1563, "that, though after my death you may have many step-dames, yet shall you never have a more natural mother than I mean to be unto you all" (Neale, 1:109).[24]

Through the years, courtiers, poets, ballad makers, and artists provided many other cult images: in Ralegh's partial list, "Cynthia, Phoebe, Flora, Diana and Aurora," to which we may add Astraea, Zabeta, Deborah, Laura, Oriana, and, of course, Belphoebe and Gloriana.[25] The gorgeous rituals of praise channeled national and religious sentiments into the worship of the prince, masked over and thus temporarily deflected deep social, political, and theological divisions in late sixteenth-century England, transformed Elizabeth's potentially disastrous sexual disadvantage into a supreme political virtue and imposed a subtle discipline upon aggressive fortune seekers. The best contemporary description of the effects of the romanticizing of royal power is by the queen's godson, Sir John Harington:

> Her mind was oftime like the gentle air that cometh from the westerly point in a summer's morn; 'twas sweet and refreshing to all around her. Her speech did win all affections, and her subjects did try to show all love to her commands; for she would say, "her state did require her to command what she knew her people would willingly do from their own love to her." Herein did she show her wisdom fully: for who did choose to

lose her confidence; or who would withhold a show of
love and obedience, when their Sovereign said it was
their choice, and not her compulsion? Surely she did
play well her tables to gain obedience thus without constraint: again, she could put forth such alterations,
when obedience was lacking, as left no doubtings
whose daughter she was.[26]

Harington's cunning description will repay close attention. It
begins with the conventional rhetoric of adoration, the familiar
language of countless panegyrics. The next sentence opens in the
same mode—we have simply turned from her mind to her
speech—but there is a subtle shift in the second clause: "her subjects did try to show all love to her commands." From mind to
speech to commands—we have moved from poetical virtue to
power. That power, however, is masked by the queen's persuasive speech, which not only transforms obedience into love but, in
the phrase "her state did require her to command," suggests that
it is *she* who is obeying an order while her subjects are privileged
to act "willingly." We then turn to the subject who thinks he is
beguiling his prince with a "show of love and obedience"—what
Castiglione called a "salutary deception"[27]—but who is in fact
being manipulated. The final sentence is almost shockingly explicit: first the picture of the queen as a clever gamester and then
the allusion to Henry VIII, the perfect picture, in Ralegh's phrase,
of a merciless prince. We have come a long way from the
gentle air of a summer's morn! Behind all the cultic shows
of love, in reserve but ready to be used when necessary, lies force.
And yet the recognition of such force is not for Harington the
decisive perception: "We did all love her," he concludes, "for she
said she loved us, and much wisdom she showed in this
matter."[28] The realism and irony remain, but they are caught up
in an appreciation of the mutual interest of both ruler and subject
in the transformation of power relations into erotic relations, an
appreciation of the queen's ability at once to fashion her identity
and to manipulate the identities of her followers.

It is to a culture so engaged in the shaping of identity, in dissimulation and the preservation of moral idealism, that Spenser
addresses himself in defining "the general intention and meaning" of the entire *Faerie Queene:* the end of all the book, he writes
to Ralegh, "is to fashion a gentleman or noble person in vertuous
and gentle discipline."[29] The poem rests on the obvious but by no
means universal assumption that a gentleman can be so fashioned,
not simply in art but in life. We will, in the remainder of this

chapter, consider the implications of one episode in this educative discipline, the destruction of the Bower of Bliss in book 2, canto 12. After a perilous voyage, as readers of *The Faerie Queene* will recall, Guyon, the knight of Temperance, arrives with his companion, the aged Palmer, at the realm of the beautiful and dangerous witch Acrasia. After quelling the threats of Acrasia's monstrous guards, they enter the witch's exquisite Bower where, aided by the Palmer's sober counsel, Guyon resists a series of sensual temptations. At the Bower's center they spy the witch, bending over a young man, and, rushing in upon her, they manage to capture her in a net. Guyon then systematically destroys the Bower and leads the tightly bound Acrasia away.

Inevitably, we will slight other moments in Spenser's vast work that qualify the perspective established by this one, but we can at least be certain that the perspective is important: like Falstaff's banishment, Othello's suicide speech, and the harsh punishment of Volpone, the close of book 2 of *The Faerie Queene* has figured in criticism as one of the great cruxes of English Renaissance literature. The destruction of Acrasia's Bower tests in a remarkably searching way our attitudes toward pleasure, sexuality, the body; tests too our sense of the relation of physical pleasure to the pleasure of aesthetic images and the relation of both of these to what Guyon calls the "excellence" of man's creation. By "tests" I do not mean that the work examines us to see if we know the right answer—the poetry of the *Faerie Queene,* as Paul Alpers has demonstrated, continually invites us to trust our own experience of its rich surface[30]—rather, this experience tends to reveal or define important aspects of ourselves. Thus when C. S. Lewis, invoking the "exquisite health" of Spenser's imagination, characterizes the Bower as a picture of "the whole sexual nature in disease," of "male prurience and female provocation," indeed of "skeptophilia," the reader familiar with Lewis's work will recognize links to his criticism of erotic passages in *Hero and Leander* and *Venus and Adonis,* links to his conception of maturity and of mental and moral health. This is not to deny that Lewis's brilliant account describes disturbing qualities that any attentive reader may recognize in the Bower, but it may help us to understand why he writes that "the Bower of Bliss is not a place even of healthy animalism, or indeed of activity of any kind," whereas Spenser depicts Acrasia and her adolescent lover reposing "after long wanton joys" and even (following Tasso) pictures droplets of sweat trilling down Acrasia's snowy breast "through langor of her late sweet toil." What for Spenser is the place "Where Pleasure dwells in sensual delights" is for Lewis the realm only of frustration; all sexual activity is in this way reserved for the Garden of Adonis and hence tied securely to reproduction.[31]

At the other extreme, Yeats dismisses the moral judgments in the canto as "unconscious hypocrisy." Spenser, he tells us, "is a poet of the delighted senses, and his song becomes most beautiful when he writes of those islands of Phaedria and Acrasia."[32] And here again the reader familiar with Yeats will recognize certain perennial interests and values. The point would be too obvious to belabor, were it not for the fact that much Spenser commentary of the past several decades treats the Bower of Bliss and comparable passages in Spenser as if they were technical puzzles to be solved, as if one could determine their meaning quite apart from their effect upon the reader: "The main subject of the bower of Bliss is disorder in the human body, the general image or picture is of the cause of that disorder, the imagery used in painting this picture is all of disorder, and the laws of decorum are satisfied."[33] A sympathetic response like Hazlitt's to the canto's "voluptuous pathos, and languid brilliancy of fancy" or a residual uneasiness about the destruction are dismissed as absurd. Indeed the Romantic readers of the poem implicitly stand charged as either degenerates or moral incompetents. To be sure, criticism has convincingly shown that the intellectual tradition behind Guyon's act of moral violence included not only Puritanism (which must, in any case, be understood as far more than a hysterical rejection of the flesh) but a rich matrix of classical and medieval thought.[34] Moreover, it has demonstrated that the description of the Bower itself is not an isolated "beauty" that Spenser, in growing uneasiness and bad faith, decided to crush, but an episode embedded in a narrative that is shaped throughout by the poet's complex moral intelligence. The Romantic critics who have been discredited by this scholarship, however, had the virtue of fully acknowledging the Bower's intense erotic appeal. It is frequently said in reply that Spenser has given us a picture of healthy sexual enjoyment in the Garden of Adonis where "Franckly each paramor his leman knowes" (3.6.41); but the comparison fails to take into consideration the fact that the Garden of Adonis, that great "seminary" of living things, has almost no erotic appeal. The issue is not whether sexual consummation is desirable in Spenser, but why the particular erotic appeal of the Bower—more intense and sustained than any comparable passage in the poem—excites the hero's destructive violence.

We are told that after an initial attractiveness the Bower becomes

stultifying, perverted, and frustrating or that the reader's task, like
the hero's, is to interpret the images correctly, that is, to recognize
the danger of "lewd loves, and wasteful luxury" embodied in the
Bower. I believe that one easily perceives that danger from the
beginning and that much of the power of the episode derives
precisely from the fact that his perception has little or no effect on
the Bower's continued sensual power:

> Upon a bed of roses she was layd,
> As faint through heat, or dight to pleasant sin,
> And was arayd, or rather disarayd,
> All in a vele of silke and silver thin,
> That hid no whit her alablaster skin,
> But rather shewd more white if more might bee.
>
> (2.12.77)

"Pleasant sin"—the moral judgment is not avoided or suspended
but neither does it establish its dominion over the stanza; rather,
for a moment it is absorbed into a world in which the normal
conceptual boundaries are blurred: languor and energy, opacity
and transparency, flesh and stone all merge. Similarly, the close of
the famous rose song—

> Gather the rose of love, whilest yet is time,
> Whilest loving thou mayst loved be with equall crime—

invites us momentarily to transvalue the word "crime," reading it
as the equivalent of "passion" or "intensity," even as we continue
to know that "crime" cannot be so transvalued. We can master the
iconography, read all the signs correctly, and still respond to the
allure of the Bower. It is, as we shall see, the threat of this absorption that triggers Guyon's climactic violence. Temperance—the
avoidance of extremes, the "sober government" of the body, the
achievement of the Golden Mean—must be constituted paradoxically by a supreme act of destructive excess.

The Bower's dangerous attractiveness is in sharp contrast to the
Cave of Mammon, where Guyon's experience, and ours, is remarkable for the complete absence of sympathetic response to the
temptation. The hero's journey through the Cave, past the fabulous displays of riches, embodies one of the basic patterns in the
life of a temperate man: to be constantly confronted with baits
which are at once spectacular and curiously easy to resist. The
consequences of succumbing to these temptations are horrible—
nothing short of being torn to pieces—but the temperate man
resists far less for fear of the evil consequences than out of genuine
indifference. That is, Mammon's offers are only attractive to those

who are going to fall—a tautology not at all alien to Spenser or to Protestant thought. Guyon faints not as an emblem of tension, the strain of resisting temptation, but from want of food and sleep.

In the Bower of Bliss, Guyon's "stubborne brest gan secret pleasaunce to embrace" (2.12.45), and he does not merely depart from the place of temptation but reduces it to ruins. To help us understand more fully why he must do so in order to play his part in Spenser's fashioning of a gentleman, we may invoke an observation made in *Civilization and Its Discontents*: "It is impossible," writes Freud, "to overlook the extent to which civilization is built up upon a renunciation of instinct, how much it presupposes precisely the nonsatisfaction (by suppression, repression, or some other means?) of powerful instincts.... Civilization behaves toward sexuality as a people or a stratum of its population does which has subjected another one to its exploitation."[35] Modern criticism would make the destruction of the Bower easy by labeling Acrasia's realm sick, stagnant, futile, and joyless, but Spenser, who participates with Freud in a venerable and profoundly significant intertwining of sexual and colonial discourse, accepts sexual colonialism only with a near-tragic sense of the cost. If he had wished, he could have unmasked Acrasia as a deformed hag, as he had exposed Duessa or as Ariosto had exposed (though more ambiguously) the enchantress Alcina, but instead Acrasia remains enticingly seductive to the end. She offers not simply sexual pleasure—"long wanton joys"—but self-abandonment, erotic aestheticism, the melting of the will, the end of all quests; and Spenser understands, at the deepest level of his being, the appeal of such an end. Again and again his knights reach out longingly for resolution, closure, or release only to have it snatched from them or deferred; the whole of *The Faerie Queene* is the expression of an intense craving for release, which is overmastered only by a still more intense fear of release.

The Bower of Bliss must be destroyed not because its gratifications are unreal but because they threaten "civility"—civilization—which for Spenser is achieved only through renunciation and the constant exercise of power. If this power inevitably entails loss, it is also richly, essentially creative; power is the guarantor of value, the shaper of all knowledge, the pledge of human redemption. Power may, as Bacon claimed, prohibit desire, but it is in its own way a version of the erotic: the violence directed against Acrasia's sensual paradise is both in itself an equivalent of erotic excess and a pledge of loving service to the royal mistress. Even when he most bitterly criticizes its abuses or records its brutalities, Spenser loves power and attempts to link his own art ever more closely with its symbolic and literal embodiment. *The Faerie Queene* is, as he insists again and again, wholly wedded to the autocratic ruler of the English state; the rich complexities of Spenser's art, its exquisite ethical discriminations in pursuit of the divine in man, are not achieved in spite of what is for us a repellent political ideology—the passionate worship of imperialism—but are inseparably linked to that ideology.

To say that Spenser worships power, that he is our originating and preeminent poet of empire, is not, in the heady manner of the late '60s, to condemn his work as shallow, craven, or timeserving. Rather, his work, like Freud's, bears witness to the deep complicity of our moral imagination even in its noblest and most hauntingly beautiful manifestations in the great Western celebration of power. Alongside Freud, we may invoke Virgil, whose profound faith in Aeneas's personal and world-historical mission and whose adoration of Augustus are tempered but never broken by a bitter sense of all that empire forces man to renounce, to flee from, to destroy. The example of Freud is useful, however, because it helps us to grasp the relation of our response to the Bower to our own contemporary preoccupations, to perceive as well those qualities in Renaissance culture which we are at this moment in our history uniquely situated to appreciate.

If all of civilization rests, as Freud argues, upon repression, nevertheless the particular civilization we produce and inhabit rests upon a complex technology of control whose origins we trace back to the Renaissance. We are no longer inclined to celebrate this period as the lifting of a veil of childish illusion, nor are we concerned to attack it in the name of a nostalgic vision of lost religious unity. The great syncretic structures of the Renaissance humanists no longer seem as intellectually compelling or as adequate to the period's major works of art as they once did, and even the imposition upon nature of an abstract mathematical logic, which Cassirer celebrates so eloquently as the birth of modern science, seems an equivocal achievement. We continue to see in the Renaissance the shaping of crucial aspects of our sense of self and society and the natural world, but we have become uneasy about our whole way of constituting reality. Above all, perhaps, we sense that the culture to which we are as profoundly attached as our face is to our skull is nonetheless a construct, a thing made, as temporary, time-conditioned, and contingent as those vast European empires from whose power Freud drew his image of repression. We sense too that we are situated at the close of the cultural movement initiated in the Renaissance and that the places in which our social and psychological world seems to be cracking apart are those structural joints visible when it was first constructed. In the midst of the anxieties and contradictions attendant upon the threatened collapse of this phase of our civilization, we respond with passionate curiosity and poignancy to the anxieties and contradictions attendant upon its rise. To experience Renaissance culture is to feel what it was like to form our own identity, and we are at once more rooted and more estranged by the experience.

If it is true that we are highly sensitive to those aspects of the Renaissance that mark the early, tentative, conflict-ridden fashioning of modern consciousness, then *The Faerie Queene* is of quite exceptional significance, for Spenser's stated intention is precisely "to fashion a gentleman or noble person in vertuous and gentle discipline." This mirroring—the conscious purpose of the work seeming to enact the larger cultural movement—may help to account for the reader's sense of encountering in Spenser's poem the process of self-fashioning itself. In the Bower of Bliss that process is depicted as involving a painful sexual renunciation: in Guyon's destructive act we are invited to experience the ontogeny of our culture's violent resistance to a sensuous release for which it nevertheless yearns with a new intensity. The resistance is necessary for Spenser because what is threatened is "our Selfe, whom though we do not see, / Yet each doth in him selfe it well perceiue to bee" (2.12.47). We can secure that self only through a restraint that involves the destruction of something intensely beautiful; to succumb to that beauty is to lose the shape of manhood and be transformed into a beast.[36]

The pleasure offered by Acrasia must be rejected with brutal decisiveness, but how exactly does one distinguish between inordinate or excessive sexual pleasure and temperate sexual pleasure? Spenser does not, after all, wish to reject pleasure entirely: if Guyon's destruction of the Bower of Bliss suggests "the extent to which civilization is built up upon a renunciation of instinct," Scudamour's seizure of Amoret in the Temple of Venus, recounted in book 4, canto 10, suggests the extent to which civilization is built upon the controlled satisfaction of instinct, upon the ability to direct and profit from the "kindly rage" of desire. Pleasure can even be celebrated, as in the nameless supplicant's hymn to Venus, provided that its legitimating function, its "end" both in the sense of purpose and termination, be properly understood:

So all things else, that nourish vitall blood,
Soone as with fury thou doest them inspire,
In generation seeke to quench their inward fire.
(4.10.46)

Spenser cannot deny pleasure, even the extreme pleasure suggested by "rage," "fury," and "fire," a legitimate function in sexuality. Quite apart from the poet's own experience and observation, it may have been extremely difficult even for figures far more suspicious of the body than Spenser to imagine an entirely pleasureless generation of children (though, as we shall see later, such a doctrine found occasional expression), for there seems to have been widespread medical belief in early modern Europe that for conception to take place, both the male and the female had to experience orgasm.[37] Virtually all of Spenser's representations of sexual fulfillment, including those he fully sanctions, seem close to excess and risk the breakdown of the carefully fashioned identity:

Lightly he clipt her twixt his armes twaine,
And streightly did embrace her body bright,
Her body, late the prison of sad paine,
Now the sweet lodge of loue and deare delight:
But she faire Lady ouercommen quight
Of huge affection, did in pleasure melt,
And in sweete rauishment pourd out her spright:
No word they spake, nor earthly thing they felt,
But like two senceles stocks in long embracement dwelt.
(3.12.45 [1590])

The distinction upon which self-definition rests at the close of book 2—between temperate pleasure and inordinate pleasure—can only be understood in terms of a further distinction between a pleasure that serves some useful purpose, some virtuous end, and a pleasure that does not. Thus the denizens of the Bower acknowledge time solely as an inducement to the eager satisfaction of desire here and now, before the body's decay, and not as the agency of purposeful direction. That direction—expressed in *The Faerie Queene* as a whole by the idea of the *quest*—is for sexuality found in the power of love to inspire virtuous action and ultimately, with the sanctification of marriage, in the generation of offspring. Generation restores the sense of linear progression to an experience that threatens to turn in upon itself, reveling in its own exquisite beauty. A pleasure that serves as its own end, that claims to be self-justifying rather than instrumental, purposeless rather than generative, is immoderate and must be destroyed, lest it undermine the power that Spenser worships.

But this way of distinguishing temperate and inordinate plea-sure is less stable than it first appears, for desire may be "quenched" in generation but is not itself temperate. On the con-trary, generation only takes place because all living beings—men and beasts—are "priuily pricked with" Venus's "lustfull powres" (4.10.45). All attempts to restrain these powers must be overcome for fruitful sexual union to occur: thus Scudamour must seize Amoret from the restraining and moderating figures—Woman-hood, Shamefastness, Modesty, Silence, Obedience, and the like—who sit at the feet of Venus's image. The fashioning of a gentleman then depends upon the imposition of control over in-escapably immoderate sexual impulses that, for the survival of the race, must constantly recur: the discriminations upon which a virtuous and gentle discipline is based are forever in danger of collapsing. Hence, I suggest, the paradox of the Knight of Temper-ance's seemingly intemperate attack upon the Bower of Bliss: Guyon destroys the Bower and ties Acrasia "in chaines of adamant"—"For nothing else might keepe her safe and sound"—in a violent attempt to secure that principle of difference necessary to fashion the self. "Excess" is defined not by some inherent imbalance or impropriety, but by the mechanism of con-trol, the exercise of restraining power. And if excess is virtually invented by this power, so too, paradoxically, power is invented by excess: this is why Acrasia cannot be destroyed, why she and what she is made to represent must continue to exist, forever the object of the destructive quest. For were she not to exist as a constant threat, the power Guyon embodies would also cease to exist. After all, we can assume that the number of people who actually suffer in any period from *melt-down* as a result of sexual excess is quite small (comparable to the number of cases of that spontaneous combustion depicted by Dickens), small enough to raise questions about the motives behind the elaborate moral weaponry designed to combat the supposed danger. The percep-tion of the threat of excess enables institutional power to have a legitimate "protective" and "healing" interest in sexuality, to exercise its constitutive control over the inner life of the individ-ual.

Self-fashioning, the project of Spenser's poem and of the culture in which it participates, requires both an enabling institution, a source of power and communal values—in *The Faerie Queene*, the court of Gloriana—and a perception of the not-self, of all that lies outside, or resists, or threatens identity. The destruction of the Bower is the fulfillment of the knight's quest—the institution has been glorified, the demonic other at once identified and destroyed—but the inherent contradictions in the relations between temperance and pleasure, restraint and gratification have been deferred rather than resolved. What appears for a moment as decisive closure gives way to renewed efforts, other quests, which, as we have already glimpsed in Scudamour, attempt to compensate for the limitations, the sacrifice of essential values, implicit in the earlier resolution.

In a remarkable study of how societies make "tragic choices" in the allocation of scarce resources (e.g. kidney machines) or in the determination of high risks (e.g. the military draft), Guido Calabresi and Philip Bobbitt observe that by complex mixtures of approaches, societies attempt to avert "tragic results, that is, results which imply the rejection of values which are proclaimed to be fundamental": these approaches may succeed for a time, but it will eventually become apparent that some sacrifice of values has taken place, whereupon "fresh mixtures of methods will be tried, structured . . . by the shortcomings of the approaches they replace."[38] These too will in time give way to others in a "strategy of successive moves" that comprises an "intricate game," a game that reflects the simultaneous perception of a tragic choice and the determination to "forget" that perception in an illusory resolution. Driven by the will to deny its own perception of tragic conflict inherent in the fashioning of civility, *The Faerie Queene* resembles such an intricate game. Thus a particular "move," here the destruction of the Bower, represents in effect a brilliant solution, constructed out of the most conventional materials and yet unmistakably original, of the uneasy, aggressive, masculine court identity fashioned by Wyatt: male sexual aggression—the hunt, the loathing, the desire to master—is yoked to the service of ideal values embodied in a female ruler, and it is through this service that identity is achieved. The conception obviously depends upon Queen Elizabeth's own extraordinary manipulation of a secular mythology infused with displaced religious veneration, yet Spenser manages to suggest that the "vertuous and gentle discipline" he chronicles is not limited by its historical circumstances. Like Elizabeth herself, Spenser appeals to an image of female power—the benevolent and nurturing life force—that transcends a local habitation and a name. But this "solution" has its costs that Spenser, as we have seen, represents with extraordinary power and that drive him to further constructions.

Each heroic quest is at once a triumph and a flight, an escape from the disillusionment glimpsed for a brief moment on the Mount of Contemplation and again at the close of the Mutabilitie Cantos. Spenser's knights live in the profound conviction that there is a moral task set for themselves by virtue of the power of Gloriana, a demonic object out there to be encountered and defeated. Each triumphant act of virtuous violence confirms this conviction, defending it from all that would undermine the rightness of the moral mission, all that would question the possibility of achieving a just, coherent, stable identity anchored in the ardent worship of power. But the destruction of the Bower of Bliss suggests the extent to which each self-constituting act is haunted by inadequacy and loss.

The experience I have just described is, insofar as the work retains its power, common to us all, embedded in each of our personal histories, though a protective cultural amnesia may have led us to forget it until we reexperience it in art. We need, at this level, bring nothing to the text but ourselves. Fuller understanding, however, requires that we confront not only personal history but the history of peoples. We must, as Clifford Geertz suggests, incorporate the work of art into the texture of a particular pattern of life, a collective experience that transcends it and completes its meaning.[39] If Spenser told his readers a story, they listened, and listened with pleasure, because they themselves, in the shared life of their culture, were telling versions of that story again and again, recording the texts on themselves and on the world around them. In this sense, it is not adequate for a cultural poetics to describe the destruction of the Bower of Bliss or any literary text as a *reflection* of its circumambient culture; Spenser's poem is one manifestation of a symbolic language that is inscribed by history on the bodies of living beings as, in Kafka's great parable, the legal sentences are inscribed by the demonic penal machine on the bodies of the condemned.

It is not possible within the scope of this chapter to outline the dense network of analogies, repetitions, correspondences, and homologies within which even this one episode of Spenser's immense poem is embedded. But I can point briefly to three reiterations by the culture of important elements of the destruction of the Bower of Bliss: the European response to the native cultures of the New World, the English colonial struggle in Ireland, and the Reformation attack on images. The examples suggest the diversity of such reiterations—from the general culture of Europe, to the national policy of England, to the ideology of a small segment of the nation's population—while their shared elements seem to bear out Freud's master analogy: "Civilization behaves towards sexuality as a people or a stratum of its population does which has subjected another one to its exploitation."

In the texts written by early explorers of the New World, a long, arduous voyage, fraught with fabulous dangers and trials, brings the band of soldiers, sailors, and religious fathers—knight, boatman, and palmer—to a world of riches and menace. The adventurer's morality is the morality of the ship, where order, discipline, and constant labor are essential for survival, and they are further united by their explicit religious faith and by an unspoken but powerful male bond. The lands they encounter are often achingly beautiful: "I am completely persuaded in my own mind," writes Columbus in 1498, "that the Terrestrial Paradise is in the place I have described."[40] So Spenser likens the Bower of Bliss to Eden itself, "if ought with Eden mote compayre," and lingers over its landscape of wish fulfillment, a landscape at once lavish and moderate, rich in abundant vegetation and yet "steadfast," "attempred," and well "disposed." If these descriptive terms are shared in the Renaissance by literary romance and travelers' accounts, it is because the two modes of vision are mutually reinforcing: Spenser, like Tasso before him, makes frequent allusion to the New World—to "all that now America men call" (2.10.72)—while when Cortes and his men looked down upon the valley of Mexico, they thought, says a participant, of Amadis of Gaule.[41] The American landscape has to European eyes the mysterious intimations of a hidden art, as Ralegh's description of the Orinoco suggests: "On both sides of this river, we passed the most beautiful country that ever mine eyes beheld: and whereas all that we had seen before was nothing but woods, prickles, bushes, and thorns, here we beheld plains of twenty miles in length, the grass short and green, and in diverse parts groves of trees by themselves, as if they had been by all the art and labor in the world so made of purpose: and still as we rowed, the Deer came down feeding by the water's side, as if they had been used to a keeper's call."[42]

Spenser, to be sure, has no need of the "as if"—he credits art as well as nature with the making of the paradisal landscape—but this difference should not suggest too sharp a contrast between an "artless" world described by the early voyagers and the poet's "artificial" Bower. The Europeans again and again record their astonishment at the Indians' artistic brilliance: "Surely I marvel

not at the gold and precious stones, but wonder with astonishment with what industry and laborious art the curious workmanship exceedeth the matter and substance. I beheld a thousand
shapes, and a thousand forms, which I cannot express in writing;
so that in my judgment I never saw anything which might more
allure the eyes of men with the beauty thereof."[43]

But all of this seductive beauty harbors danger, danger not only
in the works of art which are obviously idolatrous but in the
Edenic landscape itself. The voyagers to the New World are
treated, like Guyon and the Palmer, to mild air that "breathed
forth sweet spirit and holesom smell" (2.12.51), and they react
with mingled wonder and resistance: "Smooth and pleasing
words might be spoken of the sweet odors, and perfumes of these
countries," writes Peter Martyr, "which we purposely omit, because they make rather for the effeminating of men's minds, than
for the maintenance of good behavior."[44] Similarly, if the New
World could be portrayed as a place "In which all pleasures
plenteously abownd, / And none does others happiness envye"
(2.10.58), a Golden World, it could also serve—often in the same
text and by virtue of the same set of perceptions—as a screen onto
which Europeans projected their darkest and yet most compelling
fantasies: "These folk live like beasts without any reasonableness,
and the women be also as common. And the men hath conversation with the women who that they been or who they first meet, is
she his sister, his mother, his daughter, or any other kindred. And
the women be very hot and disposed to lecherdness. And they eat
also one another. The man eateth his wife, his children . . . . And
that land is right full of folk, for they live commonly 300 year and
more as with sickness they die not."[45] In 1582 Richard Madox, in
Sierra Leone with Edward Fenton's expedition, heard from a Por-
tuguese trader comparable stories of African customs: "He reported that near the mountains of the moon there is a queen, an
empress of all these Amazons, a witch and a cannibal who daily
feeds on the flesh of boys. She ever remains unmarried, but she
has intercourse with a great number of men by whom she begets
offspring. The kingdom, however, remains hereditary to the
daughters, not to the sons."[46]

Virtually all the essential elements of the travel narratives recur
in Spenser's episode: the sea voyage, the strange, menacing creatures, the paradisal landscape with its invisible art, the gold and
silver carved with "curious imagery," the threat of effeminacy
checked by the male bond, the generosity and wantonness of the

inhabitants, the arousal of a longing at once to enter and to destroy. Even cannibalism and incest which are the extreme manifestations of the disordered and licentious life attributed to the
Indians are both subtly suggested in the picture of Acrasia hanging over her adolescent lover:

> And oft inclining downe with kisses light,
> For fear of waking him, his lips bedewd,
> And through his humid eyes did sucke his spright,
> Quite molten into lust and pleasure lewd.
>
> (2.12.73)

In book 6 of *The Faerie Queene* Spenser offers a more explicit
version of these dark imaginings;[47] here in book 2 the violation of
the taboos is carefully displaced, so that the major threat is not
pollution but the very attractiveness of the vision. Sexual excess
has caused in Verdant a melting of the soul,[48] and this internal
pathology is matched by an external disgrace:

> His warlike armes, the idle instruments
> Of sleeping praise, were hong vpon a tree,
> And his braue shield, full of old moniments,
> Was fowly ra'st, that none the signes might see.
>
> (2.12.80)

The entire fulfillment of desire leads to the effacement of signs and
hence to the loss both of memory, depicted in canto 10 and of the
capacity for heroic effort, depicted in the figure of the boatman
who ferries Guyon and the Palmer to the Bower:

> Forward they passe, and strongly he them rowes,
> Vntill they nigh vnto that gulfe arryve,
> Where streame more violent and greedy growes:
> Then he with all his puisaunce doth stryve
> To strike his oares, and mightily doth dryve
> The hollow vessell through the threatfull wave,
> Which, gaping wide, to swallow them alyve
> In th'huge abysse of his engulfing grave,
> Doth rore at them in vaine, and with great terrour rave.
>
> (2.12.5)

The threat of being engulfed that is successfully resisted here is
encountered again at the heart of the Bower in the form not of
cannibalistic violence but of erotic absorption. Verdant, his head
in Acrasia's lap, has sunk into a narcotic slumber: all "manly"
energy, all purposeful direction, all sense of difference upon

which "civil" order is founded have been erased. This slumber corresponds to what the Europeans perceived as the *pointlessness* of native cultures. It was as if millions of souls had become unmoored, just as their ancestors had, it was thought, somehow lost their way and wandered out of sight of the civilized world. Absorbed into a vast wilderness, they lost all memory of the true history of their race and of the one God and sank into a spiritual and physical lethargy. It is difficult to recover the immense force which this charge of idleness carried; some sense may be gauged perhaps from the extraordinary harshness with which vagabonds were treated.[49]

That the Indians were idle, that they lacked all work discipline, was proved, to the satisfaction of the Europeans, by the demonstrable fact that they made wretched slaves, dying after a few weeks or even days of hard labor. And if they were freed from servitude, they merely slid back into their old customs: "For being idle and slothful, they wander up and down, and return to their old rites and ceremonies and foul and mischievous acts."[50] That the European voyagers of the sixteenth century, surely among the world's most restless and uprooted generations, should accuse the Indians of "wandering up and down" is bitterly ironic, but the accusation served as a kind of rudder, an assurance of stability and direction. And this assurance is confirmed by the vast projects undertaken to fix and enclose the native populations in the mines, in encomiendas, in fortified hamlets, and ultimately, in mass graves. A whole civilization was caught in a net and, like Acrasia, bound in chains of adamant; their gods were melted down, their palaces and temples razed, their groves felled. "And of the fairest late, now made the fowlest place."[51]

Guyon, it will be recalled, makes no attempt to destroy the Cave of Mammon; he simply declines its evil invitations which leave him exhausted but otherwise unmoved. But the Bower of Bliss he destroys with a rigor rendered the more pitiless by the fact that his stubborn breast, we are told, embraced "secret pleasance." In just this way, Europeans destroyed Indian culture not despite those aspects of it that attracted them but in part at least because of them. The violence of the destruction was regenerative; they found in it a sense of identity, discipline, and holy faith.[52] In tearing down what both appealed to them and sickened them, they strengthened their power to resist their dangerous longings, to repress antisocial impulses, to conquer the powerful desire for release. And the conquest of desire had the more power because it contained within itself a version of that which it destroyed: the power of Acrasia's sensuality to erase signs and upset temperate order is simultaneously attacked and imitated in Guyon's destruction of the exquisite Bower, while European "civility" and Christianity were never more ferociously assaulted than in the colonial destruction of a culture that was accused of mounting just such an assault.

One measure of European complicity in what they destroyed is the occurrence of apostacy or at least fantasies of apostacy. Bernal Diaz del Castillo tells one such story about a common seaman named Gonzalo Guerrero who had survived a shipwreck in the Yucatan and refused to rejoin his compatriots when, eight years later, Cortes managed to send word to him: "I am married and have three children, and they look on me as a *Cacique* here, and a captain in time of war. Go, and God's blessing be with you. But my face is tattooed and my ears are pierced. What would the Spaniards say if they saw me like this? And look how handsome these children of mine are!"[53] The emissary reminded him that he was a Christian and "should not destroy his soul for the sake of an Indian woman," but Guerrero clearly regarded his situation as an improvement in his lot. Indeed Cortes learned that it was at Guerrero's instigation that the Indians had, three years before, attacked an earlier Spanish expedition to the Yucatan.

We have, in the tattooed Spanish seaman, encountered an analogue to those disfigured beasts who try to defend the Bower against Guyon and, in particular, to Gryll, who, having been metamorphosed by Acrasia into a hog, "repyned greatly" at his restoration. Such creatures give a local habitation and a name to those vague feelings of longing and complicity that permeate accounts of a sensuous life that must be rejected and destroyed. And if the Yucatan seems too remote from Spenser's world, we need only turn to our second frame of reference, Elizabethan rule in Ireland, to encounter similar stories. In Spenser's own *View of the Present State of Ireland,* probably written in 1596, Eudoxius asks, "is it possible that an Englishman brought up naturally in such sweet civility as England affords could find such liking in that barbarous rudeness that he should forget his own nature and forgo his own nation? . . . Is it possible that any should so far grow out of frame that they should in so short space quite forget their country and their own names? . . . Could they ever conceive any such devilish dislike of their own natural country as that they would be ashamed of her name, and bite off her dug from which they sucked life?"[54] In reply, Spenser's spokesman, Irenius, speaks bitterly of those Englishmen who are "degenerated and grown almost mere Irish, yea and more malicious to the English than the very Irish themselves" (48); these metamorphosed wretches even prefer to speak Irish, although, as Eudoxius observes, "they should (methinks) rather take scorn to acquaint their tongues thereto, for it hath been ever the use of the conqueror to despise the language of the conquered, and to force him by all means to learn his."[55] Irenius locates the source of this unnatural linguistic betrayal, this effacement of signs, in the subversive power of Irish women. The rebel Englishmen will "bite off her dug from which they sucked life" because another breast has intervened: "the child that sucketh the milk of the nurse must of necessity learn his first speech of her, the which being the first that is enured to his tongue is ever after most pleasing unto him," and "the speech being Irish, the heart must needs be Irish."[56] The evil metamorphosis caused by Irish wetnurses is completed by miscegenation: "the child taketh most of his nature of the mother . . . for by them they are first framed and fashioned" (68). As the fashioning of a gentleman is threatened in book 2 of *The Faerie Queene* by Acrasia, so it is threatened in Ireland by the native women.

It is often remarked that the *View*, which Spenser wrote after his completion of *The Faerie Queene*, expresses a hardening of attitude, a harsh and bitter note brought on by years of tension and frustration. It may well reflect such a change in tone, but its colonial policies are consistent with those with which Spenser had been associated from his arrival in Ireland as Lord Grey's secretary in 1580, that is, from the time in which *The Faerie Queene* was in the early stages of its composition. When Spenser "wrote of Ireland," Yeats comments, "he wrote as an official, and out of thoughts and emotions that had been organized by the State."[57] It was not only in his capacity as an official that Spenser did so: in art and in life, his conception of identity, as we have seen, is wedded to his conception of power, and after 1580, of colonial power. For all Spenser's claims of relation to the noble Spencers of Wormleighton and Althorp, he remains a "poor boy," as he is designated in the Merchant Taylor's School and at Cambridge, until Ireland. It is there that he is fashioned a gentleman, there that he is transformed from the former denizen of East Smithfield to the 'undertaker"—the grim pun unintended but profoundly appropriate—of 3,028 acres of Munster land. From his first acquisition in 1582, this land is at once the assurance of his status—the 'Gent." next to his name—and of his insecurity: ruined abbeys, friaries expropriated by the crown, plow lands rendered vacant by famine and execution, property forfeited by those whom Spenser's superiors declared traitors.

For what services, we ask, was Spenser being rewarded? And we answer, blandly, for being a colonial administrator. But the answer, which implies pushing papers in a Dublin office through endless days of tedium, is an evasion. Spenser's own account presses in upon us the fact that he was involved intimately, on an almost daily basis, throughout the island, in the destruction of Hiberno-Norman civilization, the exercise of a brutal force that had few if any of the romantic trappings with which Elizabeth contrived to soften it at home.[58] Here, on the periphery, Spenser was an agent of and an apologist for massacre, the burning of mean hovels and of crops with the deliberate intention of starving the inhabitants, forced relocation of peoples, the manipulation of treason charges so as to facilitate the seizure of lands, the endless repetition of acts of military "justice" calculated to intimidate and break the spirit. We may wish to tell ourselves that a man of Spenser's sensitivity and gifts may have mitigated the extreme policies of ruthless men, but it appears that he did not recoil in the slightest from this horror, did not even feel himself, like his colleague Geoffrey Fenton, in mild opposition to it.[59] Ireland is not only in book 5 of *The Faerie Queene;* it pervades the poem. Civility is won through the exercise of violence over what is deemed barbarous and evil, and the passages of love and leisure are not moments set apart from this process but its rewards.

"Every detail of the huge resettlement project" in Munster, writes Spenser's biographer Judson, "was known to him as it unfolded, including its intricate legal aspects, and hence his final acquisition of thousands of acres of forfeited lands was entirely natural."[60] Natural perhaps, but equally natural that his imagination is haunted by the nightmares of savage attack—the "outrageous dreadfull yelling cry" of Maleger, "His body leane and meagre as a rake" and yet seemingly impossible to kill[61]—and of absorption. The latter fear may strike us as less compelling than the former—there is much talk, after all, of the "savage brutishness and loathly filthiness" of native customs—but the Elizabethans were well aware, as we have already seen, that many of their most dangerous enemies were Englishmen who had been metamorphosed into "mere Irish." Spenser's own career is marked by conflicting desires to turn his back on Ireland forever and to plant himself ever more firmly in Munster;[62] if the latter course scarcely represented an abandonment of English civility, it may nonetheless have felt like the beginning of the threatened transformation. I do not propose that Spenser feared such a metamorphosis on his own behalf—he may, for all we know, have been obscurely attracted to some of the very things he worked to destroy, though of this attraction our only record is his poetry's fascination with the excess against which it struggles—only that he was haunted by the fact that it had occurred over generations to so many of his countrymen. The enemy for Spenser then is as much a tenacious and surprisingly seductive way of life as it is a military force, and thus alongside a ruthless policy of mass starvation and massacre, he advocates the destruction of native Irish identity.

Spenser is one of the first English writers to have what we may call a field theory of culture, that is, the conception of a nation not simply as an institutional structure or a common race, but as a complex network of beliefs, folk customs, forms of dress, kinship relations, religious mythology, aesthetic norms, and specialized modes of production. Therefore, to *reform* a people one must not simply conquer it—though conquest is an absolute necessity—but eradicate the native culture: in the case of Ireland, eliminate (by force, wherever needed) the carrows, horseboys, jesters, and other "idlers"; transform the mass of the rural population from cowherds with their dangerous freedom of movement to husbandmen; break up the clans or sects; prohibit public meetings, councils, and assemblies; transform Irish art, prohibiting the subversive epics of the bards; make schoolchildren ashamed of their parents' backwardness; discourage English settlers from speaking Irish; prohibit traditional Irish dress; eliminate elections of chiefs, divisible inheritance, and the payment of fines to avoid capital punishment. And always in this immense undertaking, there is the need for constant vigilance and unrelenting pressure, exercised not only upon the wild Irish but upon the civilizing English themselves. "So much," writes Spenser, "can liberty and ill example do" (63) that the threat of seduction is always present, and the first inroad of this seduction is misguided compassion: "Therefore, by all means it must be foreseen and assured that after once entering into this course of reformation, there be afterwards no remorse or drawing back" (110). Pitiless destruction is here not a stain but a virtue; after all, the English themselves had to be brought from barbarism to civility by a similar conquest centuries before, a conquest that must be ever renewed lest the craving for

"liberty and natural freedom" (12) erupt again. The colonial violence inflicted upon the Irish is at the same time the force that
fashions the identity of the English.

We have returned then to the principle of regenerative violence
and thus to the destruction of the Bower of Bliss. The act of tearing
down is the act of fashioning; the promise of the opening stanza of
canto 12—"Now gins this goodly frame of Temperance / Fairely to
rise"—is fulfilled at the close in the inventory of violence:

> But all those pleasant bowres and Pallace braue,
> *Guyon* broke downe, with rigour pittilesse;
> Ne ought their goodly workmanship might saue
> Them from the tempest of his wrathfulnesse,
> But that their blisse he turn'd to balefulness;
> Their groues he feld, their gardins did deface,
> Their arbers spoyle, their Cabinets suppresse,
> Their banket houses burne, their buildings race,
> And of the fairest late, now made the fowlest place.
>
> (2.12.83)

If the totality of the destruction, the calculated absence of "remorse or drawing back," links this episode to the colonial policy of
Lord Grey which Spenser undertook to defend, the language of the
stanza recalls yet another government policy, our third "restoration" of the narrative: the destruction of Catholic Church fur-
nishings. In the *Inventarium monumentorum superstitionis* of 1566,
for example, we may hear repeated echoes of Guyon's acts:

> Imprimis one rood with Mary and John and the rest of
> the painted pictures—burnt . . . .
>
> Item our rood loft—pulled down, sold and defaced . . . .
>
> Item our mass books with the rest of such feigned fables
> and peltering popish books—burnt . . . .
>
> Item 3 altar stones—broken in pieces . . . .[63]

In 1572 Spenser, a student at Pembroke, could have witnessed a
similar scene at nearby Gonville and Caius where the authorities
licensed the destruction of "much popish trumpery." Books and
vestments, holy water stoops and images were "mangled, torn to
pieces, and mutilated"—*discerpta dissecta et lacerata*—before being
consigned to the bonfire.[64]

There is about the Bower of Bliss the taint of a graven image
designed to appeal to the sensual as opposed to the spiritual nature, to turn the wonder and admiration of men away from the

mystery of divine love. In the Bower the love survives only in the uncanny parody of the Pietà suggested by Verdant cradled in Acrasia's arms. It is not surprising then to find a close parallel between the evils of the Bower and the evils attributed to the misuse of religious images. Devotion to the representations of the Madonna and saints deflected men from the vigorous pursuit of the good, enticed them into idleness and effeminacy. With their destruction, as Hugh Latimer writes, men could turn "from lady-ness to Godliness."[65] Statues of the virgin were dismembered by unruly crowds, frescoes were whitewashed over and carvings in "Lady Chapels" were smashed, in order to free men from thrall-dom to what an Elizabethan lawyer calls, in describing the pope, "the witch of the world."[66]

But the art destroyed by Guyon does not pretend to image holy things; it is designed to grace its surroundings, to delight its viewers with its exquisite workmanship. Against such art there could be no charge of idolatry, no invocation of the Deuteronomic injunctions against graven images, unless art itself were idola-trous. And it is precisely this possibility that is suggested by Guyon's iconoclasm, for Acrasia's realm is lavishly described in just those terms which the defenders of poetry in the Renaissance reserved for imagination's noblest achievements. The Bower's art imitates nature, but is privileged to choose only those aspects of nature that correspond to man's ideal visions; its music is so per-fectly melodious and "attempred" that it blends with all of nature in one harmony, so that the whole world seems transformed into a musical "consort"; above all, the calculation and effort that lie behind the manifestation of such perfect beauty are entirely con-cealed:

> And that which all faire workes doth most aggrace,
> The art, which all that wrought, appeared in no place.

"Aggrace" has virtually a technical significance here; Castiglione had suggested in *The Courtier* that the elusive quality of "grace" could be acquired through the practice of *sprezzatura*, "so as to conceal all art and make whatever is done or said appear to be without effort and almost without any thought about it."[67]

Spenser deeply distrusts this aesthetic, even as he seems to pay homage to its central tenets; indeed the concealment of art, its imposition upon an unsuspecting observer, is one of the great recurring evils in *The Faerie Queene*. Acrasia as demonic artist and whore combines the attributes of those other masters of disguise,

Archimago and Duessa.[68] Their evil depends upon the ability to mask and forge, to conceal their satanic artistry; their defeat depends upon the power to unmask, the strength to turn from magic to strenuous virtue. Keith Thomas notes that in the sixteenth and seventeenth centuries the Protestant "emphasis upon the virtues of hard work and application . . . both reflected and helped to create a frame of mind which spurned the cheap solutions offered by magic, not just because they were wicked, but because they were too easy."[69] *Sprezzatura,* which sets out to efface all signs of "hard work and application," is a cult of the "too easy," a kind of aesthetic magic.

But what can Spenser offer in place of this discredited aesthetic? The answer lies in an art that constantly calls attention to its own processes, that includes within itself framing devices and signs of its own createdness. Far from hiding its traces, *The Faerie Queene* announces its status as art object at every turn, in the archaic diction, the use of set pieces, the elaborate sound effects, the very characters and plots of romance. For the allegorical romance is a mode that virtually by definition abjures all concealment; the artist who wishes to hide the fact that he is making a fiction would be ill-advised to write about the Faerie Queene.

If you fear that images may make a blasphemous claim to reality, that they may become idols that you will be compelled to worship, you may smash all images or you may create images that announce themselves at every moment as things made. Thus did the sixteenth-century kabbalists of Safed circumvent the Hebraic injunction against images of the Godhead;[70] their visions are punctuated by reminders that these are merely metaphors, not to be confused with divine reality itself. So too did the more moderate Protestant Reformers retain a version of the Communion, reminding the participants that the ceremony was a symbol and not a celebration of the real presence of God's body. And so does Spenser, in the face of deep anxiety about the impure claims of art, save art for himself and his readers by making its createdness explicit. Images, to be sure, retain their power, as the sensuous description of the Bower of Bliss attests, and Spenser can respond to the charge that his "famous antique history" is merely "th'aboundance of an idle braine . . . and painted forgery" by reminding his readers of the recent discoveries, of "The Indian *Peru,*" "The *Amazons* huge riuer," and "fruitfullest *Virginia*":

> Yet all these were, when no man did them know;
> Yet haue from wisest ages hidden beene:
> And later times things more vnknowne shall show.

When then should witlesse man so much misweene
That nothing is, but that which he hath seene?
What if within the Moones faire shining spheare?
What if in euery other starre vnseene
Of other worldes he happily should heare?
He wonder would much more: yet such to some
     appeare.

(2 Proem 3)

For a moment the work hovers on the brink of asserting its status as a newfound land, but Spenser immediately shatters such an assertion by invoking the gaze of royal power:

And thou, O fairest Princesse vnder sky,
In this faire mirrhour maist behold thy face,
And thine owne realmes in lond of Faery,
And in this antique Image thy great auncestry.

(2 Proem 4)

In an instant the "other world" has been transformed into a mirror; the queen turns her gaze upon a shining sphere hitherto hidden from view and sees her own face, her own realms, her own ancestry. That which threatens to exist independent of religious and secular ideology, that is, of what we believe—"Yet all these were, when no man did them know"—is revealed to be the ideal image of that ideology. And hence it need not be feared or destroyed: iconoclasm gives way to appropriation, violence to colonization. J. H. Elliott remarks that the most significant aspect of the impact of the new world upon the old is its insignificance: men looked at things unseen before, things alien to their own culture, and saw only themselves.[71] Spenser asserts that Faerie Land is a new world, another Peru or Virginia, only so that he may colonize it in the very moment of its discovery. The "other world" becomes mirror becomes aesthetic image, and this transformation of the poem from a thing discovered to a thing made, from existence to the representation of existence is completed with the poet's turn from "vaunt" to apology:

The which O pardon me thus to enfold
In couert vele, and wrap in shadowes light,
That feeble eyes your glory may behold,
Which else could not endure those beames bright,
But would be dazled with exceeding light.

(2 Proem 5)

The queen is deified precisely in the act of denying art's claim to ontological dignity, to the possession or embodiment of reality.

Such embodiment is the characteristic achievement of great drama, of Marlowe and supremely of Shakespeare, whose constant allusions to the fictionality of his creations only serve paradoxically to question the status of everything outside themselves. By contrast, Spenser's profoundly *undramatic* art, in the same movement by which it wards off idolatry, wards off this radical questioning of everything that exists. That is, if art like Shakespeare's realizes the power we glimpsed in Wyatt, the power in Althusser's words, to "make us 'perceive' . . . from *the inside*, by an *internal distance*, the very ideology" in which it is held, Spenserean allegory may be understood as a countermeasure: it opens up an internal distance within art itself by continually referring the reader out to a fixed authority beyond the poem. Spenser's art does not lead us to perceive ideology critically, but rather affirms the existence and inescapable moral power of ideology as that principle of truth toward which art forever yearns. It is art whose status is questioned in Spenser, not ideology; indeed, art is questioned precisely to spare ideology that internal distantiation it undergoes in the work of Shakespeare or Marlowe. In *The Faerie Queene* reality as given by ideology always lies safely outside the bounds of art, in a different realm, distant, infinitely powerful, perfectly good. "The hallmark of Spenserean narration," Paul Alpers acutely observes, "is confidence in locutions which are at the same time understood to be provisional."[72] Both the confidence and the provisionality stem from the externality of true value, order, meaning. For Spenser this is the final colonialism, the colonialism of language, yoked to the service of a reality forever outside itself, dedicated to "the Most High, Mightie, and Magnificent Empresse . . . Elizabeth by the Grace of God Queene of England Fraunce and Ireland and of Virginia, Defendour of the Faith."

Marlowe and the Will to Absolute Play

On 26 June 1586 a small fleet, financed by the Earl of Cumberland, set out from Gravesend for the South Seas. It sailed down the West African coast, sighting Sierra Leone in October, and at this point we may let one of those on board, the merchant John Sarracoll, tell his own story:

> The fourth of November we went on shore to a town of the Negroes, . . . which we found to be but lately built: it was of about two hundred houses, and walled about with mighty great trees, and stakes so thick, that a rat could hardly get in or out. But as it chanced, we came directly upon a port which was not shut up, where we entered with such fierceness, that the people fled all out of the town, which we found to be finely built after their fashion, and the streets of it so intricate that it was difficult for us to find the way out that we came in at. We found their houses and streets so finely and cleanly kept that it was an admiration to us all, for that neither in the houses nor streets was so much dust to be found as would fill an egg shell. We found little in their houses, except some mats, gourds, and some earthen pots. Our men at their departure set the town on fire, and it was burnt (for the most part of it) in a quarter of an hour, the houses being covered with reed and straw.[1]

This passage is atypical, for it lacks the blood bath that usually climaxes these incidents, but it will serve as a reminder of what until recently was called one of the glorious achievements of Renaissance civilization, and it will serve as a convenient bridge from the world of Edmund Spenser to the world of Christopher Marlowe.

What is most striking in Sarracoll's account, of course, is the casual, unexplained violence. Does the merchant feel that the firing of the town needs no explanation? If asked, would he have had one to give? Why does he take care to tell us why the town burned so quickly, but not why it was burned? Is there an aesthetic element in his admiration of the town, so finely built, so intricate, so cleanly kept? And does this admiration conflict with or somehow fuel the destructiveness? If he feels no uneasiness at all, why does he suddenly shift and write not *we* but *our men* set the town on fire? Was there an order or not? And, when he recalls the invasion, why does he think of rats? The questions are all met by the moral blankness that rests like thick snow on Sarracoll's sentences: "The 17th. day of November we departed from Sierra Leona, directing our course for the Straits of Magellan."

If, on returning to England in 1587, the merchant and his associates had gone to see the Lord Admiral's Men perform a new play, *Tamburlaine the Great*, they would have seen an extraordinary meditation on the roots of their own behavior. For despite all the exoticism in Marlowe—Scythian shepherds, Maltese Jews, German magicians—it is his own countrymen that he broods upon and depicts. As in Spenser, though to radically different effect, the "other world" becomes a mirror.[2] If we want to understand the historical matrix of Marlowe's achievement, the analogue to Tamburlaine's restlessness, aesthetic sensitivity, appetite, and violence, we might look not at the playwright's literary sources, not even at the relentless power-hunger of Tudor absolutism, but at the acquisitive energies of English merchants, entrepreneurs, and adventurers, promoters alike of trading companies and theatrical companies.

But what bearing does Marlowe actually have on a passage like the one with which I opened? He is, for a start, fascinated by the idea of the stranger in a strange land. Almost all of his heroes are aliens or wanderers, from Aeneas in Carthage to Barabas in Malta, from Tamburlaine's endless campaigns to Faustus's demonic flights. From his first play to his last, Marlowe is drawn to the idea of physical movement, to the problem of its representation within the narrow confines of the theater. Tamburlaine almost ceaselessly traverses the stage, and when he is not actually on the move, he is imagining campaigns or hearing reports of grueling marches. The obvious effect is to enact the hero's vision of a nature that "Doth teach us all to have aspiring minds" and of the soul that "Wills us to wear ourselves and never rest" (1 *Tam* 2.6.871, 877). But as always in Marlowe, this enactment, this realization on the level of the body in time and space, complicates, qualifies, exposes, and even mocks the abstract conception. For the cumulative effect of this restlessness is not so much heroic as grotesquely comic, if we accept Bergson's classic definition of the comic as the mechanical imposed upon the living. Tamburlaine *is* a machine, a desiring machine that produces violence and death. Menaphon's admiring description begins by making him sound like Leonardo's Vitruvian Man or Michelangelo's David and ends by making him sound like an expensive mechanical device, one of those curious inventions that courtiers gave to the queen at New Year's: a huge, straight, strongly jointed creature with a costly pearl placed between his shoulders, the pearl inscribed with celestial symbols. Once set in motion, this *thing* cannot slow down or change course; it moves at the same frenzied pace until it finally stops.

One further effect of this unvarying movement is that, paradoxically, very little progress seems to be made, despite fervent declarations to the contrary. To be sure, the scenes change, so quickly at times that Marlowe seems to be battering against the boundaries of his own medium: at one moment the stage represents a vast space, then suddenly contracts to a bed, then turns in quick succession into an imperial camp, a burning town, a besieged fortress, a battlefield, a tent. But then all of those spaces seem curiously alike. The relevant contrast is *Antony and Cleopatra* where the restless movement is organized around the deep structural opposition of Rome and Egypt, or *1 Henry IV* where the tavern, the court, and the country are perceived as diversely shaped spaces, spaces that elicit and echo different tones, energies, and even realities. In *Tamburlaine* Marlowe contrives to efface all such differences, as if to insist upon the essential meaninglessness of theatrical space, the vacancy that is the dark side of its power to imitate any place. This vacancy—quite literally, this absence of scenery—is the equivalent in the medium of the theater to the secularization of space, the abolition of qualitative up and down, which for Cassirer is one of the greatest achievements of Renaissance philosophy, the equivalent then to the reduction of the universe to the coordinates of a map:[3]

> Give me a Map, then let me see how much
> Is left for me to conquer all the world,
> That these my boys may finish all my wants.
>
> (2 *Tam* 5.3.4516–18)

Space is transformed into an abstraction, then fed to the appetitive machine. This is the voice of conquest, but it is also the voice of wants never finished and of transcendental homelessness. And though the characters and situations change, that voice is never entirely absent in Marlowe. Barabas does not leave Malta, but he is the quintessential alien: at one point his house is seized and turned into a nunnery, at another he is thrown over the walls of the city, only to rise with the words, "What, all alone?" Edward II should be the very opposite; he is, by his role, the embodiment of the land and its people, but without Gaveston he lives in his own country like an exile. Only in *Doctor Faustus* does there seem to be a significant difference: having signed away his soul and body, Faustus begins a course of restless wandering, but at the close of the twenty-four years, he feels a compulsion to return to Wittenberg.[4] Of course, it is ironic that when a meaningful sense of place finally emerges in Marlowe, it does so only as a place to die. But the irony runs deeper still. For nothing in the covenant or in any of the devil's speeches requires that Faustus has to pay his life where he originally contracted to sell it; the urge is apparently in Faustus, as if he felt there were a fatality in the place he had undertaken his studies, felt it appropriate and even necessary to die there and nowhere else. "O would I had never seen Wittenberg," he despairingly tells his friends. But the play has long before this exposed such a sense of place to radical questioning. To Faustus's insistent demands to know the "where about" of hell, Mephistophilis replies,

> Hell hath no limits, nor is circumscrib'd
> In one self place, for where we are is hell,
> And where hell is, must we ever be.
>
> (567–69)

By implication, Faustus's feeling about Wittenberg is an illusion, one of a network of fictions by which he constitutes his identity and his world. Typically, he refuses to accept the account of a limitless, inner hell, countering with the extraordinary, and in the circumstances, ludicrous "I think hell's a fable." Mephistophilis's quiet response slides from parodic agreement to devastating irony: "Aye, think so still, till experience change thy mind."[5] The experience of which the devil speaks can refer not only to torment after death but to Faustus's life in the remainder of the play: the half-trivial, half-daring exploits, the alternating states of bliss and despair, the questions that are not answered and the answers that bring no real satisfaction, the wanderings that lead nowhere. The chilling line may carry a further suggestion: "Yes, continue to think that hell's a fable, until experience *transforms* your mind." At the heart of this mental transformation is the anguished perception of time as inexorable, space as abstract. In his final soliloquy, Faustus's frenzied invocation to time to stop or slow itself gives way to horrified clarity: "The stars move still, time runs, the clock will strike" (1460). And his appeal to nature—earth, stars, air, ocean—at once to shield him and destroy him is met by silence: space is neutral and unresponsive.

Doctor Faustus then does not contradict but rather realizes intimations about space and time in Marlowe's other plays. That man is homeless, that all places are alike, is linked to man's inner state, to the uncircumscribed hell he carries within him. And this insight returns us to the violence with which we began, the violence of Tamburlaine and of the English merchant and his men. It is not enough to say that their actions are the expression of brute power, though they are certainly that, nor even that they bespeak a compulsive suspicion and hatred that one Elizabethan voyager saw as characteristic of the military mind.[6] For experiencing this limitlessness, this transformation of space and time into abstractions, men do violence as a means of marking boundaries, effecting transformation, signaling closure. To burn a town or to kill all of its inhabitants is to make an end and, in so doing, to give life a shape and a certainty that it would otherwise lack. The great fear, in Barabas's words, is "That I may vanish o'er the earth in air, / And leave no memory that e'er I was" (1.499–500). As the town where Zenocrate dies burns at his command, Tamburlaine proclaims his identity, fixed forever in the heavens by his acts of violence:

> Over my Zenith hang a blazing star,
> That may endure till heaven be dissolv'd,
> Fed with the fresh supply of earthly dregs,
> Theat'ning a death and famine to this land.
> (2 *Tam* 3.2.3196–99)

In this charred soil and the blazing star, Tamburlaine seeks literally to make an enduring mark in the world, to stamp his image on time and space. Similarly, Faustus, by violence not on others but on himself, seeks to give his life a clear fixed shape. To be sure, he speaks of attaining "a world of profit and delight, / Of power, of honor, of omnipotence" (83–84), but perhaps the hidden core of what he seeks is the *limit* of twenty-four years to live, a limit he himself sets and reiterates.[7] Time so marked out should have a quality different from other time, should possess its end: "Now will I make an end immediately," he says, writing with his blood.

But in Marlowe's ironic world, these desperate attempts at boundary and closure produce the opposite effect, reinforcing the condition they are meant to efface. Tamburlaine's violence does not transform space from the abstract to the human, but rather further reduces the world to a map, the very emblem of abstraction:

> I will confute those blind Geographers
> That make a triple region in the world,
> Excluding Regions which I mean to trace,
> And with this pen reduce them to a Map,
> Calling the Provinces, Cities and towns
> After my name and thine *Zenocrate*.
>
> (1 *Tam* 4.4.1715–20)

At Tamburlaine's death, the map still stretches out before him, and nothing bears his name save Marlowe's play (the crucial exception to which we will return).[8] Likewise at his death, pleading for "some end to my incessant pain," Faustus is haunted by eternity: "O no end is limited to damned souls" (1458).

The reasons why attempts at making a mark or an end fail are complex and vary significantly with each play, but one critical link is the feeling in almost all Marlowe's protagonists that they are *using up* experience. This feeling extends to our merchant, John Sarracoll, and his men: they not only visit Sierra Leone, they consume it. Tamburlaine exults in just this power to "Conquer, sack, and utterly consume / Your cities" (2 *Tam* 4.2.3867–68). He even contrives to use up his defeated enemies, transforming Bajazeth into his footstool, the kings of Trebizon and Soria into horses to be discarded, when they are broken-winded, for "fresh horse" (2 *Tam* 5.1.4242). In a bizarrely comic moment, Tamburlaine's son suggests that the kings just captured be released to resume the fight, but Tamburlaine replies, in the language of consumption, "Cherish thy valor still with fresh supplies: / And glut it not with stale and daunted foes" (2 *Tam* 4.1.3761–62). Valor, like any appetite, always demands new food.

Faustus's relationship to knowledge is strikingly similar; in his opening soliloquy he bids farewell to each of his studies in turn as something he has used up. He needs to cherish his mind with fresh supplies, for nothing can be accumulated, nothing saved or savored. And as the remainder of the play makes clear, each of these farewells is an act of destruction: logic, medicine, law, and divinity are not so much rejected as violated. The violence arises not only from the desire to mark boundaries but from the feeling that what one leaves behind, turns away from, *must* no longer exist; that objects endure only for the moment of the act of attention and then are effaced; that the next moment cannot be fully grasped until the last is destroyed. Marlowe writes in the period in which European man embarked on his extraordinary career of consumption, his eager pursuit of knowledge, with one intellectual model after another seized, squeezed dry, and discarded, and his frenzied exhaustion of the world's resources:[9]

> Lo here my sons are all the golden Mines,
> Inestimable drugs and precious stones,
> More worth than *Asia* and the world beside,
> And from th'Antartic Pole, Eastward behold
> As much more land which never was descried,
> Wherein are rocks of Pearl that shine as bright
> As all the Lamps that beautify the Sky,
> And shall I die, and this unconquered?
>   (2 *Tam* 5.3.4544–51)

So fully do we inhabit this construction of reality that most often we see beyond it only in accounts of cultures immensely distant from our own: "The Nuer [writes Evans-Pritchard] have no expression equivalent to 'time' in our language, and they cannot, therefore, as we can, speak of time as though it were something actual, which passes, can be wasted, can be saved, and so forth. I do not think that they ever experience the same feeling of fighting against time or of having to co-ordinate activities with an abstract passage of time because their points of reference are mainly the activities themselves, which are generally of a leisurely character . . . . Nuer are fortunate."[10] Of course, such a conception of time and activity had vanished from Europe long before the sixteenth century, but English Renaissance works, and Marlowe's plays in particular, give voice to a radically intensified sense that time is abstract, uniform, and inhuman. The origins of this sense of time are difficult to locate with any certainty. Puritans in the late sixteenth century were already campaigning vigorously against the medieval doctrine of the unevenness of time, a doctrine that had survived largely intact in the Elizabethan church calendar. They sought, in effect, to desacramentalize time, to discredit and sweep away the dense web of saints' days, "dismal days," seasonal taboos, mystic observances, and folk festivals that gave time a distinct, irregular shape; in its place, they urged a simple, flat routine of six days work and a sabbath rest.[11] Moreover, there seem, in this period, to have been subtle changes in what we may call family time. At one end of the life cycle, traditional youth groups were suppressed or fell into neglect, customs that had allowed adolescents considerable autonomy were overturned, and children were brought under the stricter discipline of the immediate family. At the other end, the Protestant rejection of the doctrine of purgatory eliminated the dead as an "age group," cutting off the living from ritualized communion with their deceased parents and relatives.[12] Such changes might well have contributed to a sense in Marlowe and some of his contemporaries that time is alien, profoundly indifferent to human longing and anxiety. Whatever the case, we certainly find in Marlowe's plays a powerful feeling that time is something to be resisted and a related fear that fulfillment or fruition is impossible. "Why waste you thus the time away?" an impatient Leicester asks Edward II, whose crown he has come to fetch. "Stay a while," Edward replies, "let me be king till night" (2045), whereupon, like Faustus,[13] he struggles vainly to arrest time with incantation. At such moments, Marlowe's celebrated line is itself rich with irony: the rhythms intended to slow time only consume it, magnificent words are spoken and disappear into a void. But it is precisely this sense of the void that compels the characters to speak so powerfully, as if to struggle the more insistently against the enveloping silence.

That the moments of intensest time-consciousness all occur at or near the close of these plays has the effect of making the heroes seem to struggle against *theatrical* time. As Marlowe uses the vacancy of theatrical space to suggest his characters' homelessness, so he uses the curve of theatrical time to suggest their struggle against extinction, in effect against the nothingness into which all characters fall at the end of a play. The pressure of the dramatic medium itself likewise underlies what we may call the *repetition compulsion* of Marlowe's heroes. Tamburlaine no sooner annihilates one army than he sets out to annihilate another, no sooner unharnesses two kings than he hitches up two more. Barabas gains and loses, regains and reloses his wealth, while pursuing a seemingly endless string of revenges and politic murders, including, characteristically, two suitors, two friars, two rulers, and, in effect, two children. In *Edward II* the plot is less overtly episodic, yet even here, after spending the first half of the play alternately embracing and parting from Gaveston, Edward immediately replaces the slain favorite with Spencer Junior and thereby resumes the same pattern, the willful courting of disaster that is finally "rewarded" in the castle cesspool. Finally, as C. L. Barber observes, "Faustus repeatedly moves through a circular pattern, from thinking of the joys of heaven, through despairing of ever possessing them, to embracing magical dominion as a blasphemous substitute."[14] The pattern of action and the complex psychological structure embodied in it vary with each play, but at the deepest level of the medium itself the motivation is the same: the renewal of existence through repetition of the self-constituting act. The character repeats himself in order to continue to be that same character on the stage. Identity is a theatrical invention that must be reiterated if it is to endure.

To grasp the full import of this notion of repetition as self-fashioning, we must understand its relation to the culturally dominant notion of repetition as a warning or memorial, an instrument of civility. In this view recurrent patterns exist in the history of individuals or nations in order to inculcate crucial moral values, passing them from generation to generation.[15] Men are notoriously slow learners and, in their inherent sinfulness, resistant to virtue, but gradually, through repetition, the paradigms may sink in and responsible, God-fearing, obedient subjects may be formed. Accordingly, Tudor monarchs ordered the formal reiteration of the central tenets of the religious and social orthodoxy, carefully specifying the minimum number of times a year these tenets were to be read aloud from the pulpit.[16] Similarly, the punishment of criminals was public, so that the state's power to inflict torment and death could act upon the people as an edifying caution. The high number of such executions reflects not only judicial "massacres"[17] but the attempt to teach through reiterated terror. Each branding or hanging or disemboweling was theatrical in conception and performance, a repeatable admonitory drama enacted on a scaffold before a rapt audience. Those who threatened order, those on whose nature nurture could never stick—the traitor, the vagabond, the homosexual, the thief—were identified and punished accordingly. This idea of the "notable spectacle," the "theater of God's judgments," extended quite naturally to the drama itself, and, indeed, to all of literature which thus takes its rightful place as part of a vast, interlocking system of repetitions, embracing homilies and hangings, royal progresses and rote learning.[18] It is by no means only timeservers who are involved here; a great artist like Spenser, as we have seen, embraces his participation in this system, though, of course, that participation is more complex than most. In Spenser's rich and subtle version of the civilizing process, the apparent repetitions within each book and in *The Faerie Queene* as a whole serve to initiate hero and reader alike into the nuances of each of the virtues, the complex discriminations that a humane moral sensibility entails, while, as we have seen, the shifting resolutions of analogous problems help to shore up values that are threatened by the shape of a prior resolution. The heroes' names and the virtues they embody both exist prior to the experiences chronicled in their books and are fully established by means of those experiences; Spenserean repetition expresses that which is already in some sense real, given by the power that exists outside the poem and that the poem celebrates.

Marlowe seems to have regarded the drama's participation in such a system—an admonitory fiction upholding a moral order—with a blend of obsessive fascination and contemptuous loathing. *Tamburlaine* repeatedly teases its audience with the *form* of the cautionary tale, only to violate the convention. All of the signals of the tragic are produced, but the play stubbornly, radically, refuses to become a tragedy. "The Gods, defenders of the innocent, / Will never prosper your intended drifts" (1 *Tam* 1.2.264–65), declares Zenocrate in act 1 and then promptly falls in love with her captor. With his dying breath, Cosroe curses Tamburlaine—a sure prelude to disaster—but the disaster never occurs. Bajazeth, the king of Arabia, and even Theridamas and Zenocrate have powerful premonitions of the hero's downfall, but he passes from success to success. Tamburlaine is proud, arrogant, and blasphemous; he lusts for power, betrays his allies, overthrows legitimate authority, and threatens the gods; he rises to the top of the wheel of fortune and then steadfastly refuses to budge. Since the dominant ideology no longer insists that rise-and-decline and pride-goes-before-a-fall are unvarying, universal rhythms, we undoubtedly miss some of the shock of Tamburlaine's career, but the play itself invokes those rhythms often enough to surprise us with their failure to materialize.

Having undermined the notion of the cautionary tale in *Tamburlaine*, part 1, Marlowe demolishes it in part 2 in the most unexpected way—by suddenly invoking it. The slaughter of thousands, the murder of his own son, the torture of his royal captives are all without apparent consequence; then Tamburlaine falls ill, and when? When he burns the Koran! The one action which Elizabethan churchmen themselves might have applauded seems to bring down divine vengeance.[19] The effect is not to celebrate the transcendent power of Mohammed but to challenge the habit of mind that looks to heaven for rewards and punishments, that imagines human evil as "the scourge of God." Similarly, in *Doctor*

Faustus, as Max Bluestone observes, the homiletical tradition is continually introduced only to be undermined by dramatic spectacle,[20] while in *Edward II* Marlowe uses the emblematic method of admonitory drama, but uses it to such devastating effect that the audience recoils from it in disgust. Edward's grisly execution is, as orthodox interpreters of the play have correctly insisted, iconographically "appropriate," but this appropriateness can only be established *at the expense of* every complex, sympathetic human feeling evoked by the play. The audience is forced to confront its insistence upon coherence, and the result is a profound questioning of the way audiences constitute meaning in the theater and in life.[21]

There is a questioning too of the way *individuals* are constituted in the theater and in life. Marlowe's heroes fashion themselves not in loving submission to an absolute authority but in self-conscious opposition: Tamburlaine against hierarchy, Barabas against Christianity, Faustus against God, Edward against the sanctified rites and responsibilities of kingship, marriage, and manhood. And where identity in More, Tyndale, Wyatt, and Spenser had been achieved through an attack upon something perceived as alien and threatening, in Marlowe it is achieved through a subversive identification with the alien. Marlowe's strategy of subversion is seen most clearly in *The Jew of Malta,* which, for this reason, I propose to consider in some detail. For Marlowe, as for Shakespeare, the figure of the Jew is useful as a powerful rhetorical device, an embodiment for a Christian audience of all they loathe and fear, all that appears stubbornly, irreducibly different. Introduced by Machiavel, the stock type of demonic villainy, Barabas enters already trailing clouds of ignominy, already a "marked case." But while never relinquishing the anti-Semitic stereotype and the conventional motif of the villain-undone-by-his-villainy, Marlowe quickly suggests that the Jew is not the exception to but rather the true representative of his society. Though he begins with a paean to liquid assets, Barabas is not primarily a usurer, set off by his hated occupation from the rest of the community, but a great merchant, sending his argosies around the world exactly as Shakespeare's much loved Antonio does. His pursuit of wealth does not mark him out but rather establishes him—if anything, rather respectably—in the midst of all the other forces in the play: the Turks exacting tribute from the Christians, the Christians expropriating money from the Jews, the convent profiting from these expropriations, religious orders competing for wealthy converts, the prostitute plying her trade and the blackmailer his. When the Governor of Malta asks the Turkish "Bashaw," "What wind drives you thus into *Malta* road?" the latter replies with perfect frankness, "The wind that bloweth all the world besides, / Desire of gold" (3.1421–23). Barabas's own desire of gold, so eloquently voiced at the start and vividly enacted in the scene in which he hugs his money bags, is the glowing core of that passion which fires all the characters. To be sure, other values are expressed—love, faith, and honor—but as private values these are revealed to be hopelessly fragile, while as public values they are revealed to be mere screens for powerful economic forces. Thus, on the one hand, Abigail, Don Mathias, and the nuns are killed off with remarkable ease and, in effect, with the complicity of the laughing audience. (The audience at the Royal Shakespeare Company's brilliant 1964 production roared with delight when the poisoned nuns came tumbling out of the house.)[22] On the other hand, the public invocation of Christian ethics or knightly honor is always linked by Marlowe to baser motives. The knights concern themselves with Barabas's "inherent sin" only at the moment when they are about to preach him out of his possessions, while the decision to resist the "barbarous misbelieving *Turks*" facilitates all too easily the sale into slavery of a shipload of Turkish captives. The religious and political ideology that seems at first to govern Christian attitudes toward infidels in fact does nothing of the sort; this ideology is clearly subordinated to considerations of profit.

It is because of the primacy of money that Barabas, for all the contempt heaped upon him, is seen as the dominant spirit of the play, its most energetic and inventive force. A victim at the level of religion and political power, he is, in effect, emancipated at the level of civil society, emancipated in Marx's contemptuous sense of the word in his essay *On the Jewish Question:* "The Jew has emancipated himself in a Jewish manner, not only by acquiring the power of money, but also because *money* has become, through him and also apart from him, a world power, while the practical Jewish spirit has become the practical spirit of the Christian nations. The Jews have emancipated themselves in so far as the Christians have become Jews."[23] Barabas's avarice, egotism, duplicity, and murderous cunning do not signal his exclusion from the world of Malta but his central place within it. His "Judaism" is, again in Marx's words, "a universal *antisocial* element of the *present time*" (34).

For neither Marlowe nor Marx does this recognition signal a turning away from Jew-baiting; if anything, Jew-baiting is intensified even as the hostility it excites is directed as well against Christian society. Thus Marlowe never discredits anti-Semitism, but he does discredit early in the play a "Christian" social concern that might otherwise have been used to counter a specifically Jewish antisocial element. When the Governor of Malta seizes the wealth of the Jews on the grounds that it is "better one want for a common good, / Then many perish for a private man" (1.331–32), an audience at all familiar with the New Testament will hear in these words echoes not of Christ but of Caiaphas and, a few lines further on, of Pilate.[24] There are, to be sure, moments of social solidarity—as when the Jews gather around Barabas to comfort him or when Ferneze and Katherine together mourn the death of their sons—but they are brief and ineffectual. The true emblem of the society of the play is the slave market, where "Every one's price is written on his back" (2.764).[25] Here in the marketplace men are literally turned, in Marx's phrase, "into *alienable,* saleable objects, in thrall to egoistic need and huckstering" (39). And at this level of society, the religious and political barriers fall away: the Jew buys a Turk at the Christian slave market. Such is the triumph of civil society.

For Marlowe the dominant mode of perceiving the world, in a society hag-ridden by the power of money and given over to the slave market, is *contempt,* contempt aroused in the beholders of such a society and, as important, governing the behavior of those who bring it into being and function within it. This is Barabas's constant attitude, virtually his signature; his withering scorn lights not only on the Christian rulers of Malta ("thus slaves will learn," he sneers, when the defeated Governor is forced into submission [5.2150]), but on his daughter's suitor ("the slave looks like a hog's cheek new sing'd" [2.803]), his daughter ("An *Hebrew* born, and would become a Christian. / *Cazzo, diabolo*" [4.1527–28]), his slave Ithamore ("Thus every villain ambles after wealth / Although he ne'er be richer than in hope" [3.1354–55]), the Turks ("How the slave jeers at him," observes the Governor of Barabas greeting Calymath [5.2339]), the pimp, Pilia-Borza ("a shaggy, totter'd staring slave" [4.1858]), his fellow Jews ("See the simplicity of these base slaves" [1.448]), and even, when he has blundered by making the poison too weak, himself ("What a damn'd slave was I" [5.2025]). Barabas's frequent asides assure us that he is feeling contempt even when he is not openly expressing it, and the reiteration of the derogatory epithet *slave* firmly anchors this contempt in the structure of relations that governs the play. Barabas's liberality in bestowing this epithet—from the

Governor to the pimp—reflects the extraordinary unity of the structure, its intricate series of mirror images: Pilia-Borza's extortion racket is repeated at the "national" level in the extortion of the Jewish community's wealth and at the international level in the Turkish extortion of the Christian tribute. The play depicts Renaissance international relations as a kind of glorified gangsterism, a vast "protection" racket.[26]

At all levels of society in Marlowe's play, behind each version of the racket (and making it possible) is violence or the threat of violence, and so here too Barabas's murderousness is presented as at once a characteristic of his accursed tribe and the expression of a universal phenomenon. This expression, to be sure, is extravagant—he is responsible, directly or indirectly, for the deaths of Mathias, Lodowick, Abigail, Pilia-Borza, Bellamira, Ithamore, Friar Jacamo, Friar Barnadine, and innumerable poisoned nuns and massacred soldiers—and, as we shall see, this extravagance helps to account for the fact that in the last analysis Barabas cannot be assimilated to his world. But if Marlowe ultimately veers away from so entirely sociological a conception, it is important to grasp the extent to which Barabas expresses in extreme, unmediated form the motives that have been partially disguised by the spiritual humbug of Christianity, indeed the extent to which Barabas is *brought into being* by the Christian society around him. His actions are always *responses* to the initiatives of others: not only is the plot of the whole play set in motion by the Governor's expropriation of his wealth, but each of Barabas's particular plots is a reaction to what he perceives as a provocation or a threat. Only his final stratagem—the betrayal of the Turks—seems an exception, since the Jew is for once in power, but even this fatal blunder is a response to his perfectly sound perception that "*Malta* hates me, and in hating me / My life's in danger" (5.2131–32).

Barabas's apparent passivity sits strangely with his entire domination of the spirit of the play, and once again, we may turn to Marx for an explication of Marlowe's rhetorical strategy: "Judaism could not create a new world. It could only bring the new creations and conditions of the world within its own sphere of activity, because practical need, the spirit of which is self-interest, is always passive, cannot expand at will, but *finds* itself extended as a result of the continued development of society" (38). Though the Jew is identified here with the spirit of egotism and selfish need, his success is credited to the triumph of Christianity which "objectifies" and hence alienates all national, natural, moral, and theoretical relationships, dissolving "the human world into a world of atomistic, antagonistic individuals" (39). The concrete emblem of this alienation in Marlowe is the slave market; its ideological expression is the religious chauvinism that sees Jews as inherently sinful, Turks as barbarous misbelievers.

The Jew of Malta ends on a powerfully ironic note of this "spiritual egotism" (to use Marx's phrase) when the Governor celebrates the treacherous destruction of Barabas and the Turks by giving due praise "Neither to Fate nor Fortune, but to Heaven" (5. 2410). (Once again, the Royal Shakespeare Company's audience guffawed at this bit of hypocritical sententiousness.) But we do not have to wait until the closing moments of the play to witness the Christian practice of alienation. It is, as I have suggested, present throughout, and nowhere more powerfully than in the figure of Barabas himself. For not only are Barabas's actions called forth by Christian actions, but his identity itself is to a great extent the product of the Christian conception of a Jew's identity. This is not entirely the case: Marlowe invokes an "indigenous" Judaism in the wicked parody of the materialism of Job and in Barabas's repeated invocation of Hebraic exclusivism ("these swine-eating Christians," etc.). Nevertheless Barabas's sense of himself, his characteristic response to the world, and his self-presentation are very largely constructed out of the materials of the dominant, Christian culture. This is nowhere more evident than in his speech, which is virtually composed of hard little aphorisms, cynical adages, worldly maxims—all the neatly packaged nastiness of his society. Where Shylock is differentiated from the Christians even in his use of the common language, Barabas is inscribed at the center of the society of the play, a society whose speech is a tissue of aphorisms. Whole speeches are little more than strings of sayings: maxims are exchanged, inverted, employed as weapons; the characters enact and even deliberately "stage" proverbs (with all of the manic energy of Breughel's "Netherlandish Proverbs"). When Barabas, intent upon poisoning the nuns, calls for the pot of rice porridge, Ithamore carries it to him along with a ladle, explaining that since "the proverb says, he that eats with the devil had need of a long spoon, I have brought you a ladle" (3.1360–62).[27] And when Barabas and Ithamore together strangle Friar Barnadine, to whom Abigail has revealed their crimes in confession, the Jew explains, "Blame not us but the proverb, Confess and be hang'd" (4.1655).

Proverbs in *The Jew of Malta* are a kind of currency, the compressed ideological wealth of society, the money of the mind.

Their terseness corresponds to that concentration of material wealth that Barabas celebrates: "Infinite riches in a little room." Barabas's own store of these ideological riches comprises the most cynical and self-serving portion:

Who is honor'd now but for his wealth?
(1.151)

Ego mihimet sum semper proximus.
(1.228)

A reaching thought will search his deepest wits,
And cast with cunning for the time to come.
(1.455–56)

             . . . in extremity
We ought to make bar of no policy.
(1.507–8)

                . . . Religion
Hides many mischiefs from suspicion.
(1.519–20)

Now will I show my self to have more of the Serpent
Than the Dove; that is, more knave than fool.
(2.797–98)

Faith is not to be held with Heretics.
(1.1076)

For he that liveth in Authority,
And neither gets him friends, nor fills his bags,
Lives like the Ass that *Æsop* speaketh of,
That labors with a load of bread and wine,
And leaves it off to snap on Thistle tops.
(5.2139–43)

For so I live, perish may all the world.
(5.2292)

This is not the exotic language of the Jews but the product of the whole society, indeed, its most familiar and ordinary face. And as the essence of proverbs is their anonymity, the effect of their recurrent use by Barabas is to render him more and more typical, to *de-individualize* him. This is, of course, the opposite of the usual process. Most dramatic characters—Shylock is the appropriate example—accumulate identity in the course of their play; Barabas loses it. He is never again as distinct and unique an individual as he is in the first moments:

Go tell 'em the Jew of *Malta* sent thee, man:
Tush, who amongst 'em knows not *Barabas?*

(1.102–3)

Even his account of his past—killing sick people or poisoning wells—tends to make him more vague and unreal, accommodating him to an abstract, anti-Semitic fantasy of a Jew's past.

In this effacement of Barabas's identity, Marlowe reflects not only upon his culture's bad faith, its insistence upon the otherness of what is in fact its own essence, but also upon the tragic limitations of rebellion against this culture. Like all of Marlowe's heroes, Barabas defines himself by negating cherished values, but his identity is itself, as we have seen, a social construction, a fiction composed of the sleaziest materials in his culture.[28] If Marlowe questions the notion of literature as cautionary tale, if his very use of admonitory fictions subverts them, he cannot dismiss the immense power of the social system in which such fictions play their part. Indeed the attempts to challenge this system—Tamburlaine's world conquests, Barabas's Machiavellianism, Edward's homosexuality, and Faustus's skepticism—are subjected to relentless probing and exposed as unwitting tributes to that social construction of identity against which they struggle. For if the heart of Renaissance orthodoxy is a vast system of repetitions in which disciplinary paradigms are established and men gradually learn what to desire and what to fear, the Marlovian rebels and skeptics remain embedded within this orthodoxy: they simply reverse the paradigms and embrace what the society brands as evil. In so doing, they imagine themselves set in diametrical opposition to their society where in fact they have unwittingly accepted its crucial structural elements. For the crucial issue is not man's power to disobey, but the characteristic modes of desire and fear produced by a given society, and the rebellious heroes never depart from those modes. With their passionate insistence on will, Marlowe's protagonists anticipate the perception that human history is the product of men themselves, but they also anticipate the perception that this product is shaped, in Lukács phrase, by forces that arise from their relations with each other and which have escaped their control.[29] As Marx writes in a famous passage in *The Eighteenth Brumaire of Louis Bonaparte:* "Men make their own history, but they do not make it just as they please; they do not make it under circumstances chosen by themselves, but under circumstances directly found, given and transmitted from the past. The tradition of all the dead generations weighs like a nightmare on the brain of the living. And just when they seem engaged in revolutionising themselves and things, in creating something entirely new, precisely in such epochs of revolutionary crisis they anxiously conjure up the spirits of the past."[30]

Marlowe's protagonists rebel against orthodoxy, but they do not do so just as they please; their acts of negation not only conjure up the order they would destroy but seem at times to be themselves conjured up by that very order. *The Jew of Malta* continually demonstrates, as we have seen, how close Barabas is to the gentile world against which he is set; if this demonstration exposes the hypocrisy of that world, it cuts against the Jew as well, for his loathing must be repeatedly directed against a version of himself, until at the close he boils in the pot he has prepared for his enemy. Similarly, Faustus's whole career binds him ever more closely to that Christian conception of the body and the mind, that divinity, he thought he was decisively rejecting. He dreams of living "in all voluptuousness" (337), but his pleasures are parodic versions of Holy Communion.[31]

Of all Marlowe's heroes, only Tamburlaine comes close to defining himself in genuinely radical opposition to the order against which he wars; he does so by virtue of a powerful if sporadic materialism that Marlowe seems to have compounded out of a strange blend of scholarly and popular heterodox elements in his culture. From academic life, Marlowe could draw upon Lucretian naturalism, with its vision of a cosmos formed by the restless clash of opposing elements; from popular culture—the culture we glimpse fleetingly in ballads, trial records, and the like—he could draw upon an unillusioned reduction of ideology to power and of power to violence.[32] From both he could derive the remarkable centrality of the body that is the play's obsessive preoccupation. The action of *Tamburlaine*—endless stabbing, chaining, drowning, lancing, hanging—is almost entirely directed toward what we may call a theatrical proof of the body's existence. In what seems a zany parody of Christ and Doubting Thomas, Tamburlaine at one point wounds himself for the edification of his sons: "Come boys, and with your fingers search my wound, / And in my blood wash all your hands at once" (2 *Tam* 3.2.3316–17). Likewise, the dying in the play—and they are legion—speak of themselves in an oddly detailed, almost clinical language, as if to insist upon the corporeal reality of their experience:

> I feel my liver pierced, and all my veins,
> That there begin and nourish every part,

> Mangled and torn, and all my entrails bathed
> In blood that straineth from their orifex.
>
> (2 *Tam* 4.3417–20)

Yet even here, I would argue, the movement toward a truly radical alternative is thwarted by the orthodoxy against which it struggles. The materialist rejection of transcendence is belied by Tamburlaine's single-minded commitment to "princely deeds" of violence. The body is affirmed only in wounding and destroying it, and this aggression ironically generates the odd note of detachment—bodilessness—that characterizes even those lines I have just quoted. A different attitude toward the flesh—sensual enjoyment, self-protection, tolerant acceptance, ease—is explicitly attacked and killed in the figure of Tamburlaine's "cowardly" (and remarkably sympathetic) son Calyphas. Tamburlaine stabs Calyphas because the "effeminate brat" possesses

> A form not meet to give that subject essence
> Whose matter is the flesh of Tamburlaine,
> Wherein an incorporeal spirit moves.
>
> (2 *Tam* 4.1.3786–88)

The Aristotelian language of the Schoolmen here signals the operation, within the bizarre and barbaric scene, of precisely those conservative principles against which Tamburlaine had seemed to be set, just as moments later the former Scythian shepherd can speak of plaguing "such peasants as resist in me / The power of heaven's eternal majesty" (2 *Tam* 4.1.3831–32).

Tamburlaine rebels against hierarchy, legitimacy, the whole established order of things, and to what end? To reach, as he declares, "The sweet fruition of an earthly crown." *Earthly* tantalizingly suggests a materialist alternative to the transcendental authority upon which all the "legitimate" kings in the play base their power, but the suggestion is not realized. Theridimas's response to Tamburlaine's declaration of purpose sounds for an instant as if it were about to confirm such an alternative, but then by a trick of syntax it veers away:

> And that made me to join with Tamburlaine,
> For he is gross and like the massy earth
> That moves not upwards, nor by princely deeds
> Doth mean to soar above the highest sort.
>
> (1 *Tam* 2.6.881–84)

Tamburlaine's will is immeasurably stronger, but its object is essentially the same as that of Mycetes, Cosroe, Bajazeth, or any of

the other princelings who strut around the stage. Part 1 ends not in
an act of revolt but in the supreme gesture of legitimacy, a proper
marriage, with the Scourge of God earnestly assuring his father-
in-law of Zenocrate's unblemished chastity. The close of part 2
may seem closer to an act of radical freedom—

> Come, let us march against the powers of heaven
> And set black streamers in the firmament
> To signify the slaughter of the gods—
>
> (2 *Tam* 5.3.4440–42)

but, as in *Faustus*, the blasphemy pays homage to the power it
insults. In just this way, several years after Marlowe wrote his
play, an illiterate visionary, condemned to death for claiming to be
Christ come in judgment upon the queen and her councillors,
demanded on the scaffold that God deliver him from his enemies:
"If not, I will fire the heavens, and tear thee from thy throne with
my hands."[33] Such acts of aggression are spectacular, but they are
ultimately bound in by the orthodoxy against which they revolt.

Marlowe stands apart then from both orthodoxy and skepticism;
he calls into question the theory of literature and history as repeatable moral lessons, and he calls into question his age's characteristic mode of rejecting those lessons. But how does he himself
understand his characters' motivation, the force that compels them
to repeat the same actions again and again? The answer, as I have
already suggested, lies in their will to self-fashioning. Marlowe's
heroes struggle to invent themselves; they stand, in Coriolanus's
phrase, "As if a man were author of himself / And knew no other
kin" (5.3.36–37). Shakespeare characteristically forces his very
Marlovian hero to reach out and grasp his mother's hand; in Marlowe's plays, with the exception of *Dido Queen of Carthage,* we
never see and scarcely even hear of the hero's parents. Tamburlaine is the son of nameless "paltry" Scythians, Faustus of "parents base of stock" (12), and Barabas, so far as we can tell, of no
one at all. (Even in *Edward II,* where an emphasis on parentage
would seem unavoidable, there is scant mention of Edward I.) The
family is at the center of most Elizabethan and Jacobean drama as
it is at the center of the period's economic and social structure;[34] in
Marlowe it is something to be neglected, despised, or violated.
Two of Marlowe's heroes kill their children without a trace of
remorse; most prefer male friendships to marriage or kinship
bonds; all insist upon free choice in determining their intimate
relations. Upon his father's death, Edward immediately sends for
Gaveston; Barabas adopts Ithamore in place of Abigail; Faustus

cleaves to his sweet Mephistophilis; and, in a more passionate love scene than any with Zenocrate, Tamburlaine wins the ardent loyalty of Theridamas.

The effect is to dissolve the structure of sacramental and blood relations that normally determine identity in this period and to render the heroes virtually autochthonous, their names and identities given by no one but themselves. Indeed self-naming is a major enterprise in these plays, repeated over and over again as if the hero continues to exist only by virtue of constantly renewed acts of will. Augustine had written in *The City of God* that "if God were to withdraw what we may call his 'constructive power' from existing things, they would cease to exist, just as they did not exist before they were made."[35] In the neutrality of time and space that characterizes Marlowe's world, this "constructive power" must exist within the hero himself; if it should fail for an instant he would fall into nothingness, become, in Barabas's words, "a senseless lump of clay / That will with every water wash to dirt" (1.450–51). Hence the hero's compulsion to repeat his name and his actions, a compulsion Marlowe links to the drama itself. The hero's re-presentations fade into the reiterated performances of the play.

If Marlowe's protagonists fashion themselves, they are, as we have seen, compelled to use only those forms and materials produced by the structure of relations in their particular, quite distinct worlds. We watch Tamburlaine construct himself out of phrases picked up or overheard: "And ride in triumph through Persepolis" (1 *Tam* 2.5.754) or "I that am term'd the Scourge and Wrath of God" (1 *Tam* 3.3.1142). Like the gold taken from unwary travelers or the troops lured away from other princes, Tamburlaine's identity is something *appropriated*, seized from others.[36] Even Edward II, with his greater psychological complexity, can only clothe himself in the metaphors available to this station, though these metaphors—the "Imperial Lion," for example—often seem little applicable. And the most haunting instance in Marlowe of this self-fashioning by quotation or appropriation occurs in *Doctor Faustus*, when the hero concludes the signing of the fatal deed with the words "*Consummatum est*" (515).

To unfold the significance of this repetition of Christ's dying words, we must restore them to their context in the Gospel of John:

> After this, Jesus knowing that all things were now accomplished, that the Scripture might be fulfilled, saith, I thirst. Now there was set a vessel full of vinegar: and

> they filled a sponge with vinegar, and put it upon hys-
> sop, and put it to his mouth. When Jesus therefore had
> received the vinegar, he said, It is finished [Consum-
> matum est]: and he bowed his head, and gave up the
> ghost. (19:28–30)[37]

As it is written in psalm 69, "and in my thirst they gave me
vinegar to drink," so it is fulfilled; Christ's thirst is not identical to
the body's normal longing for drink, but an *enactment* of that
longing so that he may fully accomplish the role darkly prefigured
in the Old Testament. The drink of vinegar is the final structural
element in the realization of his identity. Faustus's use of Christ's
words then evokes the archetypal act of role-taking; by reenacting
the moment in which Christ acknowledges the fulfillment of his
being, the magician hopes to touch upon the primal springs of
identity itself. But whatever identity Faustus can thereby achieve
is limited to the status of brilliant parody. His blasphemy is the
uncanny expression of a perverse, despairing faith, an appropriation to himself of the most solemn and momentous words available in his culture to mark the decisive boundary in his life, an
ambiguous equation of himself with Christ, first as God, then as
dying man.

"*Consummatum est*" is the culmination of Faustus's fantasies of
making an end, and hence a suicide that demonically parodies
Christ's self-sacrifice. But in the Gospel, as we have seen, the
words are a true end; they are spoken at the moment of fulfillment
and death. In *Doctor Faustus* they are rather a beginning, spoken at
the moment Faustus is embarking on his bargain. Unlike Christ,
who is his own transcendent object, and whose career is precisely
the realization of himself, Faustus, and all of Marlowe's self-
fashioning heroes, must posit an object in order to exist. Naming
oneself is not enough; one must also name and pursue a goal. And
if both the self and object so constituted are tragically bounded by
the dominant ideology against which they vainly struggle, Marlowe's heroes nevertheless manifest a theatrical energy that
distinguishes their words as well as their actions from the sur-
rounding society. If the audience's perception of radical difference
gives way to a perception of subversive identity, that too in its
turn gives way: in the *excessive* quality of Marlowe's heroes, in
their histrionic extremism, lies that which distinguishes their
self-fashioning acts from the society around them. The Turks,
friars, and Christian knights may all be driven by acquisitive desire, but only Barabas can speak of "Infinite riches in a little

room," only he has the capacity for what one must call aesthetic experience:

> Bags of fiery *Opals, Sapphires, Amethysts,*
> *Jacinths,* hard *Topaz,* grass-green *Emeralds,*
> Beauteous *Rubies,* sparkling *Diamonds,*
> And seld-seen costly stones . . . .
>
> (1.60–63)

Similarly, Theridimas may declare that "A God is not so glorious as a King," but when he is asked if he himself would be a king, he replies, "Nay, though I praise it, I can live without it" (1 *Tam* 2.5.771). Tamburlaine cannot live without it, and his reward is not only "The sweet fruition of an earthly crown" but what Plato's rival Gorgias conceives as "the magic violence of speech."[38]

It is this Gorgian conception of rhetoric, and not the Platonic or Aristotelian, that is borne out in Marlowe's heroes. For Gorgias man is forever cut off from the knowledge of being, forever locked in the partial, the contradictory, and the irrational. If anything exists, he writes, it is both incomprehensible and incommunicable, for "that which we communicate is speech, and speech is not the same thing as the things that exist."[39] This tragic epistemological distance is never bridged; instead, through the power of language men construct deceptions in which and for which they live. Gorgias held that deception—*apate*—is the very essence of the creative imagination: the tragic artist exceeds his peers in the power to deceive. Such a conception of art does not preclude its claim to strip away fraud, since tragedy "with its myths and emotions has created a deception such that its successful practitioner is nearer to reality than the unsuccessful, and the man who lets himself be deceived is wiser than he who does not."[40] In *The Jew of Malta* Barabas the deceiver gives us his own version of this aesthetic: "A counterfeit profession," he tells his daughter, "is better / Than unseen hypocrisy" (1.531–32). In the long run, the play challenges this conviction, at least from the point of view of survival: the Governor, who is the very embodiment of "unseen hypocrisy" eventually triumphs over the Jew's "counterfeit profession." But Marlowe uses the distinction to direct the audience's allegiance toward Barabas; to lie and to know that one is lying seems more attractive, more aesthetically pleasing, and more moral even, than to lie and believe that one is telling the truth.

The ethical basis of such a discrimination does not bear scrutiny; what matters is that the audience becomes Barabas's accomplice. And the pact is affirmed over and over again in Barabas's frequent, malevolently comic asides:

> LODOWICK Good *Barabas,* glance not at our holy Nuns.
> BARABAS No, but I do it through a burning zeal,
>   *Hoping ere long to set the house a fire.* [Aside]
>   (2.849–51)

Years ago, in Naples, I watched a deft pickpocket lifting a camera from a tourist's shoulder-bag and replacing it instantaneously with a rock of equal weight. The thief spotted me watching but did not run away—instead he winked, and I was frozen in mute complicity. The audience's conventional silence becomes in *The Jew of Malta* the silence of the passive accomplice, winked at by his fellow criminal. Such a relationship is, of course, itself conventional. The Jew has for the audience something of the attractiveness of the wily, misused slave in Roman comedy, always on the brink of disaster, always revealed to have a trick or two up his sleeve. The mythic core of this character's endless resourcefulness is what Nashe calls "stage-like resurrection," and, though Barabas is destined for a darker end, he is granted at least one such moment: thrown over the city walls and left for dead, he springs up full of scheming energy.[41] At this moment, as elsewhere in the play, the audience waits expectantly for Barabas's recovery, *wills* his continued existence, and hence identifies with him.

Barabas first wins the audience to him by means of the incantatory power of his language, and it is through this power too that Faustus conjures up the Prince of Deceptions and that Tamburlaine makes his entire life into a project, transforming himself into an elemental, destructive force, driving irresistibly forward: "For Will and Shall best fitteth Tamburlaine" (1 *Tam* 3.3.1139). He collapses all the senses of these verbs—intention, command, prophecy, resolution, and simple futurity—into his monomaniacal project. All of Marlowe's heroes seem similarly obsessed, and the result of their passionate willing, their insistent, reiterated naming of themselves and their objects, is that they become more intensely real to us, more present, than any of the other characters. This is only to say that they are the protagonists, but once again Marlowe relates the shape of the medium itself to the central experience of the plays; his heroes seem determined to realize the Idea of themselves as dramatic heroes.[42] There is a parallel in Spenser's Malbecco who is so completely what he is—in this case, so fanatically jealous—that he becomes the allegorical incarnation of Jealousy itself. But where this self-realization in Spenser is Platonic, in Marlowe it is Gorgian—that is, Platonism is undermined by the presence of the theater itself, the unavoidable distance between the particular actor and his role, the insistent awareness in audience and players alike of illusion.

Within the plays this awareness is intensified by the difficulties the characters experience in sustaining their lives as projects, by that constant reiteration to which, as we have seen, they are bound. For even as no two performances or readings of a text are exactly the same, so the repeated acts of self-fashioning are never absolutely identical; indeed as Gilles Deleuze has recently observed, we can only speak of repetition by reference to the difference or change that it causes in the mind that contemplates it.[43] The result is that the objects of desire, at first so clearly defined, so avidly pursued, gradually lose their sharp outlines and become more and more like mirages. Faustus speaks endlessly of his appetite, his desire to be glutted, ravished, consumed, but what is it exactly that he wants? By the end of the play it is clear that knowledge, voluptuousness, and power are each mere approximations of the goal for which he sells his soul and body; what that goal is remains maddeningly unclear. "Mine own fantasy / . . . will receive no object" (136–37), he tells Valdes and Cornelius, in a phrase that could stand as the play's epigraph. At first Barabas seems a simpler case: he wants wealth, though there is an unsettling equivocation between the desire for wealth as power and security and desire for wealth as an aesthetic, even metaphysical gratification. But the rest of the play does not bear out this desire as the center of Barabas's being: money is not finally the jealous God of the Jew of Malta. He seeks rather, at any cost, to revenge himself on the Christians. Or so we think until he plots to destroy the Turks and restore the Christians to power. Well then, he wants always to serve his own self-interest: *Ego mihimet sum semper proximus* (1.228). But where exactly is the self whose interests he serves? Even the Latin tag betrays an ominous self-distance: "I am always my own neighbor," or even, "I am always *next* to myself." Edward II is no clearer. He loves Gaveston, but why? "Because he loves me more than all the world" (372). The desire returns from its object, out there in the world, to the self, a self that is nonetheless exceedingly unstable. When Gaveston is killed, Edward has within seconds adopted someone else: the will exists, but the object of the will is little more than an illusion. Even Tamburlaine, with his firm declaration of a goal, becomes ever more equivocal.

"The sweet fruition of an earthly crown" turns out not to be what it first appears—the acquisition of kingship—for Tamburlaine continues his restless pursuit long after this acquisition. His goal then is power which is graphically depicted as the ability to transform virgins with blubbered cheeks into slaughtered carcasses. But when Tamburlaine views the corpses he has made and defines this object for himself, it immediately becomes something else, a mirror reflecting yet another goal:

> All sights of power to grace my victory:
> And such are objects fit for *Tamburlaine*,
> Wherein as in a mirror may be seen,
> His honor, that consists in shedding blood.
> (1 *Tam* 5.2.2256–59)[44]

It is Tamburlaine, in his celebrated speech "What is beauty sayeth my sufferings then?" (1 *Tam* 5.2.1941ff.), who gives the whole problem of reaching a desired end its clearest formal expression in Marlowe: beauty, like all the goals pursued by the playwright's heroes, always hovers just beyond the reach of human thought and expression. The problem of elusiveness is one of the major preoccupations of Renaissance thinkers from the most moderate to the most radical, from the judicious Hooker to the splendidly injudicious Bruno.[45] Marlowe is deeply influenced by this contemporary thought, but he subtly shifts the emphasis from the infinity that draws men beyond what they possess to the problem of the human will, the difficulty men experience in truly wanting anything. It is a commonplace that for Saint Augustine the essence of evil is that anything should be "sought for itself, whereas things should be sought only in terms of the search for God."[46] Marlowe's heroes seem at first to embrace such evil: they freely proclaim their immense hunger for something which takes on the status of a personal absolute, and they relentlessly pursue this absolute. The more threatening an obstacle in their path, the more determined they are to obliterate or overreach it: I long for, I burn, I will. But, as we have seen, we are never fully convinced by these noisy demonstrations of single-minded appetite. It is as if Marlowe's heroes wanted to be wholly perverse, in Augustine's sense, but were incapable of such perversity, as if they could not finally desire anything for itself. For Hooker and Bruno alike, this inability arises from the existence of transcendent goals—it is a proof of the existence of God; for Marlowe it springs from the suspicion that all objects of desire are fictions, theatrical illusions shaped by human subjects. And those subjects are themselves fictions, fashioned in reiterated acts of self-naming. The problem is already understood in its full complexity by Montaigne, but, as Auerbach observes, "his irony, his dislike of big words, his calm way of being profoundly at ease with himself, prevent him from pushing on beyond the limits of the problematic and into the realm of the tragic."[47] Marlowe, whose life suggests the very opposite of that "peculiar equilibrium" that distinguishes Montaigne, rushes to embrace the tragic with a strange eagerness.

Man can only exist in the world by fashioning for himself a name and an object, but these, as Marlowe and Montaigne understood, are both fictions. No particular name or object can entirely satisfy one's inner energy demanding to be expressed or fill so completely the potential of one's consciousness that all longings are quelled, all intimations of unreality silenced. As we have seen in the controversy between More and Tyndale, Protestant and Catholic polemicists demonstrated brilliantly how each other's religion—the very anchor of reality for millions of souls—was a cunning theatrical illusion, a demonic fantasy, a piece of poetry. Each conducted this unmasking, of course, in the name of the *real* religious truth, but the collective effect upon a skeptical intellect like Marlowe's seems to have been devastating. And it was not only the religious dismantling of reality to which the playwright was responding. On the distant shores of Africa and America and at home, in their "rediscovered" classical texts, Renaissance Europeans were daily confronting evidence that their accustomed reality was only one solution, among many others, of perennial human problems. Though they often tried to destroy the alien cultures they encountered, or to absorb them into their ideology, they could not always destroy the testimony of their own consciousness. "The wonder is not that things are," writes Valéry, "but that they are *what* they are and not something else."[48] Each of Marlowe's plays constitutes reality in a manner radically different from the plays that preceded it, just as his work as a whole marks a startling departure from the drama of his time. Each of his heroes makes a different leap from inchoate appetite to the all-consuming project: what is necessary in one play is accidental or absent in the next. Only the leap itself is always necessary, at once necessary and absurd, for it is the embracing of a fiction rendered desirable by the intoxication of language, by the will to play.

Marlowe's heroes *must* live their lives as projects, but they do so in the midst of intimations that the projects are illusions. Their strength is not sapped by these intimations: they do not withdraw into stoical resignation or contemplative solitude, nor do they endure for the sake of isolated moments of grace in which they are in touch with a wholeness otherwise absent in their lives. Rather they take courage from the absurdity of their enterprise, a murderous, self-destructive, supremely eloquent, playful courage. This playfulness in Marlowe's works manifests itself as cruel humor, murderous practical jokes, a penchant for the outlandish and absurd, delight in role-playing, entire absorption in the game at hand and consequent indifference to what lies outside the boundaries of the game, radical insensitivity to human complexity and suffering, extreme but disciplined aggression, hostility to transcendence.

There is some evidence, apart from the cruel, aggressive plays themselves, for a similar dark playfulness in Marlowe's own career, with the comic (and extremely dangerous) blasphemies, the nearly overt (and equally dangerous) homosexuality—tokens of a courting of disaster as reckless as that depicted in Edward or Faustus. In the life, as in the plays, the categories by which we normally organize experience are insistently called into question—is this a man whose recklessness suggests that he is out of control or rather that he is supremely in control, control so coolly mocking that he can, to recall Wyatt, calculate his own excesses? What little we know about Marlowe's mysterious stint as a double agent in Walsingham's secret service—it seems that he went to Rheims in 1587, perhaps posing as a Catholic in order to ferret out incriminating evidence against English Catholic seminarians— and what little we can gather from the contents of the Baines libel suggests, beyond estrangement from ideology, a fathomless and eerily playful self-estrangement. The will to play flaunts society's cherished orthodoxies, embraces what the culture finds loathsome or frightening, transforms the serious into the joke and then unsettles the category of the joke by taking it seriously, courts self-destruction in the interest of the anarchic discharge of its energy. This is play on the brink of an abyss, *absolute* play.

In his turbulent life and, more important, in his writing, Marlowe is deeply implicated in his heroes, though he is far more intelligent and self-aware than any of them. Cutting himself off from the comforting doctrine of repetition, he writes plays that spurn and subvert his culture's metaphysical and ethical certainties. We who have lived after Nietzsche and Flaubert may find it difficult to grasp how strong, how recklessly courageous Marlowe must have been: to write as if the admonitory purpose of literature were a lie, to invent fictions only to create and not to serve God or the state, to fashion lines that echo in the void, that echo more powerfully because there is nothing but a void. Hence Marlowe's implication in the lives of his protagonists and hence too his surmounting of this implication in the creation of enduring works of art. For the one true goal of all these heroes is to be characters in Marlowe's plays; it is only for this, ultimately, that they manifest both their playful energy and their haunting sense of unsatisfied longing.

The Improvisation of Power

Spenser and Marlowe are, from the perspective of this study, mighty opposites, poised in antagonism as radical as that of More and Tyndale in the 1530s. If Spenser sees human identity as conferred by loving service to legitimate authority, to the yoked power of God and the state, Marlowe sees identity established at those moments in which order—political, theological, sexual—is violated. If repetition for Spenser is an aspect of the patient labor of civility, for Marlowe it is the means of constituting oneself in an anonymous void. If Spenser's heroes strive for balance and control, Marlowe's strive to shatter the restraints upon their desires. If in Spenser there is fear of the excess that threatens to engulf order and seems to leave an ineradicable taint on temperance itself, in Marlowe there is fear of the order that threatens to extinguish excess and seems to have always already turned rebellion into a tribute to authority. If Spenser writes for an aristocratic and upper-middle-class audience in a self-consciously archaizing manner, thereby participating in the decorative revival of feudal trappings that characterized Elizabethan courtly ritual,[1] Marlowe writes for the new public theater in a blank verse that must have seemed, after the jog-trot fourteeners of the preceding decades, like reality itself. If Spenser holds up his "other world" to the gaze of power and says, "Behold! This rich beauty is your own face," Marlowe presents *his* and says, "Behold! This tragi-comic, magnificent deformity is how you appear in my rich art." If Spenser's art constantly questions its own status in order to protect power from such questioning, Marlowe undermines power in order to raise his art to the status of a self-regarding, self-justifying absolute.

There is not, of course, anything in Spenser or Marlowe comparable to the violent polemical exchange between More and Tyndale, but there is at least one resonant moment of conjunction that will serve to exemplify the opposition I have just sketched here. In book 1, canto 7 of *The Faerie Queene,* dismayed by the news that Redcrosse has been overthrown by the giant Orgoglio, Una providentially encounters Prince Arthur, the embodiment of Magnificence—the virtue, according to the letter to Ralegh, that "is the perfection of all the rest, and containeth in it them all." This is Arthur's first appearance in the poem, and there follows an elaborate description of his gorgeous armor, a description that includes the following stanza on his helmet's crest:

> Vpon the top of all his loftie crest,
> A bunch of haires discolourd diuersly,
> With sprincled pearle, and gold full richly drest,
> Did shake, and seem'd to daunce for iollity,
> Like to an Almond tree ymounted hye
> On top of greene *Selinis* all alone,
> With blossomes braue bedecked daintily;
> Whose tender locks do tremble euery one
> At euery little breath, that vnder heauen is blowne.
>
> (1.7.32)

As early as the late eighteenth century, a reader records his surprise to find this passage almost verbatim in part 2 of *Tamburlaine.*[2] It occurs in the scene in which Tamburlaine is drawn on stage in his chariot by the captive kings, "with bits in their mouths," the stage direction tells us, "reins in his left hand, in his right hand a whip, with which he scourgeth them." Exulting in his triumphant power, Tamburlaine baits his captives, hands over the weeping royal concubines to satisfy the lust of his common soldiers, and—his own erotic satisfaction—imagines his future conquests:

> Through the streets with troops of conquered kings,
> I'll ride in golden armor like the Sun,
> And in my helm a triple plume shall spring,
> Spangled with Diamonds dancing in the air,
> To note me Emperor of the three-fold world,
> Like to an almond tree ymounted high,
> Upon the lofty and celestial mount,

Of ever green *Selinus* quaintly decked
With blooms more white than *Hericina's* brows,
Whose tender blossoms tremble every one,
At every little breath that thorough heaven is blown.
                                        (4.3.4094–4113)

What is sung by Spenser in praise of Arthur is sung by Tamburlaine in praise of himself; the chivalric accoutrement, an emblem of Arthur's magnanimous knighthood is here part of Tamburlaine's paean to his own power lust. Lines that for Spenser belong to the supreme figure of civility, the chief upholder of the Order of Maidenhead, the worshipful servant of Gloriana, for Marlowe belong to the fantasy life of the Scythian Scourge of God. Marlowe's scene is self-consciously emblematic, as if it were a theatrical improvisation in the Spenserean manner, but now with the hero's place taken by a character who, in his sadistic excess, most closely resembles Orgoglio.[3] And even as we are struck by the radical difference, we are haunted by the vertiginous possibility of an underlying sameness. What if Arthur and Tamburlaine are not separate and opposed? What if they are two faces of the same thing, embodiments of the identical power? Tamburlaine's is the face Arthur shows to his enemies or, alternatively, Arthur's is the face Tamburlaine shows to his followers. To the Irish kern, Spenser's Prince of Magnanimity looks like the Scourge of God; to the English courtier, Marlowe's grotesque conquerer looks like the Faerie Queene.

How shall we characterize the power that possesses both faces and can pass from one to the other? In a famous passage in *The Prince,* Machiavelli writes that a prince must know well how to use both the beast and the man, and hence the ancients depicted Achilles and other heroes as educated by Chiron the centaur. This discussion is an early instance of the celebration of psychic mobility that has continued to characterize discussions of Western consciousness to the present time. Thus in his influential study of modernization in the Middle East, *The Passing of Traditional Society,* the sociologist Daniel Lerner defines the West as a "mobile society," a society characterized not only by certain enlightened and rational public practices but also by the inculcation in its people of a *"mobile sensibility* so adaptive to change that rearrangement of the self-system is its distinctive mode."[4] While traditional society, Professor Lerner argues, functions on the basis of a "highly constrictive personality" (51), one that resists change and is incapable of grasping the situation of another, the mobile personality of Western society "is distinguished by a high capacity for identification with new aspects of his environment," for he "comes equipped with the mechanisms needed to incorporate new demands upon himself that arise outside of his habitual experience" (49). Those mechanisms Professor Lerner subsumes under the single term *empathy*, which he defines as "the capacity to see oneself in the other fellow's situation" (50). In the West, this capacity was fostered first by the physical mobility initiated by the Age of Exploration, then confirmed and broadened by the mass media. "These," he writes, "have peopled the daily world of their audience with sustained, even intimate, experience of the lives of others. 'Ma Perkins,' 'The Goldbergs,' 'I Love Lucy'—all these bring us friends we never met, but whose joys and sorrows we intensely 'share'" (53). And the international diffusion of the mass media means a concomitant diffusion of psychic mobility and hence of modernization: "In our time, indeed, the spread of empathy around the world is accelerating" (52).

To test the rate of this acceleration, Professor Lerner devised a set of questions that he and his assistants put to a cross-section of the inhabitants of the Middle East, to porters and cobblers, as well as grocers and physicians. The questions began, "If you were made editor of a newspaper, what kind of a paper would you run?" and I confess myself in complete sympathy with that class of respondents who, like one shepherd interviewed in a village near Ankara, gasped "My God! How can you say such a thing?... A poor villager... master of the whole world" (24). Professor Lerner invariably interprets such answers as indicative of a constrictive personality incapable of empathy, but in fact the Turkish shepherd, with his Tamburlainian language, reintroduces the great missing term in the analysis of modernization, and that term is *power*. For my own part, I would like in this chapter to delineate the Renaissance origins of the "mobile sensibility" and, having done so, to shift the ground from "I Love Lucy" to *Othello* in order to demonstrate that what Professor Lerner calls "empathy," Shakespeare calls "Iago."

To help us return from the contemporary Middle East to the early seventeenth century, let us dwell for a moment on Professor Lerner's own concept of Renaissance origins: "Take the factor of physical mobility," he writes, "which initiated Western take-off in an age when the earth was underpopulated in terms of the world man-land ratio. Land was to be had, more or less, for the finding. The great explorers took over vast real estate by planting a

flag; these were slowly filled with new populations over generations" (65). It didn't exactly happen this way. Land does not become "real estate" quite so easily, and the underpopulation was
not found but created by those great explorers. Demographers of
Mesoamerica now estimate, for example, that the population of
Hispaniola in 1492 was 7–8 million, perhaps as high as 11 million.
Reduction to that attractive man-land ratio was startlingly sudden:
by 1501, enslavement, disruption of agriculture, and, above all,
European disease had reduced the population to some 700,000; by
1512, to 28,000.[5] The unimaginable massiveness of the death rate
did not, of course, go unnoticed; European observers took it as a
sign of God's determination to cast down the idolaters and open
the New World to Christianity.

With the passage from the sociologist's bland world of ceremonial flag-planting in an empty landscape to violent displacement
and insidious death, we have already moved toward Shakespeare's tragedy, and we move still closer if we glance at an incident recounted in 1525 by Peter Martyr in the Seventh Decade of
De orbe novo. Faced with a serious labor shortage in the gold mines
as a result of the decimation of the native population, the Spanish
in Hispaniola began to raid neighboring islands. Two ships
reached an outlying island in the Lucayas (now called the
Bahamas) where they were received with awe and trust. The
Spanish learned through their interpreters that the natives believed that after death their souls were first purged of their sins in
icy northern mountains, then borne to a paradisal island in the
south, whose beneficent, lame prince offered them innumerable
pleasures: "the souls enjoy eternal delights, among the dancings
and songs of young maidens, and among the embracements of
their children, and whatsoever they loved heretofore; they babble
also there, that such as grow old, wax young again, so that all are
of like years full of joy and mirth."[6] When the Spanish understood
these imaginations, writes Martyr, they proceeded to persuade the
natives "that they came from those places, where they should see
their parents, and children, and all their kindred and friends that
were dead: and should enjoy all kind of delights, together with the
embracements and fruition of beloved things" (625). Thus deceived, the entire population of the island passed "singing and
rejoicing," Martyr says, onto the ships and were taken to the gold
mines of Hispaniola. The Spanish, however, reaped less profit
than they had anticipated; when they grasped what had happened
to them, the Lucayans, like certain German Jewish communities
during the Crusades, undertook mass suicide: "becoming desper-

ate, they either slew themselves, or choosing to famish, gave up their faint spirits, being persuaded by no reason, or violence, to take food" (625).

Martyr, it appears, feels ambivalent about the story. He is certain that God disapproves of such treachery, since many of those who perpetrated the fraud subsequently died violent deaths; on the other hand, he opposes those who would free enslaved natives, since bitter experience has shown that even those Indians who have apparently been converted to Christianity will, given the slightest opportunity, revert to "their ancient and native vices" and turn savagely against those who had instructed them "with fatherly charity" (627). But, for our purposes, Martyr's ambivalence is less important than the power of his story to evoke a crucial Renaissance mode of behavior that links Lerner's "empathy" and Shakespeare's Iago: I shall call that mode *improvisation*, by which I mean the ability both to capitalize on the unforeseen and to transform given materials into one's own scenario. The spur-of-the-moment quality of improvisation is not as critical here as the opportunistic grasp of that which seems fixed and established. Indeed, as Castiglione and others in the Renaissance well understood, the impromptu character of an improvisation is itself often a calculated mask, the product of careful preparation.[7] Conversely, all plots, literary and behavioral, inevitably have their origin in a moment prior to formal coherence, a moment of experimental, aleatory impulse in which the available, received materials are curved toward a novel shape. We cannot locate a point of pure premeditation or pure randomness. What is essential is the Europeans' ability again and again to insinuate themselves into the preexisting political, religious, even psychic structures of the natives and to turn those structures to their advantage. The process is as familiar to us by now as the most tawdry business fraud, so familiar that we assume a virtually universal diffusion of the necessary improvisational talent, but that assumption is almost certainly misleading. There are periods and cultures in which the ability to insert oneself into the consciousness of another is of relatively slight importance, the object of limited concern; others in which it is a major preoccupation, the object of cultivation and fear. Professor Lerner is right to insist that this ability is a characteristically (though not exclusively) Western mode, present to varying degrees in the classical and medieval world and greatly strengthened from the Renaissance onward; he misleads only in insisting further that it is an act of imaginative generosity, a sympathetic appreciation of the situation of the other fellow. For when he speaks confidently of the "spread of empathy around the world," we must understand that he is speaking of the exercise of Western power, power that is creative as well as destructive, but that is scarcely ever wholly disinterested and benign.

To return to the Lucayan story, we may ask ourselves what conditions exist in Renaissance culture that make such an improvisation possible. It depends first upon the ability and willingness to play a role, to transform oneself, if only for a brief period and with mental reservations, into another. This necessitates the acceptance of disguise, the ability to effect a divorce, in Ascham's phrase, between the tongue and the heart. Such role-playing in turn depends upon the transformation of another's reality into a manipulable fiction. The Spanish had to perceive the Indians' religious beliefs as illusions, "imaginations" as Martyr's English translator calls them. Lucayan society, Martyr observes, is based upon a principle of reverent obedience fostered by a set of religious fables that "are delivered by word of mouth and tradition from the Elders to the younger, for a most sacred and true history, insomuch as he who but seemed to think otherwise, should be thrust out of the society of men" (623). The Lucayan king performs the supreme sacral functions and partakes fully in the veneration accorded to the idols, so that if he were to command one of his subjects to cast himself down from a precipice, the subject would immediately comply. The king uses this absolute power to ensure the just distribution, to families according to need, of the tribe's food, all of which is stored communally in royal granaries: "They had the golden age, *mine* and *thine*, the seeds of discord, were far removed from them" (618). Martyr then perceives the social function of Lucayan religious concepts, the native apparatus for their transmission and reproduction, and the punitive apparatus for the enforcement of belief. In short, he grasps Lucayan religion as an ideology, and it is this perception that licenses the transformation of "sacred and true history" into "crafty and subtle imaginations" (625) that may be exploited.

If improvisation is made possible by the subversive perception of another's truth as an ideological construct, that construct must at the same time be grasped in terms that bear a certain structural resemblance to one's own set of beliefs. An ideology that is perceived as entirely alien would permit no point of histrionic entry: it could be destroyed but not performed. Thus the Lucayan religion, in Martyr's account, is an anamorphic representation of Catholicism: there are "images" carried forth with solemn pomp on "the holy day of adoration"; worshipers kneel reverently before these images, sing "hymns," and make offerings, "which at night the nobles divide among them, as our priests do the cakes or wafers which women offer" (622); there are "holy relics" about which the chief priest, standing in his "pulpit," preaches; and, as we have seen, there is absolution for sin, purgatory, and eternal delight in paradise. The European account of the native religion must have borne some likeness to what the Lucayans actually believed; why else would they have danced, singing and rejoicing, onto the Spanish ships? But it is equally important that the religion is conceived as analogous to Catholicism, close enough to permit improvisation, yet sufficiently distanced to protect European beliefs from the violence of fictionalization. The Spanish were not compelled to perceive their own religion as a manipulable human construct; on the contrary, the compulsion of their own creed was presumably strengthened by their contemptuous exploitation of an analogous symbolic structure.

This absence of reciprocity is an aspect of the total economy of the mode of improvisation that I have sketched here. For what we may see in the Lucayan story is an early manifestation of an exercise of power that was subsequently to become vastly important and remains a potent force in our lives: the ownership of another's labor conceived as involving no supposedly "natural" reciprocal obligation (as in feudalism) but rather functioning by concealing the very fact of ownership from the exploited who believe that they are acting freely and in their own interest. Of course, once the ships reached Hispaniola, this concealed ownership gave way to direct enslavement; the Spanish were not capable of continuing the improvisation into the very mines. And it is this failure to sustain the illusion that led to the ultimate failure of the enterprise, for, of course, the Spanish did not want dead Indians but live mineworkers. It would take other, subtler minds, in the Renaissance and beyond, to perfect the means to sustain indefinitely an indirect enslavement.

I have called improvisation a central Renaissance mode of behavior, but the example on which I have focused is located on a geographical margin and might only seem to bear out Immanuel Wallerstein's theory that Western Europe in the sixteenth century increasingly established its ownership of the labor and resources of those located in areas defined as peripheral.[8] But I would argue that the phenomenon I have described is found in a wide variety of forms closer to home. It may be glimpsed, to suggest two significant instances, in the relation of Tudor power to Catholic symbolism and the characteristic form of rhetorical education.

The Anglican Church and the monarch who was its Supreme Head did not, as radical Protestants demanded, eradicate Catholic ritual but rather improvised within it in an attempt to assume its power. Thus, for example, in the Accession Day celebration of 1590, we are told that the queen, sitting in the Tilt gallery, "did suddenly hear a music so sweet and so secret, as every one thereat greatly marvelled. And hearkening to that excellent melody, the earth as it were opening, there appears a Pavilion, made of white Taffeta, being in proportion like unto the sacred Temple of the Virgins Vestal. This Temple seemed to consist upon pillars of porphyry, arched like unto a Church, within it were many lamps burning. Also, on the one side an Altar covered with cloth of gold; and thereupon two wax candles burning in rich candlesticks; upon the Altar also were laid certain Princely presents, which after by three Virgins were presented unto her Majesty."[9] This secular epiphany permits us to identify two of the characteristic operations of improvisation: displacement and absorption. By displacement I mean the process whereby a prior symbolic structure is compelled to coexist with other centers of attention that do not necessarily conflict with the original structure but are not swept up in its gravitational pull; indeed, as here, the sacred may find itself serving as an adornment, a backdrop, an occasion for a quite secular phenomenon. By absorption I mean the process whereby a symbolic structure is taken into the ego so completely that it ceases to exist as an external phenomenon; in the Accession Day ceremony, instead of the secular prince humbling herself before the sacred, the sacred seems only to enhance the ruler's identity, to express her power.[10]

Both displacement and absorption are possible here because the religious symbolism was already charged with the celebration of power. What we are witnessing is a shift in the institution that controls and profits from the interpretation of such symbolism, a shift mediated in this instance by the classical scholarship of Renaissance humanism. The invocation of the Temple of the Vestal Virgins is the sign of that transformation of belief into ideology that we have already examined; the Roman mythology, deftly keyed to England's Virgin Queen, helps to fictionalize Catholic ritual sufficiently for it to be displaced and absorbed.

This enzymatic function of humanism leads directly to our second instance of domestic improvisation, for the cornerstone of the humanist project was a rhetorical education. In *The Tudor Play of Mind*, Joel Altman has recently demonstrated the central importance for English Renaissance culture of the *argumentum in ut-*

ramque partem, the cultivation of the scholar's power to speak equally persuasively for diametrically opposed positions. The practice permeated intellectual life in the early sixteenth century and was, Altman convincingly argues, one of the formative influences on the early drama.[11] It is in the spirit of such rhetorical mobility that Erasmus praises More, as we have seen, for his ability "to play the man of all hours with all men" and that Roper recalls the young More's dazzling improvisations in Cardinal Morton's Christmas plays.

The hagiographical bias of Roper's and most subsequent writing on More has concealed the extent to which this improvisational gift is closely allied to a control of power in the law courts and the royal service: the mystification of manipulation as disinterested empathy begins as early as the sixteenth century. As a corrective, we need only recall More's controversial works, such as *The Confutation of Tyndale's Answer,* whose recurrent method is through improvisation to transform the heretic's faith into a fiction, then absorb it into a new symbolic structure that will ridicule or consume it. Thus Tyndale had written: "Sin we through fragility never so oft, yet as soon as we repent and come into the right way again, and unto the testament which God hath made in Christ's blood: our sins vanish away as smoke in the wind, and as darkness at the coming of light, or as thou cast a little blood or milk into the main sea." More responds by maliciously improvising on Tyndale's text: "Neither purgatory need to be feared when we go hence, nor penance need to be done while we be here, but sin and be sorry and sit and make merry, and then sin again and then repent a little and run to the ale and wash away the sin, think once on God's promise and then do what we list. For hoping sure in that, kill we ten men on a day, we cast but a little blood into the main sea." Having thus made a part of his own, More continues by labeling Tyndale's argument about penance as "but a piece of his poetry"—an explicit instance of that fictionalization we have witnessed elsewhere—and concludes, "Go me to Martin Luther . . . . While that friar lieth with his nun and woteth well he doth nought [i.e., knows he does evil], and saith still he doth well: let Tyndale tell me what repenting is that. He repenteth every morning, and to bed again every night; thinketh on God's promise first, and then go sin again upon trust of God's testament, and then he calleth it casting of a little milk into the main sea."[12]

Improvisation here obviously does not intend to deceive its original object but to work upon a third party, the reader, who might be wavering between the reformers and the Catholic

Church. If the heretic speaks of sin redeemed by God's testament as milk, More returns that milk to sin, then surpasses the simple reversal by transforming it to semen, while he turns the sea that imaged for Tyndale the boundlessness of divine forgiveness into the sexual insatiability of Luther's nun.

These perversions of the reformer's text are greatly facilitated by the fact that the text was already immersed in an intensely charged set of metaphorical transformations—that is, More seizes upon the brilliant instability of Tyndale's prose with its own nervous passage from Christ's blood to sin conceived progressively as smoke, darkness, blood, and finally milk. More's artful improvisation makes it seem that murder and lust lay just beneath the surface of the original discourse, as a kind of dark subtext, and he is able to do so more plausibly because both violence and sexual anxiety are in fact powerful underlying forces in Tyndale's prose as in More's. That is, once again, there is a haunting structural homology between the improviser and his other.

I would hope that by now *Othello* seems virtually to force itself upon us as the supreme symbolic expression of the cultural mode I have been describing, for violence, sexual anxiety, and improvisation are the materials out of which the drama is constructed. To be sure, there are many other explorations of these materials in Shakespeare—one thinks of Richard III wooing Anne[13] or, in comedy, of Rosalind playfully taking advantage of the disguise that exile has forced upon her—but none so intense and radical. In Iago's first soliloquy, Shakespeare goes out of his way to emphasize the improvised nature of the villain's plot:

> Cassio's a proper man, let me see now,
> To get this place, and to make up my will,
> A double knavery . . . how, how? . . . let me see,
> After some time, to abuse Othello's ear,
> That he is too familiar with his wife:
> He has a person and a smooth dispose,
> To be suspected, fram'd to make women false:
> The Moor a free and open nature too,
> That thinks men honest that but seems to be so:
> And will as tenderly be led by the nose . . .
> As asses are.
> I ha't, it is engender'd; Hell and night
> Must bring this monstrous birth to the world's light.
>   (1.3.390–402)[14]

We will try shortly to cast some light on why Iago conceives of his activity here as sexual; for the moment, we need only to observe all of the marks of the impromptu and provisional, extending to the ambiguity of the third-person pronoun: "to abuse Othello's ear / That he is too familiar with his wife." This ambiguity is felicitous; indeed, though scarcely visible at this point, it is the dark essence of Iago's whole enterprise which is, as we shall see, to play upon Othello's buried perception of his own sexual relations with Desdemona as adulterous.[15]

What I have called the marks of the impromptu extend to Iago's other speeches and actions through the course of the whole play. In act 2, he declares of his conspiracy, "'tis here, but yet confus'd; / Knavery's plain face is never seen, till us'd," and this half-willed confusion continues through the agile, hectic maneuvers of the last act until the moment of exposure and silence. To all but Roderigo, of course, Iago presents himself as incapable of improvisation, except in the limited and seemingly benign form of banter and jig.[16] And even here, he is careful, when Desdemona asks him to improvise her praise, to declare himself unfit for the task:

> I am about it, but indeed my invention
> Comes from my pate as birdlime does from frieze,
> It plucks out brain and all: but my Muse labours,
> And thus she is deliver'd.
>
> (2.1.125–28)

Lurking in the homely denial of ability is the image of his invention as birdlime, and hence a covert celebration of his power to ensnare others. Like Jonson's Mosca, Iago is fully aware of himself as an improviser and revels in his ability to manipulate his victims, to lead them by the nose like asses, to possess their labor without their ever being capable of grasping the relation in which they are enmeshed. Such is the relation Iago establishes with virtually every character in the play, from Othello and Desdemona to such minor figures as Montano and Bianca. For the Spanish colonialists, improvisation could only bring the Lucayans into open enslavement; for Iago, it is the key to a mastery whose emblem is the "duteous and knee-crooking knave" who dotes "on his own obsequious bondage" (1.1.45–46), a mastery invisible to the servant, a mastery, that is, whose character is essentially ideological. Iago's attitude toward Othello is nonetheless colonial: though he finds himself in a subordinate position, the ensign regards his black general as "an erring barbarian" whose "free and open nature" is a fertile field for exploitation. However galling it may be to him, Iago's subordination is a kind of protection, for it conceals his power and enables him to play upon the ambivalence of Othello's relation to Christian society: the Moor at once represents the institution and the alien, the conqueror and the infidel. Iago can conceal his malicious intentions toward "the thick-lips" behind the mask of dutiful service and hence prolong his improvisation as the Spaniards could not. To be sure, the play suggests, Iago must ultimately destroy the beings he exploits and hence undermine the profitable economy of his own relations, but that destruction may be long deferred, deferred in fact for precisely the length of the play.[17]

If Iago then holds over others a possession that must constantly efface the signs of its own power, how can it be established, let alone maintained? We will find a clue, I think, in what we have been calling the process of fictionalization that transforms a fixed symbolic structure into a flexible construct ripe for improvisational entry. This process is at work in Shakespeare's play, where we may more accurately identify it as *submission to narrative self-fashioning*. When in Cyprus Othello and Desdemona have been ecstatically reunited, Iago astonishes Roderigo by informing him that Desdemona is in love with Cassio. He has no evidence, of course—indeed we have earlier seen him "engender" the whole plot entirely out of his fantasy—but he proceeds to lay before his gull all of the circumstances that make this adultery plausible: "mark me, with what violence she first lov'd the Moor, but for bragging, and telling her fantastical lies; and she will love him still for prating?" (2.1.221–23). Desdemona cannot long take pleasure in her outlandish match: "When the blood is made dull with the act of sport, there should be again to inflame it, and give satiety a fresh appetite, loveliness in favor, sympathy in years, manners and beauties" (2.1.225–29). The elegant Cassio is the obvious choice: "Didst thou not see her paddle with the palm of his hand?" Iago asks. To Roderigo's objection that this was "but courtesy," Iago replies, "Lechery, by this hand: an index and prologue to the history of lust and foul thoughts" (2.1.251–55). The metaphor makes explicit what Iago has been doing all along: constructing a narrative into which he inscribes ("by this hand") those around him. He does not need a profound or even reasonably accurate understanding of his victims; he would rather deal in probable impossibilities than improbable possibilities. And it is eminently probable that a young, beautiful Venetian gentlewoman would tire of her old, outlandish husband and turn instead to the handsome, young lieutenant: it is, after all, one of the master plots of comedy.

What Iago as inventor of comic narrative needs is a sharp eye for the surfaces of social existence, a sense, as Bergson says, of the mechanical encrusted upon the living, a reductive grasp of human possibilities. These he has in extraordinarily full measure.[18] "The wine she drinks is made of grapes," he says in response to Roderigo's idealization of Desdemona, and so reduced, she can be assimilated to Iago's grasp of the usual run of humanity. Similarly, in a spirit of ironic connoisseurship, he observes Cassio's courtly gestures, "If such tricks as these strip you out of your lieutenantry, it had been better you had not kiss'd your three fingers so oft, which now again you are most apt to play the sir in: good, well kiss'd, an excellent courtesy" (2.1.171–75). He is watching a comedy of manners. Above all, Iago is sensitive to habitual and self-limiting forms of discourse, to Cassio's reaction when he has had a drink or when someone mentions Bianca, to Othello's rhetorical extremism, to Desdemona's persistence and tone when she pleads for a friend; and, of course, he is demonically sensitive to the way individuals interpret discourse, to the signals they ignore and those to which they respond.

We should add that Iago includes himself in this ceaseless narrative invention; indeed, as we have seen from the start, a successful improvisational career depends upon role-playing, which is in turn allied to the capacity, as Professor Lerner defines empathy, "to see oneself in the other fellow's situation." This capacity requires above all a sense that one is not forever fixed in a single, divinely sanctioned identity, a sense Iago expresses to Roderigo in a parodically sententious theory of self-fashioning: "our bodies are gardens, to the which our wills are gardeners, so that if we will plant nettles, or sow lettuce, set hyssop, and weed up thyme; supply it with one gender of herbs, or distract it with many; either to have it sterile with idleness, or manur'd with industry, why, the power, and corrigible authority of this, lies in our wills" (1.3.320–26). Confident in his shaping power, Iago has the role-player's ability to imagine his nonexistence so that he can exist for a moment in another and as another. In the opening scene he gives voice to this hypothetical self-cancellation in a line of eerie simplicity: "Were I the Moor, I would not be Iago" (1.1.57). The simplicity is far more apparent than real. Is the "I" in both halves of the line the same? Does it designate a hard, impacted self-interest prior to social identity, or are there two distinct, even opposing selves? Were I the Moor, I would not be Iago, because the "I" always loves itself and the creature I know as Iago hates the Moor he serves or, alternatively, because as the Moor I would be other than I am now, free of the tormenting appetite and revulsion that characterize the servant's relation to his master and that constitute my identity as Iago. I would be radically the same / I would be radically different; the rapacious ego underlies all institutional structures / the rapacious ego is constituted by institutional structures.[19]

What is most disturbing in Iago's comically banal and fathomless expression—as for that matter, in Professor Lerner's definition of empathy—is that the imagined self-loss conceals its opposite: a ruthless displacement and absorption of the other. Empathy, as the German *Einfühlung* suggests, may be a feeling of oneself into an object, but that object may have to be drained of its own substance before it will serve as an appropriate vessel. Certainly in *Othello*, where all relations are embedded in power and sexuality, there is no realm where the subject and object can merge in the unproblematic accord affirmed by the theorists of empathy.[20] As Iago himself proclaims, his momentary identification with the Moor is a strategic aspect of his malevolent hypocrisy:

> In following him, I follow but myself.
> Heaven is my judge, not I for love and duty,
> But seeming so, for my peculiar end.

> (1.1.58–60)

Exactly what that "peculiar end" is remains opaque. Even the general term "self-interest" is suspect: Iago begins his speech in a declaration of self-interest—"I follow him to serve my turn upon him"—and ends in a declaration of self-division: "I am not what I am."[21] We tend, to be sure, to hear the latter as "I am not what I seem," hence as a simple confirmation of his public deception. But "I am not what I am" goes beyond social feigning: not only does Iago mask himself in society as the honest ancient, but in private he tries out a bewildering succession of brief narratives that critics have attempted, with notorious results, to translate into motives. These inner narratives—shared, that is, only with the audience—continually promise to disclose what lies behind the public deception, to illuminate what Iago calls "the native act and figure" of his heart, and continually fail to do so; or rather, they reveal that his heart is precisely a series of acts and figures, each referring to something else, something just out of our grasp. "I am not what I am" suggests that this elusiveness is permanent, that even self-interest, whose transcendental guarantee is the divine "I am what I am," is a mask.[22] Iago's constant recourse to narrative then is both the affirmation of absolute self-interest and the affirmation of absolute vacancy; the oscillation between the two incompatible positions suggests in Iago the principle of narrativity itself, cut off from original motive and final disclosure. The only termination possible in his case is not revelation but silence.

The question remains why anyone would submit, even unconsciously, to Iago's narrative fashioning. Why would anyone submit to another's narrative at all? For an answer we may recall the pressures on all the figures we have considered in this study and return to our observation that there is a structural resemblance between even a hostile improvisation and its object. In *Othello* the characters have always already experienced submission to narrativity. This is clearest and most important in the case of Othello himself. When Brabantio brings before the Signiory the charge that his daughter has been seduced by witchcraft, Othello promises to deliver "a round unvarnish'd tale . . . / Of my whole course of love" (1.3.90–91), and at the heart of this tale is the telling of tales:

> Her father lov'd me, oft invited me,
> Still question'd me the story of my life,
> From year to year; the battles, sieges, fortunes,
> That I have pass'd:
> I ran it through, even from my boyish days,
> To the very moment that he bade me tell it.
> (1.3.128–33)

The telling of the story of one's life—the conception of one's life as a story[23]—is a response to public inquiry: to the demands of the Senate, sitting in judgment or, at the least, to the presence of an inquiring community. When, as recorded in the fourteenth-century documents Le Roy Ladurie has brilliantly studied, the peasants of the Languedoc village of Montaillou are examined by the Inquisition, they respond with a narrative performance: "About 14 years ago, in Lent, towards vespers, I took two sides of salted pork to the house of Guillaume Benet of Montaillou, to have them smoked. There I found Guillemette Benet warming herself by the fire, together with another woman; I put the salted meat in the kitchen and left."[24] And when the Carthaginian queen calls upon her guest to "tell us all things from the first beginning, Grecian guile, your people's trials, and then your journeyings," Aeneas responds, as he must, with a narrative of the destiny decreed by the gods.[25] So too Othello before the Senate or earlier in Brabantio's house responds to questioning with what he calls his "travel's history" or, in the Folio reading, as if noting the genre, his "traveler's history." This history, it should be noted, is not only of events in distant lands and among strange peoples: "I ran

it through," Othello declares, from childhood "To the very moment that he bade me tell it." We are on the brink of a Borges-like
narrative that is forever constituting itself out of the materials of
the present instant, a narrative in which the storyteller is constantly swallowed up by the story. That is, Othello is pressing up
against the condition of all discursive representations of identity.
He comes dangerously close to recognizing his status as a text, and
it is precisely this recognition that the play as a whole will reveal to
be insupportable. But, at this point, Othello is still convinced that
the text is his own, and he imagines only that he is recounting a
lover's performance.

In the 45th sonnet of Sidney's *Astrophil and Stella*, Astrophil
complains that while Stella is indifferent to the sufferings she has
caused him, she weeps piteous tears at a fable of some unknown
lovers. He concludes,

> Then think my dear, that you in me do read
> Of Lovers' ruin some sad Tragedy:
> I am not I, pity the tale of me.

In *Othello* it is Iago who echos that last line—"I am not what I am,"
the motto of the improviser, the manipulator of signs that bear no
resemblance to what they profess to signify—but it is Othello
himself who is fully implicated in the situation of the Sidney sonnet: that one can win pity for oneself only by becoming a tale of
oneself, and hence by ceasing to be oneself. Of course, Othello
thinks that he has triumphed through his narrative self-
fashioning:

>   she thank'd me,
> And bade me, if I had a friend that lov'd her,
> I should but teach him how to tell my story,
> And that would woo her. Upon this hint I spake:
> She lov'd me for the dangers I had pass'd,
> And I lov'd her that she did pity them.
>
>   (1.3.163–68)

But Iago knows that an identity that has been fashioned as a story
can be unfashioned, refashioned, inscribed anew in a different
narrative: it is the fate of stories to be consumed or, as we say more
politely, interpreted. And even Othello, in his moment of
triumph, has a dim intimation of this fate: a half-dozen lines after
he has recalled "the Cannibals, that each other eat," he remarks
complacently, but with an unmistakable undertone of anxiety,
that Desdemona would come "and with a greedy ear / Devour up
my discourse" (1.3.149–50).

Paradoxically, in this image of rapacious appetite Othello is recording Desdemona's *submission* to his story, what she calls the consecration of her soul and fortunes "to his honors, and his valiant parts" (1.3.253). What he has both experienced and narrated, she can only embrace as narration:

>   my story being done,
> She gave me for my pains a world of sighs;
> She swore i' faith 'twas strange, 'twas passing strange;
> 'Twas pitiful, 'twas wondrous pitiful;
> She wish'd she had not heard it, yet she wish'd
> That heaven had made her such a man.
>
>   (1.3.158–63)[26]

It is, of course, characteristic of early modern culture that male submission to narrative is conceived as active, entailing the fashioning of one's own story (albeit within the prevailing conventions), and female submission as passive, entailing the entrance into marriage in which, to recall Tyndale's definition, the "weak vessel" is put "under the obedience of her husband, to rule her lusts and wanton appetites." As we have seen, Tyndale explains that Sara, "before she was married, was Abraham's sister, and equal with him; but, as soon as she was married, was in subjection, and became without comparison inferior; for so is the nature of wedlock, by the ordinance of God."[27] At least for the world of Renaissance patriarchs, this account is fanciful in its glimpse of an original equality; most women must have entered marriage, like Desdemona, directly from paternal domination. "I do perceive here a divided duty," she tells her father before the Venetian Senate; "you are lord of all my duty,"

>   but here's my husband:
> And so much duty as my mother show'd
> To you, preferring you before her father,
> So much I challenge, that I may profess,
> Due to the Moor my lord.
>
>   (1.3.185–89)[28]

She does not question the woman's obligation to obey, invoking instead only the traditional right to transfer her duty. Yet though Desdemona proclaims throughout the play her submission to her husband—"Commend me to my kind lord," she gasps in her dying words—that submission does not accord wholly with the male dream of female passivity. She was, Brabantio tells us,

A maiden never bold of spirit,
So still and quiet, that her motion
Blush'd at her self,

(1.3.94–96)

yet even this self-abnegation in its very extremity unsettles what
we may assume was her father's expectation:

So opposite to marriage, that she shunn'd
The wealthy curled darlings of our nation.

(1.2.67–68)

And, of course, her marriage choice is, for Brabantio, an act of
astonishing disobedience, explicable only as the somnambulistic
behavior of one bewitched or drugged. He views her elopement
not as a transfer of obedience but as theft or treason or a reckless
escape from what he calls his "guardage." Both he and Iago remind Othello that her marriage suggests not submission but deception:

She did deceive her father, marrying you;
And when she seem'd to shake and fear your looks,
She lov'd them most.

(3.3.210–11)[29]

As the sly reference to Othello's "looks" suggests, the scandal of
Desdemona's marriage consists not only in her failure to receive
her father's prior consent but in her husband's blackness. That
blackness—the sign of all that the society finds frightening and
dangerous—is the indelible witness to Othello's permanent status
as an outsider, no matter how highly the state may value his services or how sincerely he has embraced its values.[30] The safe passage of the female from father to husband is irreparably disrupted,
marked as an escape: "O heaven," Brabantio cries, "how got she
out?" (1.1.169).

Desdemona's relation to her lord Othello should, of course, lay
to rest any doubts about her proper submission, but it is not only
Brabantio's opposition and Othello's blackness that raise such
doubts, even in the midst of her intensest declarations of love.
There is rather a quality in that love itself that unsettles the orthodox schema of hierarchical obedience and makes Othello perceive
her submission to his discourse as a devouring of it. We may
perceive this quality most clearly in the exquisite moment of the
lovers' reunion on Cyprus:

OTHELLO It gives me wonder great as my content
To see you here before me: O my soul's joy,

If after every tempest come such calmness,
May the winds blow, till they have waken'd death,
And let the labouring bark climb hills of seas,
Olympus-high, and duck again as low
As hell's from heaven. If it were now to die,
'Twere now to be most happy, for I fear
My soul hath her content so absolute,
That not another comfort, like to this
Succeeds in unknown fate.
DESDEMONA   The heavens forbid
But that our loves and comforts should increase,
Even as our days do grow.
OTHELLO   Amen to that, sweet powers!
I cannot speak enough of this content,
It stops me here, it is too much of joy.

                              (2.1.183–97)[31]

Christian orthodoxy in both Catholic and Protestant Europe could envision a fervent mutual love between husband and wife, the love expressed most profoundly by Saint Paul in words that are cited and commented upon in virtually every discussion of marriage:

> So men are bound to love their own wives as their own bodies. He that loveth his own wife, loveth himself. For never did any man hate his own flesh, but nourisheth and cherisheth it, even as the Lord doth the congregation: for we are members of his body, of his flesh and of his bones. For this cause shall a man leave father and mother, and shall be joined unto his wife, and they two shall be one flesh. This mystery is great, but I speak of Christ and of the congregation.[32]

Building upon this passage and upon its source in *Genesis*, commentators could write, like the Reformer Thomas Becon, that marriage is a "high, holy, and blessed order of life, ordained not of man, but of God, yea and that not in this sinful world, but in paradise that most joyful garden of pleasure." But like the Pauline text itself, all such discussions of married love begin and end by affirming the larger order of authority and submission within which marriage takes its rightful place. The family, as William Gouge puts it, "is a little Church, and a little Commonwealth . . . whereby trial may be made of such as are fit for any place of authority, or of subjection in Church or Commonwealth."[33]

In Othello's ecstatic words, the proper sentiments of a Christian

husband sit alongside something else: a violent oscillation between heaven and hell, a momentary possession of the soul's absolute content, an archaic sense of monumental scale, a dark
fear—equally archaic, perhaps—of "unknown fate." Nothing conflicts openly with Christian orthodoxy, but the erotic intensity that
informs almost every word is experienced in tension with it. This
tension is less a manifestation of some atavistic "blackness"
specific to Othello than a manifestation of the colonial power of
Christian doctrine over sexuality, a power visible at this point
precisely in its inherent limitation.[34] That is, we glimpse in this
brief moment the *boundary* of the orthodox, the strain of its control, the potential disruption of its hegemony by passion. This
scene, let us stress, does not depict rebellion or even complaint—
Desdemona invokes "the heavens" and Othello answers, "Amen
to that, sweet powers!" Yet the plural here eludes, if only slightly,
a serene affirmation of orthodoxy: the powers in their heavens do
not refer unmistakably to the Christian God, but rather are the
nameless transcendent forces that protect and enhance erotic love.
To perceive the difference, we might recall that if Augustine argues, against the gnostics, that God had intended Adam and Eve
to procreate in paradise, he insists at the same time that our first
parents would have experienced sexual intercourse without the
excitement of the flesh. How then could Adam have had an erec-
tion? Just as there are persons, Augustine writes, "who can move
their ears, either one at a time, or both together" and others who
have "such command of their bowels, that they can break wind
continuously at pleasure, so as to produce the effect of singing,"
so, before the Fall, Adam would have had fully rational, willed
control of the organ of generation and thus would have needed no
erotic arousal. "Without the seductive stimulus of passion, with
calmness of mind and with no corrupting of the integrity of the
body, the husband would lie upon the bosom of his wife," and in
this placid union, the semen could reach the womb "with the
integrity of the female genital organ being preserved, just as now,
with that same integrity being safe, the menstrual flow of blood
can be emitted from the womb of a virgin."[35] Augustine grants
that even Adam and Eve, who alone could have done so, failed to
experience this "passionless generation," since they were expelled
from paradise before they had a chance to try it. Nevertheless, the
ideal of Edenic placidity, untried but intended by God for mankind, remains as a reproach to all fallen sexuality, an exposure of
its inherent violence.[36]

The rich and disturbing pathos of the lovers' passionate reunion in *Othello* derives then not only from our awareness that Othello's premonition is tragically accurate, but from a rent, a moving ambivalence, in his experience of the ecstatic moment itself. The "calmness" of which he speaks may express gratified desire, but, as the repeated invocation of death suggests, it may equally express the longing for a final *release* from desire, from the dangerous violence, the sense of extremes, the laborious climbing and falling out of control that is experienced in the tempest. To be sure, Othello *welcomes* this tempest, with its charge of erotic feeling, but he does so for the sake of the ultimate consummation that the experience can call into being: "If after every tempest come such calmness...." That which men most fear to look upon in the storm—death—is for Othello that which makes the storm endurable. If the death he invokes may figure not the release from desire but its fulfillment—for *death* is a common Renaissance term for orgasm—this fulfillment is characteristically poised between an anxious sense of self-dissolution and a craving for decisive closure. If Othello's words suggest an ecstatic acceptance of sexuality, an absolute content, they suggest simultaneously that for him sexuality is a menacing voyage to reach a longed-for heaven; it is one of the dangers to be passed. Othello embraces the erotic as a supreme form of romantic narrative, a tale of risk and violence issuing forth at last in a happy and final tranquillity.

Desdemona's response is in an entirely different key:

> The heavens forbid
> But that our loves and comforts should increase,
> Even as our days do grow.

This is spoken to allay Othello's fear, but may it not instead augment it? For if Othello characteristically responds to his experience by shaping it as a story, Desdemona's reply denies the possibility of such narrative control and offers instead a vision of unabating increase. Othello says "Amen" to this vision, but it arouses in him a feeling at once of overflowing and inadequacy:

> I cannot speak enough of this content,
> It stops me here, it is too much of joy.

Desdemona has once again devoured up his discourse, and she has done so precisely in bringing him comfort and content.[37] Rather than simply confirming male authority, her submission eroticizes everything to which it responds, from the "disastrous chances" and "moving accidents" Othello relates, to his simplest demands,[38] to his very mistreatment of her:

> my love doth so approve him,
> That even his stubbornness, his checks and frowns, —
> Prithee unpin me, — have grace and favour in them.
>   (4.3.19–21)[39]

The other women in the play, Bianca and Emilia, both have moments of disobedience to the men who possess and abuse them—in the case of Emilia, it is a heroic disobedience for which she pays with her life.[40] Desdemona performs no such acts of defiance, but her erotic submission, conjoined with Iago's murderous cunning, far more effectively, if unintentionally, subverts her husband's carefully fashioned identity.

We will examine more fully the tragic process of this subversion, but it is important to grasp first that Othello's loss of himself—a loss depicted discursively in his incoherent ravings—arises not only from the fatal conjunction of Desdemona's love and Iago's hate, but from the nature of that identity, from what we have called his submission to narrative self-fashioning. We may invoke in this connection Lacan's observation that the source of the subject's frustration in psychoanalysis is ultimately neither the silence nor the reply of the analyst:

> Is it not rather a matter of frustration inherent in the very discourse of the subject? Does the subject not become engaged in an ever-growing dispossession of that being of his, concerning which—by dint of sincere portraits which leave its idea no less incoherent, of rectifications which do not succeed in freeing its essence, of stays and defenses which do not prevent his statue from tottering, of narcissistic embraces which become like a puff of air in animating it—he ends up by recognizing that this being has never been anything more than his construct in the Imaginary and that this construct disappoints all of his certitudes? For in this labor which he undertakes to reconstruct this construct *for another*, he finds again the fundamental alienation which made him construct it *like another one,* and which has always destined it to be stripped from him *by another.*[41]

Shakespeare's military hero, it may be objected, is particularly far removed from this introspective project, a project that would seem, in any case, to have little bearing upon any Renaissance text. Yet I think it is no accident that nearly every phrase of Lacan's critique of psychoanalysis seems a brilliant reading of *Othello*, for I

would propose that there is a deep resemblance between the construction of the self in analysis—at least as Lacan conceives it—and
Othello's self-fashioning. The resemblance is grounded in the dependence of even the innermost self upon a language that is
always necessarily given from without and upon representation
before an audience. I do not know if such are the conditions of
human identity, apart from its expression in psychoanalysis, but
they are unmistakably the conditions of theatrical identity, where
existence is conferred upon a character by the playwright's
language and the actor's performance. And in *Othello* these governing circumstances of the medium itself are reproduced and intensified in the hero's situation: his identity depends upon a constant performance, as we have seen, of his "story," a loss of his
own origins, an embrace and perpetual reiteration of the norms of
another culture. It is this dependence that gives Othello, the war-
rior and alien, a relation to Christian values that is the existential
equivalent of a religious vocation; he cannot allow himself the
moderately flexible adherence that most ordinary men have toward their own formal beliefs. Christianity is the alienating yet
constitutive force in Othello's identity, and if we seek a discursive
mode in the play that is the social equivalent of the experience
Lacan depicts, we will find it in *confession*. Othello himself invokes
before the Venetian Senate the absolute integrity of confession,
conceived, it appears, not as the formal auricular rite of penitence
but as a generalized self-scrutiny in God's presence:

> as faithful as to heaven
> I do confess the vices of my blood,
> So justly to your grave ears I'll present
> How I did thrive in this fair lady's love,
> And she in mine.
>
> (1.3.123–36)[42]

The buried identification here between the vices of the blood and
mutual thriving in love is fully exhumed by the close of the play
when confession has become a virtually obsessional theme.[43]
Theological and juridical confession are fused in Othello's mind
when, determined first to exact a deathbed confession, he comes
to take Desdemona's life:

> If you bethink yourself of any crime,
> Unreconcil'd as yet to heaven and grace,
> Solicit for it straight....
> Therefore confess thee freely of thy sin,

For to deny each article with oath
Cannot remove, nor choke the strong conceit,
That I do groan withal: thou art to die.
(5.2.26–28, 54–57)

The sin that Othello wishes Desdemona to confess is adultery, and
her refusal to do so frustrates the achievement of what in theology
was called "a good, complete confession."[44] He feels the outrage
of the thwarted system that needs to imagine itself merciful,
sacramental, when it disciplines:

thou dost stone thy heart,
And makest me call what I intend to do
A murder, which I thought a sacrifice.
(5.2.64–66)

We are at last in a position to locate the precise nature of the
symbolic structure into which Iago inserts himself in his brilliant
improvisation: this structure is the centuries-old Christian doctrine of sexuality, policed socially and psychically, as we have
already seen, by confession. To Iago, the Renaissance skeptic, this
system has a somewhat archaic ring, as if it were an earlier stage of
development which his own modern sensibility had cast off.[45]
Like the Lucayan religion to the conquistadors, the orthodox doctrine that governs Othello's sexual attitudes—his simultaneous
idealization and mistrust of women—seems to Iago sufficiently
close to be recognizable, sufficiently distant to be manipulable.
We watch him manipulate it directly at the beginning of act 4,
when he leads Othello through a brutally comic parody of the late
medieval confessional manuals with their casuistical attempts to
define the precise moment at which venial temptation passes over
into mortal sin:

IAGO To kiss in private?
OTHELLO   An unauthoriz'd kiss.
IAGO Or to be naked with her friend abed,
An hour, or more, not meaning any harm?
OTHELLO Naked abed, Iago, and not mean harm?
It is hypocrisy against the devil:
They that mean virtuously, and yet do so,
The devil their virtue tempts, and they tempt heaven.
IAGO So they do nothing, 'tis a venial slip.
(4.1.2–9)

Iago in effect assumes an extreme version of the laxist position in
such manuals in order to impel Othello toward the rigorist version
that viewed adultery as one of the most horrible of mortal sins,

more detestable, in the words of the *Eruditorium penitentiale,* "than homicide or plunder," and hence formerly deemed punishable, as several authorities remind us, by death.[46] Early Protestantism did not soften this position. Indeed, in the mid-sixteenth century, Tyndale's erstwhile collaborator, George Joye, called for a return to the Old Testament penalty for adulterers. "God's law," he writes, "is to punish adultery with death for the tranquillity and commonwealth of His church." This is not an excessive or vindictive course; on the contrary, "to take away and to cut off putrified and corrupt members from the whole body, lest they poison and destroy the body, is the law of love."[47] When Christian magistrates leave adultery unpunished, they invite more betrayals and risk the ruin of the realm, for as Protestants in particular repeatedly observe, the family is an essential component of an interlocking social and theological network. Hence adultery is a sin with the gravest of repercussions; in the words of the great Cambridge Puritan William Perkins, it "destroyeth the Seminary of the Church, which is *a godly seed* in the family, and it breaketh the covenant between the parties and God; it robs another of the precious ornament of chastity, which is a gift of the Holy Ghost; it dishonors their bodies and maketh them temples of the devil; and the Adulterer maketh his family a Stews."[48] It is in the bitter spirit of these convictions that Othello enacts the grotesque comedy of treating his wife as a strumpet and the tragedy of executing her in the name of justice, lest she betray more men.

But we still must ask how Iago manages to persuade Othello that Desdemona has committed adultery, for all of the cheap tricks Iago plays seem somehow inadequate to produce the unshakable conviction of his wife's defilement that seizes Othello's soul and drives him mad. After all, as Iago taunts Othello, he cannot achieve the point of vantage of God whom the Venetian women let "see the pranks / They dare not show their husbands" (3.3.206–7):

> Would you, the supervisor, grossly gape on,
> Behold her topp'd?
>
> (3.3.401–2)

How then, without "ocular proof" and in the face of both love and common sense, is Othello so thoroughly persuaded? To answer this, we must recall the syntactic ambiguity we noted earlier—"to abuse Othello's ear, / That he is too familiar with his wife"—and turn to a still darker aspect of orthodox Christian doctrine, an aspect central both to the confessional system and to Protestant self-scrutiny. *Omnis amator feruentior est adulter,* goes the Stoic epigram, and Saint Jerome does not hesitate to draw the inevitable inference: "An adulterer is he who is too ardent a lover of his wife."[49] Jerome quotes Seneca: "All love of another's wife is shameful; so too, too much love of your own. A wise man ought to love his wife with judgment, not affection. Let him control his impulses and not be borne headlong into copulation. Nothing is fouler than to love a wife like an adultress.... Let them show themsleves to their wives not as lovers, but as husbands."[50] The words echo through more than a thousand years of Christian writing on marriage, and, in the decisive form given them by Augustine and his commentators, remain essentially unchallenged by the leading continental Reformers of the sixteenth and early seventeenth century, by Tudor ecclesiastical authorities, and even by Elizabethan and Jacobean Puritans who sharply opposed so many conservative Anglican doctrines. There is, to be sure, in all shades of Protestantism an attack on the Catholic doctrine of celibacy and a celebration of married love, a celebration that includes acknowledgment of the legitimate role of sexual pleasure. But for Reformer as for Catholic, this acknowledgment is hedged about with warnings and restrictions. The "man who shows no modesty or comeliness in conjugal intercourse," writes Calvin, "is committing adultery with his wife," and the *King's Book,* attributed to Henry VIII, informs its readers that in lawful matrimony a man may break the Seventh Commandment "and live unchaste with his own wife, if he do unmeasurably or inordinately serve his or her fleshly appetite or lust."[51]

In the Augustinian conception, as elaborated by Raymond of Peñaforte, William of Rennes, and others, there are four motives for conjugal intercourse: to conceive offspring; to render the marital debt to one's partner so that he or she might avoid incontinency; to avoid fornication oneself; and to satisfy desire. The first two motives are without sin and excuse intercourse; the third is a venial sin; the fourth—to satisfy desire—is mortal. Among the many causes that underlie this institutional hostility to desire is the tenacious existence, in various forms, of the belief that pleasure constitutes a legitimate release from dogma and constraint. Thus when asked by the Inquisition about her happy past liaison with the heretical priest of Montaillou, the young Grazide Lizier replies with naive frankness, "in those days it pleased me, and it pleased the priest, that he should know me carnally, and be known by me; and so I did not think I was sinning, and neither did he."[52] "With Pierre Clergue," she explains, "I liked it. And so it could not displease God. It was not a sin" (157). For the peasant girl, apparently, pleasure was the guarantee of innocence: "But now, with him, it does not please me any more. And so now, if he knew me carnally, I should think it a sin" (151). A comparable attitude, derived not from peasant culture but from the troubadours, evidently lies behind the more sophisticated courtship of Romeo: "Thus from my lips, by thine my sin is purged."[53]

It should not surprise us that churchmen, Catholic and Protestant alike, would seek to crush such dangerous notions, nor that they would extend their surveillance and discipline to married couples and warn that excessive pleasure in the marriage bed is at least a potential violation of the Seventh Commandment. "Nothing is more vile," says Raymond's influential *summa*, "than to love your wife in adulterous fashion."[54] The conjugal act may be without sin, writes the rigorist Nicolaus of Ausimo, but only if "in the performance of this act there is no enjoyment of pleasure."[55] Few *summas* and no marriage manuals take so extreme a position, but virtually all are in agreement that the active *pursuit* of pleasure in sexuality is damnable, for as Jacobus Ungarelli writes in the sixteenth century, those who undertake intercourse for pleasure "exclude God from their minds, act as brute beasts, lack reason, and if they begin marriage for this reason, are given over to the power of the devil."[56]

Confessors then must determine if the married penitent has a legitimate excuse for intercourse and if the act has been performed with due regard for "matrimonial chastity," while Protestants who have rejected auricular confession must similarly scrutinize their own behavior for signs that their pleasure has been too "spacious."[57] "Lust is more spacious than love," writes Alexander Niccoles in the early seventeenth century; it "hath no mean, no bound ... more deep, more dangerous than the Sea, and less restrained, for the Sea hath bounds, but it [lust] hath none."[58] Such unbounded love is a kind of idolatry, an encroachment upon a Christian's debt of loving obedience to God, and it ultimately destroys the marital relationship as well. Immoderate love, another Puritan divine warns, "will either be blown down by some storm or tempest of displeasure, or fall of itself, or else degenerate into jealousy, the most devouring and fretting canker that can harbor in a married person's breast."[59]

These anxieties, rich in implication for *Othello*, are frequently tempered in Protestant writings by a recognition of the joyful ardor of young married couples, but there remains a constant fear of excess, and, as Ambrose observed centuries earlier, even the most plausible excuse for sexual passion is shameful in the old: "Youths generally assert the desire for generation. How much more shameful for the old to do what is shameful for the young to confess."[60] Othello himself seems eager to ward off this shame; he denies before the Senate that he seeks

> To please the palate of my appetite,
> Nor to comply with heat, the young affects
> In me defunct . . . .
>
> (1.3.262–64)[61]

But Desdemona makes no such disclaimer; indeed her declaration of passion is frankly, though by no means exclusively, sexual:

> That I did love the Moor, to live with him,
> My downright violence, and scorn of fortunes,
> May trumpet to the world: my heart's subdued
> Even to the utmost pleasure of my lord.
>
> (1.3.248–51)[62]

This moment of erotic intensity, this frank acceptance of pleasure and submission to her spouse's pleasure, is, I would argue, as much as Iago's slander the cause of Desdemona's death, for it awakens the deep current of sexual anxiety in Othello, anxiety that with Iago's help expresses itself in quite orthodox fashion as the perception of adultery.[63] Othello unleases upon Cassio—"Michael Cassio, / That came a-wooing with you" (3.3.71–72)—the fear of pollution, defilement, brutish violence that is bound up with his own experience of sexual pleasure, while he must destroy Desdemona both for her excessive experience of pleasure and for awakening such sensations in himself. Like Guyon in the Bower of Bliss, Othello transforms his complicity in erotic excess and his fear of engulfment into a "purifying," saving violence:

>   Like to the Pontic sea,
> Whose icy current and compulsive course
> Ne'er feels retiring ebb, but keeps due on
> To the Propontic and the Hellespont,
> Even so my bloody thoughts, with violent pace,
> Shall ne'er look back, ne'er ebb to humble love,
> Till that a capable and wide revenge
> Swallow them up.
>
> (3.3.460–67)

His insupportable sexual experience has been, as it were, displaced and absorbed by the act of revenge which can swallow up not only the guilty lovers but—as the syntax suggests—his own "bloody thoughts."

Such is the achievement of Iago's improvisation on the religious sexual doctrine in which Othello believes; true to that doctrine, pleasure itself becomes for Othello pollution, a defilement of his property in Desdemona and in himself.[64] It is at the level of this dark, sexual revulsion that Iago has access to Othello, access assured, as we should expect, by the fact that beneath his cynical modernity and professed self-love Iago reproduces in himself the same psychic structure. He is as intensely preoccupied with adultery, while his anxiety about his own sexuality may be gauged from the fact that he conceives his very invention, as the images of engendering suggest, as a kind of demonic semen that will bring forth monsters.[65] Indeed Iago's discourse—his assaults on women, on the irrationality of eros, on the brutishness of the sexual act— reiterates virtually to the letter the orthodox terms of Ungarelli's attack on those who seek pleasure in intercourse.

The improvisational process we have been discussing depends for its success upon the concealment of its symbolic center, but as the end approaches this center becomes increasingly visible. When, approaching the marriage bed on which Desdemona has spread the wedding sheets, Othello rages, "Thy bed, lust stain'd, shall with lust's blood be spotted" (5.1.36), he comes close to revealing his tormenting identification of marital sexuality—limited perhaps to the night he took Desdemona's virginity—and adultery.[66] The orthodox element of this identification is directly observed—

> this sorrow's heavenly,
> It strikes when it does love—
>
> (5.2.21–22)

and on her marriage bed / deathbed Desdemona seems at last to pluck out the heart of the mystery:

> OTHELLO Think on thy sins.
> DESDEMONA They are loves I bear to you.
> OTHELLO And for that thou diest.
> DESDEMONA That death's unnatural, that kills for loving.
> (5.2.39–42)

The play reveals at this point not the unfathomable darkness of human motives but their terrible transparency, and the horror of the revelation is its utter inability to deflect violence. Othello's identity is entirely caught up in the narrative structure that drives him to turn Desdemona into a being incapable of pleasure, a piece of "monumental alabaster," so that he will at last be able to love her without the taint of adultery:

Be thus, when thou art dead, and I will kill thee,
And love thee after.

$$(5.2.18–19)$$

It is as if Othello had found in a necrophilic fantasy the secret
solution to the intolerable demands of the rigorist sexual ethic,
and the revelation that Cassio has not slept with Desdemona leads
only to a doubling of this solution, for the adulterous sexual pleasure that Othello had projected upon his lieutenant now rebounds
upon himself.[67] Even with the exposure of Iago's treachery, then,
there is for Othello no escape—rather a still deeper submission to
narrative, a reaffirmation of the self as story, but now split suici-
dally between the defender of the faith and the circumcised enemy
who must be destroyed. Lodovico's bizarrely punning response to
Othello's final speech—"O bloody period!"—insists precisely
upon the fact that it was a speech, that this life fashioned as a text
is ended as a text.

To an envious contemporary like Robert Greene, Shakespeare
seems a kind of green-room Iago, appropriating for himself the
labors of others. In *Othello* Shakespeare seems to acknowledge,
represent, and explore his affinity to the malicious improviser,
but, of course, his relation to the theater and to his culture is far
more complex than such an affinity could suggest. There are
characters in his works who can improvise without tragic results,
characters who can embrace a mobility of desire—one of whose
emblems is the male actor playing a female character dressed up as
a male—that neither Iago, nor Othello, nor Desdemona can endure. Destructive violence is not Shakespeare's only version of
these materials, and even in *Othello*, Iago is not the playwright's
only representation of himself. Still, at the least we must grant
Robert Greene that it would have seemed fatal to be imitated by
Shakespeare. He possessed a limitless talent for entering into the
consciousness of another, perceiving its deepest structures as a
manipulable fiction, reinscribing it into his own narrative form.[68]
If in the late plays, he experiments with controlled disruptions of
narrative, moments of eddying and ecstasy, these invariably give
way to reaffirmations of self-fashioning through story.

Montaigne, who shares many of Shakespeare's most radical perceptions, invents in effect a brilliant mode of *non-narrative* self-
fashioning: "I cannot keep my subject still. It goes along be-
fuddled and staggering, with a natural drunkenness. I take it in
this condition, just as it is at the moment I give my attention to
it."[69] Shakespeare by contrast remains throughout his career the

supreme purveyor of "empathy," the fashioner of narrative selves, the master improviser. Where Montaigne withdrew to his study, Shakespeare became the presiding genius of a popular, urban art form with the capacity to foster psychic mobility in the service of Elizabethan power; he became the principal maker of what we may see as the prototype of the mass media Professor Lerner so admires.

Finally, we may ask, is this service to power a function of the theater itself or of Shakespeare's relation to his medium? The answer, predictably, is both. The theater is widely perceived in the period as the concrete manifestation of the histrionic quality of life, and, more specifically, of power—the power of the prince who stands as an actor upon a stage before the eyes of the nation, the power of God who enacts His will in the Theater of the World. The stage justifies itself against recurrent charges of immorality by invoking this normative function: it is the expression of those rules that govern a properly ordered society and displays visibly the punishment, in laughter and violence, that is meted out upon those who violate the rules. Most playwrights pay at least professional homage to these values; they honor the institutions that enable them to earn their keep and give voice to the ideology that holds together both their "mystery" and the society at large.

In Marlowe, as we have seen, we encounter a playwright at odds with this ideology. If the theater normally reflects and flatters the royal sense of itself as national performance, Marlowe struggles to expose the underlying motives of any performance of power. If the theater normally affirms God's providence, Marlowe explores the tragic needs and interests that are served by all such affirmations. If the Elizabethan stage functions as one of the public uses of spectacle to impose normative ethical patterns on the urban masses, Marlowe enacts a relentless challenge to those patterns and undermines employment of rhetoric and violence in their service.

Shakespeare approaches his culture not, like Marlowe, as rebel and blasphemer, but rather as dutiful servant, content to improvise a part of his own within its orthodoxy. And if after centuries, that improvisation has been revealed to us as embodying an almost boundless challenge to the culture's every tenet, a devastation of every source, the author of *Othello* would have understood that such a revelation scarcely matters. After all, the heart of a successful improvisation lies in concealment, not exposure; and besides, as we have seen, even a hostile improvisation reproduces the relations of power that it hopes to displace and absorb. This is not to dismiss the power of hatred or the significance of distinctions—it matters a great deal whether Othello or Iago, the Lucayans or the Spaniards prevail—only to suggest the boundaries that define the possibility of any improvisational contact, even contact characterized by hidden malice.

I would not want to argue, in any event, that Shakespeare's relation to his culture is defined by hidden malice. Such a case can no doubt be made for many of the plays—stranger things have been said—but it will sound forced and unconvincing, just as the case for Shakespeare as an unwavering, unquestioning apologist for Tudor ideology sounds forced and unconvincing. The solution here is not, I suggest, that the truth lies somewhere in between. Rather the truth itself is radically unstable and yet constantly stabilized, as unstable as those male authorities that affirm themselves only to be undermined by subversive women and then to be reconstituted in a different guise. If any reductive generalization about Shakespeare's relation to his culture seems dubious, it is because his plays offer no single timeless affirmation or denial of legitimate authority and no central, unwavering authorial presence. Shakespeare's language and themes are caught up, like the medium itself, in unsettling repetitions, committed to the shifting voices and audiences, with their shifting aesthetic assumptions and historical imperatives, that govern a living theater.

Criticism can legitimately show—as I hope my discussion of *Othello* does—that Shakespeare relentlessly *explores* the relations of power in a given culture. That more than exploration is involved is much harder to demonstrate convincingly. If there are intimations in Shakespeare of a release from the complex narrative orders in which everyone is inscribed, these intimations do not arise from bristling resistance or strident denunciation—the mood of a Jaques or Timon. They arise paradoxically from a peculiarly intense *submission* whose downright violence undermines everything it was meant to shore up, the submission depicted not in Othello or Iago but in Desdemona. As both the play and its culture suggest, the arousal of intense, purposeless pleasure is only superficially a confirmation of existing values, established selves. [70] In Shakespeare's narrative art, liberation from the massive power structures that determine social and psychic reality is glimpsed in an *excessive* aesthetic delight, an erotic embrace of those very structures—the embrace of a Desdemona whose love is more deeply unsettling than even a Iago's empathy.

Epilogue

A few years ago, at the start of a plane flight from Baltimore to Boston, I settled down next to a middle-aged man who was staring pensively out of the window. There was no assigned seating, and I had chosen this neighbor as the least likely to disturb me, since I wanted to finish rereading Geertz's *Interpretation of Cultures*, which I was due to teach on my return to Berkeley the following week. But no sooner had I fastened my seat belt and turned my mind to Balinese cock-fighting than the man suddenly began to speak to me. He was traveling to Boston, he said, to visit his grown son who was in the hospital. A disease had, among other consequences, impaired the son's speech, so that he could only mouth words soundlessly; still more seriously, as a result of the illness, he had lost his will to live. The father was going, he told me, to try to restore that will, but he was troubled by the thought that he would be incapable of understanding the son's attempts at speech. He had therefore a favor to ask me: would I mime a few sentences so that he could practice reading my lips? Would I say, soundlessly, "I want to die. I want to die"?

Taken aback, I began to form the words, with the man staring intently at my mouth: "I want to . . ." But I was incapable of finishing the sentence. "Couldn't I say, 'I want to live'?" Or better still (since the seat belt sign had by this time flashed off), he might go into the bathroom, I suggested lamely, and practice on himself in front of a mirror. "It's not the same," the man replied in a shaky voice, then turned back to the window. "I'm sorry," I said, and we sat in silence for the rest of the flight.

I could not do what the man had asked in part because I was afraid that he was, quite simply, a maniac and that once I had expressed the will to die, he would draw a hidden knife and stab me to death or, alternatively, activate some device secreted on board the plane that would blow us all to pieces (it's not for nothing that I have been living in California for the past ten years).

But if paranoia tinged my whole response, there were reasons for my resistance more complex than the fear of physical attack. I felt superstitiously that if I mimed the man's terrible sentence, it would have the force, as it were, of a legal sentence, that the words would stick like a burr upon me. And beyond superstition, I was aware, in a manner more forceful than anything my academic research had brought home to me, of the extent to which my identity and the words I utter coincide, the extent to which I want to form my own sentences or to choose for myself those moments in which I will recite someone else's. To be asked, even by an isolated, needy individual to perform lines that were not my own, that violated my sense of my own desires, was intolerable.

When I first conceived this book several years ago, I intended to explore the ways in which major English writers of the sixteenth century created their own performances, to analyze the choices they made in representing themselves and in fashioning characters, to understand the role of human autonomy in the construction of identity. It seemed to me the very hallmark of the Renaissance that middle-class and aristocratic males began to feel that they possessed such shaping power over their lives, and I saw this power and the freedom it implied as an important element in my own sense of myself. But as my work progressed, I perceived that fashioning oneself and being fashioned by cultural institutions—family, religion, state—were inseparably intertwined. In all my texts and documents, there were, so far as I could tell, no moments of pure, unfettered subjectivity; indeed, the human subject itself began to seem remarkably unfree, the ideological product of the relations of power in a particular society. Whenever I focused sharply upon a moment of apparently autonomous self-fashioning, I found not an epiphany of identity freely chosen but a cultural artifact. If there remained traces of free choice, the choice was among possibilities whose range was strictly delineated by the social and ideological system in force. ◢

The book I have written reflects these perceptions, but I trust that it also reflects, though in a manner more tentative, more ironic than I had originally intended, my initial impulse. For all of the sixteenth-century Englishmen I have written about here do in fact cling to the human subject and to self-fashioning, even in suggesting the absorption or corruption or loss of the self. How could they do otherwise? What was—or, for that matter, what is—the alternative? For the Renaissance figures we have considered understand that in our culture to abandon self-fashioning is to abandon the craving for freedom, and to let go of one's stubborn hold upon selfhood, even selfhood conceived as a fiction, is to die. As for myself, I have related this brief story of my encounter with the distraught father on the plane because I want to bear witness at the close to my overwhelming need to sustain the illusion that I am the principal maker of my own identity.

Notes

Introduction

1. Augustine, sermon 169, quoted in Peter Brown, *Religion and Society in the Age of Saint Augustine* (London: Faber and Faber, 1972), p. 30.

2. *Faerie Queene*, "A Letter of the Authors Expounding His Whole Intention in the Course of this Worke"; *Faerie Queene* 6.9.31; *Amoretti* 8. Citations of Spenser's poetry are to *The Works of Edmund Spenser: A Variorum Edition*, ed. Edwin Greenlaw et al. (Baltimore: Johns Hopkins University Press, 1932–57).

3. Job 31:15. The OED, from which many of the following examples are drawn, cites the late sixteenth-century translation of La Primaudaye's *French Academy:* "The seede . . . receiveth not fashion presently upon the conception, but remaineth for a time without any figure" (*sb* 2b). There is an illuminating discussion of self-fashioning by Thomas Greene, "The Flexibility of the Self in Renaissance Literature," in *The Disciplines of Criticism*, ed. Peter Demetz, Thomas Greene, and Lowry Nelson, Jr. (New Haven: Yale University Press, 1968), pp. 241–64. Greene's starting point is the assertion in Pico that man may choose to fashion *(effingere)* himself in whatever shape he prefers.

4. See David Hunt, *Parents and Children in History: The Psychology of Family Life in Early Modern France* (New York: Basic Books, 1970), p. 132. The OED cites Richard Mulcaster's *Positions:* "If the infirmity in fashion be casual . . ., exercise . . . will make that straight which was crooked" (*sb* 2a).

5. Richard Taverner, *Garden of Wisdom* (London: 1539), p. Bviii^v. I owe this reference to Richard Yanowitz, "Tudor Attitudes Toward the Power of Language" (Ph.D. diss., University of California, 1978).

6. Clifford Geertz, *The Interpretation of Cultures* (New York: Basic Books, 1973), p. 51.

7. Ibid., pp. 44, 49.

8. Karl Marx, *Grundrisse: Foundations of the Critique of Political Economy*, trans. Martin Nicolaus (New York: Vintage, 1973), pp. 110–11.

9. See Clifford Geertz, *The Interpretation of Cultures* and *Islam Observed* (New Haven: Yale University Press, 1968); James Boon, *From Symbolism to Structuralism: Levi-Strauss in a Literary Tradition* (New York: Harper & Row, 1972) and *The Anthropological Romance of Bali 1597–1972: Dynamic Perspectives in Marriage and Caste, Politics and Religion* (Cambridge: Cambridge University Press, 1977); Mary Douglas, *Purity and Danger: An Analysis of Concepts of Pollution and Taboo* (New York: Praeger, 1966) and *Natural Symbols: Explorations in Cosmology* (New York: Pantheon, 1970); Jean Duvignaud, *Change at Shebika: Report from a North African Village*, trans. Frances Frenaye (New York: Pantheon, 1970); Paul Rabinow, *Reflections on Fieldwork in Morocco* (Berkeley: University of California Press, 1977); Victor Turner, *Dramas, Fields, and Metaphors: Symbolic Action in Human Society* (Ithaca: Cornell University Press, 1974) and *The Ritual Process: Structure and Anti-Structure* (Ithaca, Cornell University Press, 1969).

10. Quoted in E. de Selincourt's introduction to *Spenser: Poetical Works*, ed. J. C. Smith and E. de Selincourt (London: Oxford University Press, 1912), p. xxxviii.

Chapter One

1. *A Dialogue of Comfort against Tribulation*, ed. Louis L. Martz and Frank Manley, *The Complete Works of St. Thomas More* 12 (New Haven: Yale University Press, 1976), p. 213. Hereafter cited as *Complete Works.*

2. *The History of King Richard III*, ed. R. S. Sylvester, *Complete Works* 3 (1963), p. 80.

3. *The Prince*, trans. Luigi Ricci, rev. E. R. P. Vincent (New York: Modern Library, 1950), pp. 64–65. Machiavelli's explanation, it should be noted, has its own elusiveness: on the one hand, there is a cold observation of something akin to a law of nature—the fox always eats the hens; on the other hand, there is smoldering outrage at the stupidity, the willfulness, of the victims.

4. In William Roper, *The Life of Sir Thomas More*, ed. Richard S. Sylvester and Davis P. Harding (New Haven: Yale University Press, 1962), p. 239. I have been deeply influenced throughout by Sylvester's seminal work; see especially, "*A Part of His Own:* Thomas More's Literary Personality in His Early Works," *Moreana* 15 (1967), pp. 29–42. See also David Bleich's psychoanalytic attempt to correlate More's writing "with particular infantile modalities" ("More's *Utopia:* Confessional Modes," *American Imago* 28 [1971], pp. 24–52).

5. The classic account of this phenomenon is Johan Huizinga, *The Waning of the Middle Ages* (London: E. Arnold, 1924).

6. On the persistence of these hopes, see Frances A. Yates, *The French Academies of the Sixteenth Century* (London: Warburg Institute, 1947), pp. 199–235; Roy Strong, *The Cult of Elizabeth* (London: Thames & Hudson, 1977), pp. 176–77.

7. Mary F. S. Hervey, *Holbein's "Ambassadors"* (London: George Bell &

Sons, 1900), p. 232. On Holbein's painting, which is in the National Gallery in London, see also Michael Levey, *The German School,* National Gallery Catalogues (London: National Gallery, 1959), pp. 46–54; Carl Georg Heise, *Hans Holbein d. J.: Die Gesandten* (Stuttgart: Philipp Reclam Jun., 1959); Ernest B. Gilman, *The Curious Perspective: Literary and Pictorial Wit in the Seventeenth Century* (New Haven: Yale University Press, 1978), pp. 98–104.

8. Jurgis Baltrušaitis, *Anamorphoses, ou perspectives curieuses* (Paris: Olivier Perrin, 1955), p. 65. The lute as a standard object in the teaching of perspective is familiar from Dürer's "Portillon" woodcut of 1525. Albrecht Dürer, *The Painter's Manual,* trans. Walter L. Strauss (New York: Abaris Books, 1977), p. 392.

9. Ficino, *Platonic Theology,* trans. Josephine I. Burroughs, in *Journal of the History of Ideas* 5 (1944): 235. On perspective in Renaissance art, see especially Samuel Y. Edgerton, Jr., *The Renaissance Discovery of Linear Perspective* (New York: Basic Books, 1975); Claudio Guillén, "On the Concept and Metaphor of Perspective," in *Comparatists at Work,* ed. Stephen G. Nichols, Jr., and Richard B. Vowles (Waltham, Mass.: Blaisdell Pub. Co., 1968), pp. 28–90; and Erwin Panofsky, "Die Perspective als symbolische Form," *Vorträge der Bibliothek Warburg* (1924–25).

10. I am, as will be clear, skeptical of Edgar R. Samuel's theory that the skull was meant to be corrected by an unidentified optical lens held by the viewer: see "Death in the Glass—A New View of Holbein's 'Ambassadors'" in *Burlington Magazine* 105 (1963), pp. 436–41.

11. See Baltrušaitis, pp. 58–76; also Fred Leeman, *Hidden Images* (New Harry N. Abrams, 1976), pp. 13–14. Levey dismisses as exceedingly unlikely the suggestion sometimes made that the skull is a punning signature: *hohle Bein* for "hollow bone." The painting in any case is manifestly a celebration of Holbein's genius.

12. Hervey, pp. 203–7.

13. Such mockery is a commonplace in representations of the "Memento mori" theme; see, for example, Breughel's "Triumph of Death." For the heraldic use of the skull, see Dürer's "Coat of Arms with a Skull" (1503) and Holbein's own "The Arms of Death" (1538).

14. We might also note the strangely ominous lute case beneath the table and the emblematic significance of the sundials. On the lute as an emblem of harmony, see John Hollander, *The Untuning of the Sky: Ideas of Music in English Poetry, 1500–1700* (Princeton: Princeton University Press, 1961).

15. See Erwin Panofsky, *Tomb Sculpture,* ed. H. W. Janson (New York: H. N. Abrams, 1964).

16. Hervey, p. 205. It is typical of the pervasive irony of Holbein's work that this substantiality should be proved by a shadow. Levey observes that the times marked on three of the faces of the polyhedral sundial differ from one another: "The variations in the cast shadows are, of course, impossible; as the times indicated are not even the same, it is difficult to

suppose anything except that different parts of the instrument were painted at different hours" (51). Possibly so; but Holbein may also be subtly furthering the unsettling of the sense of reality.

17. Professor Michael Baxandall, to whom I am indebted for several valuable suggestions, thinks that the poses are more likely to reflect the *restraint* counselled by Northern writers of behavior manuals.

18. Roper, *Life*, p. 202. Henry VIII may have been imitating Italian princes; see, for example, Vespasiano's account of the intellectual interests of Federico, Duke of Urbino, in *Renaissance Princes, Popes, and Prelates*, trans. William George and Emily Waters (New York: Harper Torchbooks, 1963), pp. 99–105. Elton's characterization occurs in "Thomas More, Councillor (1517–1529)," in *St. Thomas More: Action and Contemplation* (New Haven: Yale University Press, 1972), pp. 87–122.

19. The definition quoted by Elizabeth McCutcheon, "Denying the Contrary: More's Use of Litotes in the *Utopia*," in *Essential Articles for the Study of Thomas More*, ed. R. S. Sylvester and G. P. Marc'hadour (Hamden, Conn.: Archon Books, 1977), p. 263.

20. McCutcheon, pp. 271–72. Elsewhere in her fine article, she remarks that "we're never quite sure where we stand in the *Utopia* . . . . On the smallest syntactical level ambiguity does exist of a sort which can never be altogether resolved, and probably was not meant to be" (272). In *Self-Consuming Artifacts: The Experience of Seventeenth-Century Literature* (Berkeley: University of California Press, 1972), Stanley Fish provides a powerful critical analysis of the literary equivalent to anamorphosis; see esp. chapter 3, "The Dialectic of the Self in Herbert's Poetry," pp. 156–223.

21. Louis Marin, *Utopiques: jeux d'espaces* (Paris: Minuit, 1973), p. 81. In "Lies and the Limitable Inane: Contradiction in More's *Utopia*" (*Renaissance Quarterly* 26 [1973], pp. 173–80), Alan F. Nagel argues that More deliberately includes contradictions in his account of Utopia to call attention to its fictionality.

22. *Utopia* satisfies virtually all of the conditions of play described by Johan Huizinga, *Homo Ludens* (Boston: Beacon, 1960).

23. For an extraordinarily subtle and complex development of the implications of meditation upon an object—here a representation of God in which the eyes appear to follow one—see Nicholas of Cusa, *The Vision of God*, trans. Emma Gurney Salter (New York: J. M. Dent & Sons, 1928).

24. As Ronald Levao is demonstrating in work in progress, this theme is developed throughout Cusa's career; the most familiar expression of it is in *De docta ignorantia*.

25. *Dialogue of Comfort*, p. 133.

26. See Natalie Zemon Davis, "Holbein's *Pictures of Death* and the Reformation at Lyons," *Studies in the Renaissance* 3 (1956), pp. 97–130.

27. On the relationship between *Utopia* and More's Christianity, there has been considerable debate. The most impressive and subtle discussion, in my view, is by J. H. Hexter in his masterful introduction to the

Yale *Utopia,* ed. Hexter and Edward Surtz, S.J., *Complete Works* 4 (1965), esp. pp. lxiv–lxxxi. Hexter's argument has been endorsed by Quentin Skinner in "More's *Utopia,*" *Past and Present* 38 (1967), pp. 152–68, and in *The Foundations of Modern Political Thought,* 2 vols. (Cambridge: Cambridge University Press, 1978), 1:193ff. Skinner overstates the case, however, when he argues that More's implication is "that it may be possible to become a perfect Christian without any knowledge of the Church or its dogmas at all" (233). More is careful to have the Utopians anticipate an evolution of their religious beliefs and to depict the benign introduction of "the name of Christ, His teaching, His character, His miracles, and the no less wonderful constancy of the many martyrs" (217).

28. *Four Last Things,* in Thomas More, *The Workes . . . in the Englysh Tonge* (London, 1557), pp. 84, 81.

29. Ibid., p. 84. Cf. *Translations of Lucian,* ed. Craig R. Thompson, in More, *Complete Works* 3:1 (1974), pp. 176–77.

30. *The Latin Epigrams of Thomas More,* ed. and trans. Leicester Bradner and Charles Arthur Lynch (Chicago: University of Chicago Press, 1953), pp. 205–6.

31. Edward Hall, *Hall's Chronicle* (London: J. Johnson, 1809), p. 516.

32. J. J. Scarisbrick, *Henry VIII* (London: Penguin, 1968), pp. 33–34.

33. Noting the similarity of this anecdote to the scripted improvisation in Medwall's *Fulgens and Lucres,* R. W. Chambers remarks that "it looks as if the 'stepping in among the players' had become a popular feature, and, since there was no one like young More capable of doing it impromptu, the parts of the 'steppers-in' had to be written by the dramatist" (*Thomas More* [New York: Harcourt Brace, 1935], p. 62).

34. Nicholas Harpsfield, *The Life and Death of Sr Thomas Moore, Knight,* ed. Elsie Vaughan Hitchcock (New York: Early English Text Society, 1963), p. 38.

35. *Utopia,* p. 4.

36. *Praise of Folly,* trans. Hoyt Hopewell Hudson (New York: Modern Library, 1941), p. 2; *The Epistles of Erasmus,* trans. Francis Morgan Nichols, 3 vols. (New York: Russell & Russell, 1963), 3:392. "It would be difficult," Erasmus notes in this letter, "to find any one more successful in speaking *ex tempore,* the happiest thoughts being attended by the happiest language; while a mind that catches and anticipates all that passes, and a ready memory, having everything as it were in stock, promptly supply whatever the time, or the occasion, demands" (398). When More married, according to Erasmus, "he chose a very young girl, a lady by birth, with her character still unformed, having been always kept in the country with her parents and sisters,—so that he was all the better able to fashion her according to his own habits" (395).

37. Indeed, if G. R. Elton is correct, this habit of mind may have contributed to More's death: "It seems not unlikely, in the circumstances, that in his conversation with Riche More for once took the hypothetical manner of argument that little bit too far, saying something that made it possible to persuade the jury that treason had in fact been spoken," *Policy and Police* (Cambridge: Cambridge University Press, 1972), pp. 416–17.

On More and Tudor training in the "moral cultivation of ambivalence," see Joel Altman, *The Tudor Play of Mind: Rhetorical Inquiry and the Development of Elizabethan Drama* (Berkeley: University of California Press, 1978), esp. pp. 31–106.

38. William Tyndale, *An Answer to Sir Thomas More's Dialogue*, in *The Works of the English Reformers: William Tyndale and John Frith*, ed. Thomas Russell, 3 vols. (London: Ebenezer Palmer, 1831), 2:15. Cf. p. 196. To which More replies, "And as for my poetry verily I can little else, and yet not that neither. But it had been good for Tyndale's soul and a thousand souls beside that he had meddled but with poetry instead of holy scripture all the days of his life," *The Confutation of Tyndale's Answer*, ed. L. Schuster, R. Marius, J. Lusardi, and R. J. Schoeck, in *Complete Works* 8 (1973), p. 176.

39. See Peter R. Allen, "*Utopia* and European Humanism: The Function of the Prefatory Letters and Verses," *Studies in the Renaissance* 10 (1963), pp. 91–107.

40. See, more recently, Jerry Mermel, "Preparations for a Politic Life: Sir Thomas More's Entry into the King's Service," *Journal of Medieval and Renaissance Studies* (1977), pp. 53–66. See likewise David M. Bevington, "The Dialogue in *Utopia*: Two Sides to the Question," *Studies in Philology* 58 (1961), p. 507: "It is central to an understanding of the dialogue to realize that in 1515–16 More perceived a dilemma. He gave expression to it in a pattern of two alternatives: Hythlodaeus's wariness of all Machiavellianism as an earnest of future ill intent, and *persona* More's cautiously idealistic tendency to seize upon any ray of hope as a basis for gradual improvement."

41. J. H. Hexter, *More's "Utopia": The Biography of an Idea* (Princeton: Princeton University Press, 1952), p. 28, reiterated in the introduction to the Yale *Utopia*, p. xix. For suggestive reflections on the relation of the two parts and on several of the aspects of More's work discussed here, see Marin, *Utopiques*, and Fredric Jameson, "Of Islands and Trenches: Neutralization and the Production of Utopian Discourse" (review of Marin), *Diacritics* (1977), pp. 2–21.

42. In this respect *Utopia* is, as Russell Ames has argued, the work of a "city" man; there is no spokesman for the aristocracy, and Hythlodaeus's searing attack on kings and warriors stands virtually unchallenged (see Ames, *Citizen Thomas More and His Utopia* [Princeton: Princeton University Press, 1949]), but also J. H. Hexter's persuasive criticisms (*Utopia*, pp. liv–lvii).

43. See, in his commendatory letter to Lupset, William Budé's satiric description of "the object of legal and civil arts and sciences": "with spiteful and watchful cunning a man should behave toward his neighbor, with whom he is joined by rights of citizenship and sometimes of family, so as always to be taking something or other away, drawing it away, shaving it away, swearing it away, squeezing it out, beating it out, scooping it out, twisting it out, shaking it out" (etc.) (7).

44. C. B. Macpherson, *The Political Theory of Possessive Individualism: Hobbes to Locke* (London: Oxford University Press, 1962). Alan Macfarlane

has argued that as early as the thirteenth century England was in effect "a capitalist-market economy without factories." That is, "there were already a developed market and mobility of labour, land was treated as a commodity and full private ownership was established, there was very considerable geographical and social mobility, a complete distinction between farm and family existed, and rational accounting and the profit motive were widespread" (*The Origins of English Individualism: The Family, Property, and Social Transition* [Oxford: Blackwell, 1978], pp. 195–96). Consequently, suggests Macfarlane, "the majority of ordinary people in England from at least the thirteenth century were rampant individidualists" (163).

45. As Hexter and Surtz note (*Utopia*, p. 404), the Henrician "Acte concernyng Artificers & Labourers" specifies labor daybreak to night from mid-September to mid-March; before 5:00 A.M. to between 7:00 and 8:00 P.M. from mid-March to mid-September.

46. One should note that in Utopia, as in Tudor culture generally, the concern is not only to ensure a high level of productivity but to avoid idleness, which is thought to be the nursery of vice and sedition.

47. Slavery remained a statutory punishment in Tudor England; see, for example, Proclamation 329, "Providing Penalty for Rumors of Military Defeat" (3 Edward VI), in Paul L. Hughes and James F. Larkin, *Tudor Royal Proclamations,* 2 vols. (New Haven: Yale University Press, 1964), 1:456.

48. *Utopia,* p. xli.

49. See Lawrence Stone, *The Family, Sex and Marriage in England 1500–1800* (New York: Harper & Row, 1977), pp. 426–32.

50. "The Rise of the Nuclear Family in Early Modern England: The Patriarchal Stage," in *The Family in History,* ed. Charles E. Rosenberg (Philadelphia: University of Pennsylvania Press, 1975), p. 25.

51. The Utopians divide pleasure between the soul and body, the former being higher. The pleasures of the body are in turn divided between overall health and the joys of the senses; again the former are higher. The joys of the senses are in turn divided between those that possess "a secret but remarkable moving force" (such as music) and those that derive from the bodily organs; the former are higher. The pleasures derived from the organs are divided between those generated by renewal (i.e. eating and drinking) and those generated by discharge; it is in this last and lowest category that the Utopians place sexual intercourse. It is difficult not to see this whole scheme as specifically designed to put sexuality in this category.

52. Natalie Zemon Davis, "Ghosts, Kin, and Progeny: Some Features of Family Life in Early Modern France," *Daedalus* 106 (1977): 87.

53. On More's kneeling, see Roper, p. 221; on "the arrow of family fortunes in historical time," see Davis, "Ghosts," p. 92.

54. T. C. Price Zimmermann, "Confession and Autobiography in the Early Renaissance," in *Renaissance Studies in Honor of Hans Baron,* ed. Anthony Molho and John A. Tedeschi (Florence: G. C. Sansoni, 1971), pp. 123–24.

55. William J. Bouwsma, in "Anxiety and the Formation of Early Modern Culture" (unpublished essay), has explored the psychological consequences of urban development in the Renaissance.

56. *The Essayes of Michael Lord of Montaigne*, trans. John Florio, 3 vols. (London: J. M. Dent, 1910), 1:254–55.

57. There is a haunting transformation of the idea of the "shop" near the close of More's life. On 12 June 1535, More's books were taken from him and he was informed of the Council's decision to increase the rigor of his confinement. From that day, according to Thomas Stapleton, "he kept the blinds of his windows drawn down day and night. His gaoler asked why he acted thus. He answered: 'Now that the goods and the implements are taken away, the shop must be closed'" (*The Life and Illustrious Martyrdom of Sir Thomas More*, trans. Philip E. Hallett (London: Burns Oates & Washbourne, 1928), p. 140.

58. See Shlomo Avineri, "War and Slavery in More's *Utopia*," *International Review of Social History* 7 (1962), p. 58: "His [the slave's] is the lot of a moral *pariah*, and the condition of slavery has less social than moral significance."

59. See Julian Pitt-Rivers, "Honour and Social Status," in J. G. Peristiany, ed., *Honour and Shame: The Values of Mediterranean Society* (Chicago: University of Chicago Press, 1966), p. 27: Honor "is only irrevocably committed by attitudes expressed in the presence of witnesses, the representatives of public opinion."

60. *Honor and Shame*, p. 9.

61. *Honor and Shame*, p. 228.

62. For the distinction between guilt and shame, see Helen Merrell Lynd, *On Shame and the Search for Identity* (New York: Harcourt Brace, 1958), and, especially, Paul Ricoeur, *The Symbolism of Evil*, trans. Emerson Buchanan (Boston: Beacon Press, 1967).

63. George Cavendish, *The Life and Death of Cardinal Wolsey*, ed. Richard S. Sylvester and Davis P. Harding (New Haven: Yale University Press, 1962), p. 166.

64. "The Life of John Picus, Earl of Mirandula," in *The English Works of Sir Thomas More*, ed. W. E. Campbell, 2 vols. (reprint of Rastell's 1557 edition; London: Eyre and Spottiswoode, 1931), 1:379, 356.

65. *Thomas More's Prayer Book. A Facsimile Reproduction of the Annotated Pages*, transcription and translation by Louis L. Martz and Richard S. Sylvester, Elizabethan Club Series 4 (New Haven: Yale University Press, 1969), p. 205.

66. Harpsfield, pp. 85–86.

67. Chambers, *Thomas More*, p. 128.

68. Characteristically, More deflates the fantasy; the letter concludes: "I was going to continue with this fascinating vision, but the rising Dawn has shattered my dream—poor me!—and shaken me off my throne and summons me back to the drudgery of the courts. But at least this thought gives me consolation: real kingdoms do not last much longer" (*St. Thomas More: Selected Letters*, ed. Elizabeth Frances Rogers [New Haven: Yale University Press, 1961], p. 85).

69. *Selected Letters,* p. 76: "Some time ago I sent you my *Nowhere;* I am most anxious to have it published soon and also that it be handsomely set off with the highest of recommendations, if possible, from several people, both intellectuals and distinguished statesmen."

70. Still, "impiety" here means not heretical belief (for which, More states explicitly, the Utopians have no physical punishment) but immoral behavior.

71. *Responsio ad Lutherum,* ed. John M. Headley, trans. Sister Scholastica Mandeville, *Complete Works* 5:1 (1969), pp. 305–7.

72. *Responsio,* p. 119.

73. John Foxe, *Acts and Monuments,* ed. Josiah Pratt, 8 vols. (London: George Seely, 1870), 4:643.

74. *Dialogue Concerning Heresies,* in *English Works,* ed. Campbell, 2:322.

75. On Erasmus's conception of the *consensus fidelium,* see James K. McConica, "Erasmus and the Grammar of Consent," *Strinium Erasmianum* 2 (1969): 77–99. On More's relation to Erasmus's biblical scholarship, see Richard C. Marius, "Thomas More's View of the Church," in *Confutation,* pp. 1351–52. On *consensus* in More's thought, see Marius, p. 1292; John Headley, "More Against Luther: The Substance of the Diatribe," in *Responsio,* pp. 732–74; André Prévost, *Thomas More et la crise de la pensée européene* (Paris: Maison Mame, 1969), pp. 158–60; Rainer Pineas, *Thomas More and Tudor Polemics* (Bloomington: Indiana University Press, 1968).

76. Tyndale may argue that the churchmen are like the scribes and pharisees, mired in error, but More can show him (with a wry glance at the Reformer's own method) "the plain scriptures, in which God hath made many such plentious promises of his assistence with his Holy Spirit in his church, perpetually to keep it from all damnable errors, by teaching it and leading it into every truth that though he suffer many great pieces of people to fall out thereof, and so little and little the body to be minished and made a small flock in comparison, till his pleasure shall be to increase it again, yet shall he never neither suffer it to be destroyed nor the flock that remaineth how many branches soever the devil blow off, to be brought unto the scarcity either of faith or virtue, that the synagogue of the Jews was at Christ's coming" (*Confutation,* pp. 616–17).

77. Ibid., p. 617. "These heretics," More writes, "be almost as many sects as men, and never one agreeth with other, so that if the world were to learn the right way of them, that matter were much like, as if a man walking in a wilderness that fain would find the right way toward the town that he intended, should meet with a many of lewd mocking knaves, which when the poor man had prayed them to tell him the way, would get them into a roundel turning them back to back, and then speak all at once, and each of them tell him, 'this way,' each of them pointing forth with his hand the way that his face standeth" (772).

78. *Responsio,* p. 599.

79. *Responsio,* pp. 619–21. No one, I trust, will be surprised to learn that Luther and Tyndale were not, after all, defenders of the liberty of the individual.

80. *Responsio*, p. 413.

81. Thus More can attack the anonymous author of the heretical *Supper of the Lord* as "Master Masker": "And verily as we see sometime, that such as walk in visors, have much the less fear and shame, both what they do and what they say, because they think themself unknown: so do these folk oftentimes little force [i.e. care] what they write that use to put out their books, and set not their names unto them" (*Answere . . . to the Poysened Booke* [London: W. Rastell, 1534], B6ᵛ–B7ʳ).

82. *Confutation*, p. 178.

83. "I say therefore in these days in which men by their own default misconstrue and take harm of the very Scripture of God, until men better amend, if any man would now translate *Moria* [i.e. *The Praise of Folly*] into English, or some works either that I have myself written ere this, albeit there be none harm therein, folk yet being (as they be) given to take harm of that that is good, I would not only my darling's books but mine own also, help to burn them both with mine own hands" (*Confutation*, p. 179).

84. McConica, p. 89.

85. *Responsio*, pp. 259, 141.

86. Cf. Columbus, *Journals and Other Documents on the Life and Voyages of Christopher Columbus*, trans. and ed. Samuel Eliot Morison (New York: Heritage Press, 1963), p. 65. More objects to violent or even strident attempts at conversion; see *Utopia*, p. 219.

87. E. M. Cioran, *The New Gods*, trans. Richard Howard (New York: Quadrangle, 1974), p. 17.

88. *Responsio*, p. 311.

89. *Confutation*, p. 62.

90. G. R. Elton, "Sir Thomas More and the Opposition to Henry VIII," *Bulletin of the Institute of Historical Research* (London University) 41 (1968), pp. 19–34.

91. Roper, p. 225. Elton comments suggestively on this incident in "Sir Thomas More and the Opposition to Henry VIII," pp. 25–26.

92. *Hall's Chronicle*, p. 780.

93. *Selected Letters*, p. 211.

94. Chambers, p. 336.

95. Chambers, pp. 336–37.

96. *Selected Letters*, p. 213.

97. *Selected Letters*, p. 222.

98. *Selected Letters*, pp. 251–52.

99. Roper, p. 216.

100. See Chambers, p. 306.

101. *Hall's Chronicle*, p. 317.

102. We may note the identical point made in accounts of Protestant martyrdoms; see, for example, Foxe's account of Dr. Taylor, Vicar of Hadley: "All the way Dr. Taylor was joyful and merry, as one that accounted himself going to a pleasant banquet or bridal" (Foxe, *Acts and Monuments* 6:695).

103. See *Selected Letters*, pp. 224ff; *The Correspondence of Sir Thomas*

More, ed. Elizabeth Frances Rogers (Princeton: Princeton University Press, 1947), pp. 514–32.

104. *De Tristitia Christi*, ed. and trans. Clarence H. Miller, in *Complete Works* 14 (1976), p. 249.

105. *Selected Letters*, p. 225. More describes his own timorousness in a letter to Margaret; see *Selected Letters*, pp. 239–42.

106. *De Tristitia*, p. 253. See the remark of G. E. Haupt: "It is not too much to say that to some extent More sees Christ in his own image or at least emphasizes those aspects of the life of Christ which are most relevant to his own situation. There can, for instance, be little doubt that More is much more interested in the mental anguish of Christ in the garden than in the crucifixion itself" (*Treatise on the Passion, Treatise on the Blessed Body, Instructions and Prayers*, in *Complete Works* 13 [1976], p. clxxvii).

107. See Louis L. Martz, "Thomas More: The Sacramental Life," *Thought* 52 (1977), pp. 300–318.

Chapter Two

1. John Foxe, *Acts and Monuments* 4:702. The account of Bainham's martyrdom occurs on pages 697–706. On Foxe's book, see William Haller, *The Elect Nation: The Meaning and Relevance of Foxe's "Book of Martyrs"* (New York: Harper & Row, 1964).

2. *The Apologye of Syr Thomas More, Knyght*, ed. Arthur I. Taft (London: Early English Text Society, 1930), p. lxxxv. In this work of 1533 More specifically denies some of the charges of maltreatment of heretics that are repeated in Foxe's account, but More does not deny the imprisonment of heretics in his Chelsea house.

3. R. W. Chambers' translation in *Thomas More* (New York: Harcourt Brace, 1935), p. 286.

4. *Confutation*, p. 16. More speaks of Hitton as "the devil's stinking martyr of whose burning Tyndale maketh boast" (p. 17). On More as persecutor, see Leland Miles, "Persecution and the *Dialogue of Comfort*: A Fresh Look at the Charges Against Thomas More," *Journal of British Studies* 5 (1965), pp. 19–30.

5. Chambers, p. 178. See the account of John Tewkesbury's imprisonment in Foxe, 4:689.

6. Roper, p. 238.

7. *Confutation*, p. 710.

8. Foxe, 3:730.

9. Foxe, 3:281. Foxe says he is using Tyndale's edition. On the conduct of heresy investigations in the fifteenth and early sixteenth century, see John A. F. Thomson, *The Later Lollards, 1414–1520* (London: Oxford University Press, 1965), pp. 220–38. On Thorpe and early Lollardry, see K. B. McFarlane, *John Wycliffe and the Beginnings of English Non-conformity* (London: English Universities Press, 1952).

10. Foxe repeatedly refers to the archbishop of Canterbury, Thomas Arundel, as "Caiaphas"; for example, see 3:326, where he is described as "sitting in Caiaphas's room."

11. Foxe, 3:334–35. The primary thrust of Oldcastle's gesture is against the so-called worship of images, but the heretical position frequently contains the related sense of the presence of the sacred in the everyday. Thus in 1509 John Blomstone was accused of asserting "that it was foolishness to go on pilgrimage to the image of our Lady of Doncaster, Walsingham, or of the Tower of the city of Coventry: for a man might as well worship the blessed Virgin by the fire-side in the kitchen, as in the aforesaid places, and as well might a man worship the blessed Virgin, when he seeth his mother or sister, as in visiting the images; because they be no more but dead stocks and stones" (Foxe, 4:133).

12. Foxe, 3:542.

13. So, similarly, certain radicals in our century have welcomed and even attempted to induce repressive violence as proof that state institutions rested not on democratic consent but on force.

14. See Robert J. Lifton, *Thought Reform and the Psychology of Totalism* (New York: Norton, 1961). Lifton's subject is brainwashing in China; there are, of course, in the West ample scriptural and patristic sources justifying the persecution of heretics.

15. Quoted in Henry Kamen, *The Rise of Toleration* (London: Weidenfeld & Nicolson, 1967), pp. 13–14. In the struggle against the Donatists, Augustine develops a subtle conception of the relationship between physical constraint and the free soul:

> "You should not consider this constraint in itself, but the quality of the object to which one is constrained, whether it is good or bad. It is not that a man can become good in spite of himself, but the fear of suffering which he hates either makes him throw aside the obstinacy which held him back, or helps him to recognize the truth he did not recognize. Consequently, this fear leads him to reject the falsehood he championed or to seek the truth he did not know; thus he will come to attach himself voluntarily to what he first rejected."

Quoted in Joseph Lecler, *Toleration and the Reformation*, trans. T. L. Westow, 2 vols. (New York: Association Press, 1960), 1:56.

16. Michel Foucault, *Discipline and Punish: The Birth of the Prison*, trans. Alan Sheridan (New York: Pantheon, 1977), p. 29.

17. For the theatricality of executions, see Samuel Y. Edgerton, Jr., "*Maniera* and the *Mannaia:* Decorum and Decapitation in the Sixteenth Century," in *The Meaning of Mannerism*, ed. Franklin W. Robinson and Stephen G. Nichols, Jr. (Hanover, N.H.: University Press of New England, 1972), pp. 67–103.

18. See Nicolas Perella, *The Kiss, Sacred and Profane* (Berkeley: University of California Press, 1969).

19. Both sides frequently cited 2 Cor. 11:14: "for Satan himself is transformed into an angel of light." The notion that the religious community is threatened by what Peter Brown calls "a sinister *Doppelgänger*" has been traced back to the Dead Sea Scrolls; see Brown, *Augustine of Hippo* (Berkeley: University of California Press, 1969), p. 213, and W. H. C. Frend,

Martyrdom and Persecution in the Early Church (Oxford: Blackwell, 1965), p. 61.

20. The setting—a warehouse in Bow-lane—suggests not only the secrecy of the conventicle, but the important connection between the early Protestant community in England and the merchant class through whose international ties prohibited books could be smuggled from the continent.

21. Foxe, 5:421.

22. There is not enough evidence about the letters Bainham wrote at the time of his public return to heresy to be very clear about their part in this process: perhaps he felt that a letter to the bishop was necessary to cancel his written abjuration. But he also wrote to his brother, apparently in bold, even reckless, terms: at the second interrogation, Bainham retracted certain things he had written to his brother, saying "he did it by ignorance, and he did not oversee his letters" (4:703). There are two ways to interpret this retraction: either Bainham was once more wavering between saving his life and defending his Protestant convictions or, alternately, he had, in the great emotional release of his "relapse," written and said things to which he did not, in his more sober moments, subscribe. In this case, the denials at the second interrogatory must be seen not as hopeless attempts to save himself, but as attempts to state with precision just what he firmly believed in and was willing to die for; i.e. to distinguish, in the manner of Frith, between necessary dogma and adiaphora.

23. Sigmund Freud, "Inhibitions, Symptom and Anxiety" (1926), in *Standard Edition of the Complete Works*, trans. James Strachey, 24 vols. (London: Hogarth Press, 1959), 20:119. See also "Notes upon a Case of Obsessional Neurosis" (1909), *Standard Edition* 10:235–36.

24. Indeed, as Freud's reference to magic suggests, it seems likely that *he* developed the concept of undoing at least partly from analogous symbolic processes in religion; it would seem difficult to turn an analogy drawn from a phenomenon into an explanation of that phenomenon.

25. Seymour Byman, "Ritualistic Acts and Compulsive Behavior: The Pattern of Tudor Martyrdom," *American Historical Review* 3 (1978), p. 627. Much of what Byman cites as evidence of "compulsive behavior" seems to me quite unconvincing. Thus where Foxe writes that after dinner Ridley "used to sit an hour or thereabouts, talking, or playing at the chess," Byman comments that "in order to cope with doubt, Ridley carefully scheduled even his chess games" (631).

26. See Thomas N. Tentler, *Sin and Confession on the Eve of the Reformation* (Princeton: Princeton University Press, 1977). Tentler's fine book has largely superseded Henry Charles Lea's *A History of Auricular Confession and Indulgences in the Latin Church*, 3 vols. (Philadelphia: Lea Brothers, 1896), still useful, however, for its massive detail. There are powerful speculations upon the importance of this material in Michel Foucault, *La volonté de savoir* (Paris: Gallimard, 1976).

27. *The Obedience of a Christian Man*, in William Tyndale, *Doctrinal*

Treatises and Introductions to Different Portions of The Holy Scriptures, ed.
Henry Walter (Cambridge: Parker Society, 1848), p. 263. More quotes this
passage in the *Confutation* and remarks that "Luther, that was Tyndale's
master, as lewd as he is, played never the blasphemous fool against confession so far yet as Tyndale doth. For Luther, albeit he would make every
man, and every woman too, sufficient and meetly to serve for a confessor,
yet confesseth he that shrift is very necessary, and doth much good, and
would in no wise have left it" (*Confutation,* p. 89).

All citations of the *Obedience* are to the Parker Society text.

28. There are, of course, exceptions of which the most famous is
Luther's autobiographical remarks which he published as a Preface to the
Wittenberg edition of his Latin works. Byman (p. 633) cites an account of
the practice of the Marian martyr John Bradford: "He used to make unto
himself an ephemeris or a journal, in which he used to write all such
notable things as wither he might see in that book the signs of his smitten
heart" (Thomas Sampson, Preface to Bradford, *Two Notable Sermons Made
by That Worthy Martyr of Christ Master John Bradford* [London, 1574]).

29. "The Work of Art in the Age of Mechanical Reproduction," in *Il-
luminations,* ed. Hannah Arendt, trans. Harry Zohn (New York: Schocken,
1969), pp. 217–51. On the significance of the printed book, see especially
Elizabeth L. Eisenstein, *The Printing Press as an Agent of Change: Com-
munications and Cultural Transformations in Early Modern Europe,* 2 vols.
(New York: Cambridge University Press, 1972).

30. It is tempting to speculate that these works may have been read
silently far more often than other books and manuscripts; after all, one
must exercise extreme caution with prohibited books. If this were so, it
might give readers still more of the sense that the books were occurring
deep within their own minds, away from all external manifestation. There
is, however, no substantial evidence for such silent reading, and we must
recall the importance for someone like Bainham of his fellow believers.

31. Thus the Protestants could accept, in a sense, the Catholic symbolism of the flames of the *auto-da-fé* as symbolic of hell, but reinterpret
this descent into hell as the prologue to an ascent to heaven.

32. See, for example, *Confutation,* pp. 22–23: "Another is there also,
whom his [Tyndale's] unhappy books have brought unto the fire, Thomas
Bilney." In the heretic Tewkesbury's house, More writes, "was found
Tyndale's book of Obedience . . . and his wicked book also of The Wicked
Mammom." More claims that Tewkesbury, who was burned at Smithfield
during More's chancellorship, would not have become a heretic "if Tyndale's ungracious books had never come in his hand. For which the poor
wretch lieth now in hell and crieth out on him, and Tyndale, if he do not
amend in time, . . . is like to find him when they come together, an hot
firebrand burning at his back, that all the water in the world will never be
able to quench" (*Confutation,* p. 22).

33. Tyndale's authorship of the English *Enchiridion* is uncertain; see
Anne O'Donnell, "A Critical Edition of the 1534 English Translation of
Erasmus' Enchiridion militis Christiani" (Ph.D. diss., Yale University,

1972), pp. 51–58. I am indebted for this reference and for other biblio-graphical assistance to Professor Donald J. Millus of Coastal Carolina College.

According to Norbert Elias's remarkable study of the development of manners, *The Civilizing Process* (trans. Edmund Jephcott [New York: Uri-zen Books, 1978]), Erasmus's most influential work of this kind, and one of the most important in the period, was the *De civilitate morum puerilium.*

34. *Lectures on Genesis* II, 65; quoted in William J. Bouwsma, "Anxiety and the Formation of Early Modern Culture," unpublished.

35. See Lawrence Stone, *The Causes of the English Revolution, 1529–1642* (New York: Harper & Row, 1972); Immanuel Wallerstein, *The Modern World-System: Capitalist Agriculture and the Origins of the European World-Economy in the Sixteenth Century* (New York: Academic Press, 1974); Eric Kerridge, *The Agricultural Revolution* (New York: A. M. Kelley, 1968); Bouwsma, "Anxiety."

36. In Arthur F. Kinney, ed., *Elizabethan Backgrounds: Historical Docu-ments of the Age of Elizabeth I* (Hamden, Conn.: Archon, 1975), p. 63.

37. J. J. Scarisbrick, *Henry VIII* (London: Penguin, 1968), p. 325.

38. In the first edition of the *Exposition of 1 John*, Tyndale even went so far as to hint that the king had contracted syphilis; see Donald Millus, "Tyndale on the First Epistle of Saint John," *Moreana* 13 (1976), pp. 40–41.

39. *The exposition of the Fyrste Epistle of seynt Ihon, with a Prologge before it:* by W. T. (Antwerp: M. de Keyser, 1531), p. Fl^r.

40. *The Parable of the Wicked Mammon* (1527), in *Doctrinal Treatises*, p. 42.

41. *Exposition of the Fyrste Epistle of seynt Ihon*, p. El^r. Tyndale can, however, counsel his readers, in the prologue to the 1525 New Testament, to "counterfeit Christ" (*Doctrinal Treatises*, p. 20).

42. This evaluation of Tyndale may be traced at least as far back as Abednego Seller's *History of Passive Obedience since the Reformation* (Amsterdam: Theodore Johnson, 1689), p. 20. For a useful discussion of the distinction between conservative and radical Protestants, see Quentin Skinner, *The Foundations of Modern Political Thought* 2:73–81.

43. More, *Dialogue Concerning Tyndale*, in *The English Works of Sir Thomas More* 2:257. See *Obedience*, p. 332: if a prince commands us "to do evil, we must then disobey, and say, 'We are otherwise commanded of God.'" "So far yet are the worldly powers and rulers to be obeyed only," writes Tyndale in the prologue to the 1525 New Testament, "as their commandments repugn not against the commandment of God; and then, ho" (in *Doctrinal Treatises*, p. 25).

44. "A Table, expounding certain words in the First Book of Moses, called Genesis," in *Doctrinal Treatises*, p. 407.

45. It is nonetheless significant that when he turns to someone for help, Tyndale finds Humphrey Monmouth, a wealthy cloth merchant, who supplies him with food, a place to live, and money. Still, this does not mean that Protestantism is the "party" of the middle class; the issue is clearly much more complicated. See Stone, *Causes of the English Revolu-*

tion, pp. 58–117; Christopher Hill, *Society and Puritanism in Pre-Revolutionary England,* 2d ed. (New York: Schocken Books, 1967); Michael Waltzer, *The Revolution of the Saints* (Cambridge, Mass.: Harvard University Press, 1965); Skinner, *Foundations,* vol. 2.

46. *Dialogue Concerning Tyndale,* p. 112.

47. "A Pathway into the Holy Scripture," in *Doctrinal Treatises,* p. 17. The "Pathway" is a revised version, published separately, of the 1525 Prologue; the following quotations are from the original version. Cf. Luther, *De servo arbitrio (On the Bondage of the Will)* [1525], in *Luther and Erasmus: Free Will and Salvation,* ed. E. Gordon Rupp et al. (Philadelphia: Westminster Press, 1964).

48. *Dialogue Concerning Tyndale,* pp. 206–11.

49. Quoted in W. Schwarz, *Principles and Problems of Biblical Translation* (Cambridge: Cambridge University Press, 1955), p. 10.

50. It is worth noting perhaps that Tyndale apparently took to heart More's criticism of his rendering of *presbyter* as *senior;* in later editions of the New Testament, the word is changed to *elder.*

51. J. F. Mozley, *William Tyndale* (London: Society for Promoting Christian Knowledge, 1937), pp. 147–50. The story is related in Hall's *Chronicle.*

52. "Prologue to the Book of Genesis," in *Doctrinal Treatises,* p. 405. The figure of 50,000 copies is that of H. W. Hoare, *Our English Bible,* rev. ed. (London: John Murray, 1911), p. 161; see also Arthur S. Herbert, *Historical Catalogue of Printed Editions of the English Bible: 1525–1961* (London: British and Foreign Bible Society, 1968).

53. This effect must have been heightened by the fact that children first learned to read from Latin primers and hence "must have thought of reading, from the very beginning, as something artificial, set apart in a realm of its own" (Susan Noakes, "The Fifteen Oes, the *Disticha Catonis,* Marculfius, and Dick, Jane, and Sally," in *The University of Chicago Library Society Bulletin* 2 [1977], p. 7). The vernacular then may have been powerfully linked to the earliest experiences of language.

In a remarkable work in progress, Walter Kerrigan is exploring the psychosexual implications for literature of Latin as the "father tongue" and English as the "mother tongue" (forthcoming in *Psychiatry and the Humanities,* ed. Joseph Smith, vol. 4).

54. In *Doctrinal Treatises,* p. 400. The Scripture is not only a defense; God's word, writes Tyndale in the preface to *The Parable of the Wicked Mammon,* "is the right weapon to slay sin, vice, and all iniquity" (in *Doctrinal Treatises,* p. 41).

55. For the royal proclamations against Tyndale's translation, see *Tudor Royal Proclamations* 1:181–86, 193–97. The latter proclamation, 22 Henry VIII (1530), declares "that having respect to the malignity of this present time, with the inclination of people to erroneous opinions, the translation of the New Testament and the Old into the vulgar tongue of English should rather be the occasion of continuance or increase of errors among the said people than any benefit or commodity toward the weal of their

souls, and that it shall now be more convenient that the same people have the Holy Scripture expounded to them by preachers in their sermons." It warns that henceforth those who "buy, receive, keep, or have" the Old or New Testament in English, French or Dutch "will answer to the King's highness at their uttermost perils" (196–97).

56. Hugh Latimer, *Sermons,* ed. George Elwes Corrie, 2 vols. (Cambridge: Parker Society, 1844), 1:222. The focus of Bilney's fear, it should be added, was not the book but the stake.

57. Foxe, 4:653.

58. *Confutation,* p. 359.

59. See Lawrence Stone, "Literacy and Education in England, 1640–1900," *Past and Present* 42 (1969), p. 101. See also Stone, "The Educational Revolution in England, 1560–1640," *Past and Present* 28 (1964), pp. 49–80.

60. *Tudor Royal Proclamations,* 1:297.

Elizabeth concurred and commanded that her clergy "shall discourage no man from the reading of any part of the Bible either in Latin or in English, but shall rather exhort every person to read the same with great humility and reverence as the very lively word of God and the special food of man's souls . . . ." (*Tudor Royal Proclamations* 2:119).

61. Quoted in Thomas Laqueur, "The Cultural Origins of Popular Literacy in England, 1500–1850," *Oxford Review of Education* 2 (1976), p. 262.

62. Laqueur, p. 262.

63. John Bunyan, *Grace Abounding to the Chief of Sinners* (1666), ed. Roger Sharrock (London: Oxford University Press, 1966), p. 32.

64. Foxe, 3:719–20. In the *Histoire de la mappemonde papistique* (Geneva, 1567), the Lyons engraver Pierre Eskrich depicts Protestant pastors breaking down the walls of the papal city with books (see Natalie Zemon Davis, "The Sacred and the Body Social in Sixteenth-Century Lyon," forthcoming).

65. For the larger argument of *sola scriptura* vs. *sola ecclesia,* see George H. Tavard, *Holy Writ or Holy Church: The Crisis of the Protestant Reformation* (London: Burns & Oates, 1959).

66. See John S. Coolidge, *The Pauline Renaissance in England: Puritanism and the Bible* (Oxford: At the Clarendon Press, 1970). The principle of "feeling faith," so confidently affirmed by the *Obedience,* would soon be at the center of the debate over the precise nature of religious observance that raged for decades between the Puritans and the Anglican establishment. The breadth and vagueness of the formulation in Tyndale suggests that he, at least, did not intend it to suggest that only those actions may be undertaken that have *explicit* sanction in the Bible. Notwithstanding his insistence on covenant and contract, he does not solely or even primarily turn to Scripture in the manner, for example, that Orthodox Jews turn to the *Shulchan Aruch,* as a detailed code of action. Tyndale does not *exclude* such a use of Scripture—on the contrary, its case histories do serve as infallible guides to correct behavior—but rather he includes it in a larger and more flexible identification with the sacred.

67. *Dialogue Concerning Heresies,* 2:112–13.

68. *An Answer to Sir Thomas More's Dialogue,* ed. Henry Walter (Cambridge: Parker Society, 1850), p. 49.

69. *Confutation,* p. 723.

70. Erasmus, *Enchiridion Militis Christiani: The Manual of the Christian Knight,* trans. William Tyndale? (London: Methuen & Co., 1905), p. 146. One should note that the issues involved in the interpretation of the Bible are by no means new in the Reformation; for medieval arguments, see especially M.-D. Chenu, *Nature, Man, and Society in the Twelfth Century,* trans. Jerome Taylor and Lester K. Little (Chicago: University of Chicago Press, 1957).

71. *Confutation,* pp. 165–66. It should be noted that Tyndale is only granting for the sake of argument the notion that *congregation* is a more general term than *church.*

72. *Confutation,* pp. 220–21.

73. Quoted from *The English Hexapla* (London: Samuel Bagster & Sons, 1848). This is the most convenient starting point for comparative analysis of early English translations.

74. "A Prologue Upon the Epistle of St Paul to the Romans," in *Doctrinal Treatises,* p. 505.

75. *Confutation,* p. 9.

76. "Prologue to Genesis," *Doctrinal Treatises,* p. 404.

77. Quoted in F. F. Bruce, *History of the Bible in English,* 3d ed. (New York: Oxford University Press, 1978), p. 20.

78. "Preface to the Five Books of Moses" (1530), in *Doctrinal Treatises,* p. 395.

79. Quoted in Robert Demaus, *William Tindale,* pop. ed., revised by Richard Lovett (London: The Religious Tract Society, 1925), pp. 357–58.

80. Foxe, 5:117; I have followed Demaus and Mozley in altering the indirect discourse given in Foxe to direct discourse.

81. *The Paraclesis,* trans. John C. Olin, in Erasmus, *Christian Humanism and the Reformation: Selected Writings,* ed. Olin (New York: Harper & Row, 1965), p. 97.

82. "The Parable of the Wicked Mammon," in *Doctrinal Treatises,* p. 37.

83. Quoted in Mozley, *William Tyndale,* p. 250.

84. It is not known for whom Phillips was working; see Mozley, *William Tyndale,* pp. 294–342.

85. Mozley, *William Tyndale,* p. 334.

86. Ibid., p. 339.

87. Foxe, 5:127.

88. See William A. Clebsch, *England's Earliest Protestants, 1520–1535* (New Haven: Yale University Press, 1964), p. 191; L. J. Trinterud, "A Reappraisal of William Tyndale's Debt to Martin Luther," *Church History* 21 (1962), pp. 24–45.

89. *Doctrinal Treatises,* p. 13.

90. "On His Own Ignorance and That of Many Others," trans. Hans Nachod, in *The Renaissance Philosophy of Man,* ed. Ernst Cassirer, Paul

Oskar Kristeller, and John Herman Randall, Jr. (Chicago: University of Chicago Press, 1948), p. 105.

91. *Doctrinal Treatises*, p. 403; see Clebsch, *England's Earliest Protestants*, p. 182.

92. C. S. Lewis, *English Literature in the Sixteenth Century, Excluding Drama* (Oxford: At the Clarendon Press, 1954), p. 190.

93. *The Parable of the Wicked Mammon*, in *Doctrinal Treatises*, p. 103.

94. *Obedience*, p. 161.

95. "A Table," in *Doctrinal Treatises*, p. 407.

96. *Expositions and Notes on Sundry Portions of The Holy Scriptures, together with the Practice of Prelates*, ed. Henry Walter (Cambridge: Parker Society, 1849), p. 268.

97. *Answer to Sir Thomas More's Dialogue*, p. 157; see also pp. 166, 188, 193.

Chapter Three

1. See E. G. Rupp, *Studies in the Making of the English Protestant Tradition (Mainly in the Reign of Henry VIII)* (Cambridge: Cambridge University Press, 1947), p. 132: "Excerpts from an heretical Primer were condemned by the bishops in 1530 because 'he puttith in the book of the vii Psalmes, but he leveth owt the whole Litany, by which apperith his erronyous opynyon agenst praying to saints latanie.' . . . This agrees with More's statement about Joye's Primer 'wherein the Seven Psalms be set in without the Litany and the Dirige is left.'" Rupp notes further that "the first publication to bear Luther's name and authority had been his edition of these Seven Penitential Psalms, and all that we know of this Primer suggests contact with the doctrines of the Reformers."

2. On Protestantism and Wyatt's version of the psalms, see especially H. A. Mason, *Humanism and Poetry in the Early Tudor Period* (London: Routledge & Kegan Paul, 1959), pp. 209–21; Robert G. Twombly, "Thomas Wyatt's Paraphrase of the Penitential Psalms of David," in *Texas Studies in Language and Literature* 12 (1970), pp. 345–80.

3. Psalm 51, lines 503–5. Wyatt had similarly added the phrase "the heart's forest" to his translation of Petrarch, "The long love that in my thought doth harbor."

Line numbers for Wyatt's poetry refer to those given in *Collected Poems of Sir Thomas Wyatt*, ed. Kenneth Muir and Patricia Thomson (Liverpool: Liverpool University Press, 1969). For a book-length critique of this edition, see H. A. Mason, *Editing Wyatt* (Cambridge: Cambridge Quarterly Publications, 1972). I have consulted Richard Harrier, *The Canon of Sir Thomas Wyatt's Poetry* (Cambridge, Mass.: Harvard University Press, 1975), and *Sir Thomas Wyatt: Collected Poems*, ed. Joost Daalder (London: Oxford University Press, 1975).

4. Both Aretino and Campensis stress at this point that outward deeds are *signs* of the inner state of contrition (see *Collected Poems*, Commentary, p. 378); though he elsewhere concurs, Wyatt takes this opportunity to infuse his version with the spirit of Luther's famous *Prologue to Romans*,

as translated by Tyndale: "If the law were fleshly, and but man's doctrine, it might be satisfied, and stilled with outward deeds. But now is the law ghostly, and no man fulfilleth it, except that all that he doth spring of love from the bottom of the heart." Good works spring naturally from faith, but they may not by themselves be taken as the assurance of anything; everything depends upon the state of the heart which in turn depends upon the will of God. (Cf. Mason, *Humanism and Poetry*, pp. 215–19.)

5. Apart from the Judeo-Christian West, we should recall, most of the great civilizations of the world have placed overwhelming emphasis not on the isolated member but on the conformity of every element to its role in the society; the dominant ideology of Hinduism, for example, begins from the standpoint of the total hierarchical structure and then moves to the particular, constituent parts. See Louis Dumont, *Homo Hierarchicus: The Caste System and Its Implications,* trans. Mark Sainsbury (Chicago: University of Chicago Press, 1970), p. 4.

6. Ricoeur, *The Symbolism of Evil,* pp. 103–4.

7. In *Medieval Handbooks of Penance,* trans. and ed. John J. McNeill and Helena M. Gamer (New York: Columbia University Press, 1938), p. 315. See Oscar D. Watkins, *A History of Penance,* 2 vols. (London: Longmans, 1920), 2:58.

8. See Thomas N. Tentler, *Sin and Confession on the Eve of the Reformation* (Princeton: Princeton University Press, 1977), pp. 16–27; John Bossy, "The Social History of Confession in the Age of the Reformation," *Transactions of the Royal Historical Society,* 5th ser., 25 (1975), pp. 21–38.

9. "Treatise Concerning the Fruitful Sayings of David the King and Prophet in the Seven Penitential Psalms," in *The English Works of John Fisher, Bishop of Rochester,* ed. John E. B. Mayor (London: Early English Text Society, 1876), p. 24.

10. "Est autem multis modis huis Psalmi cognitio tum necessaria tum utilis: Continet enim doctrinam de praecipuis nostrae Religionis capitibus, de Poenitentia, de Peccato, de Gratia, et Justificatione, Item du Cultu quem nos praestare debemus." Quoted in Mason, *Humanism and Poetry,* p. 217.

11. The point is worth emphasizing because the hard-won and precious bourgeois myth that the inner life is somehow divorced from the legitimate exercise of power has been read backward into history so that the Spanish Inquisition or the Puritan witch trials have seemed only obscene aberrations. The fourteenth-century legislation that decrees it high treason to "compass or imagine the Death of . . . the King" does not deem it useful or important to distinguish between "imagine" as a subjective, inner state and "imagine" as the designing of a "real" plot (Leon Radzinowicz, *A History of English Criminal Law and Its Administration from 1750* [London: Stevens & Sons, 1948] 1:7).

12. *English Works of John Fisher,* p. 33.

13. The personal intensity of the penitential psalms then must not be viewed as something Wyatt somehow tacked on to conventional material; rather, Wyatt's inwardness in these poems is itself largely the product of

the total discursive field constituted by other versions of the psalms and by related doctrinal and devotional treatises. If the distinctive voice seems intermittent, the failure is not caused by the dead weight of "impersonal" convention, but by the inadequacies of a poetic technique still in the early stages of development. As his contemporaries understood, Wyatt had virtually to invent for English poetry a language suited to his expressive ends; those ends are "his own" precisely by virtue of the power of the convention.

14. Raymond Southall, *Literature and the Rise of Capitalism* (London: Lawrence & Wishart, 1973), p. 22.

15. Mason, *Humanism and Poetry*, pp. 202–9. Surrey, in *Wyatt: The Critical Heritage*, ed. Patricia Thomson (London: Routledge & Kegan Paul, 1974), p. 28.

16. Ralegh, *History of the World* (London, 1614), p. C4^v. Ralegh wrote of Henry VIII that "if all the pictures and patterns of a merciless prince were lost in the world, they might all again be painted to the life out of the story of this king" (A4^v).

17. Mason, *Humanism and Poetry*, p. 216, suggests that the imagery here and at lines 345–48 reflects the horror of those who witnessed the "first deadly onslaughts" of syphilis; if so, the physical revulsion has been absorbed into the depiction of a moral state. It is adulterous sexual desire that is itself the disease, the filth that must be purged by suffering.

18. Cf. Luther on the will: "Thus the human will is . . . like a beast of burden. If God rides it, it wills and goes where God wills. . . . If Satan rides it, it wills and goes where Satan wills; nor can it choose to run to either of the two riders or to seek him out, but the riders themselves contend for the possession and control of it" (*Luther and Erasmus: Free Will and Salvation,* trans. and ed. E. Gordon Rupp [London: The Library of Christian Classics, 1969], p. 140). See also Wyatt to his son, "the chiefest and infallible ground [of virtue] is the dread and Reverence of God," in *Life and Letters of Sir Thomas Wyatt,* ed. Kenneth Muir (Liverpool: Liverpool University Press, 1963), pp. 38–39.

19. Maurice Merleau-Ponty, *The Primacy of Perception,* ed. James M. Edie (Evanston: Northwestern University Press, 1964), p. 5.

20. In trying to grasp the origins of this pervasive suspicion of the body, it is tempting to invoke the state of both medical science and personal hygiene in the sixteenth century: men and women endured a daily level of physical discomfort, indeed quite often excruciating pain, that is for us all but unimaginable. Theological objections aside, the phenomenological celebration of the body might well have seemed to most men a slender reed on which to base a conception of human identity. But without dismissing the miseries of ulcers, tumors, gastrointestinal disorders, and toothaches, I think it likely that the attitude of Wyatt and others in his situation was far more powerfully influenced by cultural forces, above all by their experience of power.

21. "Who List His Wealth and Ease Retain," line 16.

22. *Life and Letters,* pp. 39–40.

23. For powerful reflections upon perception and the sense of the body, see Michael Fried, "The Beholder in Courbet: His Early Self-Portraits and Their Place in His Art," *Glyph* 4 (1978), pp. 84–129.

24. See Wyatt to his son: "God hath of his goodness chastised me and not cast me clean out of his favor" (*Life and Letters*, p. 40).

25. *Life and Letters*, p. 35.

26. Donald Friedman, "The 'Thing' in Wyatt's Mind," *Essays in Criticism* 16 (1966), p. 377. The satires echo as well the contrast between outward and inward: see, for example, "Mine Own John Poins," 10–13.

27. "Mine Own John Poins," 76. One should note that the negation is qualified by the rhetorical insistence on the speaker's *inability*, on what he *cannot* do.

28. Thus for Wyatt it is not God but "fortune" that has given rulers the right "to strike the stroke," while submission in the psalms has no reference to secular authority.

29. As Wyatt's early nineteenth-century editor, George Frederick Nott, observes, these lines are imitated and enlarged from Persius's third Satire (*Wyatt: The Critical Heritage*, pp. 71–72).

30. Seneca, *Letters from a Stoic*, trans. Robin Campbell (London: Penguin, 1969), Letter 65, p. 124. "I am too great," Seneca writes, "was born to too great a destiny to be my body's slave. So far as I am concerned that body is nothing more or less than a fetter on my freedom. I place it squarely in the path of fortune, letting her expend her onslaught on it, not allowing any blow to get through it to my actual self. For that body is all that is vulnerable about me: within this dwelling so liable to injury there lives a spirit that is free" (123). See Wyatt's sonnet, "Farewell, Love, and all thy laws forever," in which the speaker invokes "Senec and Plato" as his guides in the passage from the bondage of the body to the liberty of the mind. Wyatt urged his son to study Seneca's moral philosophy (*Life and Letters*, p. 43).

31. Jürgen Habermas, *Knowledge and Human Interests*, trans. Jeremy J. Shapiro (Boston: Beacon Press, 1971), p. 282.

32. Daniel Javitch, *Poetry and Courtliness in Renaissance England* (Princeton: Princeton University Press, 1978), pp. 119–40.

33. W. J. Courthope, in *Wyatt: The Critical Heritage*, p. 104.

34. Ibid., pp. 44, 71, 104, 165. See, too, Patricia Thomson, *Sir Thomas Wyatt and His Background* (Stanford: Stanford University Press, 1964), p. 270: "There is no reason why both his amorous and his satirical poetry should not be enjoyed. But if I were called, as in an examination, to admire one at the expense of the other, I should look askance at the love poetry, as Yeats did at his 'Stolen Child': 'that is not the poetry of insight and knowledge but the poetry of longing and complaint.' And certainly the satires are Wyatt's greatest achievement in the poetry of insight and knowledge. In the long run courtly wisdom was a richer source of inspiration than courtly love."

35. Raymond Williams, *The Country and the City* (New York: Oxford University Press, 1973), p. 54.

36. Edward Hall, *Chronicle* (London: J. Johnson, 1808), p. 597.

37. In 1517 Brian, whom Cromwell nicknamed "vicar of hell," had married a wealthy widow (as he was to do again later in his career). He furthered the interests of his cousin, Anne Boleyn (cf. Wyatt, "A Spending Hand," line 63), then upon her fall, hastened to protect his position by working zealously for her conviction.

38. *Sir Thomas Wyatt and His Background,* p. 185.

39. *Wyatt: The Critical Heritage,* p. 25.

40. Ibid., p. 34.

41. Javitch, *Poetry and Courtliness,* p. 68.

42. Mason, *Humanism and Poetry,* p. 171. "By a little application," Mason comments, "we could compose a dictionary of conventional phrases which would show that many of these poems of Wyatt's are simply strung together from these phrases into set forms." I would argue that conventionality is not in this period the enemy of genuine poetic activity, but one of its essential ingredients.

43. C. S. Lewis, *English Literature in the Sixteenth Century, Excluding Drama* (Oxford: At the Clarendon Press, 1954), p. 230. The influence of the court has been treated more seriously and probingly by Patricia Thomson, *Sir Thomas Wyatt and His Background,* and by Raymond Southall, *The Courtly Maker* (Oxford: Blackwell, 1964).

44. For what bizarre social occasion was Henry VIII himself supplying material when he proudly displayed a "tragedy" he had written on the subject of the adultery and fall of Anne Boleyn? (J. J. Scarisbrick, *Henry VIII* [London: Penguin, 1968], p. 455). Was this meant to be a grand show of indifference? an aesthetic triumph over the pain and humiliation of betrayal? was it an attempt to make sense of the horrifying turn of events, to impose the coherence and dignity of tragedy upon them? was it a demonstration of prescience and power, a magical assertion that he himself had "written" the whole history? Henry apparently told the bishop of Carlisle, to whom he showed his "tragedy," that he had long expected the present turn of events. The tragedy has not survived, but the anecdote is haunting: it suggests a far different and more disturbing range of possibilities for the functions of court art than is suggested by after-dinner music.

45. Harrier, *Canon,* pp. 37–38, thinks it unlikely the poem is by Wyatt. I use the Devonshire manuscript's reading of the final word; the Blage manuscript gives *worse.*

46. We might note that this accords unpleasantly well with Wyatt's treatment of his wife, whom he publicly denounced for adultery. Obviously, the denunciation heightened the "mock" of being a cuckold, but he evidently did not care about this as much as he cared about his revenge.

47. Lewis, *English Literature,* p. 229.

48. On "sociosis," see J. H. van den Berg, *The Changing Nature of Man* (New York: Norton, 1961).

49. *Humanism and Poetry,* p. 171.

50. We might take this occasion to remark that the major achievements of all three of the figures we have considered thus far are intimately

associated with the Continent, in three quite distinct cultural forms: for More, humanism; for Tyndale, the Reformation; and for Wyatt, courtliness. These cultures overlapped in important respects, but they were far more strikingly at each other's throats. This is most evident in the struggle between More and Tyndale, but they in turn were both set passionately against the world in which Wyatt participated, Europe in what we may call, after Pocock, its quintessentially Machiavellian moment.

51. The nature of the relation between the prince's body and the power of the state is, of course, extremely complex: see Ernst H. Kantorowicz, *The King's Two Bodies: A Study in Mediaeval Political Theology* (Princeton: Princeton University Press, 1957): "It is evident that the doctrine of theology and canon law, teaching that the Church and Christian society in general, was a *'corpus mysticum* the head of which is Christ' has been transferred by the jurists from the theological sphere to that of the state the head of which is the king" (pp. 15–16).

See also Georg Rusche and Otto Kirchheimer, *Punishment and Social Structure* (New York: Columbia University Press, 1939); John Bellamy, *Crime and Public Order in England in the Later Middle Ages* (London: Routledge & Kegan Paul, 1973); Foucault, *Discipline and Punish.*

52. Louis Dumont, *From Mandeville to Marx: The Genesis and Triumph of Economic Ideology* (Chicago: University of Chicago Press, 1977), p. 35.

53. "I find no peace and all my war is done," 11; the poem is a translation of Petrarch, *Rime* cxxxiv. Wyatt characteristically intensifies the *causal* relation of love and hate: Petrarch had written, "Et ho in odio me stresso et amo altrui." One might add that in Wyatt's psalms, when King David turns his love to God, he does so by removing it from Bathsheba and abasing himself. Indeed if Renaissance diplomacy may be usefully invoked in a reading of the love lyrics, it has an equal bearing upon the penitential psalms, which are permeated with the spirit of subtle, devious negotiations with an overpowering, irascible, and dangerous ally.

54. It is doubtful that this poem, which appears in the Blage manuscript, is by Wyatt.

55. Quoted in Garrett Mattingly, *Renaissance Diplomacy* (Baltimore: Penguin, 1964), p. 95. Compare Bernard du Rosier's treatise on diplomacy, written in 1436: "The business of an ambassador is peace.... An ambassador labors for the public good.... An ambassador is sacred because he acts for the general welfare" (quoted in Mattingly, p. 42).

56. Quoted in Hugh Trevor-Roper, "The Intellectual World of Sir Thomas More," *American Scholar* 48 (1978/79), p. 28.

57. *Life and Letters,* p. 157.

58. Tottel, all too typically, wrecks the effect of the poem by entitling it, "Complaint for true love unrequited."

59. *Life and Letters,* p. 135.

60. Mattingly, *Renaissance Diplomacy*, p. 217.

61. Ibid., p. 186.

62. Perhaps Charles created the stir about the word simply to avoid talking about Brancetour (though he did so by the end of the conversa-

tion). Both Henry VIII and Cromwell chose to interpret the discussion of the word, however, as an assertion of precedence over both the English and French kings; at least they tried to use the emperor's words to sow dissension between him and Francis I (*Life and Letters,* p. 139).

63. The restraint extends even to the choice of "And" in line 11 instead of "For" as a lead-in to the description of the collar. "For" would have presented the final lines as a clear explanation of the poet's situation; "And" invites the reader to draw his own conclusion.

64. See Richard Bernheimer, *Wild Men in the Middle Ages: A Study in Art, Sentiment, and Demonology* (Cambridge, Mass.: Harvard University Press, 1952); *The Wild Man Within: An Image in Western Thought from the Renaissance to Romanticism,* ed. Edward Dudley and Maximillian E. Novak (Pittsburgh: University of Pittsburgh Press, 1972).

65. Thus Petrarch's "stanchi di mirar, non sazi" is not so much contradicted as confirmed by Wyatt's "The vain travail hath wearied me so sore," while Petrarch's "libera" becomes Wyatt's "wild."

66. "The Mind in the Poem: Wyatt's 'They Flee from Me,'" *Studies in English Literature* 7 (1967), p. 4.

67. See also Michael McCanles, "Love and Power in the Poetry of Sir Thomas Wyatt," *Modern Language Quarterly* 29 (1968), pp. 145–60. My view of Wyatt is close to McCanles's, particularly to his suggestion in a footnote that "it could be shown that the overriding concern of all Wyatt's poetry, including the Satires and the translation of the Psalms, is adjustment to a court and to a society in which the drive to power is dominant" (p. 148, n. 4).

68. Friedman, "The Mind in the Poem," p. 9.

69. "A Letter on Art in Reply to André Daspre," in *Lenin and Philosophy and Other Essays,* trans. Ben Brewster (New York: Monthly Review Press, 1971), pp. 222–23.

70. Surrey, in *Wyatt: The Critical Heritage,* p. 31.

71. *Life and Letters,* pp. 198–99. Wyatt remarks, "Because I am wont sometime to rap out an oath in an earnest talk, look how craftily they have put in an oath to the matter to make the matter seem mine."

72. Mason, *Humanism and Poetry,* pp. 190–91: "We have a number of poems in Wyatt's own hand and some of these contain Wyatt's second and even third thoughts. These 'corrections,' taken by and large, show that, as he worked over them, Wyatt made his lines more 'rugged,' 'difficult,' and less like Surrey's or the Tottel version."

It is tempting, following the lead of Christopher Caudwell, to see Wyatt's poetic technique as a direct outcome of his social position: "This 'individualism' of the bourgeois, which is born of the need to dissolve the restrictions of feudal society, causes a tremendous and ceaseless technical advance in production. In the same way it causes in poetry a tremendous and ceaseless advance in technique" (*Illusion and Reality* [New York: International Publishers, 1937], p. 60). From this perspective, the seizure of Church lands and treasure and the development of new poetic techniques are both manifestations of "primitive accumulation," the earliest stage of capitalism.

The difficulties inherent in such an interpretation outweigh the advantages. It takes considerable sleight of hand to present Wyatt as a typical representative of the bourgeoisie, his acquisition of monastic lands does not have a clear relation to his political let alone poetic career, the invocation of capitalism in a description of the 1530s requires an act of faith I personally shrink from. But the Marxist interpretation has the virtue of insisting that Wyatt's life is not rigidly compartmentalized, insisting, as I have argued through this chapter, that poetry and power are deeply intertwined. I believe it is fundamentally correct to link the drive toward technical experimentation and mastery in Wyatt with his manifestation of individuality and this individuality in turn with fundamental historical and economic developments of the period: Henry VIII's ambitions, the accumulation of wealth, the changes in Tudor government that moved England decisively away from feudalism and toward the modern state.

For an attempt to construct a Marxist reading of Wyatt, see Raymond Southall, *Literature and the Rise of Capitalism,* chap. 2.

73. "So Unwarely Was Never No Man Caught," 3–4.

Chapter Four

1. Natalie Zemon Davis, "The Sacred and the Body Social in Sixteenth-Century Lyon."

2. We should also remind ourselves that the full integration of public career and writing, such as we described in More or Wyatt, may be viewed in a figure like Ralegh, while the Tyndalean rituals of disobedience and absolute submission to the Word continue in the lives and deaths of nonconformists like Henry Barrow.

3. Jacob Burckhardt, *The Civilization of the Renaissance in Italy* (1860). For criticism of Burckhardt, see Wallace Ferguson, *The Renaissance in Historical Thought* (Boston: Houghton Mifflin, 1948), chaps. 7–11.

4. See Paul O. Kristeller, *Renaissance Thought: The Classic, Scholastic, and Humanist Strains* (New York: Harper & Row [Harper Torchbooks], 1961); Hanna H. Gray, "Renaissance Humanism: The Pursuit of Eloquence," in *Renaissance Essays,* ed. Kristeller and Philip P. Wiener (New York: Harper & Row [Harper Torchbooks], 1968), pp. 199–216. On relations between rhetoric and other fields, see Rosemond Tuve, *Elizabethan and Metaphysical Imagery* (Chicago: University of Chicago Press, 1947); Jerrold Seigel, *Rhetoric and Philosophy in Renaissance Humanism* (Princeton: Princeton University Press, 1968); Nancy S. Streuver, *The Language of History in the Renaissance* (Princeton: Princeton University Press, 1970). On rhetoric in the English school curriculum, see T. W. Baldwin, *William Shakespere's Small Latine and Lesse Greeke,* 2 vols (Urbana, Ill.: University of Illinois Press, 1944).

5. On the theatricality of Renaissance culture, see Jean Duvignaud, *Sociologie du théâtre: Essai sur les ombres collectives* (Paris: Presses Universitaires de France, 1965).

6. See Norbert Elias, *The Civilizing Process,* p. 73: "The problem of behavior in society had obviously taken on such importance in this period that even people of extraordinary talent and renown did not disdain to

concern themselves with it.... Erasmus' treatise [*De civilitate morum puerilium*] comes at a time of social regrouping. It is the expression of the fruitful transitional period after the loosening of the medieval social hierarchy and before the stabilizing of the modern one."

7. *The Covrte of Civill Courtesie...Out of Italian by S. R. Gent* (London, 1577). The full title is revealing: "Fitly furnished with a pleasant port of stately phrases and pithy precepts: assembled in the behalf of all young Gentlemen, and others, that are desirous to frame their behavior according to their estates, at all times and in all companies: thereby to purchase worthy praise of their inferiors, and estimation and credit among their betters."

8. Stephen Guazzo, *The Civile Conversation*, trans. George Pettie and Bartholomew Young, ed. Sir Edward Sullivan, 2 vols. (London: Constable, 1925), 1:86ff; Castiglione, *The Book of the Courtier*, trans. Charles S. Singleton (New York: Anchor, 1959), p. 294.

9. Philibert de Vienne, *The Philosopher of the Court*, trans. George North (London, 1575), p. 13. See C. A. Mayer, "L'Honnête Homme. Molière and Philibert de Vienne's 'Philosophe de Court,'" *MLR* 46 (1951), pp. 196–217, and Pauline Smith, *The Anti-Courtier Trend in Sixteenth Century French Literature* (Geneva: Droz, 1966).

10. Philibert's Court Philosopher commends to his readers "the understanding of all Arts and liberal Sciences, whereby we become right Courtiers" (p. 29). We must be skilled in music, dancing, and poetry; we should have "some pretty sprinkled judgment in the commonplaces and practices of all the liberal sciences, chopped up in hotchpot together" out of which we may stock our conversation; likewise, we should have "store of histories, to pass the time meet for any company" or, what is just as good, "certain sudden lies and inventions of our own forging" (p. 30).

11. Cf. Machiavelli, *The Prince*: "if one could change one's nature with time and circumstances, fortune would never change" (p. 93). For Proteus, see A. Bartlett Giamatti, "Proteus Unbound: Some Versions of the Sea God in the Renaissance," in *The Disciplines of Criticism*, ed. Peter Demetz, Thomas Greene, and Lowry Nelson, Jr. (New Haven: Yale University Press, 1968), pp. 437–75.

12. Daniel Javitch, "*The Philosopher at Court:* A French Satire Misunderstood," *Cmparative Literature* 23 (1971), pp. 97–124. There is similar ambiguity about Robert Laneham's *Letter* (1575), ed. F. J. Furnivall (New York: Duffield, 1907).

13. Quoted in Stephen J. Greenblatt, *Sir Walter Ralegh: The Renaissance Man and His Roles* (New Haven: Yale University Press, 1973), p. 24. The official occasion for this effusion is a letter to Robert Cecil about bills for the coats of the Queen's Guards.

14. Quoted in Greenblatt, *Sir Walter Ralegh*, pp. 76–77.

15. *Memoirs of the Life of Robert Cary*, ed. John, Earl of Corke and Orrery (London: R. & J. Dodsley, 1759), p. 103.

16. "On the Fortunate Memory of Elizabeth Queen of England," trans. James Spedding, in *The Works of Francis Bacon*, ed. Spedding and Robert Ellis, 14 vols. (London: Longman, 1857–74), 6:317.

17. See David M. Bergeron, *English Civic Pageantry, 1558*–1642 (London: Edward Arnold, 1971); Frances A. Yates, *Astraea: The Imperial Theme in the Sixteenth Century* (London: Routledge & Kegan Paul, 1975); Roy Strong, *The Cult of Elizabeth: Elizabethan Portraiture and Pageantry* (London: Thames & Hudson, 1977). For the queen's Tudor predecessor, see Sydney Anglo, *Spectacle, Pageantry, and Early Tudor Policy* (Oxford: At the Clarendon Press, 1969). For the "Platonic politics" of the Stuart reigns, see Stephen Orgel, *The Illusion of Power: Political Theater in the English Renaissance* (Berkeley: University of California Press, 1975).

18. Quoted in Allison Heisch, "Queen Elizabeth I: Parliamentary Rhetoric and the Exercise of Power," *Signs: Journal of Women in Culture and Society* 1 (1975), p. 39.

19. Accession speech, quoted in Heisch, p. 33. Plowden and Coke, quoted in Kantorowicz, *The King's Two Bodies*, p. 13.

20. The religious element emerges most clearly in Elizabeth's conservative stance in the Vestarian Controversy.

21. Quoted in J. E. Neale, *Elizabeth I and Her Parliaments, 1584–1601*, 2 vols. (London: Jonathan Cape, 1965), 2:119. Referred to in text as "Neale."

22. Godfrey Goodman, Bishop of Gloucester, *The Court of King James the First*, ed. J. S. Brewer, 2 vols. (London: R. Bentley, 1839), 1:163 (italics mine). We would do well to remember that in 1588, with widespread fear of assassination attempts, any royal appearance before a crowd was a courageous act.

23. *The Quenes maiesties passage through the citie of London to Westminster the day before her coronacion* [1559], ed. James M. Osborn (New Haven: Yale University Press, 1960), pp. 28, 46. On Queen Mary's accession, see *The Chronicle of Queen Jane and of Two Years of Queen Mary*, ed. John G. Nichols, Camden Society, 48 (London: Royal Historical Society, 1850), p. 14: "The Queen's Grace stayed at Allgate Street before the stage where the poor children stood, and heard an oration that one of them made, but she said nothing to them."

24. Yates, *Astraea*, comments, "The bejewelled and painted images of the Virgin Mary had been cast out of churches and monasteries but another bejewelled and painted image was set up at court, and went in progress through the land for her worshippers to adore" (p. 79).

25. Ralegh, "Now we have present made," in Walter Oakeshott, *The Queen and the Poet* (London: Faber, 1960), p. 205. See Roy Strong, *The Cult of Elizabeth* and *The Portraits of Queen Elizabeth I* (Oxford: At the Clarendon Press, 1963); E. C. Wilson, *England's Eliza* (Cambridge, Mass.: Harvard University Press, 1939). The richest compilation of materials remains *The Progresses and Public Processions of Queen Elizabeth*, ed. John Nichols, 3 vols. (London: J. Nichols, 1823).

26. *The Letters of Epigrams of Sir John Harington*, ed. Norman E. McClure (Philadelphia: University of Pennsylvania Press, 1930), p. 122.

27. *The Book of the Courtier*, p. 294.

28. *Letters*, p. 125. "I write from wonder and affection," he remarks (p. 126).

29. We may note that in 1589 (the date of the letter), Ralegh is perhaps

the supreme example in England of a gentleman not born but fashioned.

30. Paul J. Alpers, *The Poetry of "The Faerie Queene"* (Princeton: Princeton University Press, 1967), and "How to Read *The Faerie Queene*," in *Essays in Criticism* 18 (1968), pp. 429–43.

31. C. S. Lewis, *The Allegory of Love* (New York: Oxford University Press [first published 1936]), p. 332. Lewis's description of the Bower has been discussed by Graham Hough, *A Preface to "The Faerie Queene"* (New York: Norton, 1963).

32. *Essays and Introductions* (London: Macmillan & Co., 1961), p. 370.

33. N. S. Brooke, "C. S. Lewis and Spenser: Nature, Art and the Bower of Bliss," in *Essential Articles for the Study of Edmund Spenser*, ed. A. C. Hamilton (Hamden, Conn.: Archon Books, 1972), p. 28. Typical of much recent criticism is the observation by M. Pauline Parker that the Bower's "painted golden ivy is used where the real plant could have grown and should have grown," indeed the ivy is "alive only with the horrible energy of corruption" (*The Allegory of "The Faerie Queene"* [Oxford: Clarendon, 1960], pp. 42, 152).

34. See especially Merritt Y. Hughes, "Spenser's Acrasia and the Circe of the Renaissance," *Journal of the History of Ideas* 4 (1943), pp. 381–99; Robert M. Durling, "The Bower of Bliss and Armida's Palace," *Comparative Literature* 6 (1954), pp. 335–47; James Nohrnberg, *The Analogy of "The Faerie Queene"* (Princeton: Princeton University Press, 1976), pp. 490–513.

35. Sigmund Freud, *Civilization and Its Discontents*, trans. James Strachey (New York: Norton, 1962), pp. 44, 51.

36. For modern versions, see Samuel Z. Klausner, "A Collocation of Concepts of Self-Control," in *The Quest for Self-Control: Classical Philosophies and Scientific Research*, ed. Klausner (New York: Free Press, 1965), pp. 9–48.

37. Natalie Zemon Davis, "'Women's History' in Transition: The European Case," *Feminist Studies* 3 (1976), p. 89 and the refs. in note 31.

38. Guido Calabresi and Philip Bobbitt, *Tragic Choices* (New York: Norton, 1978), p. 195.

39. Clifford Geertz, "Art as a Cultural System," *Modern Language Notes* 91 (1976), pp. 1473–99.

40. Christopher Columbus, *Journals and Other Documents*, p. 287.

41. Tasso, *Gerusalemme Liberata* (book 15, stanzas 28ff.), relates the quest for the realm of Armida to Columbus's voyages. Spenser's Maleger carries arrows "Such as the *Indians* in their quiuers hide" (2.11.21). Bernal Diaz del Castillo recalls the first reaction to the sight of the Aztec capital in *The Conquest of New Spain*, trans. J. M. Cohen (Baltimore: Penguin, 1963), p. 214. On Spenser and the New World, see Roy Harvey Pearce, "Primitivistic Ideas in the *Faerie Queene*," *Journal of English and Germanic Philology* 45 (1945), pp. 139–51; A. Bartlett Giamatti, "Primitivism and the Process of Civility in Spenser's Faerie Queene," in *First Images of America: The Impact of the New World on the Old*, ed. Fredi Chiappelli, 2 vols. (Berkeley: University of California Press, 1976), 1:71–82.

42. Ralegh, *The Discovery of Guiana*, ed. V. T. Harlow (London: Argonaut Press, 1928), p. 42.

43. Peter Martyr, *The Decades of the New World,* trans. Michael Lok, in *A Selection of Curious, Rare, and Early Voyages and Histories of Interesting Discoveries chiefly published by Hakluyt . . .* (London: R. H. Evans and R. Priestly, 1812), p. 539.

44. Ibid., p. 530.

45. *Of the newe landes,* in *The First Three English Books on America,* ed. Edward Arber (Birmingham: Turnbull and Spears, 1885), p. xxvii; cf. Wilberforce Eames, "Description of a Wood Engraving Illustrating the South American Indians (1505)," *Bulletin of the New York Public Library* 26 (1922), pp. 755–60.

46. Elizabeth Story Donno, ed., *An Elizabethan in 1582: The Diary of Richard Madox, Fellow of All Souls,* Hakluyt Society, Second Series, No. 147 (London: Hakluyt Society, 1977), p. 183. The editor notes that "in the older maps the mountains of the moon figure as a range extending across the continent from Abyssinia to the Gulf of Guinea."

47. At 6.8.43, the cannibals who capture Serena consider raping her, but they are stopped by their priests.

48. Compare Redcrosse who, when he dallies with Duessa, is described as "Pourd out in loosnesse on the grassy grownd, / Both carelesse of his health, and of his fame" (1.7.7).

49. On vagabonds, see Frank Aydelotte, *Elizabethan Rogues and Vagabonds* (London: Frank Cass & Co., 1913).

50. Martyr, *Decades,* p. 628. On charges of idleness, see Edmund S. Morgan, *American Slavery, American Freedom: The Ordeal of Colonial Virginia* (New York: Norton, 1975).

51. Cortes "had ordered that all houses should be pulled down and burnt and the bridged channels filled up; and what he gained each day was thus consolidated. He sent an order to Pedro de Alvarado to be sure that we never crossed a bridge or gap in the causeway without first blocking it up, and to pull down and burn every house" (Bernal Diaz, *Conquest,* p. 369).

52. I am indebted here to Richard Slotkin, *Regeneration through Violence: The Mythology of the American Frontier, 1600–1860* (Middletown, Conn.: Wesleyan University Press, 1973).

53. Bernal Diaz, *Conquest,* p. 60.

54. *A View of the Present State of Ireland,* ed. W. L. Renwick (Oxford: Clarendon, 1970), pp. 48, 64, 65. Our primary purpose is to explore aspects of Elizabethan policy in Ireland as a reiteration of a characteristic cultural pattern rather than to detail the direct influence of Ireland upon *The Faerie Queene;* for the latter, see M. M. Gray, "The Influence of Spenser's Irish Experiences on *The Faerie Queene,*" *Review of English Studies* 6 (1930), pp. 413–28; Pauline Henley, *Spenser in Ireland* (Folcroft, Pa.: Folcroft Press, 1920).

55. Ibid., p. 67. Cf. Louis-Jean Calvet, *Linguistique et colonialisme: Petit traité de glottophagie* (Paris: Payot, 1974) and Stephen J. Greenblatt, "Learning to Curse: Aspects of Linguistic Colonialism in the Sixteenth Century," in *First Images of America* 2:561–80.

56. *View,* pp. 67–68. Children "draweth into themselves together with

their suck, even the nature and disposition of their nurses, for the mind followeth much the temperature of the body; and also the words are the image of the mind, so as they proceeding from the mind, the mind must be needs effected with the words" (p. 68).

57. Yeats, *Essays and Introductions*, p. 372.

58. R. Dudley Edwards, *Ireland in the Age of the Tudors: The Destruction of Hiberno-Norman Civilization* (London: Croom Helm, 1977); Nicholas P. Canny, *The Elizabethan Conquest of Ireland: A Pattern Established, 1565–76* (Hassocks, Sussex: Harvester Press, 1976); David Beers Quinn, *The Elizabethans and the Irish* (Ithaca: Cornell University Press, 1966). For an apologetic account of Spenser's involvement, see Pauline Henley, *Spenser in Ireland;* for an enigmatic indication of Spenser's personal profit from the Smerwick massacre, see Anna Maria Crinò, "La Relazione Barducci-Ubaldini sull'Impresa d'Irlanda (1579–1581)," *English Miscellany* 19 (1968), pp. 339–67.

59. Alexander C. Judson, *The Life of Edmund Spenser* (Baltimore: Johns Hopkins University Press, 1945), pp. 107–8.

60. Ibid., p. 116. The reference to the "fennes of Allan" in 2.9.16 indicates that it was written after Spenser acquired New Abbey, a ruined Franciscan friary in County Kildare, in 1582 (see Josephine Waters Bennett, *The Evolution of "The Faerie Queene"* [Chicago: University of Chicago Press, 1942], p. 131n.).　·

61. It has been frequently noted that Maleger and his band resemble accounts in Spenser's *View* and in other reports on Ireland of Irish kerns.

62. We should perhaps note in this connection that Guyon leaves the Bower immediately after its destruction: "But let vs hence depart," says the Palmer, "whilest wether serues and wind" (2.12.87).

63. Quoted in Philip Hughes, *The Reformation in England*, 3 vols. (New York: Macmillan, 1954), 3:408.

64. John Venn, *John Caius* (Cambridge: Cambridge University Press, 1910), p. 37. In a letter of the vice-chancellor, Dr. Byng, to the chancellor, Lord Burghley, dated 14 December 1572, the "trumpery" is catalogued: "vestments, albes, tunicles, stoles, manicles, corporas clothes, with the pix and sindon, and canopie, besides holy water stoppes, with sprinkles, pax, sensars, superaltaries, tables of idolles, masse bookes, portuises, and grailles, with other such stuffe as might have furnished divers massers at one instant." The Latin account is from John Caius, *The Annals of Gonville and Caius College*, ed. John Venn, Cambridge Antiquarian Society Octavo Series no. 40 (Cambridge, 1904), p. 185. Caius adds that iconoclasts used hammers to smash certain objects.

65. Quoted in John Phillips, *The Reformation of Images: Destruction of Art in England, 1535–1660* (Berkeley: University of California Press, 1973), p. 80.

66. Keith Thomas, *Religion and the Decline of Magic* (London: Weidenfeld and Nicolson, 1971), p. 69.

67. *The Book of the Courtier*, trans. Singleton, p. 43. On *sprezzatura*, see Wayne A. Rebhorn, *Courtly Performances: Masking and Festivity in Castig-*

lione's "Book of the Courtier" (Detroit: Wayne State University Press, 1978), pp. 33–40.

68. On demonic artists, see A. Bartlett Giamatti, *Play of Double Senses: Spenser's Faerie Queene* (Englewood Cliffs, N.J.: Prentice-Hall, 1975), pp. 106–33. We may observe that Spenser seems on occasion to invoke positive versions of self-concealing art:

> Then came the Bride, the louely *Medua* came,
> Clad in a vesture of vnknowen geare,
> And vncouth fashion, yet her well became;
> That seem'd like siluer, sprinckled here and theare
> With glittering spangs, that did like starres appeare,
> And wau'd vpon, like water Chamelot,
> To hide the metall, which yet euery where
> Bewrayd it selfe, to let men plainely wot,
> It was no mortall worke, that seem'd and yet was not.
>
> (4.11.45)

Spenser's suspicions of aesthetic concealment can be allayed by its use in a virtuous context, but we might also note that in this instance the device both hides and does not hide its own artifice. The art is designed to seem natural and yet at the same time to let men plainly know, through a kind of "self-betrayal," that it is not natural. For conflicting arguments on the status of artifice in Spenser, see C. S. Lewis, *The Allegory of Love*, pp. 326–33, and Hans P. Guth, "Allegorical Implications of Artifice in Spenser's *Faerie Queene*," *Publication of the Modern Language Association* 76 (1961), pp. 474–79.

69. Keith Thomas, *Religion and the Decline of Magic*, p. 275.

70. See Gershom Scholem, *Sabbatai Sevi* (Princeton: Princeton University Press, 1973).

71. J. H. Elliott, *The Old World and the New, 1492–1650* (Cambridge: Cambridge University Press, 1970).

72. Paul Alpers, "Narration in *The Faerie Queene*," *English Literary History* 44 (1977), p. 27.

Chapter Five

1. "The voyage set out by the right honourable the Earle of Cumberland, in the yere 1586.... Written by M. John Sarracoll marchant in the same voyage," in Richard Hakluyt, ed., *The Principal Navigations, Voyages, Traffiques & Discoveries of the English Nation*, 12 vols. (Glasgow: James MacLehose & Sons, 1903–5), 11:206–7. On the English in Sierra Leone prior to this voyage, see P. E. H. Hair, "Protestants as Pirates, Slavers, and Proto-missionaries: Sierra Leone 1568 and 1582," *Journal of Ecclesiastical History* 21 (1970), pp. 203–24. On the region in this period, see Walter Rodney, *A History of the Upper Guinea Coast, 1545–1800* (Oxford: At the Clarendon Press, 1970).

2. At the opening of *Tamburlaine* there is a wry reminder of how exotic Europe would appear to a Persian: "*Europe*, where the Sun dares scarce appear, / For freezing meteors and congealed cold" (1 *Tam* 1.1.18–19).

Quotations of Marlowe's plays with the exception of *Doctor Faustus,* are modernized from *The Works of Christopher Marlowe,* ed. C. F. Tucker Brooke (Oxford: Clarendon Press, 1910). Quotations of *Doctor Faustus* are modernized from the A text of W. W. Greg's *Marlowe's "Doctor Faustus" 1604–1616: Parallel Texts* (Oxford: At the Clarendon Press, 1950). My own reading of the play supports recent arguments for the superiority of the A text; see Fredson Bowers, "Marlowe's *Doctor Faustus:* The 1602 Additions," (*Studies in Bibliography* 26 [1973], 1–18) and Constance Brown Kuriyama (*English Literary Renaissance* 5 [1975], 171–97).

On the relationship of Spenser and Marlowe, see Douglas Bush, "Marlowe and Spenser," *Times Literary Supplement,* 28 May 1938, p. 370; T. W. Baldwin, "The Genesis of Some Passages which Spenser Borrowed from Marlowe," *English Literary History* 9 (1942), pp. 157–87, and reply by W. B. C. Watkins in *ELH* 11 (1944), 249–65; John D. Jump, "Spenser and Marlowe," *Notes and Queries* 209, new ser. 11 (1964), pp. 261–62. See also Georg Schoeneich, "Der literarische Einfluss Spensers auf Marlowe" (Diss., Halle, 1907).

3. See Ernst Cassirer, *The Individual and the Cosmos in Renaissance Philosophy,* trans. Mario Domandi (New York: Barnes & Noble, 1963), esp. chap. 1, "Nicholas Cusanus." In *Doctor Faustus* Marlowe plays upon the residual religious symbolism of the Elizabethan stage (though this is more true of the B text than the A text), but he does so only to subvert it, locating hell psychologically rather than spatially.

On maps in Marlowe, see Ethel Seaton, "Marlowe's Map," *Essays and Studies by Members of the English Association* 10 (1924), pp. 13–35; Donald K. Anderson, Jr., "Tamburlaine's 'Perpendicular' and the T-in-O Maps," *Notes and Queries* 21 (1974), pp. 284–86.

4. Here, as elsewhere in my discussion of *Doctor Faustus,* I am indebted to conversations with Edward Snow and to his essay, "Marlowe's *Doctor Faustus* and the Ends of Desire," in *Two Renaissance Mythmakers: Christopher Marlowe and Ben Jonson,* ed. Alvin B. Kernan (Baltimore: Johns Hopkins University Press, 1977), pp. 70–110.

5. The agreement depends, in part, on the pun on Aye/I (the latter is the reading of the A and B texts). "Experience" may also have the sense of "experiment," as if Faustus's whole future were a test of the proposition that hell is a fable.

6. See Richard Madox's Diary for 14 December 1582: "Although the soldiers are strong and sufficiently courageous, they are utterly inept at trading and the exploring of unknown lands. Because, indeed, being always among enemies and in a hostile place, they believe they are [here] exposed to the usual dangers; for this reason they can never enter into dealings with others without suspicion. Suspicion, however, breeds hatred and hatred open war, and thus those they ought to attract and attach to themselves by human kindness and clemency, they frighten off by impudence and malice, and in this way all love perishes. Especially because of ignorance of languages, each is a barbarian to the other" (*An*

Elizabethan in 1582, ed. Donno, p. 186). In the light of this passage, perhaps the odd conjunction of admiration and destructiveness in Sarracoll's account may be traced to the difference between the merchant's view of the town and the view (and consequent actions) of the soldiers who were with him.

7. Snow, "Marlowe's *Doctor Faustus* and the Ends of Desire," p. 101.

8. The futility of naming cities after oneself was a commonplace in the period; see, for example, Ralegh's *History of the World* (1614):

> This was that *Seleucia,* whereto *Antigonus the great* who founded it, gave the name of *Antigonia:* but *Seleucus* getting it shortly after, called it *Seleucia;* and *Ptolemie Evergetes* having lately won it, might, if it had so pleased him, have changed the name into *Ptolemais.* Such is the vanity of men, that hope to purchase an endless memorial unto their names, by works proceeding rather from their greatness, than from their virtue; which therefore no longer are their own, than the same greatness hath continuance. (V, v, 2, p. 646)

9. The cutting edge of this career was the conquest of the New World where fertile lands, rich mines, and whole peoples were consumed in a few generations. It is estimated that the Indian population of New Spain (Mexico) fell from approximately 11 million in 1519 to approximately 1.5 million in 1650, and there are similarly horrifying figures for Brazil. In 1583 a Jesuit, José de Anchieta, observed of the latter that "the number of people used up in this place from twenty years ago until now seems a thing not to be believed" (quoted in Immanuel Wallerstein, *The Modern World-System* [New York: Academic Press, 1974], 80, n. 75); appropriately, it is on this great enterprise (among others) that the dying Tamburlaine, with infinite pathos, reflects.

10. E. E. Evans-Pritchard, *The Nuer* (Oxford: At the Clarendon Press, 1940), p. 103; quoted in E. P. Thompson, "Time, Work-Discipline, and Industrial Capitalism," *Past and Present* 38 (1967), p. 96.

11. See Keith Thomas, *Religion and the Decline of Magic* (London: Weidenfeld & Nicolson, 1971), p. 621; likewise, Christopher Hill, *Society and Puritanism in Pre-Revolutionary England,* 2d ed. (New York: Schocken, 1967), chap. 5.

12. See Natalie Zemon Davis, "Some Tasks and Themes in the Study of Popular Religion," in *The Pursuit of Holiness in Late Medieval and Renaissance Religion,* eds. Charles Trinkaus and Heiko A. Oberman (Leiden: E. J. Brill, 1974), pp. 307–36. I am also indebted to Professor Davis's essay, "Ghosts, Kin and Progeny: Some Features of Family Life in Early Modern France," *Daedalus* 106 (1977), pp. 87–114.

13. On time in *Doctor Faustus,* see Max Bluestone, "Adaptive Time in *Doctor Faustus,*" in *From Story to Siege: The Dramatic Adaptation of Prose Fiction in the Period of Shakespeare and his Contemporaries* [*Studies in English Literature,* n. 70] (The Hague: Mouton, 1974), pp. 244–52; David Kaula,

"Time and the Timeless in *Everyman* and *Dr. Faustus*," *College English* 22 (1960), pp. 9–14.

14. C. L. Barber, "'The form of Faustus' fortunes good or bad,'" *Tulane Drama Review* 8 (1964), p. 99.

15. For a typical expression of this view, see Ralegh's *History:* "The same just God who liveth and governeth all things for ever, doth in these our times give victory, courage and discourage, raise and throw down Kings, Estates, Cities, and Nations, for the same offences which were committed of old, and are committed in the present: for which reason in these and other the afflictions of *Israel,* always the causes are set down, that they might be as precedents to succeeding ages" (II, xix, 3, pp. 508–9).

16. See, for example, the Edwardian proclamations: #287 and #313, in *Tudor Royal Proclamations,* 1:393–403, 432–33.

17. This characterization of the period's legal procedure is Christopher Hill's: "The Many-Headed Monster in Late Tudor and Early Stuart Political Thinking," in *From the Renaissance to the Counter-Reformation: Essays in Honor of Garrett Mattingly,* ed. Charles H. Carter (New York: Random House, 1965), p. 303. Hill's view is close to Thomas More's in *Utopia:* Thieves "were everywhere executed, . . . as many as twenty at a time being hanged on one gallows" (*Utopia,* p. 61). Statistics are inexact and inconsistent, but, for example, 74 persons were sentenced to death in Devon in 1598, and the average number of executions per year in London and Middlesex in the years 1607–1616 was 140 [Douglas Hay, "Property, Authority and the Criminal Law," in Hay et al., *Albion's Fatal Tree* (New York: Random House, 1975), p. 22n].

18. The *Mirror for Magistrates* is typical for its tireless repetition of the same paradigm of retributive justice, while both tragedy and comedy are quite characteristically conceived by Sidney, in the *Apology for Poetry,* as warnings and lessons. This conception continues to dominate sociological theories of literature; see, for example, Elizabeth Burns, *Theatricality* (New York: Harper & Row, 1973), p. 35.

19. On English Renaissance attitudes toward the Koran, see Samuel C. Chew, *The Crescent and the Rose: Islam and England during the Renaissance* (New York: Oxford University Press, 1937), esp. pp. 434ff.

20. Max Bluestone, "*Libido Speculandi:* Doctrine and Dramaturgy in Contemporary Interpretations of Marlowe's *Doctor Faustus,*" in *Reinterpretations of Elizabethan Drama,* ed. Norman Rabkin (New York: Columbia University Press, 1969), p. 82.

21. There is perceptive exploration of this aspect of Marlowe's work by J. R. Mulryne and Stephen Fender, "Marlowe and the 'Comic Distance,'" in *Christopher Marlowe: Mermaid Critical Commentaries,* ed. Brian Morris (London: Ernest Benn, 1968), 49–64.

22. There is a discussion of this and other productions of Marlowe's play in James L. Smith, "*The Jew of Malta* in the Theatre," in *Christopher Marlowe: Mermaid Critical Commentaries,* pp. 1–23.

23. *On the Jewish Question* in Karl Marx, *Early Writings,* trans. and ed. T. B. Bottomore (New York: McGraw-Hill, 1963), p. 35. For a fuller explora-

tion of the relation between Marx's essay and Marlowe's play, see Stephen J. Greenblatt, "Marlowe, Marx, and Anti-Semitism," *Critical Inquiry* 5 (1978), pp. 291–307.

24. G. K. Hunter, "The Theology of Marlowe's *The Jew of Malta*," *Journal of the Warburg and Courtauld Institute* 27 (1964), p. 236.

25. Shylock attempts to make this a similarly central issue in the trial scene, but, as we might expect, the attempt fails (*Merchant of Venice*, 4.1.90–100).

26. For a modern confirmation of such a view, see Frederic C. Lane, *Venice and History* (Baltimore: Johns Hopkins University Press, 1966).

27. For the Jew as devil, see Joshua Trachtenberg, *The Devil and the Jews: The Medieval Conception of the Jew and Its Relation to Modern Anti-semitism* (New Haven: Yale University Press, 1943).

28. In a sense, Marlowe uses his hero-villains as satirist figures: he has them expose the viciousness of the world and then reveals the extent to which they are no different from what they attack. Recall Duke Senior to Jaques:

> Mos mischievous foul sin, in chiding sin,
> For thou thyself hast been a libertine,
> As sensual as the brutish sting itself;
> And all th'embossed sores and headed evils
> That thou with license of free foot hast caught,
> Wouldst thou disgorge into the general world.
>   (*As You Like It*, 2.7.64–69)

29. See Georg Lukács, *History and Class Consciousness*, trans. Rodney Livingstone (Cambridge, Mass.: MIT Press, 1971), p. 15. The fountain-head of all modern speculation along these lines is Vico's *New Science*.

30. *Eighteenth Brumaire*, in *The Marx-Engels Reader*, ed. Robert C. Tucker (New York: Norton, 1972), p. 437.

31. See C. L. Barber, " 'The form of Faustus' fortunes good or bad,' " esp. p. 107. This does not, however, establish Holy Communion as the healthy, proper end that Faustus should be pursuing; on the contrary, Marlowe may have regarded Holy Communion as itself perverse. There are, in *Doctor Faustus* and throughout Marlowe's works, the elements of a radical critique of Christianity, a critique similar to that made with suicidal daring in 1584 by Giordano Bruno's *Expulsion of the Triumphant Beast (Lo spaccio de la bestia trionfante)*. Here, in a scarcely veiled satirical allegory of the life of Christ, the Greek gods, sensing a waning of their reputation on earth, decide to send Orion to restore their credit among men. This Orion

> knows how to perform miracles, and . . . can walk over the waves of the sea without sinking, without wetting his feet, and with this, consequently, will be able to perform many other fine acts of kindness. Let us send him among men, and let us see to it that he give them to understand all that I want and like them to understand: that white is black, that the human intellect, through which they seem to see best, is blindness, and that that which according to reason seems ex-

cellent, good, and very good, is vile, criminal, and extremely
bad. I want them to understand that Nature is a whorish
prostitute, that natural law is ribaldry, that Nature and Divinity cannot concur in one and the same good end, and that
the justice of the one is not subordinate to the justice of the
other, but that they are contraries, as are shadows and
light . . . . With this he [Orion] will persuade them that philosophy, all contemplation, and all magic that could make them
similar to us, are nothing but follies, that every heroic act is
only cowardice, and that ignorance is the best science in the
world because it is acquired without labor and does not cause
the mind to be affected by melancholy. (*Expulsion,* trans. and
ed. by Arthur D. Imerti [New Brunswick: Rutgers University
Press, 1964], pp. 255–56.)

32. On the materialism of peasant culture, see Carlo Ginzburg, *Il for-
maggio e i vermi: Il cosmo di un mugnaio del '500* (Torino: Einaudi, 1976).

33. William Hacket, quoted in Richard Bauckham, *Tudor Apocalypse*
[Courtenay Library of Reformation Classics 8] (Sutton Courtenay Press,
1978), p. 203.

34. See C. L. Barber, "The Family in Shakespeare's Development: The
Tragedy of the Sacred," a paper delivered at the English Institute, Sep-
tember, 1976; also Peter Laslett, *The World We Have Lost* (New York:
Scribner's, 1965).

35. *The City of God,* trans. Henry Bettenson (London: Penguin, 1972), II,
xii, 26, p. 506. See Georges Poulet, *Studies in Human Time,* trans. Elliott
Coleman (Baltimore: Johns Hopkins University Press, 1956), p. 19.

36. Cf. Julian Pitt-Rivers, "Honour and Social Status": "The victor in
any competition for honour finds his reputation enhanced by the humiliation of the vanquished . . . . It was believed at one time in Italy by the
common people that one who gave an insult thereby took to himself the
reputation of which he deprived the other. The Church of England hymn
puts the pont succinctly:

> Conquering Kings their titles take
> From the foes they captive make"
> (In J. G. Peristiany, ed., *Honour and Shame,* p. 24.)

37. The Vulgate is worth quoting for its subtle play on *consummo:*
"Postea sciens Iesus quia omnia consummata sunt, ut consummaretur
Scriptura, dixit: Sitio. Vas ergo erat positum aceto plenum; illi autem
spongiam plenam aceto hyssopo circumponentes obtulerunt ori eius.
Cum ergo accepisset Iesus acetum, dixit, Consummatum est. Et inclinato
capite, tradidit spiritum."

38. See Mario Untersteiner, *The Sophists,* trans. Kathleen Freeman
(Oxford: Blackwell, 1954), p. 106. Untersteiner's account of the place of
tragedy in Gorgias has considerable resonance for a student of Marlowe:

> If Being and knowledge are tragic, life will be tragic. The most
> universal form of art will be that which by means of "decep-
> tion" can give knowledge of the tragic element revealed by

ontology and epistemology. The perfect form of art will be, therefore, tragedy, which, better than any other manifestation of poetry, achieves a penetrating understanding of the irrational reality, by means of that "deception" which favours an irrational communicability of that which is not rationally communicable: the effect of this conditional knowledge of the unknowable and of this partial communication of the incommunicable is pleasure. (Pp. 187–88)

39. Kathleen Freeman, *Ancilla to the Pre-Socratic Philosophers* (Cambridge, Mass.: Harvard University Press, 1948), p. 129.

40. Untersteiner, p. 113. See Thomas G. Rosenmeyer, "Gorgias, Aeschylus, and *Apate*," *American Journal of Philology* 76 (1955), pp. 225–60.

41. Thomas Nashe, "An Almond for a Parrat," in *The Works of Thomas Nashe*, ed. Ronald B. McKerrow, 5 vols. (London: A. H. Bullen, 1905), 3:344. See Stephen J. Greenblatt, "The False Ending in *Volpone*," *Journal of English and Germanic Philology* 75 (1976), p. 93.

42. "With complete assurance and certainty," writes Georg Lukács, tragedy "solves the most difficult problem of Platonism: that of discovering whether individual things have their own Idea and their own Essence. And the reply which it gives reverses the order in which the question is put, since it shows that it is only when what is individual—that is to say, a particular living individual—is carried to its final limits and possibilities that it conforms to the Idea and begins really to exist." (Quoted in Lucien Goldmann, *The Hidden God*, trans. Philip Thody [London: Routledge & Kegan Paul, 1964], p. 59.) Marlowe's heroes are extremists of the kind called for by this conception of tragedy, but Marlowe treats their extremism with considerable irony.

43. Gilles Deleuze, *Différence et répétition* (Paris: Presses Universitaires de France, 1968), p. 96. The idea seems to originate with Hume.

44. In the very moment of Tamburlaine's triumph, a gap is opened between the self and its object, indeed a gap *within* both self and object. Similarly, when one of his admirers says that Tamburlaine is "In every part proportioned like the man, / Should make the world subdued to Tamburlaine" (1 *Tam* 2.1.483–84), his words inadvertently touch off a vertiginous series of repetitions and differences.

45. Richard Hooker, *Of the Laws of Ecclesiastical Polity*, 2 vols. (London: J. M. Dent [Everyman's Library], 1907), 1:I, xi, 4, pp. 257–58:

For man doth not seem to rest satisfied, either with fruition of that wherewith his life is preserved, or with performance of such actions as advance him most deservedly in estimation; but doth further covet, yea oftentimes manifestly pursue with great sedulity and earnestness, that which cannot stand him in any stead for vital use; that which exceedeth the reach of sense; yea somewhat above the capacity of reason, somewhat divine and heavenly, which with hidden exultation it rather surmiseth than conceiveth; somewhat it seeketh, and what that is directly it knoweth not, yet very intentive desire thereof doth so incite it, that all other known delights and

> pleasures are laid aside, they give place to the search of this
> but only suspected desire.... For although the beauties,
> riches, honours, sciences, virtues, and perfections of all men
> living, were in the present possession of one; yet somewhat
> beyond and above all this there would still be sought and
> earnestly thirsted for.

Giordano Bruno, *The Heroic Frenzies,* trans. Paul E. Memo, Jr., University
of North Carolina Studies in Romance Languages and Literatures, no. 50
(1964), pp. 128–29:

> Whatever species is represented to the intellect and com-
> prehended by the will, the intellect concludes there is another
> species above it, a greater and still greater one, and con-
> sequently it is always impelled toward new motion and
> abstraction in a certain fashion. For it ever realizes that ev-
> erything it possesses is a limited thing which for that reason
> cannot be sufficient in itself, good in itself, or beautiful in
> itself, because the limited thing is not the universe and is not
> the absolute entity, but is contracted to this nature, this
> species or this form represented to the intellect and presented
> to the soul. As a result, from that beautiful which is com-
> prehended, and therefore limited, and consequently beautiful
> by participation, the intellect progresses toward that which is
> truly beautiful without limit or circumspection whatsoever.

There are strikingly similar passages in Cusa and Ficino. The philosophical origins of all these expressions are to be found in Plato and Augustine.

46. Kenneth Burke, *The Rhetoric of Religion* (Berkeley: University of
California Press, 1961), p. 69.

47. Erich Auerbach, *Mimesis,* trans. Willard R. Trask (Princeton:
Princeton University Press, 1968 ed.), p. 311. The relevance of this pas-
sage to the present context was suggested to me by my colleague Paul
Alpers.

48. Paul Valéry, *Leonardo Poe Mallarmé,* trans. Malcolm Cowley and
James R. Lawler (Princeton: Princeton University Press, 1972) [vol. 8 of
The Collected Works of Paul Valéry, ed. Jackson Mathews, Bollingen Series
45], p. 93.

Chapter Six

1. On the feudal revival, see Arthur B. Ferguson, *The Indian Summer of
English Chivalry* (Durham, N.C.: Duke University Press, 1960), Frances A.
Yates, "Elizabethan Chivalry: The Romance of the Accession Day Tilts,"
in *Astraea: The Imperial Theme in the Sixteenth Century* (London: Rout-
ledge, 1975), pp. 88–111, and Roy Strong, *The Cult of Elizabeth: Elizabethan
Portraiture and Pageantry* (London: Thames and Hudson, 1977).

2. John Steevens, cited in Spenser, *Variorum* 1:252.

3. It is not certain who borrowed from whom, though I think the dominant view, that Marlowe borrowed from Spenser, is quite likely. See

chapter 5, note 2, above. For the parallels between Spenser and Marlowe, see also Charles Crawford, "Edmund Spenser, 'Locrine,' and 'Selimus,'" *Notes and Queries* (9th ser.) 7 (1901), pp. 61–63, 101–3, 142–44, 203–5, 261–63, 324–25, 384–86.

4. Daniel Lerner, *The Passing of Traditional Society: Modernizing the Middle East* (New York: Free Press, 1958; rev. ed. 1964), p. 49.

5. The figures are from Sherburne Cook and Woodrow W. Borah, *Essays in Population History: Mexico and the Caribbean* (Berkeley: University of California Press, 1971), pp. 376–411.

6. Peter Martyr (Pietro Martire d'Anghiera), *De Orbe Novo*, trans. M. Lok, p. 623. The Seventh Decade was finished in the middle of 1525. On Peter Martyr, see Henry R. Wagner, "Peter Martyr and His Works," *Proceedings of the American Antiquarian Society* 56 (1946), pp. 238–88. There is a rather pallid modern translation of *De Orbe Novo* by Francis A. MacNutt (New York: Putnam's, 1912).

7. It is the essence of *sprezzatura* to create the impression of a spontaneous improvisation by means of careful rehearsals. Similarly, the early English drama often strove for this effect; see, for example, *Fulgens and Lucres* where the seemingly incidental conversation of "A" and "B" is fully scripted.

8. Immanuel Wallerstein, *The Modern World System*.

9. Roy Strong, *The Cult of Elizabeth: Elizabethan Portraiture and Pageantry*, p. 153.

10. As an example of the operation of displacement in the visual arts, one may consider Breughel's *Christ Bearing the Cross*, where the mourning figures from Van der Weyden's great *Descent from the Cross* are pushed out to the margin of the canvas and the swirling, festive crowd all but obscures Christ. Similarly, for absorption we may invoke Dürer's self-portrait of 1500, where the rigidly frontalized, verticalized, hieratic figure has taken into itself the Christ Pantocrator.

11. Joel B. Altman, *The Tudor Play of Mind*. See also Jackson I. Cope, *The Theater and the Dream: From Metaphor to Form in Renaissance Drama* (Baltimore: The Johns Hopkins University Press, 1973), esp. chaps. 4–6. Cope argues brilliantly for the central importance of improvisation in the drama of the Renaissance, but for him improvisation is in the service finally of "a real coherence" of "the eternal order" of the myths of renewal (p. 210). One passes, by means of an apparent randomness, a chaotic flux, to a buried but all-powerful form. Improvisation is the mask of providence, and Cope concludes his study with a discussion of *The Tempest* as a "mythic play" of natural resurrection and Christian doctrine. I would argue that the final effect of improvisation in Shakespeare is the reverse: we always begin with a notion of the inescapability of form, a sense that there are no surprises, that narrative triumphs over the apparent disruptions, that even the disruptions serve narrative by confirming the presence of the artist as a version of the presence of God. And through improvisation we pass, only partially and tentatively, to a sense that in the very acts of homage to the great formal structures, there open up small

but constant glimpses of the limitations of those structures, of their insecurities, of the possibility of their collapse.

12. *Confutation,* 8:1, pp. 90–92. My attention was drawn to this passage by Professor Louis L. Martz who discussed it in a lecture at the Folger conference "Thomas More: The Man and His Age." On More's "art of improvisation" see Martz, "The Tower Works," in *St. Thomas More: Action and Contemplation,* pp. 63–65.

13. Richard III virtually declares himself an improviser: "I clothe my naked villainy / With odd old ends stol'n forth of holy writ" (1.3.335–36). He gives a fine demonstration of his agility when he turns Margaret's curse back on herself. Behind this trick perhaps is the fact that there were in the popular culture of the Renaissance formulaic curses and satirical jigs into which any names could be fitted; see Charles Read Baskervill, *The Elizabethan Jig and Related Song Drama* (Chicago: University of Chicago Press, 1929), pp. 66–67.

14. All citations of *Othello* are to the Arden edition, ed. M. R. Ridley (Cambridge, Mass.: Harvard University Press, 1958). Iago's description of Cassio, "a finder out of occasions" (2.1.240–41), is a far more apt description of himself as an improviser.

15. This interpretation is argued powerfully in an unpublished essay, "On the Language of Sexual Pathology in *Othello,*" by Edward Snow of George Mason University. A similar case is made by Arthur Kirsch in a sensitive psychoanalytic study, "The Polarization of Erotic Love in *Othello*" (*Modern Language Review* 73 [1978], pp. 721–40). Kirsch suggests that what becomes insupportable for Othello is "the fulsomeness of his own sexual instincts and, as his verbal and physical decomposition suggests, his jealous rage against Cassio is ultimately a rage against himself which reaches back to the elemental and destructive triadic fantasies which at one stage in childhood govern the mind of every human being" (p. 737).

16. Iago's performance here, which Desdemona unnervingly characterizes as "lame and impotent," is one of the ways in which he is linked to the playwright or at least to the Vice-like "presenter" of a play; see Bernard Spivack, *Shakespeare and the Allegory of Evil: The History of a Metaphor in Relation to His Major Villains* (New York: Columbia University Press, 1958).

17. One might argue that Shakespeare, like Marx, sees the exploiter as doomed by the fact that he must reduce his victim to nothingness, but where Marx derives a revolutionary optimism from this process, Shakespeare derives the tragic mood of the play's end.

18. For Iago's "corrosive habit of abstraction," see Maynard Mack, "The Jacobean Shakespeare: Some Observations on the Construction of the Tragedies," in *Stratford-upon-Avon Studies: Jacobean Theatre* 1 (1960), p. 18. For Iago as a "portrait of the artist," see Stanley Edgar Hyman, *Iago: Some Approaches to the Illusion of His Motivation* (New York: Atheneum, 1970), pp. 61–100.

19. The vertigo intensifies if we add the sly preceding line: "It is as sure

as you are Roderigo, / Were I the Moor, I would not be Iago." One imagines that Roderigo would unconsciously touch himself at this point to make sure that he *is* Roderigo.

Iago is a master of the vertiginous confounding of self and other, being and seeming:

> Men should be what they seem,
> Or those that be not, would they might seem none.
>
> (III, iii, 130–31)
>
> He's that he is; I may not breathe my censure,
> What he might be, if, as he might, he is not,
> I would to heaven he were!
>
> (IV, i, 267–69)

20. See, for example, Theodor Lipps:

> The specific characteristic of esthetic pleasure has now been defined. It consists in this: that it is the enjoyment of an object, which however, so far as it is the object of *enjoyment*, is not an object, but myself. Or, it is the enjoyment of the ego, which however, so far as it is esthetically enjoyed, is not myself but objective.
>
> Now, all this is included in the concept empathy. It constitutes the very meaning of this concept. Empathy is the fact here established, that the object is myself and by the very same token this self of mine is the object. Empathy is the fact that the antithesis between myself and the object disappears, or rather does not yet exist. ("Empathy, Inner Imitation, and Sense-Feelings," in *A Modern Book of Esthetics,* ed. Melvin Rader [New York: Holt, Rinehart and Winston, 1960], p. 376.)

To establish this "fact," Lipps must posit a wholly esthetic dimension and what he calls an "ideal," as opposed to a "practical" self. In *Othello* there is no realm of the purely esthetic, no space defined by the intersection of negative capability and the willing suspension of disbelief, and no separation of an "ideal" from a "practical" self.

21. To complicate matters further, both declarations occur in a cunning performance for his dupe Roderigo; that is, Iago is saying what he presumes Roderigo wants to believe.

22. Thus Iago invokes heaven as the judge of his self-interested hypocrisy, for *self* and *interest* as stable entities both rely ultimately upon an absolute Being.

23. Elsewhere too, Othello speaks as if aware of himself as a character: "Were it my cue to fight," he tells the incensed Brabantio and his own followers, "I should have known it, / Without a prompter" (1.2.83–84). His acceptance of the commission to fight the Turks is likewise couched in an inflated diction that suggests he is responding to a cue:

> The tyrant custom, most grave senators,
> Hath made the flinty and steel couch of war
> My thrice-driven bed of down: I do agnize
> A natural and prompt alacrity

I find in hardness, and would undertake
This present wars against the Ottomites.

(1.3.229–34)

24. Emmanuel Le Roy Ladurie, *Montaillou: The Promised Land of Error,*
trans. Barbara Bray (New York: Braziller, 1978), pp. 8–9. In a review essay,
Natalie Zemon Davis calls attention to the narrative structure of the testimony, a structure she attributes not to the pressure of the Inquisition
but to the form of village culture: "Some of these details were probably
remembered over the decades—good memories are part of oral culture—
but most form a reconstructed past: from a general memory of an event, a
narrative is created that tells with verisimilitude how the events could
have unfolded. The past is a story" ("Les Conteurs de Montaillou," *Annales: Economies, Sociétés, Civilisations* 34 [1979], p. 70).

On narrativity as a mode, see Louis Marin, *Utopiques: jeux d'espaces;*
Svetlana Alpers, "Describe or Narrate? A Problem in Realistic Repre-
sentation," *New Literary History* 7 (1976–77), pp. 15–41; Leo Bersani, "The
Other Freud," *Humanities in Society* 1 (1978), pp. 35–49.

25. *The Aeneid of Virgil,* trans. Allen Mandelbaum (New York: Bantam
Books, 1972), bk. 1, lines 1049–51.

26. I very reluctantly accept the Quarto's *sighs* for the Folio's *kisses;* the
latter need not, as editors sometimes claim, suggest an improbable im-
modesty but rather may express Othello's perception of Desdemona's
nature, hence what her love has given him. Moreover, the frank eroticism
of *kisses* is in keeping with Desdemona's own speeches; it is Othello who
emphasizes a pity that she voices nowhere in the play itself. On the other
hand, *sighs* admits a simpler reading and by no means excludes the erotic.

There is another interpretive problem in this speech that should be
noted: the last two lines are usually taken as a continuation of Desdemona's actual response, as recalled by Othello. But they may equally
be his interpretation of her feelings, in which case they may say far more
about Othello than about Desdemona. A competent actor could suggest
either possibility. There is a further ambiguity in the *her* of "made her
such a man": I hear *her* as accusative, but the dative cannot be ruled out.

27. William Tyndale, *Obedience,* p. 171, and above, chapter 2.

28. Both the Folio and the Second Quarto read "You are the Lord of
duty," but the paradox of an absolute duty that must nevertheless be
divided is suggestive.

29. Iago is improvising on two earlier remarks of Brabantio:

and she, in spite of nature,
Of years, of country, credit, everything,
To fall in love with what she fear'd to look on?

(1.3.96–98)

and

Look to her, Moor, have a quick eye to see:
She has deceiv'd her father, may do thee.

(1.3.292–93)

In a society deeply troubled by clandestine marriage, the circumstances of Desdemona's union already brand her as faithless, even at the moment Othello stakes his life upon her faith, while, quite apart from these circumstances, it would seem for the male psyche depicted in the play that the very act of leaving her father borders obscurely on sexual betrayal.

30. See George K. Hunter, "Othello and Colour Prejudice," *Proceedings of the British Academy 1967* 53 (1968), pp. 139–63; Leslie A. Fielder, *The Stranger in Shakespeare* (New York: Stein & Day, 1972), chap. 3.

A measure of the complex significance of Othello's blackness may be taken from a glance at the competing interpretive possibilities of Desdemona's "I saw Othello's visage in his mind" (1.3.252):

> "Do not be surprised that I have married an older black man who looks to you grotesque and terrifying. I have married not a face, a complexion, but a mind: a resolute, Christian mind."

> "I saw Othello's valuation of himself, his internal image, the picture he has in his mind of his own face. I saw how much he had at stake in his narrative sense of himself, how much his whole existence depended upon this sense, and I was deeply drawn to this 'visage.'"

> "I saw Othello's visage—his blackness, his otherness—in his mind as well as his complexion: there is a unity in his being. I am subdued to precisely this quality in him."

31. Ridley, in the Arden edition, adheres to the Quarto's "calmness" at line 185. Most editors prefer the Folio's "calms."

32. Ephesians 5.28–32, as cited in the marriage liturgy (*The Book of Common Prayer 1559*, ed. John Booty [Charlottesville: University of Virginia Press, 1976], p. 297). The passage is quoted by Arthur Kirsch, "The Polarization of Erotic Love in *Othello*," p. 721, who draws conclusions closely parallel to some of my own, though he differs in emphases and methodology.

33. Becon and Gouge are cited in William and Malleville Haller, "The Puritan Art of Love," *Huntington Library Quarterly* 5 (1941–42), pp. 44–45, 46.

34. From its inception, Christianity competed fiercely with other sexual conceptions and practices. For a detailed and moving study of one episode in this struggle, see Le Roy Ladurie's *Montaillou*. Michel Foucault has attempted the beginnings of a modern history of the subject in *La volonté de savoir*.

35. *The City of God*, trans. Marcus Dods (New York: Modern Library, 1950), bk. 14, chap. 24, pp. 473–75.

36. For the inherent violence of sexuality, see Lucretius, *The Nature of the Universe*, trans. Ronald Latham (Baltimore: Penguin, 1951): "Lovers' passion is storm-tossed, even in the moment of fruition, by waves of delusion and incertitude. They cannot make up their mind what to enjoy first with eye or hand. They clasp the object of their longing so tightly that

the embrace is painful. They kiss so fiercely that teeth are driven into lips. All this because their pleasure is not pure, but they are goaded by an underlying impulse to hurt the thing, whatever it may be, that gives rise to these budding shoots of madness" (pp. 163–64).

37. Richard Onorato has called my attention to the way Iago, who is watching this scene, subsequently uses the word *content*. 'nothing can, nor shall content my soul," he tells himself, "Till I am even with him, wife, for wife" (2.1.293–94). Later, when under his influence Othello has bade "farewell content" (3.3.354), Iago proffers the consoling words, "Pray be content" (3.3.457).

38. When Othello asks Desdemona to leave him a little to himself, she replies, "Shall I deny you? no, farewell, my lord" (3.3.87).

39. "Prithee unpin me" requires that the actress, as she speaks these words, call attention to Desdemona's erotic submission to Othello's violence.

40. As Gabrielle Jackson pointed out to me, Emilia feels that she must explain her refusal to observe her husband's commands to be silent and go home:

> Good gentlemen, let me have leave to speak,
> 'Tis proper I obey him but not now:
> Perchance, Iago, I will ne'er go home.
>
> (5.2.196–98)

The moment is felt as a liberating gesture and redeems her earlier, compliant theft of the handkerchief, but it is both too late and fatal. The play does not hold out the wife's disobedience as a way of averting tragedy.

41. Jacques Lacan, *The Language of the Self: The Function of Language in Psychoanalysis (Discours de Rome)*, trans. Anthony Wilden (Baltimore: The Johns Hopkins University Press, 1968), p. 11.

42. In effect, Othello invokes larger and larger spheres of self-fashioning: Othello to Desdemona, Othello to Desdemona and Brabantio, Othello to the Senate, Othello to heaven. We might add that the narrative element in formal auricular confession may have been heightened by the fact that confessors were instructed not to interrupt the penitent but to let him begin with a full and circumstantial account.

43. The word *confession* and its variants (*confess'd, confessions*) is repeated eighteen times in the course of the play, more often than in any other play in the canon.

44. See Thomas N. Tentler, *Sin and Confession on the Eve of the Reformation,* and chapter 2, above.

45. This is a frequent response in the literature of colonialism; we have encountered it in Spenser's *View of the Present State of Ireland,* where he sees the Irish as living in certain respects as the English did before the civilizing influence of the Norman Conquest.

46. Tentler, p. 229. The *Eruditorium penitentiale* points out that in cases of necessity it is possible to kill or steal justifiably, "but no one may fornicate knowingly without committing a mortal sin." Tentler observes, "This kind of thinking is an exaggeration even of medieval puritanism.

Yet it is also true that the climate of religious opinion allowed and perhaps even encouraged such exaggerations."

Cf. Francis Dillingham, *Christian Oeconomy or Household Government* (London: John Tapp, 1609): "Julius Caesar made a law that if the husband or the wife found either in adultery, it should be lawful for the husband to kill the wife or the wife the husband. Death then by the light of nature is fit punishment for adulterers and adulteresses" (p. 13).

47. George Joye, *A Contrarye (to a certayne manis) Consultacion: That Adulterers ought to be punyshed wyth deathe. Wyth the solucions of his argumentes for the contrarye* (London: n.p., 1559?), pp. G4^v, A4^v. "The sacred integrity therefore of this Christ's holy church, the inviolable honor of holy matrimony ordained of God, the preservation of the private and public peace, all honesty, godly zeal to virtue, to the salvation of our souls and to God's glory should constrain every Christian heart to counsel, to exhort and to excite all Christian magistrates to cut off this contagious canker of adultery from among us, lest in further creeping, . . . it daily corrupteth the whole body of this noble realm so that it else be at last so incurable that . . . neither the vice nor yet the just remedy will be suffered" (A6^v).

The death penalty for adulterers was briefly adopted by the Puritan Parliament in the seventeenth century; see Keith Thomas, "The Puritans and Adultery: the Act of 1650 Reconsidered," in *Puritans and Revolutionaries: Essays in Seventeenth-Century History*, ed. Donald Pennington and Keith Thomas (Oxford: At the Clarendon Press, 1978), pp. 257–82.

48. William Perkins, *A Godly and Learned Exposition of Christs Sermon in the Mount* (Cambridge: Thomas Pierson, 1608), p. 111. See Robert V. Schnucker, "La position puritaine à l'égard de l'adultère," *Annales: Economies, Sociétés, Civilisations* 27 (1972), pp. 1379–88.

49. Quoted, with a mass of supporting material, in John T. Noonan, Jr., *Contraception: A History of Its Treatment by the Catholic Theologians and Canonists* (Cambridge, Mass.: Harvard University Press, 1966), p. 80. The Stoic marital doctrine, Noonan observes, "joined the Stoic distrust of pleasure and the Stoic insistence on purpose" (p. 47); early Christians embraced the doctrine and hardened its formulation in combatting the gnostic sects.

50. Noonan, p. 47.

51. John Calvin, *Institutes of the Christian Religion*, bk. 2, chap. 8, section 44, quoted in Lawrence Stone, *The Family, Sex and Marriage in England 1500–1800*, p. 499; *The King's Book, or a Necessary Doctrine and Erudition for Any Christian Man* (1543), ed. T. A. Lacey (London: Society for Promoting Christian Knowledge, 1932), pp. 111–12. See likewise John Rogers, *The Glasse of Godly Loue* (1569), ed. Frederick J. Furnivall, New Shakespeare Society, ser. 6, no. 2 (London: N Trübner, 1876), p. 185:

> Also there ought to be a temperance between man and wife, for God hath ordained marriage for a remedy or medicine, to assuage the heart of the burning flesh, and for procreation, and not beastly for to fulfill the whole lusts of the devilish mind and wicked flesh; for, though

> ye have a promise that the act in marriage is not sin
> . . . yet if ye take excess, or use it beastly, vilely, or in-
> ordinately, your mistemperance makes that ill which is
> good (being rightly used), and that which is clean, ye
> defile through your abusing of it.

In the seventeenth century, William Perkins informs his readers that the "holy manner" in marital intercourse involves moderation, "for even in wedlock, excess in lusts is not better than plain adultery before God." "This is the judgment of the ancient Church," notes Perkins, citing Ambrose and Augustine, "that Intemperance, that is, immoderate desire even between man and wife, is fornication" (*Christian Oeconomie*, trans. Thomas Pickering [London: Felix Kyngstone, 1609], pp. 113–14).

52. Le Roy Ladurie, *Montaillou*, p. 151. In fact the priest, who was, in Le Roy Ladurie's words, "an energetic lover and incorrigible Don Juan" (p. 154), held a somewhat different position. "One woman's just like another," he told Grazide's mother, "The sin is the same, whether she is married or not. Which is as much as to say that there is no sin about it at all" (p. 157). Le Roy Ladurie interprets his views on love as follows: "Starting from the Cathar proposition that 'any sexual act, even between married persons, is wrong,' he applied it to suit himself. Because everything was forbidden, one act was no worse than another" (pp. 158–59).

53. 1.5.107. Le Roy Ladurie quotes from the *Brévaire d'amour*: "A lady who sleeps with a true lover is purified of all sins . . . the joy of love makes the act innocent, for it proceeds from a pure heart" (p. 159).

See Friar Laurence's warnings to Romeo about excessive love:

> These violent delights have violent ends
> And in their triumph die, like fire and powder,
> Which, as they kiss, consume . . . .
> Therefore love moderately: long love doth so.
>
>   (2.6.9–14)

54. Tentler, p. 174.

55. Tentler, p. 181: "hoc est in executione ipsius actus nulla voluptatis delectatione teneatur."

56. Tentler, p. 183. According to the *King's Book*, over those who have violated married chastity, "the Devil hath power, as the angel Raphael said unto Thobit, They that marry in such wise that they exclude God out of their hearts, and give themselves unto their own carnal lusts, as it were an horse or a mule, which have no reason; upon such persons the Devil hath power" (p. 112).

For a humanist's version of these notions, see the following aphorisms from Juan Luis Vives's *Introductio ad Sapientam:*

> The pleasure of the body is, like the body itself, vile and
>   brutal.
> Sensual delectation bores the soul and benumbs the intellect.
> Sensual delectation is like robbery, it vilifies the soul. This is
>   the reason why even the most corrupted man seeks secrecy
>   and abhors witnesses.

> Sensual pleasure is fleeting and momentaneous, totally be-
>   yond any control and always mixed with frustration.
> Nothing debilitates more the vigor of the our intellect than
>   sexual pleasure.
> (Carlos G. Noreña, *Juan Luis Vives* [The Hague: Martinus
> Nijhoff, 1970], p. 211)

For an attenuated modern version, see the first televised speech delivered from the Sistine Chapel on 27 August 1978 by Pope John Paul I; the
pope prayed that families "may be defended from the destructive attitude
of sheer pleasure-seeking, which snuffs out life" (*S.F. Chronicle*, 28 August 1978, p. 1).

57. In the early seventeenth century, Samuel Hieron counsels married
couples to recite the following prayer before going to bed: "Allay in us all
sensual and brutish love, purifying and sanctifying our affections one
towards another, that we may in nothing dishonor this honorable state,
nor pollute the bed of marriage . . . but may use this thine ordinance in the
holy sort, that carnal lusts may be slaked and subdued, nor increased or
inflamed thereby" (*A Helpe Unto Devotion*, 3d ed. [London: H.L., 1611], p.
411).

58. *A Discourse of Marriage and Wiving* (London, 1620), quoted in
Ronald Mushat Frye, "The Teachings of Classical Puritanism on Conjugal
Love," *Studies in the Renaissance* 2 (1955), pp. 156–57.

59. William Whately, *A Bride-bush* (London, 1619), quoted in Frye, p.
156.

60. Noonan, p. 79.

61. A major textual crux, and I have taken the liberty, for the sake of
clarity and brevity, to depart from Ridley's reading which is as follows:

>   the young affects
> In my defunct, and proper satisfaction.

As Ridley says, "after all the discussion, Othello's meaning is moderately
clear. He is too mature to be subjugated by physical desire"; but he goes
on to read *proper* as "justifiable," where I would read it as "my own."
Ridley's *moderately* should be emphasized.

62. Yet another crux: the Quarto reads "very quality" instead of "utmost pleasure." I find the latter more powerful and persuasive, particularly in the context of Desdemona's further mention (l. 255) of "The rites
for which I love him."

Iago twice echoes Desdemona's declaration: "It was a violent com-
mencement in her, and thou shalt see an answerable sequestration"
(1.3.342–43) and again "Mark me with what violence she first loved the
Moor" (2.1.221).

63. Desdemona is, in effect, a kind of mirror reversal of Cordelia: where
the latter is doomed in the first act of the play by her refusal to declare her
love, the former is doomed precisely for such a declaration.

Professor Spivack, along with most critics of the play, sees Iago as the enemy of the religious bond in marriage (pp. 49–50); I would argue that it is precisely the nature of this bond, as defined by rigorists, that torments Othello.

64. On "property" see Kenneth Burke, *A Grammar of Motives* (Berkeley: University of California Press, 1969): "Iago may be considered 'consubstantial' with Othello in that he represents the principles of jealousy implicit in Othello's delight in Desdemona as a private spiritual possession. Iago, to arouse Othello, must talk a language that Othello knows as well as he, a language implicit in the nature of Othello's love as the idealization of his private property in Desdemona. This language is the dialectical opposite of Othello's; but it so thoroughly shares a common ground with Othello's language that its insinuations are never for one moment irrelevant to Othello's thinking. Iago must be cautious in leading Othello to believe them as true: but Othello never for a moment doubts them as *values*" (p. 414). As so often happens, I discovered that Burke's brilliant sketch had anticipated the shape of much of my argument. Burke has an essay on the ritual structure of the play in *Hudson Review* 4 (1951), pp. 165–203.

65. I have read two powerful unpublished essays that analyze the male sexual anxieties in the play at a level prior to or beneath the social and doctrinal one discussed here: Edward Snow, "On the Language of Sexual Pathology in *Othello*" and C. L. Barber, "'I'll pour this pestilence into his ear'; *Othello* as a Development from Hamlet."

66. In act 4, Othello had first thought of poisoning Desdemona and then was persuaded by Iago to "strangle her in her bed, even the bed she hath contaminated" (4.1.203–4). The blood he fantasizes about later may be simply an expression of violence (as he had earlier declared, "I will chop her into messes" [4.1.196]), but it is tempting to see it as a projection of the blood that marked her loss of virginity and hence, in his disturbed formulation, as "lust's blood." For a sensitive exploration of the anxiety over virginity, staining, and impotence in *Othello*, see Stanley Cavell, "Epistemology and Tragedy: A Reading of *Othello*," *Daedalus* 108 (1979), pp. 27–43.

67. Like Oedipus, Othello cannot escape the fact that it is he who has committed the crime and must be punished.

We should, in all fairness, call attention to the fact that Othello in the end views his wife as "chaste," but the language in which he does so reinforces the orthodox condemnation of pleasure:

> cold, cold my girl,
> Even like thy chastity.
>
> (5.2.276–77)

Indeed the identification of the coldness of death with marital chastity seems to me a *confirmation* of the necrophilic fantasy.

68. Shakespeare's talent for entering into the consciousness of others and giving supreme expression to incompatible perspectives has been a

major preoccupation of criticism since Coleridge and Keats. For a recent exploration, see Norman Rabkin's concept of "complementarity": *Shakespeare and the Common Understanding* (New York: Free Press, 1967).

In *The Anxiety of Influence* (New York: Oxford University Press, 1973), Harold Bloom remarks, "Shakespeare is the largest instance in the language of a phenomenon that stands outside the concern of this book: the absolute absorption of the precursor" (p. 11).

69. "Of Repentance," in *The Complete Essays of Montaigne*, trans. Donald M. Frame (Stanford: Stanford University Press, 1958), pp. 610–11. It is hardly irrelevant for our purposes that Montaigne describes this method in an essay in which he rejects the confessional system.

70. On pleasure and the threat to established order, see Georges Bataille, *Death and Sensuality: A Study of Eroticism and the Taboo* (New York: Walker & Co., 1962), and Mikhail Bakhtin, *Rabelais and His World*, trans. Helene Iswolsky (Cambridge, Mass.: MIT Press, 1968).

See also Herbert Marcuse, *Eros and Civilization* (New York: Random House, 1955); Michel Foucault, *Discipline and Punish;* Leo Bersani, *A Future for Asyanax: Character and Desire in Literature* (Boston: Little, Brown and Company, 1976).

In work in progress, Jonathan Crewe of Berkeley is investigating comparable issues in the work of Thomas Nashe.

Index

Perella, Nicolas, 269 n. 18
Peristiany, J. G., 50, 265 n. 59
Perkins, William, 247, 303 n. 48,
  304 n. 51
Persius, 279 n. 29
Peter, Saint, 62, 83, 87, 108
Petrarch, Francesco, 110, 145–46,
  148–50, 166, 275–76 n. 90, 276
  n. 3, 281 n. 53, 282 n. 65
Philibert de Vienne, 163–65, 284
  n. 9, 284 n. 10
Phillips, Henry, 108, 275 n. 84
Phillips, John, 288 n. 65
Pico della Mirandola, 36, 51–52, 258
  n. 3
Pineas, Rainer, 266 n. 75
Pitt-Rivers, Julian, 265 n. 59, 294
  n. 36
Plato, 36, 42, 44, 58, 109, 164, 215,
  217, 279 n. 30, 296 n. 45
Plowden, Edmund, 167
Pocock, J. G. A., 281 n. 50
Poins, John, 129–32 passim
Poulet, Georges, 294 n. 35
Prévost, André, 266 n. 75
Protestantism, 17, 113, 126, 141, 276
  n. 2; and authority, 98–99; and
  Bible, 93–94, 96–99; and Catholic
  ritual, 60, 230, 271 n. 31; and
  community, 82–83, 159; emphasis on inwardness of, 52, 78, 115,
  156; iconoclasm in, 85, 179,
  188–90; and martyrdom, 74–84;
  and penitence, 115, 118–19; rejection of purgatory in, 200; and
  sexuality, 247–49; and social
  class, 270 n. 20, 272–73 n. 45. *See
  also* Heretics; Luther; Puritanism; Tyndale
Pseudo-Dionysius, 101
Puritanism, 171, 199, 248, 249, 274
  n. 66, 277 n. 11, 303 n. 47
Purvey, John, 105
Puttenham, George, 136
Pynson, Richard, 59

Quinn, David Beers, 288 n. 58

Rabinow, Paul, 4, 259 n. 9
Rabkin, Norman, 307 n. 68
Radzinowicz, Leon, 277 n. 11
Ralegh, Sir Walter, 121, 140, 165,
  168–69, 180, 278 n. 16, 283 n. 2,
  285 n. 25, 285–86 n. 29, 286 n. 42,
  290 n. 8, 292 n. 15
Rastell, William, 68
Raymond of Peñaforte, 248–49
Rebhorn, Wayne A., 288–89 n. 67
Regino (monk), 117, 277 n. 7
Rhetoric, 253; and Bible transla-
  tion, 102–5; Gorgias's conception
  of, 215; in humanist education,
  162
Rich, Richard, 68, 262 n. 37
Richard III, 13, 124
Ricoeur, Paul, 265 n. 62
Ridley, Nicholas, 270 n. 25
Rodney, Walter, 289 n. 1
Rogers, John, 303–4 n. 51
Role-playing: and colonialism, 228;
  in court of Henry VIII, 28–29; in
  life of More, 13–14, 26–27, 29–31,
  36–37, 72, 112, 158, 160, 231; in
  Othello, 235; and Wyatt, 129–30,
  161. *See also* Improvisation;
  Self-fashioning
Roper, Margaret More, 16, 31, 45,
  52, 72, 268 n. 105
Roper, William, 21, 29–30, 32, 45,
  52–53, 55, 67, 70, 75, 231, 259
  n. 4, 264 n. 53
Rosenmeyer, Thomas G., 295 n. 40
Rosier, Bernard du, 281 n. 55
Roy, William, 107
Royal Shakespeare Company, 204,
  207
Rupp, E. G., 276 n. 1
Rusche, Georg, 281 n. 51
Russell, Sir John, 140

Sampson, Thomas, 271 n. 28
Samuel, Edgar R., 260 n. 10
Sandys, Edwin (archbishop), 3
Sarracoll, John, 193–94, 198, 289
  n. 1, 291 n. 6
Satires (Wyatt's), 116, 127–35, 279
  n. 29; admired, 131, 279 n. 34;
  "Mine Own John Poins," 128–30,
  132–33, 279 n. 26, 279 n. 27, 279
  n. 28; "My Mother's Maids,"
  128–29, 131–32, 279 n. 29; negation in, 127–28, 279 n. 27; attitude toward power in, 127–28,
  130, 132–35, 279 n. 28; attitude